Churches
That Make
a Difference

Churches That Make a Difference

Reaching Your Community with Good News and Good Works

Ronald J. Sider, Philip N. Olson,
and Heidi Rolland Unruh

Baker Books
A Division of Baker Book House Co
Grand Rapids, Michigan 49516

Published by Baker Books
a division of Baker Book House Company
P.O. Box 6287, Grand Rapids, MI 49516-6287

Third printing, December 2003

Printed in the United States of America

Library of Congress Cataloging-in-Publication Data

Sider, Ronald J.
    Churches that make a difference : reaching your community with good news and good works / Ronald J. Sider, Philip N. Olson, and Heidi Rolland Unruh.
       p.   cm.
    Includes bibliographical references.
    ISBN 0-8010-9133-0 (paper)
    1. Church work—United States. 2. Church charities—United States. I. Olson, Philip N. II. Unruh, Heidi Rolland. III. Title.
BV4403.S53   2002
253—dc21   2001043751

For current information about all releases from Baker Book House, visit our web site:
http://www.bakerbooks.com

To our spouses

Arbutus Sider
Holly Olson
Jim Unruh

who daily show us the love of God in word and deed

Contents

Acknowledgments

"A threefold cord is not quickly broken," says Ecclesiastes 4:12. The threefold authorship of this book, we hope, has produced a much stronger work than any of us could have created alone. Each of us wrote first drafts of portions of the book, with Heidi drafting the majority. Together we reviewed, argued about, and revised the material, so that the final version in its entirety speaks for each of the authors.

We owe a special debt to many people and organizations. We are very grateful to all the wonderful congregations, pastors, and ministry leaders who participated in the Congregations, Communities, and Leadership Development Project. We hope others are as inspired by their vision, faith, witness, courage, and compassion as we have been. Our appreciation also goes out to the many, many unsung heroines and heroes of holistic ministry whom we have yet to meet.

The project would not have been possible without funding support from the Lilly Endowment and the John Templeton Foundation. We also gratefully acknowledge the work of the team of researchers who conducted the fieldwork in the churches, whose careful data gathering and insightful field notes and reports provided the foundation for our analysis. Dr. Paul Light, as data analyst and project consultant, was particularly helpful throughout the project. We were also aided and encouraged by input from evaluators Dr. Katie Day and Dr. Harold Dean Trulear, an advisory council of local religious leaders, a consulting council of professionals in the field of congregational studies, and consultations with researchers at the Center for Social and Religious Research at Hartford Seminary. We note that the opinions expressed in this book are those of the authors and do not necessarily reflect the views of the foundations, researchers, or consultants who supported our work.

Our editors at Baker have been more than gracious, for which we are grateful. We also thank Eastern Baptist Theological Seminary for providing a home for the project, and Evangelicals for Social Action for freeing time for Phil to write. Both organizations share a mission of equipping church leaders to answer the call outlined in this book. We are each also grateful to our home churches—Oxford Circle Mennonite Church, First Presbyterian Church of Mount Holly, and Norristown New Life/Nueva Vida Mennonite Church, respectively—for embracing the holistic vision. Each of us has had special support from various individuals. Phil thanks Wendy Moluf, director of Servant Development at First Presbyterian Church, for supplying information on church ministries and resources. Heidi thanks her prayer partner Dawn Graham for her assurance, "We'll keep praying until it's done."

An Astonishing Opportunity

Never in our lifetime—perhaps not anytime in the last one hundred years—has the possibility of explosive growth in holistic ministry[1] been so promising. Today, a historic opportunity beckons Christians eager to love the whole person the way Jesus did.

For decades, most academics, journalists, and policy experts ignored or dismissed the role of religion in solving social problems. Health care and social work professionals were taught to be morally neutral and "objective" and to see a spiritual dimension in their work as inappropriate for professional care. Secular foundations and government insisted that for Christian social service agencies to receive funding, they would have to water down or abandon the explicitly religious aspects of their work.

Today the situation is dramatically different. By the end of the 1990s, policy elites were desperate for new solutions to urban brokenness and poverty. Neither the liberal nor the conservative approaches of the preceding decades had ended widespread poverty in the richest nation in human history. People realized that the level of social decay—failing schools, violence, broken families, poverty—in all America's great cities was both a moral outrage and a threat to democracy. Increasingly, policy experts agreed with Senator Daniel Moynihan, who said in his lectures at Harvard that "we do not have a clue" what social policies could solve these problems.

As this dismay about the failure of past efforts spread, more and more reports began to surface about the astonishing effectiveness of some faith-based approaches. Studies of Teen Challenge's Christ-centered drug and alcohol rehab

11

program revealed recovery rates far higher than in most secular programs.[2] The Ten Point Coalition, a faith-based response to gang violence led by Rev. Eugene Rivers, has dramatically reduced youth homicides in a gritty Boston neighborhood.[3] Prison Fellowship has reduced prisoners' recidivism rates.[4] Faith-based mentoring teams seem to have played a crucial role in enabling Ottawa County in Michigan to help every recipient move off the welfare rolls.[5] Lawndale Community Center's holistic faith-based health center and other programs have witnessed a 60 percent drop in infant mortality rates in a desperately poor section of Chicago—prompting newspaper headlines and careful exploration by federal health officials.[6]

Too much of the evidence is still anecdotal. We urgently need far more extensive scholarly evaluation of holistic faith-based providers. But there is enough emerging evidence to suggest the possibility that holistic organizations sometimes succeed where almost everything else has failed.

Along with the renewed interest in faith-based social services has been a growing awareness of the positive impact of faith on people's lives. When David Larson studied psychiatry in the late 1960s, he was taught that religious beliefs were harmful to mental health. Dr. Larson's careful research over the last several decades has proven his teachers to be quite wrong. Study after study by Dr. Larson and others indicate that religious people enjoy better mental and physical health, stay married longer, and avoid socially destructive behaviors such as alcohol abuse.[7] Faith also helps people counter the influence of a negative environment. A secular Harvard economist was astounded to learn in the 1980s that church attendance was the best indicator of which young inner-city African American males would escape the syndrome of gangs, drugs, and prison.[8] Highly religious people are also more than twice as likely to volunteer to help others.[9] All this suggests that helping people develop a strong faith and ties to a church community helps their chances of developing a better quality of life and becoming productive citizens.

In the late 1990s, religion returned to the public spotlight in a dramatic way. Secular journalists, academics, and public policy experts developed an amazing new openness to an expanded role for faith-based organizations (FBOs) in overcoming poverty. This growing public embrace crystalized in the 2000 presidential campaign when both leading candidates declared that FBOs would be central to their administration's programs to reduce poverty. In his second week in office, President George W. Bush established a new White House Office on Faith-Based and Community Initiatives, naming a prominent Catholic academic, University of Pennsylvania political scientist John DiIulio, as head of the new office. President Bush moved quickly to promote expanded opportunities and funding for FBOs in ways that he hoped would both respect people's right to religious freedom and protect the religious integrity of FBOs. This dramatic development presents both opportunity and danger.[10]

It is much too early to know how this new initiative will turn out, and there is still considerable controversy surrounding issues of government funding for FBOs. What is abundantly clear, however, is that the broader society is dramatically more open to a major role for FBOs in addressing social problems than in the past several decades. A 2001 poll sponsored by the Pew Charitable Trusts found that 75 percent of those surveyed supported the idea of government funding for FBOs. Today the church faces a historic window of opportunity. This window, however, will not remain open for long unless large numbers of Christians quickly step forward. In five years, if we fail to respond, policy circles will conclude that the turn to faith-based approaches was a failure. They will look elsewhere for solutions. But at present, the larger society is looking to people of faith to demonstrate the power of faith in overcoming society's toughest problems.

Another important development also strengthens the potential for holistic ministry. The twentieth century saw a divisive argument between social gospel churches that focused one-sidedly on social action, and evangelistic churches that insisted that leading people to Christ was the only truly important mission of the church. The tragic results of that long argument have not entirely disappeared, but we have made great progress. Evangelical leaders today widely agree that biblical churches must combine word and deed, doing both evangelism and social ministry. Scores of historic evangelical congregations that focused almost exclusively on evangelism twenty years ago are now immersed in social engagement—without losing their evangelistic passion. Thousands of grassroots holistic ministries have emerged. Based on a national survey, sociologist Chris Smith concluded recently that "evangelicals may be the most committed carriers of a new Social Gospel."[11] At the same time, mainline denominations have been engaged in conversations about the importance of evangelism. To an increasing degree, the church in America is ready to embark on a vast expansion of holistic ministry.

That is not to say that all is well today. We do not pretend that most congregations are now enthusiastically leading scores of people to Christ each year and also ministering to the social needs around them. Large numbers of local church leaders still need to catch the vision of loving the whole person the way Jesus did. Many thousands of congregations need help to put into practice the holistic vision they have begun to embrace. More and more church leaders are asking, What will it take for our congregation to develop effective holistic ministry? How do we take the first—or second and third—steps? What problems will we face? Where can we get help?

That is what this book is all about. The following chapters lay out the different components needed for effective holistic ministry. Of course, there is no simple formula, and there is no substitute for hard work, urgent prayer, and radical dependence on the Holy Spirit. But there is a great deal that any congregation today can learn from the last few decades, which have seen a wonderful expansion of vibrant, thriving holistic ministries.

We had the privilege of becoming closely acquainted with some of these ministries through a study called the Congregations, Communities, and Leadership Development Project. This study, funded by the Lilly Endowment and the Templeton Foundation,[12] explored the integration of evangelism and social ministry in fifteen congregations in the Philadelphia area. From these in-depth case studies, conducted by researchers Averil Clarke, Joan Hoppe-Spink, Paula McCosh, Kesha Moore, Timothy Nelson, Jill Witmer Sinha, and Gaynor Yancey, come most of the illustrations used in this book. (For a profile of and contact information for these fifteen churches, see appendix A.)[13]

Besides the study, we also draw on our extensive experience in networking, consulting, and writing about holistic ministry. Phil was the mission pastor for thirteen years at First Presbyterian Church in Mount Holly, New Jersey, which has been a pioneer in holistic ministry for three decades (and is one of the congregations we studied). Phil now directs Network 9:35, a resourcing and networking ministry for churches and FBOs, and is also vice president for church relations at Evangelicals for Social Action. As founder and president of Evangelicals for Social Action and professor of theology and culture at Eastern Baptist Seminary, Ron has been speaking, writing, and teaching about the church's calling to combine evangelism and social action for over thirty years. Heidi has researched and written about the role of FBOs and along with Ron directed the Congregations, Communities, and Leadership Development Project.

We believe the next few decades could see an explosion of holistic ministry that will draw millions to personal faith in Christ, restore broken people to wholeness, and renew entire neighborhoods and societies. Never has the need been greater or the opportunity more clear. This book represents our best effort to help the church seize this historic moment.

An Overview of the Book

The purpose of this book is to help congregations develop more biblical, effective, dynamic holistic ministries. Part 1 lays the foundation for outreach mission by exploring the meaning and biblical basis for holistic ministry, illustrating what this looks like in diverse churches. It develops a holistic perspective on evangelism and social ministry and describes how they can be interwoven.

Part 2 builds on this foundation by examining the essential components of a holistic congregation (see the overview of the holistic congregation below). Love for God and neighbor, a commitment to reaching out beyond the walls of the church, spiritual and relational vitality within the congregation, a visionary leadership team, mission-centered organizational practices, and ministry partnerships—these pieces are all vital to a church that wants to fulfill its biblical mission of loving its community in wholeness.

How does a church put the pieces together? Part 3 addresses this question, laying out several key steps in the three stages of developing a holistic ministry vision (see the overview below). The last chapter deals with common challenges facing churches in the process of establishing holistic outreach.

Below we set out the framework for two concepts central to this book: the characteristics of a holistic congregation and the stages in holistic ministry development. While the book does not cover every point in detail, key ideas are highlighted in the chapters indicated in parentheses.

The Holistic Congregation

Holistic ministry takes place in a holistic church. If you have been to such a church, you recognize it. If you are not in one, you sense something is missing. There is an indescribable quality about a church committed to living out the gospel that whispers to your spirit: Yes, this is how Christ meant his followers to live together. The church may not be perfect—come to think of it, no church is!—and the vision may not be fully realized, but the active presence of the Spirit can be felt, bringing renewal, growth, and transformation both within the church and in the community. A Christian community that is spiritually dynamic, sacrificially caring, boldly prophetic, and lovingly nurturing is God's chosen vessel for authentic change in persons and in society.

Holistic congregations can take many forms, but they share certain attributes in common: a holistic understanding of the church's mission, dynamic spirituality, healthy congregational dynamics, and holistic ministry practice.

Holistic Understanding of the Church's Mission (chaps. 1–5)

The holistic church:

- teaches a ministry vision that integrates discipleship, evangelism, and social action, and works toward both spiritual and social transformation.
- supports a spectrum of social action that includes charity, compassion, community development, public policy, and justice advocacy, addressing both individual and systemic sources of human problems.
- sees ministry as fundamentally relational, seeking to develop long-term relationships with ministry recipients and welcoming them into church fellowship.
- views mission as both local and global in scope.

Dynamic Spirituality (chaps. 6–7)

The holistic church:

- centers congregational life around passionate worship of the Triune God, celebrating salvation by grace through faith in Christ and relying on the power of God's Spirit for fruitful ministry.
- is led by the inspired and authoritative Word of God and grounded in the teachings of historic Christian orthodoxy.
- nurtures individual members in a deepening spiritual life of worship, prayer, study, and mutual discipleship.
- shares God's self-sacrificial love for the lost, lonely, and broken and cultivates a commitment toward outreach as an expression of worship.

Healthy Congregational Dynamics (chaps. 8–9)

The holistic church:

- cultivates loving, accountable, reconciling relationships within the congregation.

- balances outreach with internal nurture, discipling and uniting members through participation in the church's mission.
- selects, develops, and upholds church leaders with faith, vision, courage, integrity, and a passion for holistic mission.
- places every area of individual and congregational life under the lordship of Jesus Christ, without distinction between "sacred" and "secular."

Holistic Ministry Practice (chaps. 10–11)

The holistic church:

- calls, trains, equips, and organizes members for ministry, building on the full range of spiritual gifts.
- sustains ministry through mission-centered organizational systems, effective resource management, and visionary planning.
- ministers with an informed appreciation for its community context and with a spirit of sacrificial servanthood, humility, and boldness in relationship to the community.
- seeks unity in ministry with other expressions of the body of Christ and serves alongside all through whom God is at work in the world.

When all the pieces are put together, a holistic congregation results: a church that practices both evangelism and social ministry; balances nurture and outreach; knows and loves its community; clearly communicates its theology and specific vision for holistic mission; integrates the holistic vision into the internal life of the church; builds its ministry on a base of spiritual maturity and healthy, loving relationships; and calls and equips its members to action.

Stages in Holistic Ministry Development

No church will travel the same path to becoming a holistic congregation. Each congregation starts in a different place, has a unique makeup and character, and ministers to a particular community. While there are no simple 1-2-3 steps to holistic ministry, there are three distinct phases that most churches experience along the way. Some of the points under each phase may follow in sequence; others may develop simultaneously.

Stage 1: Setting the Stage

- *Prepare the leadership team* (chap. 9): Develop a team of leaders (clergy and lay) who share spiritual passion, a holistic theology, and positive working relationships.
- *Prepare the congregation* (chaps. 6, 8): Strengthen the congregation's spiritual vitality, relational health, and holistic theology.
- *Nurture a commitment to outreach* (chap. 7): Develop an "outreach-minded" focus and build bridges of belonging and love with the community.
- *Know your congregation* (chap. 12): Assess your congregation's identity, beliefs, organizational systems, and ministries in terms of strengths and weaknesses for building holistic ministry.
- *Assess the community context* (chap. 12): Define your community of ministry and become familiar with its demographics, culture, systems, assets, and needs.

Stage 2: Unleashing the Vision

- *Seek God's vision* (chap. 12): Reflect on your congregation and community assessments, wait prayerfully on the Holy Spirit's guidance, and begin developing your holistic ministry vision.
- *Share the vision with the congregation* (chap. 13): Cultivate the congregation's understanding and sense of ownership of the ministry vision.
- *Rally the congregation around the vision* (chap. 13): Equip and recruit members to connect to the outreach vision in practical ways, while keeping a healthy balance with worship, discipleship, and internal nurture.
- *Organize for ministry* (chap. 10): "Plan the work and work the plan" for strategic implementation of your ministry vision, adjusting the organizational systems as necessary to be consistent with your mission.
- *Gather ministry resources and partners* (chaps. 10, 11): Generate the necessary assets of funds, space, personnel, and skills and develop relationships with other groups who share common goals.

Stage 3: Sustaining the Vision

- *Address fears and conflicts* (chap. 14): Respond to clashes and concerns in constructive ways, helping your congregation adjust to the changes associated with a change in mission focus.
- *Develop new leaders* (chap. 9): Identify and train potential leaders to meet expanding program needs and to invest in the next generation of ministry.

- *Build ongoing accountability:* With feedback from the congregation, the community, and mentors (individuals and churches), evaluate whether ministries are holistic, effective, and faithful to your unique calling.
- *Maintain a fresh vision:* Continually adapt priorities and projects in light of the changing congregational and community context for ministry, while affirming your core holistic mission.
- *Keep growing:* Celebrate the work of God in and through your congregation and seek God's guidance for the next stage in ministry.

Each church must prayerfully consider where it is in the process, where its strengths and weaknesses lie, and what its next steps should be. Some churches have a heart for holistic ministry, but their efforts falter for lack of stable leadership and internal unity. Their priority is strengthening the spiritual and organizational health of their congregation, setting the stage so that leaders and laypeople can effectively fulfill the vision God has given them. Other churches have strong leaders and are wonderfully nurturing, but all of their ministry is focused inward; these churches need to work on teaching holistic theology and developing a love for the community. Some churches have most of the pieces in place but lack direction. They need a process for seeking God's vision, supported by information about the congregation and the community.

Wherever your congregation is now, the key is to commit yourself by faith to take the next step in reaching your community with Good News and good works.

Part 1

Understanding Holistic Ministry

chapter one

What Does Holistic Ministry Look Like?

Inside of our churches we are to be a reflection of the coming kingdom, and we are to be doing the work of the kingdom—a work of justice, of love, of healing, of hope and transformation.[1]

What is holistic ministry?

We could start with a definition or theological explanation. But for most people, real illumination and inspiration come from seeing principles in action. In our study of churches in the Philadelphia area, we were privileged to observe a variety of wonderful models. No single illustration would suffice to explain holistic ministry. The following four snapshots illustrate how the Good Samaritan's robe comes in many sizes and colors.

Faith Assembly of God: Compassion Evangelism

Ethnicity: mainly African American
Size: 100 avg. attenders
Founded: 1981
Location: inner-city Philadelphia
Denomination: Assembly of God

As the men and women enter the church basement on a chill February day, they are greeted warmly by name. Linda, the program director, seems to be everywhere, giving out hugs and telling jokes to the people who have come in for food, as well as to the other staff. A woman enters and signs in on the attendance form, next to a stack of Christian tracts and flyers with the church's monthly activity calendar. Sharon, a motherly volunteer, listens to the woman share her anxieties about an upcoming court date involving her children. Sharon calls over to Linda, "Come over here and pray with us!" Linda reassures the woman that God listens to prayer and will take care of her situation. As they finish praying for the woman's family, both volunteers hug her and speak more encouraging words.

As more people gather in the room, Linda announces that anyone who wants to can join in the prayer circle. They all hold hands, and a volunteer prays for all the prayer requests that have been shared. Then the volunteers give out food bags, while some people browse through the clothes hanging on a portable rack. Around noon, those who are still in the room are invited upstairs to the sanctuary for a worship service, led by the pastor. The sound of singing accompanied by tambourines wafts downstairs. Meanwhile, volunteers are preparing a hot meal, mopping the floor, putting the pantry in order, and setting up tables and chairs. After the service concludes, the group returns downstairs to share a hot lunch.

With many senior citizens, people on public assistance, and recovering substance abusers in the neighborhood, food ministries are an important way (though not the only way) that Faith Assembly of God shares Christ's love with the community. Faith serves a hot lunch three days a week to an average of thirty-five people each meal and provides up to two bags of dry groceries each month to people who meet income requirements. The church does not have a large budget—about two-thirds of the food comes from state grants, private foundations, and food bank donations—but the congregation supplies ample volunteers for the ministry.

"We're trying to reach their souls and spirits as well as just feed their bellies," says Linda. Some of the volunteers first came to the church through the food ministry, and so they know from personal experience how groceries can become a vehicle for imparting both spiritual life and nutrition. One volunteer's prayer for the program is that "a little part of God's Spirit will go in every bag of food, so that we might know Jesus and tell someone about Jesus today." The friendly, caring atmosphere brings people back as much as their need for food. People know they will always be treated with dignity, unlike the treatment received from other bureaucratic programs, where the attitude, according to Linda, is, "Get in line, show us your ID, okay, next."

Linda once was impressed by a quote from T. D. Jakes: "They want to see your scars." A former drug addict who shot out all the veins in her arm before Christ redeemed her spirit and reclaimed her body, Linda gives the women she meets reason to trust her by showing them her scars. Women naturally confide in her and are encouraged by her testimony as an overcomer. When women come in looking abused or stressed, Linda says, "It gives me an opportunity to approach them in love. I don't push the 'You're going to hell' message. I try to show them how much God loves them and that they're precious in his sight." But without the food ministry, Linda might not have the opportunity to get to know them.

Processing food bags is the easy part. Loving people in Jesus' name is the hard part. Linda describes the struggles and the rewards of loving needy people who present themselves as unlovable:

> We have to love. No matter what, you have to love them. . . . Whether they're drunk, whether they're high, it doesn't matter. I have one gentleman that will come in . . . and he'll say, "I'm drunk!" . . . And inside of me sometimes I'd like to smack him, thinking, "What's the matter with you!" I would never show it on the outside. And the main thing I can do is to just talk to him and say, "You know that you don't have to be like this. God has a better plan." . . . When he's out there, this man knows he can come here. He knows that if he stumbles into the church drunk, he's not gonna be talked to rudely, he's not gonna be pushed aside. . . . Because who did Jesus associate with? We're not gonna tell people, "You can't come here like that." No, we say, "Come here like that." Then we can get through to them.

The pastor, Rev. Richard Smith, estimates that in one year, directly or indirectly, the church's food ministry has helped twenty-five people come to a new or renewed Christian faith. The ministry increases people's receptiveness to the gospel in several ways. Through the weekly daytime worship services, people who do not attend services regularly get used to the idea and feel of being in church. Knowing some songs and familiar faces makes it easier for them to show up for church on Sunday. The food ministry also becomes a bridge to other church ministries as the volunteers get to know people and identify their other needs.

For example, several of the residents in the church's Men's Home for recovering substance abusers first entered the church's doors to receive food aid. Lloyd found out about Faith Assembly of God through one of his drug buddies who went there for food. The ministry took care of his hunger, but he realized he needed something deeper. He attended an evening church service where he became convinced of God's saving power. Looking back, he attributes his conversion to the prayers and spiritual warfare of people in the church. He eventually became the leader of the Men's Home.

In the summertime, a weeklong tent crusade also combines food and worship, serving up to four hundred meals and food bags each day! The tent crusade and regular outdoor Sunday services "knock the church walls down," allowing unchurched people in the community to watch services from their doorstep or from windows. These services often feature testimonies from people who came to the church via the food ministry, showing local residents they have something in common with church members.

Dorothy, a resident in the nearby low-income housing complex, at first said no when people from Faith knocked on her door to invite her to the tent revival. But when they kept coming back each day, she finally agreed to go, just to get rid of them. She did not come forward for salvation at the revival, but that fall she started attending church, and one Sunday she felt a need to come clean and change her life. After a few months, her boyfriend started attending church. He too accepted Christ, and they got married. The thing about Faith Assembly that has made the biggest impact on her, Dorothy says, is the pastor's compassionate love. "He lives it. You can see him do it. He never does not feed if someone is hungry."

Dorothy's back problems keep her from full-time employment, but she receives a small stipend for her work with Peacemakers, a foundation-funded program started by the church in response to the fights and drive-by shootings endangering neighborhood youth. Wearing bright orange vests, Dorothy and other volunteers stand on street corners watching over the children making their way to and from school. Every weekday afternoon, teens in the program gather at the church to hang out with staff and rehearse skits, rap songs, and puppet shows that teach about peacemaking and safety and are performed at local schools and neighborhood events. In the summer, a special "Peace Celebration," open to the community, features Christian music groups, mime, testimonies, and, of course, food.

God's love, made tangible through food, hugs, and prayers, is what invites and sustains many broken people along the slow, ongoing path of personal transformation.

Media Presbyterian: Holistic Ministry in the Suburbs

Ethnicity: Anglo
Size: 400 avg. attenders
Founded: 1850
Location: Philadelphia suburb
Denomination: PC (USA)

Can a church be holistic if it is not in the inner city? Media Presbyterian, nestled neatly in the heart of a comfortable Philadelphia suburb, demonstrates that it is not only possible but that the rewards to church and community are just as great when the social needs are not as obvious or close at hand.

Rev. Bill Borror's vivid, Christ-centered preaching lays a strong foundation for holistic ministry. He consistently reminds the congregation, "The purpose of the church is to be an instrument for redemption." Sermons and teachings emphasize the mission of the church, which is to evangelize and to reach out to needy neighbors, whether that means a neighboring family struggling with divorce or the neighboring impoverished community of Chester.

"Holistic ministry is incarnational ministry. . . . It's God's people fleshing out the truth of the gospel," says Rev. Borror. This means making a personal commitment to service, not simply donating money from a distance (though the church does this as well—fully one-third of its budget goes to mission work far and near!). The Faith in Action committee was formed with the goal of involving at least half the congregation in some form of hands-on ministry. Church members are recruited for an array of service projects: running summer day camps for kids in inner-city neighborhoods; wielding a hammer in the Carpenter's Club to help elderly and low-income home owners; covering books and reading to children in the library of an urban Christian elementary school; visiting "throwaway parents" in nursing homes; linking professionals in the church (including many retirees) with nonprofit organizations needing skilled consultation.

The value of these ministries lies not only in helping people outside the church but in enriching the spiritual life of church members and expanding their relationships outside their cultural comfort zone. One of the goals of Faith in Action, says the committee chair, is that "everybody who participates in urban ministry knows somebody there on a first name basis." Rev. Borror has modeled this in his friendship with Bishop Dickie Robbins, the pastor of Life in Christ Cathedral of Faith in neighboring Chester, Pennsylvania. In the world's eyes, these two men and churches have little in common. But "United in Christ, Laboring in Love," as a banner heralds their joint work on a housing rehab project, the congregations witness to the community about their oneness in Christ. (See chapter 11 for more on their partnership.)

A major focus of Media's outreach is an annual Habitat for Humanity "blitz build" project in rural North Carolina. In 1999, 150 members and friends of the church spent a week of their summer vacation sweating and sawing together to give a low-income family a home. They completed the entire house from the foundation up, as well as several smaller rehab projects. One man, on whose trailer home Media Presbyterian members built a handicap ramp for his wife, was skeptical at first. He couldn't believe there were people out there who were willing to help him regardless of who he was or what he had done. "Why would you want to do this?" he would ask. "Well, because Christ directs us to," came the answer. "Oh, it's that simple?" Over the course of the week, volunteers at his site watched him soften. He allowed the volunteers to pray with him, and he even prayed himself. "I never really knew what or who Christians were before," the man said, "but now I do." Though he did not make a public profession of faith, it was clear that the church's presence had a dramatic impact on his life.

Another evangelistic outcome of their service is their witness to the surrounding community. "The secular world and school districts and politicians can't say that what is here at this church isn't real," says Rev. Borror. "They can't dismiss us as merely being another cultural clique, or a socioeconomic ghetto. We may not be doing things they are comfortable with, or they understand, but they cannot write us off as being insignificant and not impacting our community." After a television news story about their Habitat project spotlighted their faith as their motive for service, a member commented, "I just hope somebody watched that newscast who may be frustrated with [televangelists] and said, 'Hey, maybe all these Christians aren't such bad people after all.'"

Media Presbyterian members know well that spiritual and social needs are not limited to the inner city or the rural poor. Though the scars may be less visible than in poor areas, people in their community have been wounded by the maladies of middle-class culture: divorce, substance abuse, domestic violence, eating disorders. In a society driven by materialistic values, many kids are bounced from activity to activity without parental supervision or attention. Rev. Borror describes the result as "the fragmentation of the youth culture." In one year, their community reeled from the deaths of five high school students in an auto accident, several youth suicides (the youngest in sixth grade), and a murder. In the aftermath, Rev. Borror and Media's youth pastor came to be known as unofficial chaplains for the community—hosting funerals for unchurched families, providing counseling for the local school district, and inviting youth to participate in the church's active youth group. The church also hosts several support groups, such as for those dealing with divorce and grief.

Media Presbyterian has also become attuned to the "hidden" poverty of the suburbs. People regularly call the church with urgent requests for food or a month's rent. Church members in social work positions, such as one woman who works for the local public school, also refer families with special needs to the church. Through the deacons and Rev. Deb Miller, the church's associate pastor for holistic ministries, the church either meets the needs or refers people to other appropriate agencies. By helping people, says a deacon, the church is planting "seeds of goodness" that may eventually bear spiritual fruit, even if they never see the person again. "You can't make people understand," she explains, "but you can say we do this as a representation of Christ's love."

One particularly needy group the church has encountered are grandparents who for various reasons end up raising their grandchildren. The grandparents face multiple stressors—fixed incomes, failing health, depleted energy, and adult children in crisis. One grandmother asked the church to host their Second Time Around support group, and Media welcomed them with open arms. Every year, the church throws a Christmas party for the families and buys gifts for the children. The youth pastor leads a parenting class for grandparents raising teenagers. If a grandparent needs home repairs, they call on Media's Carpenter's Club. In emergencies the church helps out with food, medicine, or financial counseling, and the pastor's office is open for personal counseling or prayer. Says the group's coordinator, "There's not one thing I wouldn't go to the church about . . . and they wouldn't find a way to help. We know they're there for us, and we're so grateful." While Media puts no pressure on the group to join the church, three of the families in the group now attend worship services.

Evangelism in their suburban context is most effective, Media Presbyterian Church has found, when it is low-key. Up-front strategies such as Evangelism Explosion tend to alienate people. Rev. Borror stresses the importance of lifestyle evangelism: "Evangelism is to take place in your neighborhoods, the PTA, the soccer fields, the workplace." For example, when one deacon's company was going through a difficult time, another contractor asked him, "How do you stay so calm in this rat-race business?" The deacon's answer surprised him. "It's simple. I have a very strong faith, and the Lord continues to direct my life. I feel sorry for people who don't have that. It's much easier for me, having the ability to let go of certain things and entrust them to the Lord."

Another innovative way that Media witnesses to its community is through what Steve Sjogren calls *servant evangelism*. During summer street fairs, the church hosts a booth that gives out cups of cold water. A brochure available at the booth asks on its cover, "Why would a church offer free water on State Street?" Inside, along with biblical passages about Jesus, the text concludes: "We just thought that you might be thirsty for the water in the cup or for the water from which you will thirst no more." The results are not immediate or dramatic, but still meaningful, as the chair of the evangelism committee explains. "Later, when someone is in crisis or hurt, they will remember—'Hey, they were out there giving out cold water, so maybe I'll go to the church and talk to someone.'"

As Media celebrated its 150th anniversary in 2000, a longtime member of the church reflected, "There is a spirit here in this church that will keep on bringing new members in, a lively program that will serve the people and do what Christ wants us to do—which is to reach out into the world, serve those who are in need, and broadcast the Good News to everyone."

New Creation Lutheran Church/Iglesia Luterana Nueva Creación: The Empowering Gospel

Ethnicity: Hispanic and Anglo
Size: 75 avg. attenders
Founded: 1994

Location: inner-city Philadelphia
Denomination: Lutheran

Worship services at New Creation Lutheran Church often close with the small congregation holding hands in a circle and singing the simple song "God Is So Good." Like everything else in the service, the song is bilingual, and the circle symbolizes the diverse congregation's unity in Christ. In his benediction, Rev. Patrick Cabello Hansel charges the congregation to spend their week "inviting others who do not know Christ, and working for peace and justice."

The sanctuary space surrounds the congregation with affirmations of the church's mission. Hanging in the sanctuary is a banner with the church's butterfly logo and theme verse, "En Cristo Somos Una Nueva Creación/In Christ We Are a New Creation" (2 Cor. 5:17). Behind the pulpit is a colorful handmade quilt with urban and biblical scenes intermingled. Another prominently displayed banner depicts a dove surrounded by olive branches hovering over a city skyline, with Jesus' well-known saying from Luke 4—with a slight change in the words to claim Jesus' mission as their own: "The Spirit of the Lord has anointed *us* to preach good news to the poor."

New Creation's community cries out for good news. The neighborhood is plagued by generational poverty, family dysfunction, and accompanying high rates of violence, single parenthood, and substance abuse. A lack of structure and stability, at both the family and institutional levels, keeps people's lives in a state of chaos. Deportation is a constant threat to many undocumented immigrants, adding to the high rates of unemployment and transience. A lack of positive role models and productive activities stunts the potential of the booming population of children and youth. Insidious racism has lowered residents' expectations and demeaned their self-esteem. The neighborhood suffers from neglect by police, elected officials, and city services such as street cleaning and trash pickup. Many in the community are secularized Catholics lacking a strong spiritual foundation.

In this setting, says Rev. Hansel, "The mission of the church is not simply to save souls but to transform the community." Although the church is relatively new, and its resource base and membership are still small (literally—over half the members are under age eighteen), the church has developed a reputation for helping the community. Rev. Hansel believes the role of the church is to sustain a compassionate, empowering, transformational presence in the midst of poverty and hopelessness. As people experience God's love through the church's demonstration and proclamation of the gospel, they are freed and empowered to work for change. Rev. Hansel explains:

> Transformation generally takes place first within the individual coming to an awareness of being loved and forgiven by a gracious God, and then being transformed and the evil or oppression taken away from them. . . . That individual transformation leads to involvement in justice and the building of a community.

New Creation helps people come to know God's love and grace both through its daily incarnational witness and through more direct evangelistic efforts such as flyers, street festivals, and Bring-a-Friend Sunday, as well as celebrations traditional to the Latino culture, such as Three Kings Day and First Communion. The church also shares the gospel in the context of social programs. For example, the summer camp celebrates "Christmas in July" each year, giving the counselors an opportunity to tell children the story of Christ. Prayer is a regular feature of all the church's ministries.

Rev. Hansel believes that social ministry can be disempowering when it focuses on "responding to need, rather than energizing what people's gifts are." People came to Christ deaf, blind, and leprous; Christ invited them to follow him and become evangelists and healers. The people who come to New Creation to receive ministry are recruited to minister to others. People who are aided by the church's food program find it difficult to refuse the ministry coordinator when she urges them to spend a few hours volunteering for the church. "We're giving food to you," she coaxes. "You can at least give your time." Through the church, residents come to view themselves as community assets and learn the power of working together to accomplish common goals.

One innovative grant-funded ministry, the Pre-Work program, exemplifies this empowerment approach. The program simultaneously tackles unemployment, community decay, and a lack of wholesome activities for youth by hiring preteens and adult supervisors (some just leaving welfare) to work in various community service and entrepreneurship projects. Youth tend a garden cultivated in an empty lot, work at the church's summer day camp, maintain the church and community center, paint flowers over graffiti at local playgrounds, write for the community newspaper, and run a small snack food business. The youth also learn how to advocate for their community—for example, how to report abandoned cars to the police.

Rev. Hansel looks for opportunities to raise the youths' awareness of justice issues. For example, on a field trip, their van got stuck behind a garbage truck in an upscale neighborhood. The kids were surprised to see the garbage workers set the cans back where they found them, instead of throwing them into the street, and pick up garbage that they dropped. Rev. Hansel led a discussion as to why this does *not* happen in their neighborhood, and what they might do to change things.

The program also encourages youth to focus on personal development by training them in conflict resolution, integrity, and other matters of character. They learn the value of prayer and church fellowship, the necessity of seeking forgiveness from God and forgiving others. The youth also learn to integrate faith with service. When asked what the program taught them about God, one young girl responded: "When we help people, we're doing something God wants us to do."

Community beautification is another important expression of the church's mission. Co-pastor Luisa Cabello Hansel explains:

> One of the more aggressive ways that people express themselves, their anger, their dissatisfactions, is through graffiti. . . . When we first saw the church and all the walls around covered with graffiti, that was a sign of a lack of hope that our children were going to see every day. . . . Painting flowers and butterflies— signs of hope—is giving the children a message that life can be better than what they used to see.

Now the church walls are covered with colorful murals instead of graffiti. Similarly, the community garden is a living symbol of the new creation the church is becoming through Christ. Rev. Hansel attests, "When you take care of the creation, the creation responds. We planted our garden, and birds came back, butterflies came back, wildflowers came back. It's like it says in Romans 8: 'The whole creation is waiting for the revealing of the children of God.'"

New Creation's transformational vision looks beyond its neighborhood. Through an ecumenical coalition called Philadelphia Interfaith Action, New Creation joins with other churches to work for change on social issues that affect the entire city, such as community policing, affordable housing, and welfare reform. Their involvement reflects a belief that God loves the whole city and desires to see it flourish. As one church attender expressed it, "Social change comes from an understanding that we are all children of God and that this is not the way God wants things." Even when the congregation does not see specific improvements in the neighborhood or personal circumstances, their involvement with community organizing reinforces the church's message of perseverance and hope in God.

Hope sustains Rev. Hansel through times of discouragement and weariness. "God is going to transform the world, and we plant little seeds of that, and the church is a gardener," he says. "The youth in the Pre-Work program, the murals, or getting a few people jobs—those are all signs. The same way that people forgiving each other is a sign. It's a long process, but I do believe that transformation's coming, and it's coming here."

Tenth Presbyterian Church: Sharing the Transforming Word of God

Ethnicity: majority Anglo; some Asian and African American
Size: 1,150 avg. attenders
Founded: 1829
Location: downtown Philadelphia
Denomination: Presbyterian Church of America

The prayer meeting had ended, and the small group of Tenth Presbyterian Church members were bundling up in their coats to go home. They were about to step around a lump of blanket huddled on the church steps when something stopped them short. Here they had been in God's presence in prayer, while right outside the church was one of God's children, suffering in the cold. One member turned to another and said, "We need to do something about that."

Later, the prayer group approached the deacons and said, "What can you do?" The deacons wisely answered, "What do *you* want to do?" And so the church members began praying and reflecting about how the church could be a good neighbor, not only to this one particular person but to the growing population of homeless men and women in the downtown area around the church. At first, the response was to start a feeding program. The church soon realized, however, that the most important thing they could do was to establish relationships and to share the Word of God with the people they fed.

From that small seed, ACTS (Active Compassion through Service) has grown into a ministry that now involves roughly 20 percent of the congregation. ACTS aims "to educate, motivate, and equip the members of Tenth to imitate Christ in attitude, humility and service, and to be good stewards of their God-given resources and talents."[2] An array of ministries provides abundant opportunities to serve: dinners and Bible studies for homeless guests, after-school tutoring, nursing home visitation, a worship service for people with HIV, single parent/divorce support groups, and a racial reconciliation fellowship. The mission of ACTS is nothing less than the "total transformation of individuals in the name of Jesus. It seeks to be a prophetic witness of Christ's love to those who suffer from spiritual and physical poverty."

One of the principles underlying the diverse ACTS ministries is the goal of nurturing relationships between Christian volunteers and needy members of the community. At the monthly Community Dinner, for example, the homeless guests (not "clients"!) do not line up to receive meals served on trays cafeteria-style. Instead, they are seated at tables with attractive, full place settings and served family style, sitting beside church members who share the meal and dinner conversation. A worship service before the meal provides spiritual nourishment for many guests who would never dream of entering the church on Sunday morning. The setting and the worship service affirm guests' dignity, and the relationships forged over the meal help guests become more receptive to the message of the Word. For more substantive spiritual guidance, guests are invited to the weekly Fellowship Bible Study, which includes a less formal meal. The Community Dinner draws about 120 homeless persons; about 25 attend the Fellowship Bible Study.

The relational approach to evangelism is rooted in Christ's model of incarnational love and sacrificial servanthood. Dr. David Apple, director of ACTS, explains:

> Just as Jesus became a servant of others, washing others' feet, not being afraid to be vulnerable, not being afraid to come alongside people who are hurting, not being afraid of coming alongside someone who may smell—we're called to be advocates, to come alongside and be available. Servanthood means to be available to people, and to know that God is in charge of our time and our resources.

ACTS is as much about discipling Christians to a deeper commitment as it is about serving those outside the church. Engaging the church in mercy ministry, says Dr. Apple, requires "converting those who call themselves believers." To become a servant and friend to someone very different from you is to embark on a pilgrimage of discipleship. The impact of the gospel is seen equally in how it transforms street people's social circumstances and how it transforms church members' innate self-centeredness into Christlike love for the marginalized.

Dr. Apple's own pilgrimage to holistic ministry began with his salvation experience. "I was saved in a small, black church, through the witness of former drug addicts, recovering alcoholics, former prostitutes, and people who had nothing physically, but showed me that they had everything, because of Jesus Christ." Because of their witness, and because of struggles he has faced in his own life, he says, "My calling, my passion, is to be available to God to help the poor."

Dr. Apple explains why evangelism and discipleship are central to this mission.

> If someone has no friends, has no support, then he or she is going to find themselves feeling abandoned and hopeless. Why try? The systemic solution is escape—whether it's escape through chemicals, your drug of choice, or sexual promiscuity. All of them are some form of self condemnation, because we're punishing ourselves for the situation that we are in. . . . But all of that, I believe, has a spiritual solution, because . . . there's no condemnation if we know that we are covered with the righteousness of Christ. So even if we have absolutely nothing, the starting point for renewal is spiritual. . . . It's only in Christ that people finally possess the freedom to finally look beyond themselves for a source of healing.

People with habitual needs should be offered services, skills, and economic opportunities, but in Dr. Apple's experience, unless the spiritual bondage is broken, this assistance may be of little benefit. As a matter of stewardship, Tenth Church does not duplicate services already provided by other Christian and secular agencies. Rather, by building ongoing, supportive, Christ-centered relationships with people, ACTS's ministries help empower people to take advantage of other resources effectively. Progress with homeless guests is slow, but the fruits become evident over time. Dr. Apple can point to "several homeless guests who because of becoming a new creature are able to assume new characteristics and able to take off old labels and assume responsible citizenship."

One of these men used to sleep on the steps of a synagogue a block from Tenth Church. For years, he was addicted to crack cocaine, alcohol, and other chemicals. He was, in Dr. Apple's words, "a walking dead man." A couple of ACTS volunteers befriended him and from time to time would bring him sandwiches and blankets and invite him to church. He began to come occasionally to Tenth Church for the meals and the warmth—but for several years refused other help. Finally, as Dr. Apple puts it, "He got sick and tired of being sick and tired." He began attending Bible studies, opening up to his church friends, and learning about Jesus.

ACTS volunteers led the man to a profession of saving faith and helped him enter a Christian drug recovery program. After several episodes of relapse and treatment, he became drug-free. He reunited with the mother of his children, and they married and bought a home. His wife and two teenage daughters became believers. He stood before a judge and paid old outstanding fines, saying, "The person who did all these things, I'm not that person anymore." The former crack addict who slept on the synagogue steps now volunteers with ACTS, sharing the gospel with people with whom he used to share drugs.

One woman who attended the Fellowship Bible Study accepted Christ before she died of AIDS. Tenth Church members attended her funeral service. Their caring caught the attention of the secular respite home where she had lived, and they invited ACTS to start a Bible study and worship service at the home. Because of the relationship that they had nurtured with this woman, the church gained credibility and access to a population that desperately needs and is open to the gospel, but one that rarely trusts the church. Says a Tenth Church volunteer who ministers at the home, "We have a responsibility to everyone, but especially those whose life span is going to be shorter than everyone else's."

Inner-city areas are often places of alienation, where commuters pass by homeless people in alleys and doorways on their way in for a day's work or an evening's entertainment. When Tenth Church faced the decision as to whether to sell its property and move to the suburbs, following the trail of so many other white urban churches, the congregation decided to remain. They have stayed, not just to keep a piece of real estate but to be a witness and servant in the city. Church bulletins proclaim, "This church opens wide her doors and offers her welcome in the name of the Lord Jesus Christ." Homeless men, suburbanites, HIV sufferers, international students, young urban families—all have accepted the invitation.

Patterns of Ministry among Holistic Congregations

As the above stories illustrate, there is no one template for "the holistic church." Although holistic congregations have common theological roots and share several key characteristics, each church grows out of different soil—its denomination, community context, leadership, available resources, ethnic heritage, congregational culture—and bears different fruit. Each church's journey toward holistic ministry is unique and is marked by different joys and challenges. A church's ministry is also shaped by a sense of its particular calling and by a range of theological beliefs that shade how holistic mission is interpreted and implemented.

This means that holistic churches are quite diverse. You cannot predict where they will be found, or what ethnic group will fill the pews, or whether they will sing hymns or contemporary choruses, or which political party they will endorse. Nor can you associate holistic churches with a particular type of ministry. In fact, churches that foster a holistic mission may not all agree on the "right" priorities for ministry or on the best ways to share the gospel. But they will all affirm that the church must share the gospel and that community outreach is a priority.

In our study of fifteen churches in the greater Philadelphia area that engage in community ministry, we were surprised at first by this diversity among holistic churches. After interviewing many church leaders and ministry participants and observing dozens of ministries, we began to notice patterns in the forms that holistic ministry takes in different churches. You might think of these patterns as musical themes in a complex symphony—distinct but interweaving motifs held together by an integral melodic line. Each theme focuses on a particular dimension of holistic mission. A congregation is likely to combine various aspects of several themes, and different individuals or programs within a congregation may lean toward different themes. In fact, a church that focuses exclusively on one ministry theme alone is not truly holistic. However, a church may identify most strongly with two or three of the themes. The key is to blend these themes in a balance that is appropriate to the needs of the community, the spiritual gifts and resources of the members, and the vision and calling of the church.

1. *Focus on ministries of personal spiritual transformation as a path to social change.* The first pattern or ministry theme emphasizes transforming society one life at a time—as Glenn Loury puts it, "one by one from the inside out."[3] Spiritual renewal empowers change in every area of a person's life, and the transformation of individuals in turn serves as the seed of lasting change at a community level.

In working with individuals who struggle with deep-rooted behavioral and psychological issues—such as drug addiction, long-term welfare dependency, or generational domestic abuse—spiritual renewal and a process of holistic discipleship may be necessary to produce fundamental life changes. Vibrant personal faith endows life with meaning and purpose. It overcomes the grip of nihilism and despair. It assures forgiveness, canceling feelings of guilt and failure. It brings a new sense of dignity and worth that counters the stigmatizing effects of poverty. It strengthens a moral framework for lifestyle, character, and attitude. And it offers hope for the future, motivating positive steps toward change. Christian faith is more than positive thinking or self-help therapy. Spiritual rebirth releases a supernatural power that breaks the stranglehold of evil forces and transforms the very core of broken persons. This spiritual liberation can then bring about emotional, relational, physical, and financial deliverance.

Renewal ministries are especially important for people who have been systematically demeaned, such as minorities, explains a ministry leader at Christian Stronghold Baptist Church:

> The strongest issue that you see . . . is that they will not have finished high school, and will have a poor self image and a lack of hope. They have been oriented to a negative lifestyle because that's the only way that they see they can survive on the streets. . . . So what I'm looking at with them is to help them to define themselves as God sees them.

Without attention to internal barriers to empowerment, social ministry often has limited impact. Social ministry may alter people's circumstances, but unless there is inner change, the root problems will manifest themselves in other forms.

Shirley, a counselor with Cookman United Methodist's welfare-to-work program, learned this the hard way. After she accepted Christ in prison, she quit her drug habit. In prison, she took computer and office skills training and enrolled in college classes. After her release, she got a job and stabilized her family life. But she did not follow through with discipleship and church fellowship, and within a few years she was back in prison for forgery. Even though she no longer used drugs, she still had a "dope fiend mentality," as she describes it, because she had not resolved the spiritual issues at the root of her addiction. She then realized that she could not succeed without God and that she had to make a decision: "His way or no way." Shirley now helps the women she counsels understand that without surrendering their lives to God, they might get a job, but if they leave the other parts of their lives in shambles, they will eventually face some moral or social challenge that they do not have the ability in themselves to resolve.

Spiritual renewal is not a magic wand that immediately resolves all of a Christian's problems. Sometimes a person does experience instantaneous deliverance after turning his or her life over to Christ—but most often, as in Shirley's case, it takes years of slow progress and patient discipling. Getting right with God is seldom *by itself* sufficient to turn a person or a community around, but it is a fertile starting place. Discipleship becomes a solid foundation for social services, such as family counseling, GED classes, financial seminars, job training, and health education, that empower people to build new lives.

In addition, the loving support of members of a congregation is essential to the ongoing transformation of broken people. Many people who have adopted habitual, destructive patterns will experience lasting change only if other Christians walk prayerfully with them over an extensive period of time, holding them accountable, challenging them to take the next step, showing grace when they stumble, and celebrating new patterns of behavior.

2. *Focus on social services ministries as a door to evangelism.* The second holistic ministry theme or pattern sounds at first like the opposite of the first: Helping to meet people's social needs lays a foundation for spiritual nurture.

People's immediate needs—whether financial, physical, relational, or emotional—may eclipse their felt need for God. People are less likely to absorb the message that God loves them and wants to turn their lives around if they are worried about paying overdue rent, struggling to learn English as a second language, or surviving an abusive relationship. As a staff member at Christian Stronghold Baptist Church notes, "By going out to the community and meeting their felt needs, that gives us the opportunity to spread the Good News of Jesus Christ. . . . People become very curious why you are helping them. It gives us an opportunity to change the conversation to Christ." By helping people overcome physical hunger, the church can help create in them a new awareness of their spiritual hunger. Bringing stability into people's lives clears a space for them to reflect on their relationship with God.

Jesus saw a person's need as a window of opportunity to invite him or her to embark on a journey of transformation. Jesus fed the five thousand (John 6:5–13) and then invited the crowd to eat of the bread of life (6:27). After a dramatic healing, Jesus commissioned a demon-possessed social outcast to return to his hometown as an evangelist (Luke 8:27–39). In his first encounter with a paralyzed man (John 5:5–14), Jesus told him, "Stand up, take your mat and walk" (v. 8); in his second encounter, Jesus admonished him, "You have been made well! Do not sin any more" (v. 14).

Meeting a pressing need is also a way of making the gospel tangible. Caring for physical needs has symbolic meaning as well as practical importance. Jesus recognized this when he instructed his disciples to follow his example by washing one another's feet. Humble service communicates Christ's love in a way that transcends words. Heidi once sat beside a man at a Christian homeless shelter in Chicago as he poured out his doubts about faith. "There are so many religions out there. How am I supposed to believe that this one is right? How do I know that what the Christians say is true?" he asked. Heidi thought for a moment. "Well, who was it that gave you dinner tonight?" The man got the point. When people see love in action, they are better able to believe in a loving God. As people's needs are met in Christ's name, they catch a glimpse of Jehovah Jireh, the great Provider.

Beyond simply distributing goods or services, holistic social ministries also create opportunities for Christians to build relationships with those who are served. People who have repeatedly been hurt or abandoned do not easily let people into their lives. Gaining a hearing for the gospel message may require overcoming barriers of trust or culture by cultivating a caring, nurturing track record over time. David Apple says of Tenth Presbyterian Church's ministry to homeless persons, "The first goal is that each worker be a friend to each guest in order to establish trust. If there is no trust then there can be no ministry."[4] You can tell people that God loves them, but until they see it demonstrated, they may not understand or believe it.

Compassion ministries feed people while teaching them that they don't live by bread alone (John 6:27). The ultimate desire in holistic social ministries is to see people brought into the fullness of life in Christ. But this does not mean that social compassion is pointless unless someone becomes a Christian because of it. When Jesus healed a group of ten lepers, only one returned to thank him for his mercy. Yet this did not discourage Jesus from continuing his ministry of healing. The church similarly bears a responsibility to meet people's needs regardless of how they respond to Christ. Otherwise social ministry is reduced to a means to an end, a utilitarian evangelistic tool. Compassion must never be used as a bribe. "The LORD is good to all, and his compassion is over all that he has made" (Ps. 145:9). Holistic churches model God's extravagant love by extending aid in the same spirit of gracious, patient compassion.

3. *Focus on ministries of reconciliation that witness to unity in Christ*. Theologian Vinay Samuel asserts, "One sign and wonder, biblically speaking, that alone can prove the power of the gospel is that of reconciliation."[5] The assurance of the gospel is that Christ has broken down the dividing wall of hostility between different people groups (Eph. 2:14). The peace between God and humanity accomplished by the cross is inseparable from the peace that should prevail among God's people.

Only by the power of the Spirit can holistic churches take on the seemingly intractable divisions of race. "Generations of racism have left deep, deep scars on the soul of the black community," writes Bishop George McKinney.[6] The historical abuses and ongoing assault on minority communities have produced "a very deep, very broad reservoir of rage seething in the guts of most black people today." While other types of ministries address the symptomatic consequences of this rage, such as violence, addictions, and family instability, ministries of reconciliation allow God's redemptive power to flow to the root of the anger. Authentic reconciliation goes beyond superficial friendships or token integration to create new patterns of fellowship based on repentance, spiritual healing, and Christlike love. Holistic congregations create an environment where Christians can work through the stages of racial reconciliation, as summed up by Spencer Perkins and Chris Rice: "admit, submit, commit."[7]

One of the signs of authentic reconciliation is multicultural worship. Such worship anticipates John's glorious vision: "There was a great multitude that no one could count, from every nation, from all tribes and peoples and languages, standing before the throne and before the Lamb" (Rev. 7:9). Some culturally homogenous congregations enter into "sister church" relationships outside their ethnic group; some congregations share building space and hold occasional joint worship celebrations (for example, helping a new immigrant congregation take root in the community); some congregations become fully integrated, from the leadership team to the language of worship to the foods served at fellowship meals. Reconciliation in holistic churches extends beyond ethnicity to other barriers to unity, such as economic class, physical and mental abilities, and family status. Sunday at 11:00 is still the most segregated hour in America—but not in holistic congregations that embrace God's delight in the diversity of humankind. Such churches become "a little picture of what heaven will be like."

Cross-cultural "yokefellows" in ministry—such as the relationship between Chris Rice and the late Spencer Perkins, or an effective urban-suburban church partnership—provide powerful models of reconciliation. True cross-cultural partnerships bring a power and credibility to ministry, especially in ethnically diverse communities. When people hear that Jesus is Lord over all, they may not be inclined to believe it; when they see diverse followers of Jesus working together for the good of others, they cannot deny the evidence that "the Lord is one" (Mark 12:29). Jesus indicated the evangelistic impact of Christian unity: "By this everyone will know that you are my disciples, if you have love for one another" (John 13:35).

Cross-cultural personal relationships are an important fruit of reconciliation, but it does not stop there. Holistic reconciliation also means examining and changing entrenched social patterns that keep members of the congregation segregated from others (especially other Christians) who are different. This could mean forming a study group to examine how racism has affected the family history and current lives of church members (for better and for worse), fostering changes in the local community to make it more open to diversity, lobbying for public policies that promote racial justice, or supporting the relocation of "missionaries" from the congregation to forge relationships within other ethnic communities. Such actions, immersed in prayer, have a transforming ripple effect from the congregation to society.

4. *Focus on community development to express God's love for whole persons and communities.* The first two patterns focus largely on individuals. Their programs provide material assistance, help develop skills, nurture behavioral

change, or offer relational support for individuals. But individuals live in communities. If the community is unhealthy, the people who live there will continue to fight an uphill battle to realize the quality of life God intended for them. Often people have needs that go beyond personal transformation or a specific service, such as the need for affordable housing, jobs, health care, and safe places for children to play. Holistic social and economic development ministries address people's needs at the community level.

Community development ministries work to shape the community to be more consistent with God's design for shalom. They help guard against paternalism and break cycles of dependency by creating opportunities for people to become self-sufficient. As a matter of stewardship, development ministries redistribute public and private resources (e.g., through access to assets such as loans and grants) on behalf of the most vulnerable in society. They leave a legacy of new or renewed institutions, such as schools, credit unions, and health clinics, that give community residents the opportunity to build a better future for themselves and their children. By inviting the participation of residents, these ministries increase people's investment in their community and empower them to address their own problems.

Just because community development achieves "secular" results does not mean it has no spiritual roots or fruits! Holistic community development is distinct from a secular model of development, which tempts agencies to "engage in 'projects' rather than 'ministry,' to focus on results rather than discipleship, [and] ties the church to a dominant culture rather than to a theology of sacrifice."[8] Holistic ministries integrate a spiritual component in several ways. Flowing out of the mission Jesus modeled and taught, guided by a Spirit-led vision for outreach, inspired by passionate worship, and strengthened through prayer, holistic community development integrates concerns for people's social and spiritual well-being. Community development ministry serves as a tangible expression of the Good News the church proclaims in evangelism. It nurtures an environment that affirms the church's message of God's love and human dignity. By identifying the church with the good things happening in the community, it points people to the reign of Christ. It creates new opportunities for church members to come into relationship with non-Christians in the context of ministry, and it makes community residents more receptive to invitations to attend church or to hear the gospel.

Holistic community development also guards the fruits of evangelism. Faith-based development ministry relieves the conditions that drive people to despair, abuse, or crime. It also recognizes the dilemma faced by residents of distressed communities who experience a radical spiritual transformation. As they achieve greater stability in their personal lives, they naturally want to move out of the community to create a better life for their children. Community development ministry builds the church by giving people hope and a purpose for remaining where they are and becoming part of the solution.

5. *Focus on justice ministries that embody the empowering message of the gospel.* Where there is injustice, service and community development ministries may significantly improve the living conditions of residents, but they do not get to the root of the problem. Racism—"America's original sin," as Sojourners' Jim Wallis describes it—along with sexism, political corruption, failing schools, environmental abuses, corrupt criminal justice systems, and unfair economic structures all undermine the good created by converted individuals and effective community development. Unjust systems and institutions block people's access to opportunities, stunt their human dignity, and rob them of shalom. Darrell Guder describes the church's calling to pursue justice:

> Shalom envisions the full prosperity of a people of God living under the covenant of God's demanding care and compassionate rule. In the prophetic vision, peace like this comes hand in hand with justice. Without justice, there can be no real peace, and without peace, no real justice. Indeed, only in a social world full of a peace grounded in justice can there come the full expression of joy and celebration.[9]

Through advocacy ministries, churches grapple with the reality of social sin and follow in the prophetic tradition of serving as "God's voice," proclaiming a biblical perspective on institutional or systemic social problems. Sometimes churches are able to work within channels of official power, sometimes they organize together to exert pressure from outside the system or create alternatives to the system, and sometimes they raise a lone voice of protest, witness, or solidarity. Advocacy ministries might lobby for higher earned income tax credits, or confront city officials about zoning regulations that restrict affordable family housing, or educate the public about an upcoming proposal to legalize gambling. The goal of holistic advocacy ministries is not to force change through violence or threats but to speak the truth in love and overcome evil with good.

Holistic ministries of systemic reform well up from a deep fountain of spiritual commitment. They integrate spiritual nurture and support evangelism in the same ways as community development ministries. They also call Christians to grieve over sin and the brokenness it begets and remind us afresh of our need for the whole gospel. Worship services renew those who seek justice with a celebration of God's promise that all of creation's goodness will one day be restored.

6. *Focus on reaching skeptics by demonstrating that the church makes a difference.* The patterns or themes discussed so far show how serving people in Christ's name helps people grasp the breadth and depth of God's love for them and

nurtures those served on a journey of personal transformation. But the evangelistic impact of social outreach ministry doesn't stop there. Others are watching from the wings.

The evangelical church's witness has been sadly tarnished by decades of infighting and skepticism about social ministry. Stereotypes of fallen television preachers, abortion clinic-bombing fundamentalists, and finger-pointing political activists leap all too easily to mind in association with the word *Christian*. The church is often perceived as self-serving, hypocritical, and irrelevant. Cynicism and alienation can be just as much a barrier to evangelism as hunger and homelessness. Holistic ministry in the spirit of Christlike servanthood challenges the unbelieving community's perception of the church and Christianity by modeling a meaningful alternative. The holistic church stands out like the "city on a hill" that glorifies God, a beacon of integrity and hope. "Let your light shine before others, so that they may see your good works and give glory to your Father in heaven" (Matt. 5:16).

Letting the church's light shine also creates opportunities for personal evangelism. In our materialistic, me-first culture, sacrificial service is a curiosity! Many people can't help but wonder why that bunch of Christians should care so much about helping others. Imagine a Media Presbyterian church member having a conversation with a coworker after just returning from the church's annual Habitat for Humanity mission trip in North Carolina.

"Yeah, we really enjoyed our Caribbean cruise. So what did you do?"

"I built a house."

"What?"

"Well, our family went to North Carolina, along with about 150 others from our church, and we spent a week putting up a house for a poor family there."

"Now, why would you go and do something like that?"

This secular coworker has just handed the church member an evangelistic opening equivalent to, "So, tell me about Jesus."

Developing a reputation for social activism makes churches especially attractive to spiritual seekers who value justice and compassion without knowing the God of shalom. The church's lack of concern about social issues led many social activists in the 1960s and 1970s to think they had to leave the church to make a difference in the world. Many disillusioned activists are now seeking ways to bring together social concerns with spiritual fulfillment. Baby boomers, especially, crave a sense of belonging to a meaningful effort to improve society.[10] Younger generations are also showing an increasing attraction to activism. Churches that combine word and deed, that minister to body, soul, and spirit, draw in people who hunger for more than superficial Christianity.

Rev. Jim Kraft notes that when new members of First Presbyterian Church are asked why they decided to join the church, "A significant number talk about the fact that they heard about our church's ministries—'There's a church that's doing something. . . . It's trying to help people. That's the kind of church we want to be associated with.'" The director of Servant Development at First Presbyterian concurs. "I think people today are not interested in a lot of hypocrisy, and they are not impressed with a lot of 'sounding good,' but not living out the Christian faith. When they see what we are doing, that draws them in, because they know we are trying to put it into action."

Conclusion

The churches profiled in this book are truly remarkable—and yet there is nothing special about them. Any church can become a center of healing, hope, and shalom in its community. Any church can be used by God to provide food and job training to people in need; to break the bondage of substance abuse, racial prejudice, and materialism; to restore families and rebuild homes; to reform culture and advocate for justice, while sharing the Good News of God's amazing grace. Any church—including *your* church—can make a difference by serving the kingdom and witnessing to Christ the King. How? We hope the rest of this book will provide some answers.

chapter two

The Church's Calling
to Holistic Ministry

To spread the kingdom of God is more than simply winning people to Christ. It is also working for the healing of persons, families, and relationships. It is doing deeds of mercy and seeking justice. It is ordering lives and relationships and institutions and communities according to God's authority to bring in the blessedness of the kingdom. The presence of the kingdom of God is the means for the renewal of the entire world and all the dimensions of life.[1]

The early twentieth century saw a bitter falling-out between fundamentalists and followers of the so-called social gospel. The division has affected the church to this day. One branch, quoting the Great Commission, claims that nothing is as important as leading individuals to a saving relationship with Jesus Christ. These Christians see evangelism as the primary task of the church. The other side points to the parable of the sheep and the goats in Matthew 25:31–46. There Jesus declares to those who fail to meet people's needs, "You that are accursed, depart from me!" (v. 41). This side stresses that the calling of Christians is to care for those who are poor and to seek justice. Both sides have it partly right—but neither has the whole picture. These selective readings of Scripture and interpretations of the church's mission have led to lopsided Christianity.

Holistic ministry overcomes this long-standing divide by reaching out with the whole gospel in both word and deed. Holistic Christians love not only "in word or speech, but [also] in truth and action" (1 John 3:18). The coordinator of evangelism and outreach at Germantown Church of the Brethren sums it up: "Love is an action word. People want to see action, not hear so much mouth. You can't tell somebody about the love of Jesus Christ if you don't have the love in your heart. The love is what draws people to Christ." Without social ministry, evangelism can be perceived as just "so much mouth." Without the gospel, social activism is stripped of the Holy Spirit's transforming power.

This chapter takes a closer look at the church's calling to share the gospel through both Good News and good works.

Why Do Holistic Ministry? The Model and Teaching of Jesus

Virtually every strand of biblical truth calls Christians to link word and deed in proclaiming and demonstrating the Good News of Christ's reign. Jesus' example, Jesus' commands, and Jesus' gospel reveal that Christians are to love the whole person the way our Lord and Master did.

Jesus' Example

Jesus knew better than anyone that each person he encountered had an immortal soul in need of salvation. Yet story after story in the Gospels depicts Jesus devoting many hours of potential preaching time to healing sick bodies. Of course, he also preached and taught. But the space that the Gospel writers devote to stories of healing tells us that God incarnate had a high view of the importance of meeting people's physical needs. Furthermore, the texts often point out that Jesus ministered because he had compassion on hurting people (Matt. 14:14; 15:32; 20:34; Mark 1:41). He did not perform acts of healing simply to entice people to hear his message. If Jesus is our only perfect example, then the church today must combine word and deed out of compassionate love for the world.

But Jesus' ministry went beyond touching individuals. Though Jesus did not start a political party or reform campaign, his teachings and practices made it clear that his new messianic community would feature radically different social, economic, and political arrangements. In all kinds of ways, Jesus challenged the status quo of his time: its view of women, wealth, power, leadership, and violence.[2] Jesus' example calls the church to follow in pursuing a new vision of a just, peaceful, and equitable society.

Jesus' example also teaches us that holistic ministry is incarnational. Jesus lived among the people whom he taught and healed. Rev. Luisa Cabello Hansel of New Creation Lutheran Church explains. "Jesus didn't send a messenger, didn't just reach out a hand to pull us up, but Jesus came *himself*. He became like one of us and lived among us." After the resurrection, Jesus sent his indwelling Spirit so that he could continue to be present in the world through his followers. Just as Jesus took on the form of a servant (Phil. 2:7), Christians are to be humble ambassadors of Christ's healing presence in word and deed.

Jesus' Commands

When Jesus sent out the Twelve on their first independent preaching mission, he told them "to proclaim the kingdom of God and to heal" (Luke 9:2). When Jesus sent out the Seventy, he told them to "cure the sick who are there, and say to them, 'the kingdom of God has come to you'" (Luke 10:9). That combination of preaching and healing was exactly what Jesus had modeled, according to Matthew's summary of Jesus' ministry: "Jesus went about all the cities and villages, teaching in their synagogues, and proclaiming the Good News of the kingdom, and curing every disease and every sickness" (Matt. 9:35).

As Jesus prepared to leave his disciples, he told them to carry on his mission in the world: "As the Father has sent me, so I send you" (John 20:21). Jesus' final instructions in the Great Commission in Matthew 28 also point to word and deed. We fulfill the basic command of making disciples in a twofold way: by baptizing those who accept the gospel and by "teaching them to obey everything that [Jesus has] commanded you" (v. 20). What did Jesus command his disciples to do? Both to heal and to preach. If Jesus regularly combined word and deed and then commanded his followers to do the same, biblical Christians dare not focus only on evangelism or only on social ministry.

Jesus' Gospel

If Jesus had defined the gospel only as the forgiveness of sins, then we could focus all our energy and resources on inviting sinners to accept God's forgiveness through the cross. Lost souls could receive salvation and be on their way to eternal life while refusing to change any other part of their lives—whether their adulterous activity, racist behavior, or acts of economic injustice. People could accept the gospel as if it were a one-way ticket to heaven and then live as they wished until they get there.

Instead, Jesus repeatedly said the gospel is the Good News of the kingdom (e.g., Luke 4:43; 16:16). What did Jesus mean?

Centuries before, the prophets had spoken of the future Messiah who would usher in the messianic kingdom or reign of God. This kingdom would be characterized by renewed right relationships with God and neighbor, as God mercifully bestowed forgiveness and created justice for all, especially poor persons (e.g., Isa. 9:1–7; 11:1–9; Jer. 31:31–34). Jesus the Messiah fulfilled the prophesies by offering transformed relations with both God (vertical transformation) and neighbor (horizontal transformation). Jesus welcomed sinners, assuring them of the heavenly Father's eagerness to forgive prodigal sons and daughters.

Accepting divine forgiveness was the only way to enter Jesus' messianic king-dom. Divine forgiveness, however, was not all there was to Jesus' gospel. Jesus also taught and demonstrated that his dawning kingdom was beginning to trans-form horizontal socioeconomic relationships wherever people accepted him.

Jesus taught his followers to pray daily, "Your kingdom come. Your will be done, *on earth* as it is in heaven" (Matt. 6:10, emphasis added). The second sen-tence explains the first. Jesus' messianic kingdom arrives when God's will is done on earth. That is why, when John the Baptist sent messengers to ask if Jesus was the expected Messiah, Jesus replied, "Go and tell John what you hear and see: the blind receive their sight, the lame walk, the lepers are cleansed, the deaf hear, the dead are raised, and the poor have good news brought to them" (Matt. 11:4–5). The fact that faith in Jesus was transforming the broken lives of diseased and impoverished people was evidence that Jesus was the Messiah. It was also a cen-tral part of what Jesus meant by his proclamation of the gospel of the kingdom.

Jesus made it clear that his new messianic kingdom was good news for poor and broken persons: "Blessed are you who are poor, for yours is the kingdom of God" (Luke 6:20; cf. Luke 4:18). Jesus' parable in Luke 14 tells us that we are to invite especially those who are marginalized into the kingdom: "Bring in the poor, the crippled, the blind, and the lame" (v. 21). Jesus brings good news not only to the souls of those who are poor, marginalized, sick, imprisoned, and handicapped but to their physical and relational condition as well. Our sharing of the gospel is flatly unbiblical unless our words and actions present the won-derful vertical and horizontal transformation worked by Jesus' gospel.

Since our Lord's gospel is the Good News of the kingdom, not only for-giveness of sins, biblical Christians will combine word and deed the way Jesus did. Biblical Christians will incarnationally demonstrate God's special concern for poor and marginalized persons the way Jesus did. Biblical Christians will lovingly challenge what is wrong in the status quo the way Jesus did. Biblical Christians will both preach and live the gospel the way Jesus did.

Why Do Holistic Ministry? Biblical Doctrines

The example, command, and gospel of Jesus Christ do not stand alone. Key biblical doctrines—the biblical view of persons, sin, salvation, conversion, heaven, and eschatology—also summon the church to holistic mission.

Human Nature

People Are Body-Soul Unities

According to the Bible, people are body-soul beings created for community. "Your hands have made me and fashioned me, an intricate unity," declares Job

(10:8 NKJV). We are neither good souls trapped in evil bodies, nor soul-less bodies destined to rot and disappear forever. The spirit, the body, the mind, and the emotions are all part of what it means to be created in the image of God, together making up the total human package.

For centuries, a Platonic view of persons as souls encased in insignificant bodies has distorted the church's mission. This view has tempted Christians to belittle the goodness of the body and the material world and has often justified a one-sided preoccupation with "saving souls." In contrast, the Bible tells us that bodily existence is intended to be wonderfully good. God gathered up clay, worked it into a human shape, breathed life into it, and declared the first human being "very good." In fact, the human body is so good that the Creator became flesh, rose bodily from the dead, and promised to return someday to complete his victory over evil by bodily resurrecting believers. Because the body is central to the way the Creator made persons, a one-sided preoccupation with the spiritual side of humanity that neglects persons' physical well-being is heretical.

Equally wrong and destructive is the modern secular view that human beings are merely socioeconomic, material animals. Created in the very image of God, we are far more than complex physical machines. We are also spiritual beings, invited to live forever in the presence of the living God. That is why Jesus said it is better to lose the whole world than to lose our relationship with God (Mark 8:34–38). Any one-sided preoccupation with material well-being, or any illusion that we can solve human problems merely by changing the socioeconomic environment, neglects the biblical truth about human nature. It is wrong to think that we can eliminate poverty or end destructive social behavior *merely* by changing the social environment, offering quality education, modifying economic incentives, registering more voters, or lobbying politicians. Unless we address the whole person, we can get at only part of the problem.

Some evangelistic churches regard social concerns as a distraction from their spiritual mission. Some social ministries, on the other hand, focus on people's needs to the exclusion of their spiritual condition. Holistic ministries, however, respond to every dimension of human need. God loves not only our spirits but our whole selves. Ministering to a person's material needs is one way of communicating God's love. And leading someone to a right relationship with God has a profound effect on a person's psychological, physical, social, and economic well-being as well.

People Are Made for Community

People are body-soul unities made for community. God created people to be connected by webs of social relationships. Individual lives are woven together in a complex fabric of families, cultures, ethnic groups, social institutions, and political and economic structures. People cannot be abstracted from their social settings. If my family dynamics are unhealthy, if all the good jobs have left my community, if my ethnic group is discriminated against, if my nation is facing a moral crisis—then my life will not be all that God intended, regardless of my individual prosperity or spiritual peace. We cannot be the whole persons intended by God unless we enjoy righteous, wholesome relationships with our families and neighbors. Therefore, a biblical understanding of persons should lead the church to seek both spiritual renewal and social renewal, including institutional development, structural reform, and creation care.

Holistic ministry thus means attending to the needs of individuals while also working toward the shalom of community and nation. A clue to this balance is given in the prophet Jeremiah's letter to the captives in Israel. Jeremiah passed on the Lord's instructions to the exiles: "Build houses and live in them; plant gardens and eat what they produce. Take wives and have sons and daughters" (Jer. 29:5–6). The exiled Israelites were to provide for basic necessities such as food and housing and to rebuild their shattered family lives. Then God called them to go a step farther: "Seek the welfare of the city where I have sent you into exile, and pray to the LORD on its behalf, for in its welfare you will find your welfare" (v. 7). As the Israelites worked to meet personal and family needs, they were also to seek the good of their new home city. God's plan for the Israelites rested not just on their personal well-being but on their becoming a positive influence on the wider society. Church ministries that focus solely on individuals will miss God's vision for the healing of their community.

Sin

Sin is both vertical and horizontal, an offense against both God and neighbor. Sin is arrogant rebellion against the Lord of the universe, a violation of God's law. Divine forgiveness is the only solution, and sinners desperately need to embrace the Good News that the only Son of God died for our sins. Sin also violates our sisters and brothers in the human family. Addressing sin requires repentance, restitution, and reconciliation of broken relationships with our neighbors. That is why the Bible often commands offenders to make restitution to their victims (Lev. 6:5; 24:18, 21; Num. 5:7).

Sin is also both personal and social. Lying, stealing, and committing adultery are examples of personal sins that usually affect a relatively small number of people directly connected with the person who sins. On the other hand, knowingly participating in racist or economically unjust laws and institutions (e.g., racial profiling, apartheid, inadequate payment of workers) is a social sin that can crush large numbers of people.[3] The rebellion and selfishness in the heart of every person is the root of both personal and social sin. But when sinful choices such as the unfair treatment of someone from another race or class or gender are repeated again and again over time, they slowly become embedded in society's customs and laws and take on a life of their own.

Christians often argue whether the causes of people's problems originate in social structures or in personal choices. For example, take a young, urban African American male in prison for dealing drugs. A person with a one-sided focus on social sin will point to the persistent racism that limits African Americans' vocational opportunities and crushes their self-esteem, failing urban schools that graduate students who cannot read, and the lack of decent jobs and public transportation in the inner city. A person with a one-sided preoccupation with personal sin will point to the person's lack of respect for the law, his unwillingness to accept a traditional job, and his disregard for moral authority. Each view is partially right but incomplete.

A holistic view of persons in community understands that individual responsibility and social justice are not an either-or. God holds individuals responsible for their own sinful choices, even when the social context for those choices is oppressive and unfair. God also holds each member of society accountable to help create just, wholesome communities, regardless of whether people are personally responsible for the injustice. Holistic ministries thus reach out to individuals with compassion while working to correct unjust structures. A church's after-school program may bless a few individual children and improve their grades, but we also must ask why the school systems for poor and minority kids are regularly inferior to educational systems in upper-middle-class neighborhoods. God may use a Christian prison ministry to convert individual inmates, but God also wants us to ask whether the prison system is fair and effective.

Individuals need to hear the glorious gospel that God freely forgives all who repent. Individuals need to experience the Spirit's transforming grace that changes liars and adulterers into truthful neighbors and faithful spouses. Without that inner divine healing of broken persons, no amount of good legislation to correct social injustice will be adequate. At the same time, because sin has been institutionalized in our customs and laws, simply converting individuals without also correcting unjust institutions is inadequate—like converting slave owners without challenging slavery. Only the biblical combination of evangelism and social action can redeem the devastation of sin in our communities.

Salvation

Salvation involves the whole person, body and soul. Salvation also includes the restoration of wholesome community among Christians. Its effects spill over into the entire social order. At Christ's return, even the creation itself will be restored to wholeness (Rom. 8:19–23). Should we expect any less from our

Creator/Redeemer, who created people as body-soul unities made for community and then resolved to redeem us from the evil that personal and social sin brought into God's good world?

Salvation Is for the Whole Person

At the center of the biblical teaching on salvation is the glorious gift of justification through faith in Christ. It is only because Jesus took our place on the cross that we dare to look into the face of our holy God as forgiven sinners, confident that we will live forever in his awesome presence. If a renewed personal relationship with God were all there was to God's salvation, we would gladly embrace it. Repeatedly, persistently, however, the Bible teaches that salvation is something far broader.[4]

The Old Testament words for salvation show that salvation has strong social and physical aspects. God's salvation includes liberation from oppression, material prosperity, justice for those in poverty, and the continued historical existence of the redeemed community, the people of Israel. The same is true in the New Testament. In Luke, for example, the words for salvation refer to forgiveness for a fallen woman (7:50), the healing of a Gentile soldier's servant (7:3), and the restoration to life of a dead girl (8:50). Salvation touches and restores every area of individual and community life.

Salvation Impacts the Whole Creation

While salvation is a personal experience, it also has global and cosmic implications. Each of us must personally respond to the invitation to become a child of God. A nation cannot accept Christ as its Savior and be born again. At the same time, Scripture shows that God is concerned with the restoration of whole communities, cities, and societies (see, for example, Jonah 4:11). God's transforming power extends both to individuals and to the social structures of which they are a part.

Indeed, the entire creation is ultimately destined for wholeness under Christ. David Apple writes:

> His mission was as large as the creation. His redeeming power reaches to wherever the curse of sin is found. He has come to rescue the entire cosmos, in all its dimensions and activities, from the bonds of sin. So God has entered into His creation in order to reclaim it. He successfully challenges those forces that threaten to pervert and distort all those things once pronounced good.[5]

God has "a plan for the fullness of time, to gather up *all things* in him, things in heaven and things on earth" (Eph. 1:10, emphasis added). We anticipate Christ's final, complete redemption by taking care of the "things on earth" that are under his reign.

Salvation Is Both Vertical and Horizontal

The vertical dimension of salvation—the reconciliation of humanity with God—must be accompanied by a horizontal dimension. The story of the exodus helps us understand the relationship between our salvation and our calling to holistic ministry. The Israelites' miraculous experience of liberation marked the start of a new covenant relationship with God. At the same time, God gave the Israelites a system of laws to govern how they should live, covering not only ritual religious requirements but every aspect of life—business, family relationships, sexual morality, public health. There was a direct connection between God's saving intervention on their behalf and the way they were to treat others, especially the most vulnerable among them. God cared about their suffering in Egypt, but he did not deliver them just for the sake of improving their own lot. The Israelites were to live out their deliverance in a way that expressed the full scope of God's plan for human society and also served as a witness to the surrounding nations.

The story of Zacchaeus further illustrates how Jesus' salvation goes hand in hand with a commitment to pursue righteous relationships with others. When this wicked tax collector enmeshed in an evil social system came face-to-face with Jesus, he quickly decided to repay everything wrongly taken from people and then donated large sums to poor people. At the end of the story, Jesus declared: "Today salvation has come to this house" (Luke 19:9). There is not a single word in the text about forgiveness of sins (although, of course, Jesus must have forgiven the rascal). What the text emphasizes is the radical change in Zacchaeus's social and economic relationships after he encountered Jesus face-to-face.

Too often, churches today might preach cheap grace to a Zacchaeus, offering forgiveness and acceptance from God without calling for any change in his lifestyle and business practices. Again and again, however, the Bible insists that we cannot enjoy a right relationship with God without also pursuing right relationships with our neighbors. In the Lord's Prayer, Jesus instructs us to pray: "Forgive us our debts, as we also have forgiven our debtors" (Matt. 6:12). In the astonishing parable of the unmerciful servant, the king angrily throws the ungrateful wretch into prison for not imitating the king's mercy. Jesus bluntly concludes by condemning those who want justification without conversion: "So my heavenly Father will also do to every one of you, if you do not forgive your brother or sister from your heart" (Matt. 18:35; cf. Matt. 6:14–15).

Both Jeremiah and John teach that peace with God is inseparable from doing justice for poor people and helping those in need (Jer. 22:13–16; 1 John 3:17). The prophets harshly denounced the Israelites because they thought they could please God with their liturgical worship while they continued oppressing the poor. God's angry reply is harsh: "I hate, I despise your festivals" (Amos 5:21; cf. Isa. 1:10–15; 58:3–7). Matthew 25:31ff. draws the inevitable conclusion:

Those who do not feed the hungry and clothe the naked "go away into eternal punishment" (v. 46).

These texts do not teach works-righteousness. No amount of good deeds in noble social action can earn divine forgiveness. The only way to enter Jesus' kingdom is by accepting it as a gift (Luke 12:32). But kingdom people embrace kingdom values. Sixteen times the New Testament calls Jesus Savior. Four hundred times it calls him Lord. We will not receive Christ's unmerited forgiveness if we persist in rejecting him as Lord of our whole lives. We must "work out" our salvation through lifelong discipleship that pursues purity and justice (Phil. 2:12). The God who made us for community insists that a right relationship with God is inseparable from right relationships with our neighbors.

Conversion

The experience of salvation begins with conversion—an inner spiritual renewal that changes external behavior. The Greek words for conversion (*epistrepho* and *metanoia*) refer to a turning around, a change of mind, the transformation of every aspect of behavior that displeases God. That is possible only in the power of the Holy Spirit. The New Testament offers a radical hope that the Holy Spirit can powerfully transform broken people.

Because of this power of the gospel to change lives from the inside out, holistic ministry views people from a transformational perspective. The casework approach to social ministry labels people according to their needs: Homeless. Alcoholic. Child abuser. Welfare mom. From this casework perspective, ministry means meeting the presenting need by providing goods or services. Meeting needs is vitally important—but if the church stops there, it has not fulfilled its calling to minister the whole gospel.

God knows each of us by name, not by need (Isa. 43:1)! God focuses not on a person's present circumstances but on the divine plan for his or her future. "Do not remember the former things, or consider the things of old. I am about to do a new thing; now it springs forth, do you not perceive it?" (Isa. 43:18–19). Holistic ministry thus looks beyond the need to the "new thing" that God desires to do in each person's life by the Lord's own power and goodness (Titus 3:5). Rev. Bill Borror explains what this means in the ministry of Media Presbyterian Church: "We offer people new beginnings—whether it be in their careers, or their marriage, or those desperate acts that haunt them, or the things that have been done against them. We accept people at the point where they are, but we also believe God changes people."

Consequently, the aim of holistic ministry is not just to help people but to invite them into a process of transformation through conversion and regeneration by the Spirit. Secular agencies may be effective in meeting people's presenting needs. People who do not know the Lord might succeed in becoming drug-free or financially independent. But only when people are reborn through the Holy Spirit do they also become wholly new creations, receiving from Jesus abundant life both in this world and in the next (John 10:10).

Further, as people are transformed, they become vessels for God's love to spill over onto others. A drug dealer comes to faith and ends up becoming a volunteer coach for a church-sponsored urban basketball league. A materialistic entrepreneur is converted and launches a credit union for poor families. The one ministered to becomes the minister, the comforted becomes the comforter (2 Cor. 1:4). Those who experience conversion not only enjoy more personal well-being and joy, but they also slowly transform their families, neighborhoods, nations, and world. Rev. Luisa Cabello Hansel, co-pastor of New Creation Lutheran Church, puts it succinctly: "God makes us whole, and God makes us instruments to bring wholeness to our community."

That is why we dare not keep our social ministries separate from our evangelism and rob people of opportunities to experience this life-giving transformation. Nor should we reduce conversion to a onetime act of profession of faith in Christ, without also nurturing people in the changes in lifestyle and values that accompany true repentance and lead to wholeness. As a New Covenant church leader put it, "When God is put in his proper place, then many other things are put in their proper places."

Heaven

Holistic ministry balances a longing for our eternal home with God in heaven and love for God's creation in the here and now. It is said about certain Christians: "They're so heavenly minded that they're no earthly good." "Heavenly minded" lopsidedness often produces a "fire insurance" version of evangelism, which focuses exclusively on leading people to the point of asking Jesus to give them eternal life in heaven after they die. Certainly, the angels cheer each time God writes a person's name in the Book of Life! The problem comes when lopsided Christians ignore the fact that before people get to heaven, they have to live on earth. Christians should imitate God's loving concern for every moment of a person's earthly sojourn (Ps. 139:15–16). A First Presbyterian Church leader put it this way: "You don't give birth to a baby and leave him on the street."

Of course, the other extreme—a sole focus on improving people's quality of life in the here and now—is just as damaging to the whole gospel, if not more so. Some even downplay or deny the existence of heaven and hell, saying that Christianity's main purpose is to help us live this life in a more loving, moral, and spiritual way. But Jesus warned that on the day of judgment, he would reject those who had done good deeds on earth but never professed Christ as their Savior (Matt. 7:22–23). Jesus urged, "Do not work for the food that perishes, but for the food that endures for eternal life, which the Son of

Man will give you" (John 6:27). As Bethel Temple's director of community development notes, "It's no good to have a nice car and live in a nice house, and still be going to hell when you die."

Eschatology

Finally, the biblical teaching on eschatology—the doctrine about Christ's second coming and the culmination of history—points to combining evangelism and social action. Some Christians take the promise of "new heavens and a new earth" (2 Peter 3:13) to mean that trying to fix the problems in the world is simply a waste of time. Such efforts are taken to be as futile as rearranging deck chairs on the *Titanic*. In fact, some say, the worse things get here, the closer Christians get to their ultimate redemption.

The New Testament, however, tells us something different about the future.[6] At the end of history, God does not destroy his creation but restores it to wholeness: "The creation itself will be set free from its bondage to decay and will obtain the freedom of the glory of the children of God" (Rom. 8:21). In the final judgment, the glory of human civilization will be purged of evil and taken up into Christ's kingdom (Rev. 21:24–27). The physical and social dimensions of creation have enduring value to God, so they should have value to us now.

In contrast, other Christians believe that God has left the ultimate fate of the world in human hands and that it is up to the church's social action to bring about the glorious future of peace, prosperity, and righteousness glimpsed by the prophets of old. The biblical record makes it clear, however, that human effort can never "fix" the problems of the world. Fortunately, we are not called to save the world. Our mission is to be faithful to God's command to love it.

Because we love the world, we labor and long for it to be renewed. But we know that no matter how hard we work or how much we love and sacrifice, only Christ's return will set things finally right. We look forward to that mysterious future day when all evil will be destroyed and Christ will reign in glory. In the meantime, as stewards and heralds of his kingdom, we must continue to do Christ's work until he comes.

> We wait, not with hands folded, but as God's copycats, modeling his love for the city (Luke 10:2). As the community called into being by God's reign, we are to anticipate the shalom of the new city through our corporate life and witness in the present. We are to be "impatient" with brokenness and oppression, because we know the wholeness and mercy in Christ that await the cities of our world.[7]

We trust that our service pleases God and has eternal significance in some way we cannot yet fathom. Even when the problems in our communities seem unfixable apart from Christ's return, holistic ministry means "always excelling in the work of the Lord, because you know that in the Lord your labor is not in vain" (1 Cor. 15:58).

We must also keep in mind that only those who hear and believe the message of salvation can share in the joy of the redeemed in the New Jerusalem. Christians must therefore continue to announce the coming of a day of judgment and invite people to accept Christ as Lord today so that they can enter his kingdom when it comes in its fullness.

Everywhere we look, the Bible calls us to combine Good News and good works. Jesus' gospel of the kingdom announced the arrival of a comprehensive salvation that transforms the whole person, body and soul. In the new redeemed community of Jesus' disciples, God began to reverse both the personal and the social aspects of sin. At his return, Christ promised, he would complete his victory and make "all things new" (Rev. 21:5). Knowing what Christ has done in the past, how the Spirit is moving in the present, and where history is headed, believers invite others to participate in this wholeness. We witness and work, loving the whole person the way Jesus did. We build congregations committed to following the Jesus who preached and healed. Enthusiastically embracing both evangelism and social ministry is the only way to be faithful to our Lord.[8]

Why Do Holistic Ministry? Practical Benefits

What happens when we apply this theological mandate to our church's ministry? We discover that there are also practical benefits to taking a holistic approach. John Perkins summarizes the mutually reinforcing relationship between evangelism and social ministry: "Evangelism creates the committed people, the concern for the needs of people and the broad community base from which to launch social action. Social action, in turn, fleshes out the Lordship of Christ, reaching people's spiritual needs through their felt needs and developing an indigenous economic base for the work."[9] Spiritual and social ministry, when woven together, yield a stronger fabric than either strand alone. Here we summarize the way that Good News and good works are intertwined.

Social ministry provides a vehicle or foundation for spiritual nurture.

- Social ministry draws in people (both as recipients of ministry and as ministry volunteers) who would not otherwise meet Christians, thus creating new opportunities for friendship evangelism.
- Meeting felt needs may help recipients become more aware of their spiritual needs and more receptive to the gospel.
- Lovingly caring for people's social needs puts flesh on the message of God's love, helping hurting persons grasp the meaning of the Good News.

- Social ministries help overcome barriers of mistrust or cultural differences by building a credible foundation of compassion and trust.
- Social action makes Christianity more attractive to others in the community by showing that faith is relevant to contemporary problems.

Evangelism enhances the outcomes of social ministry. New or renewed faith makes community ministries more effective by:

- giving people new hope, motivation, dignity, and self-esteem.
- healing scars from past negative experiences and relationships.
- freeing people from spiritual bondage to evil forces and self-destructive patterns.
- teaching new moral principles and guidelines for healthy living.
- introducing people to the Holy Spirit's miraculous power that enables people to live differently, to overcome obstacles, and to persevere.
- addressing the personal sinful choices as well as the structural injustices that produce poverty and social need.
- transforming the status of people from "victims" to "overcomers in Christ," empowering them to give back to the community as part of the solution.
- bringing people into a community of faith that provides emotional, physical, and spiritual support, in a context of mutual accountability.

Evangelism builds the church's capacity for social ministry.

- Evangelism that leads people to fellowship in a holistic church expands the community of dedicated Christian servants.
- The people who have experienced God's powerful deliverance are often the most zealous about offering hope and help to others.
- The testimonies of new people coming to Christ through social ministry revitalize and energize the church's commitment to holistic ministry, reviving a passion for evangelism and reminding ministry supporters that their gifts of time and money are investments with eternal rewards.
- Social barriers are broken when a congregation comes to see those served not only as "recipients" but as brothers and sisters in Christ.
- Evangelism leads the wealthy and powerful to repent and dedicate their resources to serving needy persons and restoring social justice.

Tenth Memorial Baptist Church knows the benefits of combining words and action. The church's S.W.A.T. (Saints With A Testimony) team goes door-to-door in the community and passes out evangelistic tracts, seeking to bring neighborhood people to Christ. When people hear what church they are from, their testimony has added credibility. Tenth Memorial is known as a church that is rebuilding the community—literally. New town homes line the block facing the church, their tidy porches and grassy backyards in sharp contrast with the crumbling, grimy row houses on the other sides of the block. Down the street, a well-kept high-rise provides secure, affordable housing for seniors. Neighborhood residents know they can come to Tenth Memorial for food bags or for help preparing for their GED exam. With a gift for organizing, Pastor Bill Moore helped to establish the first African American–owned credit union, a Black Clergy association that responds to political and social issues, and other agencies and coalitions.

Rev. Moore explains the link between these social ministries and the church's evangelism:

> Revitalizing the community is a way to accent the reality of the Christian witness. To talk about Jesus feeding the hungry and clothing the naked, and then to send people away from our churches . . . who are hungry, who are ill-fed, who are ill-clothed, and not to do anything about it, negates the witness of the gospel. . . . It's Jesus, but it's also Jesus and potatoes and greens, and Jesus and a good, decent house, so that it helps to bring alive what we articulate from the pulpit.

In Rev. Moore's ministry, the Word of God has "come alive" in a powerful way for many. In his first four years as pastor, Tenth Memorial recorded five hundred decisions for Christ! Holistic churches like Tenth Memorial make a difference, both here and now in their community and in the eternal kingdom to come.

The Whole Gospel for the Whole Person through Whole Churches

The root meaning of the word *holistic* is *whole,* from the Greek *holos.* Christians recognize that the world is broken and incomplete, falling far short of the glory God intended at the dawn of creation. As Christ is making us whole, both as individuals and as Jesus' new kingdom community, God's Spirit works through us to bring wholeness to others.

We can thus summarize the church's call to holistic ministry: *Reaching your community with the whole gospel for the whole person through whole churches.*[10]

Reaching Your Community with the Whole Gospel . . .

The *whole gospel,* as we have seen, brings salvation in its fullest sense—forgiveness of sins, inner conversion of individuals, physical well-being, the transformation of social and economic relationships, the renewal of communities, and the ultimate triumph of Christ over the forces of evil on a cosmic scale. Living out this gospel in our churches means modeling God's concern for the total well-being of people and communities. It means an incarnational lifestyle of integrity, compassion, and invitation. It means loving neighbors both far and near, especially those who are most needy and least lovable, with the same joyous abandon that Jesus displayed. It means sharing good news, both for this life and for the life after death, and anticipating the time when Christ will renew all creation while also continuing now to do Christ's work in this world. Through holistic ministry, Christ's redeemed community responds to the world's brokenness by proclaiming the joy of a right relationship with God in Christ, participating in the Spirit's ongoing work of personal and social restoration, and providing a foretaste of the coming of God's kingdom in its fullness.

God's salvation is comprehensive. We are finite. We tend to want to break God's work down into smaller chunks that are easier to understand and to manage. Thus, the church's presentation of the gospel has been fractured. Different segments of the church have emphasized different aspects of the Good News, and some have claimed to possess the *only* true meaning of the gospel. But God's glorious work of redemption in Christ far exceeds any system or box we try to contain it in—it accomplishes "far more than all we can ask or imagine" (Eph. 3:20). If our understanding of the gospel is too narrow, we limit the ways that God can use us in his kingdom. Not only that, but we cut ourselves off from others who are also doing God's work. Holistic churches acknowledge the sinfulness of divisions in the church and minister in the power of the full gospel.

. . . for the Whole Person . . .

Holistic ministry views persons through God's eyes, as body-soul wholes created to live in wholesome community. Thus, the church ministers to every dimension of human need and seeks wholeness at every level of society—individuals, families, communities, nations, and the global human family. Holistic ministry values every person as a unique and marvelous creation, bought by Christ, called to be the Lord's own possession, destined for eternity. Because of the Spirit's power to make all things new, a transformational perspective sees people in terms of their potential rather than their problems.

Holistic ministry breaks down the barriers between those serving and those being served. Ministry does not feature perfect people who have it all together, reaching out to miserable, needy sinners. Rather, we recognize that we are all on a journey of transformation together, "from one degree of glory to another" (2 Cor. 3:18). Each of us has contributed to the pain and suffering and decay in the world. We thus serve with a posture of gratitude and humility, acknowledging our own brokenness before the cross. We recognize that ministering Christ's wholeness to others is part of what makes us whole.

... through Whole Churches

Holistic ministry takes place in holistic congregations, where disciples of Christ live out their salvation in loving fellowship. Individual Christians are, of course, called to acts of compassion and witness, but the corporate expression of mission is indispensable. Building a healthy church and creating dynamic outreach are not conflicting priorities, because when the church is functioning rightly as the body of Christ, it will also serve as the hands and feet of Christ in the world.

Because the church plays a key role in God's redemptive plan, the goal of holistic ministry is not just to bring persons to Christ but to welcome them into a congregation of his followers. Christians should not be satisfied with establishing great para-church ministries. Para-church ministries fill an important role, but they are not a substitute for a worshiping, discipling congregation. Holistic churches welcome those who are served with open arms. They also call and equip new believers to join in the church's mission.

A holistic approach also means that the whole church pulls together toward a unifying ministry vision that recognizes the unique gifts of each individual member. Each Christian bears fruit only as a branch of the larger vine. "There are many members, yet one body" (1 Cor. 12:20). Just as the eye needs the hand to get the job done, the evangelist needs the church member with social work skills, the youth minister needs the accountant, and the outgoing organizer who plans the outreach concert needs the shy volunteer who cleans up afterward. And in the same way, each individual congregation needs the ministry of the whole community of the redeemed.

Conclusion

We are called to reach our communities with the whole gospel for the whole person through whole churches. This calling makes us bold in sharing God's glorious salvation through word and deed. Not that our ministries presume to "save" others or "fix" the world! But as Jesus told his followers, "As the Father has sent me, so I send you" (John 20:21). As the Father is loving and compassionate, forgiving and merciful, so too we should model these qualities in our relationships with others. As the Father desires that all should have abundant life, we too should help others realize their potential for living as God intended. As the Father urges that "justice roll down like waters" (Amos 5:24), we too must work toward creating the kind of society that pleases God. As the Creator of all takes delight in his work and promises to renew the earth, we too should serve as responsible, creative stewards over the earth's resources. As God incarnate in Christ appealed to all to receive the Good News, our work and witness is an invitation to others: "See what love God has for the world! Come, turn to God and be made whole. Come, join with our community of faith as we follow Christ in holistic mission."

chapter three

Making Evangelism Central

A ministry of Christian community development without evangelism is like a body without a soul.[1]

Glen Kehrein worked hard in inner-city Chicago starting one social ministry after another, expecting that his actions would bring people to Christ. After ten years, Circle Community Center had grown, but few of those served had become Christians. "Not many people asked why we were doing what we were doing," Glen admitted.[2] Then Raleigh Washington, a church planter with a passion for sharing the gospel, joined Glen, and evangelism quickly became central in all aspects of the community center. By the end of the next ten years, hundreds of people had come to faith in Christ, and a thriving congregation of about 350 people worshiped every Sunday in the community center's gym.

As Glen discovered, evangelism rarely happens by osmosis. A prevalent myth in many churches is that if you give non-Christians a chance to rub shoulders with Christians, they'll catch a dose of the gospel. This myth is sometimes used to justify not making any special effort to provide evangelism programs or training. It allows churches to feel that they are obeying the Great Commission just by doing good deeds for Christ's sake. "Our actions speak for us," some churches say. "Everything we do is evangelism." What this often means is that the church may be doing a lot of social ministry but very little evangelism. Faith can and should be catching! But Christians are fooling themselves if they think their faith will simply rub off on society.

One reason many Christians prefer to let their good deeds do their witnessing for them is that evangelism simply makes people uncomfortable. "The word *evangelism* kind of unnerves me," admitted one woman on a church evangelism committee, "and I think it unnerves a lot of people. . . . When you say 'evangelism,' people think, Holy Roller." Many associate evangelism with aggressive, insensitive, pound-you-over-the-head-with-a-big-Bible, won't-take-no-for-an-answer proselytizing. There are some valid reasons for this. A recent survey found that 44 percent of non-Christian adults who have had an evangelistic encounter with evangelicals came away with a negative impression![3] Sadly, for every new believer transformed by the liberating Good News of Christ, others have been turned off to Christ by offensive soul-winning strategies. The proper response to this is not to abandon evangelism but to emphasize appropriate evangelism.

It may seem like an odd strategy to insist that evangelism be central to your church's outreach, especially if outreach is an unfamiliar venture. But to approach mission piecemeal (e.g., starting with the social ministry, then adding a spiritual dimension) reinforces the false separation between evangelism and social action. A holistic approach places spiritual nurture and social care on an equal footing from the start.

This doesn't mean you should expect your congregation to go from 0 to 60 in its evangelism before the next church council meeting. Like everything else in God's kingdom, a zeal for evangelism may start as small as a mustard seed, but when properly nourished and promoted, it grows to bear fruit a hundredfold. Making evangelism and discipleship central requires a fundamental decision to make proclamation of the Good News a central component of all your ministry and then an investment of time and resources to develop your congregation's evangelistic gifts. Significant evangelism simply does not happen in a church without planning, praying, teaching, training—and more praying!

What Is Evangelism?

Here is our definition of evangelism: Sharing Jesus' gospel by word and deed with non-Christians with the intention and hope that they will embrace the message and repent, accept and follow Christ, and join a Christian church community for ongoing discipleship.[4]

Several parts of this definition are especially important.

First, as indicated above, we share the gospel by word *and* deed, not word *or* deed. Modeling the gospel through personal piety, acts of kindness, and the pursuit of justice is powerful and can draw people to Christ—*if* they learn why you are doing what you do. The Bible does assure us that in some cases nonbelievers may be won "without a word" by our witness (1 Peter 3:1). But more typically, "faith comes by hearing" (Rom. 10:17). Loving acts need the complement of the verbal presentation of Christ's life, death, and resurrection. If people don't ask, and Christians never tell, how will anyone ever know the gospel? If your church does good deeds without verbally pointing to Christ, how will people know to praise God rather than you for your aid? Social action by itself is not evangelism. Conversely, of course, proclamation alone may ring hollow, if there is nothing of tangible substance to back it up.

The above definition also highlights the hope that those who hear the Word will "embrace the message" of the Christian gospel and "repent." The message of the Christian gospel centers on Christ. This may sound obvious, but it is important because participants in outreach programs can get stuck talking about God's love in a generic sense. They fall short of preaching the Christ who proclaimed, "Repent, for the kingdom of heaven is at hand!" and "Come, follow me!" We are not advocating a fire-and-brimstone approach that majors in telling people just how wretched and sinful they are. The bedrock of the Good News is Christ's incarnation of God's love to a broken world. But accepting that love brings more than warm feelings and enhanced self-esteem. The powerful love of a just and holy God calls for repentance, or a radical turning away from personal and social sin through the power of the Holy Spirit. Sincere repentance does not merely make people more "spiritual"; it breaks the bondage of sin and death in the name of Jesus.

Also, note that evangelism does not stop when someone accepts Christ. The Great Commission is very clear: "Go therefore and make disciples" (Matt. 28:19). The ultimate goal of evangelism is not to win converts but to make disciples. By discipleship, Jesus meant a life of total, unconditional submission to him as Master. Conversion is not just an initial decision but a lifelong process, "a once-in-a-lifetime choice that takes a lifetime to do."[5] As David Apple of Tenth Presbyterian Church puts it, "It's one thing to say, 'He saved me from my sins.' It's another thing to say, 'He's my Lord and owns everything that I have.'" It is disingenuous to present conversion merely as a quick fix or feel-good answer to all of someone's problems. Such evangelism is like a glossy ad making fabulous promises—with fine print that goes undiscovered until after the new convert starts attending church.[6] Evangelism focused on decisions without discipleship has led to the present tragic reality: Great numbers of people call themselves Christians but show little evidence of it in their morals and actions.

Discipleship-oriented evangelism is concerned not only with nonbelievers but also with lukewarm believers and Christians who have left the church. Part of the task of evangelism is to discern where someone is in his or her faith journey. The goal is to help that person "take the next logical step in his or her relationship with God" (using a phrase from Dr. Ben Johnson's evangelism training seminar). This approach is especially critical with many street

Sharing the Gospel with People with HIV

A member of Tenth Presbyterian Church leads a worship service and Bible study for people with HIV/AIDS. Here he reflects on their spiritual needs.

Almost all of the people with HIV/AIDS have a belief in God. When life knocks you down, you tend to reach out to something greater than yourself. But I'd say probably a small percentage actually know the truth of who God is and have come to a point of accepting him as Lord and Savior. The other category is people who have accepted the Lord, but their walk with him isn't strong. Others acknowledge there's a God but are skeptical of anyone who would talk to them about God because they've heard it so often. When you're on the streets, almost everyone who wants to help you also wants to tell you why they're helping you. Whether it's the cults that prey on these people, or whether it's a real Bible-believing evangelical church—they all are giving them a message, so that people get immune to the message after a while. They're cordial, and they'll accept it and nod their head. But it's more or less so they can accept what you're there to give them.

Because people with HIV feel ostracized from the church, they tend to get their theology on the streets, which is a mixture of Christianity, Islam, Jehovah's Witness, New Age stuff, and other cults. Consequently, they have a belief that they know God's will, that they're ready for the Lord when he's ready to come take them. But unfortunately, that's not really the case.

Some years back, when my ex-wife and I were separated, I used to get my daughter every other weekend. When Sunday came and it was time to go home, in my daughter's eyes, as long as she had her favorite teddy bear in the bag, she was ready to go. I had to explain to her, "No, first we have to put some of your clothes in, your personal belongings, your toys, and your teddy bear—and *then* you're ready to go." That's how I see what we're doing in this ministry. I consider it an honor and a privilege to be able to go there and minister to them, to help them get their bags packed for their final trip home.

people who have been "over-evangelized"—they have heard the gospel presented so many times, with so little practical effect, that it has lost its meaning (see sidebar, "Sharing the Gospel with People with HIV"). What such people need is not just an altar call but a way to be connected with a church for ongoing discipleship.

Evangelism thus includes bringing a person into a Christian church community. The radical life of obedience preached by Christ is impossible without the teaching, accountability, and *koinonia* (fellowship) of a loving church community. After studying Americans' religious beliefs and behavior, sociologist Dr. Robert Wuthnow concluded that "religious inclinations make very little difference unless a person becomes involved in some kind of organized religious community."[7] If you make converts but fail to help them connect with a biblical, supportive, worshiping congregation, then you have not completed the evangelistic mandate.

This does not always mean bringing new or rededicated Christians into *your* church. Evangelism adds to the body of Christ, but it is not the same as a church growth strategy. Many activities that pass as evangelism—sending flyers to new community residents, following up with church visitors, and so on—actually fall under member recruitment. Often such measures are most successful with Christians who are just looking for a new church. But successful evangelism is not measured by church transfers.

A Holistic Approach to Evangelism

How holistic is your church's understanding and practice of evangelism? Sadly, many churches try to communicate a holistic gospel in one-sided ways. Evangelism ministries and training must be founded on a full biblical understanding of the gospel, or they will stunt the effectiveness of ministry and pass on a truncated gospel to new believers.

One sign of a lack of holism is evangelism that is divorced from service ministries and the broader social concerns of our world. Many congregations with training and gifts in evangelism are simply not doing much social ministry. Or if they are, they too often keep the budgets, staff, and program activities for evangelism and social outreach separate. They often fail to train their staff and volunteers in service ministries to be sensitive to spiritual needs and to pray for opportunities to share their faith. (We address this issue in more detail in the following chapter on integrating evangelism and social ministry.)

Another indicator that an evangelism program is not holistic is a lack of attention to people's "non-spiritual" dimensions. It is tragic when evangelism ministries turn a blind eye to people's physical and social needs. An exclusively spiritual focus costs evangelists opportunities to demonstrate the sincerity of their care and to communicate God's love in concrete ways. The Spirit can turn even simple tangible expressions of social concern into parables for kingdom truths. At worst, insensitivity to social realities in the context of evangelism can be downright offensive. For example, many churches use colored bracelets as evangelistic aids, on which each color symbolizes a step in the plan for salvation. Unfortunately, many of these bracelets' color schemes reinforce the racist association of "black" with "sin." Using such a tool with African Americans shows a lack of sensitivity to the demeaning experiences of racism they have endured. Holistic evangelism loves the whole person and takes their needs and social context into account.

A lack of holism is often rooted in an individualistic, exclusively head-oriented understanding of sin, the gospel, salvation, and conversion. In this understanding, the goal of evangelism is the spiritual renewal of the individual based on his or her acceptance of propositional truths. Such evangelism centers on getting people simply to *say* the A, B, Cs—yielding a mental conversion that does not transform the heart, hands, and feet. A common formula goes something like this:

A Acknowledge your sinfulness (usually defined exclusively in terms of personal sins with no sense of the larger, systemic sins that also have entrapped or victimized us).

B Believe that Jesus died on the cross in your place for your sins, receive him by faith as Savior and Lord, and enter into an abundant life both now and for eternity.

C Confess to God and others what you have done in A and B.

The gospel is as simple as A, B, C but not as simplistic as A, B, C. As discussed in chapter 2, the gospel is good news beyond forgiveness of personal sins. It is the Good News of God's kingdom.

Timothy Keller, pastor of Redeemer Presbyterian Church in Manhattan, writes, "The kingdom means bringing the kingship of Christ in both word and deed to broken lives."[8] God has established the crucified and risen Christ as the King over earth and heaven (Col. 1:20). Jesus' reign promises a final victory over evil, injustice, poverty, decay, and death—not just for individuals but for the entire creation. Evangelism, or proclaiming the Good News of the kingdom, means announcing that individuals can share in Christ's cosmic redemption by submitting themselves to Christ's lordship. It means an invitation to join Jesus' new community, the church, which is now making the kingdom visible by caring for those who are poor, restoring communities and creation, and loving the whole person the way Jesus did.

The hoped-for fruit of evangelism is, therefore, more than a onetime experience of believing the right truths and saying the right words. Salvation indeed brings unmerited forgiveness and a renewed personal relationship between a person and Jesus. But it also (as the story of Zacchaeus in Luke 19:2–10 shows) entails the transformation of socioeconomic relationships consistent with the upside-down values of the kingdom of God. Evangelism divorced from social ministry and concern for the whole person robs the gospel of the full implications of Christ's lordship, both in bringing wholeness to every area of a new believer's life and in calling new believers to become agents of God's restoration of creation.

Explains David Apple, "Conversion is not only a change of mind or heart as far as a person's convictions and relationship to God are concerned, but also a commitment to join what is understood to be God's program of change for the world."[9] When we are "born again" into God's kingdom, God makes us living models and messengers of hope to the world. God charges his redeemed ones with a mission of redemption: "I have called you in righteousness, I have taken you by the hand and kept you; I have given you as . . . a light to the nations, to open the eyes that are blind, to bring out the prisoners from the dungeon" (Isa. 42:6–7). In his first public sermon, Jesus declared this to be his mission (Luke 4:16–19). Evangelism thus is the first step in a calling to follow Jesus into holistic ministry.

Evangelism Types

What does evangelism look like? Holistic evangelism can take many forms. The following chart organizes evangelism by the nature of the relationship between those sharing and those receiving the gospel. It also recognizes two variations of most types, depending on whether the presentation is primarily verbal or nonverbal.

EVANGELISM TYPES

Evangelism Type	Nature of Relationship with Recipient	Nature of Evangelistic Activity	
		Verbal (explicit)	Modeled (implicit)
Network Evangelism	natural relational network (friends, family, coworkers, etc.)	share your testimony with a colleague, invite your cousin to church, offer to pray with a neighbor	"lifestyle evangelism"—live in such a way that the people who know you will see you are different
Contact Evangelism	intentional personal contact for the purpose of evangelism with little or no prior relationship	tract distribution, street witnessing, door-to-door visits	"kindness evangelism"—giving out cold water at fairs, free car wash at the church (with no explicit or extended verbal message)
Service Evangelism	contact in context of service provision or community development	sermon at a soup kitchen, devotional at a youth basketball practice, prayer with a GED student	"kindness evangelism"—Habitat for Humanity work project, painting murals over graffiti (with no explicit or extended verbal message)

Continued

Evangelism Types Continued Evangelism Type	Nature of Relationship with Recipient	Nature of Evangelistic Activity	
		Verbal (explicit)	Modeled (implicit)
Sanctuary Evangelism	contact in context of regular church activities	altar calls in worship services, evangelistic message in a Bible study or youth group, seeker-friendly worship services	regular church activities that draw people to God (e.g., exuberant worship)
Special Event Evangelism	contact via a special event to which non-Christians are invited	evangelistic crusade, open-air worship service, play or concert with a spiritual message	"pre-evangelism"—housing seminar or health fair sponsored by the church (with no explicit or extended evangelistic message)
Media Evangelism	contact via broadcast media	sharing the gospel via television, radio, newspaper, or Internet	"pre-evangelism"—parenting film series based on a biblical worldview without any explicit call to faith
Prayer Evangelism	prayer (with or without the recipient's knowledge)	intercessory prayer on behalf of non-Christians	

Which of these evangelistic methods are most appropriate for your church? That question must be prayerfully discerned by your leadership team in conjunction with the assessment of your congregation, study of your community, and inventory of spiritual gifts, as will be discussed further in chapter 12.

Christian Stronghold Baptist Church illustrates how a church can combine a range of evangelistic methods and styles. A strong emphasis on network evangelism equips members to reach those within their relational circle, particularly the members of their own families. The church also has well-organized programs of telephone and door-to-door evangelism, which target both the area immediately around the church and members' own neighborhoods ("block evangelism"). Community ministries meet felt needs while presenting the gospel. Most worship services end with an altar call to allow attendees to respond to the invitation of Christ, whether to make a first-time profession of faith or to affirm a rededication to faith and church membership. The church hosts special events, such as Family Day and Men's Breakfasts, designed to bring people into the church, where they can hear an evangelistic message. Church volunteers print and distribute a community newspaper with articles covering local events, useful information, and a biblical perspective on social and moral issues, along with an invitation to attend Christian Stronghold. The variety of approaches allows the church to reach a wide variety of people.

New Wineskins

Whatever evangelism strategies your church practices, they should be adapted to fit the unique and ever-evolving cultural and demographic context of your ministry. As Moody Memorial Church pastor Michael Allen writes, "Although the very essence of the message, namely, who Jesus is and what He did, cannot change, the presentation of the message must."[10]

Each of the evangelism types described above has the potential for endless innovative variation—not just for the sake of being trendy but for the sake of "incarnational witness." In the incarnation, Jesus was "found in human form" (Phil. 2:7) in order to minister to humans. If we are to connect meaningfully with a group of people, we have to be found in their form: We have to interact with them in the context of their culture, interests, lifestyles, concerns, and needs. This doesn't mean we have to become *like* them, any more than Jesus had to become a sinner to save sinners. But to be holistic, we have to enter their world as a witness and a servant, following the example set by the great evangelist Paul: "I have become all things to all people, that I might by all means save some" (1 Cor. 9:22).

What are some of the creative, incarnational forms of evangelism that churches have developed recently? *Seeker services,* or "sanctuary evangelism" that is friendly to unchurched people, make the gospel message more understandable and applicable by avoiding church jargon, making facilities more accessible, stripping liturgical scripts, and contemporizing worship. *E-vangelism,* in the "media evangelism" category, is the communication of the gospel through Internet technology, such as web sites and chat rooms exploring Christianity. Ideally, E-vangelism ministries build not only a bridge to the gospel for those in the digital generation but also a bridge to relationships with church members who can address their needs on a more personal level. *Christian coffeehouses* have reemerged as an effective tool for reaching people unwilling to step inside a church building, showing up in suburban shopping centers and malls and featuring Internet cafés and Christian music videos. *"Kindness Conspiracy" evangelism,* a term coined by Steve Sjogren (www.kindness.com/index.html), unleashes "low risk/high grace" "service evangelism" (not a lot of personal risk to the evangelist but a lot of room for God to act). People involved in this ministry share the love of Jesus in a host of practical ways: cleaning the toilets at local businesses; throwing birthday parties for residents at a homeless shelter; handing out coffee at busy bus stops; taping quarters to parking meters along with a church information card. *Open-air evangelism* literally takes the gospel to the streets through stirring testimonies

Three Ways of Taking the Gospel to the Streets

Providence, RI

How can a congregation reach people who normally don't give Christ and Christianity a second thought? North Providence Assembly of God has discovered ways to draw a crowd of people along Providence's popular "river walk" in order to share the gospel. Paul Conway, a former street missionary who is now the youth pastor at NPAG, explains, "Our primary goal is to raise faith questions for people strolling by. If those observing our activities go beyond that, we rejoice and go with them as far as they're willing to go in such a public setting. Yes, sometimes people even ask us to pray with them for salvation."

NPAG has discovered that "the abnormal attracts," and that it helps to rise a bit above the crowd, like on a ladder or small platform. NPAG also plays on popular cultural icons as inventive vehicles for ministry. In one event, living mannequins representing characters from the popular movie *Titanic* posed while another church member led the gathering crowd in a trivia quiz: "How much did a ticket on the *Titanic* cost?" "How much did a link on the anchor chain weigh?" This became a springboard to a brief presentation of the gospel. One man in the crowd recognized his need for a "lifeboat" and prayed with the presenter.

NPAG members are commonly sighted along the river walk, doing uncommon things: handing out roses (with an attached Scripture about Jesus, "the rose of Sharon," and an invitation to church), putting on magic shows, displaying works of art with a religious message, and providing hot drinks in cold weather. Such efforts use members' gifts of artistry and outgoing personalities to turn people's eyes to Christ.

Philadelphia, PA

On Tuesday evenings in the summer, volunteers from Bethel Temple Community Bible Church set up a stage and sound system on the street, often at known drug corners. Other volunteers canvass the area with evangelistic tracts, inviting people to the coming open-air service. Meetings feature music, testimonies (often from neighborhood residents now living changed lives), a gospel presentation, an altar call, and follow-up distribution of Christian literature.

From her window, Clarisa heard Rev. Luis Centeno preaching one week. His preaching stirred her, but "I was too scared to go down and talk to the people there," she recalls. A single mother of three, Clarisa would leave her children alone in the house while she went out with her boyfriend and used drugs. She sank into a deep depression after her boyfriend left her for another woman. She knew she needed God in her life, but she was not yet ready to respond. She prayed, "God, if you really love me, send this pastor back again." Rev. Centeno returned the next week. That evening, Clarisa went outside and turned her life over to Christ.

Since that point, her life has turned around—with a new church family, a new home, and a new marriage to another member of Bethel Temple.

Nashville, TN

The people who work in live music venues usually don't go home until the wee hours on Saturday, and they rarely get up for church on Sunday. So Belmont Church takes the gospel to them. On "Dancing in the District" open-air concert nights in the glitzy downtown area, volunteers park a specially outfitted bus (with "Isaiah 58—Ministry-in-Motion" on the side) behind one of the music stages. As a variety of secular and Christian bands entertain tourists and residents on hot summer nights, volunteers from Belmont Church provide a meal and Christian counsel to the band members and roadies.

Later in the evening, volunteers serve a hot meal to the homeless people who live along the riverfront, sitting beside them and sharing the gospel as they eat. The bus also doubles as a mobile medical clinic, with medical staff trained not only to deal with health needs but also to talk about faith. Belmont Church has looked beyond the glamour of Nashville to connect with two overlooked people groups in practical ways.

and preaching, often accompanied by music, puppet shows, cookouts, or other attention getters. *Arts ministries* include worship bands that play in parks or at community events, choirs that visit hospitals and nursing homes, rap groups that minister at youth hangouts, and mime and drama troupes that catch people's attention on street corners. Other ministries show up at secular performing arts venues such as concerts, where people pass out evangelistic tracts and provide free rides home to sloshed concert-goers. (See sidebar, "Three Ways of Taking the Gospel to the Streets.")

Consider the groups in your community who have not been reached by traditional evangelism methods. Look for innovative ways to connect with them on their turf, so that your church can become an incarnational vessel for the healing, transforming presence of Christ.

Assessing Your Church's Evangelism

The first step for a church seeking to revitalize its evangelism is to take a careful, critical look at how it has been (or has not been) fulfilling the Great Commission. Examine your church's evangelism ministries. If any of the following indicators are true, you should probably reassess your evangelistic strategy:

- All your church's evangelism eggs are in one basket (e.g., the only targets of witness are people in members' relational networks).
- Your evangelism is either wholly explicit (all words) or wholly implicit (all deeds).
- You have no form of evangelism that brings members in contact with hurting people (such as service evangelism or evangelistic events targeted at troubled youth).
- You have no form of evangelism that encourages the formation of deeper relationships of witness (e.g., you distribute flyers in the neighborhood and pray for people but never get to know any non-Christians personally).
- Evangelism is happening only in official church programs (not in members' daily lives), or evangelism is happening only individually and spontaneously (not in an organized, planned way).
- A small group of people is responsible for most of the church's evangelism.
- Your evangelism methods have not changed in the last ten years.

Examine not only *what* you are doing in evangelism but also *how* you are doing it. Do evangelists treat those with whom they share the gospel with condescension or respect, condemnation or loving-kindness? Are non-Christians viewed as unique individuals to be understood and loved or merely as "targets"? Do evangelists show respect for other faiths while presenting Christian truth? Is the evangelistic message presented in a cookie-cutter fashion or in a way that is relevant to people's felt needs and issues? Does the invitation to faith feel friendly or confrontational? In the end, a church's evangelistic techniques may not matter as much as the spirit with which they are carried out.

Next, look beyond specific evangelism ministries to consider how every aspect of your church life relates to evangelism—front door, side door, and back door.

What is happening through the "front door" ministry—i.e., worship services—of your church? Are your services meaningful to guests as well as "insiders"? Are your "get to know us" materials (mission/vision statements, brochures, road sign, etc.) designed with the nonchurched in mind, or are they thoroughly in "Christian-speak"? Is evangelism limited to a single point in the service, such as an altar call or call for decision, or is it a process? As a process, evangelism begins with prayer before the service starts, moves through the parking lot (reserve those choice spots for guest parking!), flows through the greeting of worship guests, influences every part of the service itself, and inspires follow-up with guests after the service.

What is happening through the "side door" ministries of your church? Is there an evangelistic dimension to your Sunday school or education hour?

How are small groups turned "inside out" so that unchurched acquaintances are not excluded? Can your church handle some (perhaps even controversial) recovery groups? Most churches make room for AA, but what about SLAA (Sex/Love Addicts Anonymous, a.k.a., St. Augustine's Society)? How about an evangelistically infused job seekers support group or single parenting fellowship?

Also check who is going out your church's "back door." The evangelism ministry of Tenth Memorial Baptist Church formed a "Back Door Committee" to prevent people from "coming into the church through the front door and leaving out the back door." The committee helps new converts, especially those from their street evangelism, to connect with church services and discipling resources. The pastor, Rev. Moore, also works with his congregation to give a warm welcome to new converts and "to teach people in the congregation that Jesus identified with the least among us." He wants to keep the church from giving the mixed message, "God wants you in his family, but we're not comfortable with you in our church."

The most important question is whether pain for the lost and passion for Christ are a part of the heartbeat of your congregation. The whole life of your congregation is to exude the Good News of God's kingdom. Sharing the gospel, says Rev. Joel Van Dyke of Bethel Temple Community Bible Church, "should be as natural as breathing."

Evangelism Training

People who are not trained in evangelism are less likely to do evangelism. And people who do evangelism without training are less likely to do evangelism well.

Training should never elevate an evangelistic method over an evangelistic lifestyle. Some evangelism training programs teach Christians to "do it by the book." They tout a formulaic method, usually propositional rather than relational in style, in which "stick to it" equals success. The popularity of such methods is understandable, because many prefer the comfort of a canned, memorized presentation to the unknown of a free-flowing presentation of the gospel. But only a flexible, organic approach to evangelism is consistent with each Christian's calling to whole-life discipleship and adequate for the cutting-edge realities of holistic ministry.

An ongoing, hands-on training is also important. Some absorb the basic ideas but fall down on the day-to-day implementation because they have no on-the-job training or modeling. "Show me" beats "tell me" any day. Role playing in training can help people break the ice of initial discomfort and learn to think on their feet. Evangelists-in-training also need to see their leaders setting an example in action, not just at the front of the class. Ongoing feedback is also important; provide a forum in which congregants can share their evangelism experiences and discuss the questions and issues that arise. Churches should emulate a lifelong learning model of education, posing evangelism not just as a course to be completed but as a craft to be continually practiced and perfected.

Christian Stronghold's evangelism training program provides an example of how to marry classroom learning, hands-on involvement, and personal spiritual growth. One typical member signed up for an evangelism course to learn to share her faith with her family. To meet a class requirement, she became a trainee in the Block Evangelism ministry, in which volunteers share the gospel door-to-door in a chosen neighborhood. As a trainee she was given the role of prayer partner, working alongside another church member who had already completed the training. She was grateful just to be able to watch and pray at first. As she practiced her skills and slowly overcame her fears, she also saw firsthand how the program nurtures volunteers' spiritual and personal growth. The ministry gave her transportation to the evangelism site when necessary and served a light breakfast. Volunteers shared a Bible study and prayed for one another before, during, and after the ministry. She appreciated that the group took time to debrief after each evangelism experience, discussing the difficulties and joys they encountered, or any other aspect of their lives. She formed friendships with the other trainees and volunteers. Gradually she lost the feeling that she was entering new and hostile territory. Instead, her focus shifted to the benefits of the ministry to herself, to the church, and to the recipients. After completing the class she decided to continue participating in the Block Evangelism ministry.

Are evangelism tools available in your church? Most people need something in their hand to pass along, even if they simply say, "My pastor told me to give this to you!" Using evangelism aids involves a paradox: Diligently have your tools and testimony ready, but rely totally on the Holy Spirit. The power of our witness is in Spirit and truth, not in the package. No matter how smooth our presentation or how creative and cool our paraphernalia, we cannot "make" anything happen. Yet as we are obedient, God graciously uses us as channels of his Good News, and he gives us spiritual gifts, skills, talents, and creativity to share the gospel. What Christ commands, the Spirit empowers.

Because holistic ministry shares the gospel across racial, ethnic, and economic barriers, evangelism training should include a cross-cultural component. In our "tossed salad" (a metaphor that has replaced the "melting pot") society, it is both unethical and shortsighted to assume that you will minister only to people who are like you. For example, a study of Portland, Oregon, revealed the presence of 108 ethnic groups! "Pentecost has come to the doorstep of virtually every city in our land," writes church consultant Jack Dennison. "It is time to put on the missionary hat and approach the work of intracity evangelism with the same cross-cultural preparation that missionaries do before entering a foreign culture."[11] Without diversity training grounded in familiarity with the culture of the community, you will inevitably neglect, mislead, or offend. For example, one suburban church ran a weekly children's club in a subsidized housing project. The chosen theme was "I am the Good Shepherd." The aim was to introduce kids to Jesus, but because the occupation of shepherd was unknown to them, it left many children puzzled. They were less able to connect to Jesus on their own terms.

It is particularly important to train participants in social ministries to be sensitive to the spiritual needs of those they serve, even when people deny or do not recognize their need for Christ. A volunteer food ministry coordinator at Faith Assembly shares her sorrow over those who accept only the physical food: "I've cried because my heart feels compassion and fear for them, because they're going to answer for it. To come here and accept all that God has to give, but then to reject him—that's a frightening thing. . . . So, we just pray for them. We hope that the Lord would open their eyes to see." Evangelism training encourages ministry participants to perceive the spiritual dynamics of a person's situation and to share their faith with the same dedication and commitment as they share other forms of aid.

One critical goal of training is to help church members understand evangelism as a way of life, rather than a special calling or program. While an evangelism task force that plans and leads the church's evangelistic work is important, evangelism must be seen as the responsibility of every Christian. Christians tend to look at Billy Graham and say, "Now there's an evangelist!" But the men and women who pray for each Billy Graham crusade, who organize the logistics behind the scenes, and who distribute Christian literature to new converts all make an equally important contribution to a revival's evangelistic harvest. Thus, in a sermon about evangelism, Bishop Dickie Robbins had everyone in the Life in Christ congregation repeat, "*I* am an evangelist." The purpose of training is not to discover who has the gift of evangelism but to discern how each member's gifts can best be used in support of evangelism.

Finally, training should address people's motivation for evangelism. We are not to evangelize out of guilt or with a spirit of self-righteous martyrdom. Evangelists must not be like Jonah—who ultimately obeyed and delivered the message but cared little what happened to the people who heard it. Why evangelize? Because the gospel is the best treasure we have to share with our neighbors. And because Jesus said so.[12] Doing evangelism with the right motives means harmonizing the Great Commission with the Great Commandment: making disciples because you love your neighbor and long for the reign of God.

Developing Holistic, Relational Evangelism

While evangelistic events that reach groups (such as revivals and seeker services) are important ingredients in a church's evangelism strategy, research consistently shows that the most effective faith-sharing takes place in the context of relationships. "The kingdom is relational. Mission is about rebuilding relationships," writes Jayakumar Christian. "A kingdom-based missiology offers a healing alternative to a community whose relationships have become a source of hurt."[13] In contrast, churches sometimes make evangelism sound like a sporting event, stressing "soul-winning" and keeping track of conversion "scores."

How can a congregation embrace an understanding and practice of evangelism that heals wounds, rebuilds relationships, and restores hope? Following are three key evangelism steps: Pray, listen, and look.

Pray . . . before Anything Else

"Prayer is the key to unlock relationships," says a lay leader at New Covenant Church. "Prayer is what will draw, change, and cause people to be committed in their relationship with the Lord." Because salvation is God's work, we must permeate all our evangelistic activity with prayer. Prayer starts before we meet someone: Ask that God might give you a longing to share the gospel and lead you to someone whom he is drawing to faith. Prayer continues silently while we are meeting with someone: "Lord, what do you have in store for this encounter? Help me to serve you while serving this one who is loved by you. Help me to listen and understand what she is really trying to say. Is there more going on here than meets the eye?" Nor does prayer stop after your encounter with the person has ended. You lift the person into God's presence, bind the power of sin, and ask God to water the seed you have sown.

One way of bathing your evangelistic outreach in prayer is to establish Lighthouses of Prayer in the homes, schools, or workplaces of church members. Lighthouse materials help guide members in praying for their neighbors, caring for them through acts of kindness, mercy, and hospitality, and appropriately sharing faith. (Check out www.lighthousemovement.com for information and resources.)

Listen . . . Really Listen

One church member we interviewed recalled a home visit from a minister soon after her family had started attending his church. They talked with the minister for three hours about their background and spiritual lives. At the end of the conversation, the minister asked if she and her husband would like to accept Christ. They were taken aback. Had the minister not heard anything they had told him about their faith, or did he just not believe them? Did he consider the visit wasted unless he checked "Invite to receive salvation" off his list? "I'm not saying people shouldn't be evangelistic," she reflects, "but he never stopped to listen to my husband and me. . . . The church just had a mission that they were going to convert everybody." Her family soon found another church.

Most of us tend to act before we think and speak before we listen. When you talk with unchurched people, focus on *their* questions and opinions, without having an agenda. The temptation in proclamational evangelism is to try to take the conversation where *we* want it to go. This is particularly problematic with formulaic gospel presentations. Sometimes we listen just to find the weaknesses in an argument or a spiritual "soft spot" to attack. Don't be more interested in getting out your piece than in getting inside the heart and mind of the person God has placed before you. Ask thoughtful, open-ended, non-inquisitional questions.

Remember, "evangelism takes place best when the target community is treated not as a project, but as a people who have dignity and deserve respect."[14] People can figure you out. They won't reveal what they truly believe or are feeling inside if they sense you are taking advantage of their vulnerability. No one wants to feel like the "catch of the day."

Look . . . for a Way to Serve, Connect, Invite, and Fellowship

Look for a way to serve. "Little acts of kindness transform people's lives," says Rev. Bill Borror. After you've *listened,* really *listened,* and as you continue to pray without ceasing, look for an avenue of service that will touch the heart of the person you are seeking to reach. If you are meeting the person in the context of a social service ministry, look for ways that you can go the extra mile to bless the person. Imagine yourself in that person's shoes, and see if there is a practical way that you can touch his or her life.

Recognize that a person's surface or presenting needs may not be the deepest need. Eating too much or not enough might cover an addiction. Laziness might signal depression or a mental or emotional disability. A broken arm might be one of a series of "accidents" that indicates abuse. A food shortage could indicate poor budgeting skills or under-employment. A persistent health problem might mean an unsafe work environment. Fits of anger could be the tip of an iceberg related to repressed rage at experiences of racism or classism. A poor self-image might come from a confused sexual identity. Realize, too, that even those who on the surface seem to be doing pretty well still have needs: the need for meaning, the need for intimacy, the need for a challenge, the need to make a difference in their world—and most important, the need to know the living God.

Serve with humility. Don't come storming into a person's life with the attitude, "You needy person—me helper." Don't paternalistically presume, "You have the problem and I have the answer." And don't panic or feel like a failure if, on this occasion, God does not open a door to a verbal witness to accompany the action witness. Do the good deed simply to do the good deed, without worrying about the other person's response. Trust God that over time, as your relationship with that person develops, you will be able to share personally, deeply, and intimately why you do what you do and in whose name you do it.

Look for a way to connect. No two people are alike—which means that no two "gospel presentations" should be alike. In the Gospels, Jesus never related the gospel to any two people in the same way. He told Simon Peter and Andrew, "Follow me, and I will make you fish for people" (Matt. 4:19). He told the religious leader Nicodemus, "You must be born from above" (John 3:7). He told the rich ruler, "Sell all that you own and distribute the money to the poor" (Luke 18:22). He told the woman caught in adultery, "Go your way, and from now on do not sin again" (John 8:11). He told the man beseeching healing for his son, "All things can be done for the one who believes" (Mark 9:23). And who knows what Jesus told Zacchaeus after he invited himself over for dinner, but the crowd saw a transformed man after that dinner party (Luke 19:2–9).

When the opportunity for connection comes, many people become anxious and freeze up. They may be afraid of where the other person will take the conversation. They may worry about not having all the "right" answers (as if we have to have an answer for everything!). Like Jesus, who calmly listened for his Father's voice in every situation, we can simply trust the Spirit for guidance (Matt. 10:19–20). God is with you and in you, so relax and let the living waters flow. Don't get uptight about covering every key doctrine or failing to recall a memorized verse. A person's salvation is not on the line because of your performance. After all, the task of Christians is simply to announce the Good News. We can't save anyone. It's God's job to save people.

Look for a way to invite. Ask the Lord to show you how you can help that person with whom you are cultivating a relationship to "take their next logical step in their relationship with God." In Faithful Witnesses, Dr. Richard Armstrong, professor emeritus at Princeton Theological Seminary, suggests that there are scores of intermediary steps that help a person move forward in his or her spiritual journey but stop short of asking him or her to trust in Christ as personal Savior and Lord.[15] We can graciously extend invitations such as:

- "We have a great single's group that meets at a restaurant downtown. May I pick you up next Monday night?"
- "Would it be okay if I prayed with you right now about what you just told me, so that we can ask Jesus to help you carry that burden?"

- "We offer a lunchtime Bible study every Friday for students in our GED and computer training classes. May I sign you up?"
- "Since you are dealing with the death of your spouse, would you be interested in attending our church's grief support group?"
- "Would you like to read this book that will tell you more about Jesus?"
- "God's Spirit can empower you to take a stand for what's right at your workplace. Do you want to tap into that power source?"

Remember that the journey from unbelief (whether atheism, agnosticism, rebellion, or other faiths) is a long one. Each invitation to make a small decision is but one of a series of steps a person takes on the pilgrimage to faith. Do not expect instant results. Successful evangelism often involves an extended process of overcoming a person's resistance to the gospel. An associate pastor of Christian Stronghold Baptist Church explains:

> The people that come down the aisle don't usually come based on that first time of hearing the gospel of salvation. . . . The planting and watering process takes place, and God gives the increase at a certain point of time. . . . Then that seventh time when the gospel is preached, the person comes forward.

Evangelism calls for boldness and persistence (such as not giving up on someone after an initial expression of disinterest) but not pushiness. Depend on God to lead you to issue the invitation appropriate for each step of a person's journey, and thank God for giving you the opportunity to encourage the pilgrim.

Look for a way to fellowship. Follow-up is essential. Don't use hit-and-run tactics. People rightly expect that if we truly care about them we will come through for them. Robert Linthicum refers to this as an "evangelism of respect."[16] In the business world, clients look for and appreciate customer service as they make their choices. The same is true for people who are looking to us for a "good deal"—in other words, a quality relationship. This is particularly the case in situations involving social dysfunction, which have taught people not to trust. The founder of an evangelistic ministry in a Philadelphia housing project advises:

> You've got to understand something about inner-city ministry. You cannot go in and be with people for a few weeks and then leave. . . . If you go in and give them clothes or something, they will come in and take it. But they still will not trust you. You have to be there for them week after week, and month after month. Then they will finally start trusting you. It was like Jesus with the disciples. He was with them for three years, twenty-four hours a day.

Most people, not only poor people, simply won't tolerate it if you come in, do your "Christian" thing, and walk away patting yourself on your spiritual back. What makes evangelism meaningful is "not just how many hands get raised," says Rev. Joel Van Dyke, "but how many relationships can be formed where people get led into a relationship with Christ because of people naturally loving them."

One way to make yourself available is through a mentoring relationship, or coming alongside someone with wisdom, models, inspiration, prayer, connections, aid, or whatever it takes to help that person move in a positive direction. Mentoring relationships form the core of the youth evangelism ministry of Bethel Temple Community Bible Church. A youth leader (who himself became a Christian through another Bethel mentor) describes the process:

> Just building the relationship is what counts the most. . . . Not forcing Jesus into it, but showing his love and being an example. Taking them out and playing hand ball, playing a sport, doing something they like, just being a friend. . . . Of course they see me in the church, so they know I'm gonna come at them. Someday, sometime I'm gonna tell them. So I build a relationship first, and then I say, "Let me tell you more about Jesus."

As Bethel Temple mentors know well, this process takes great amounts of time, energy, and patience. Holistic ministry cannot always be scheduled, writes Amy Sherman. "Relationships take time; they sometimes require spontaneity. Our busyness and tight schedules become barriers to outreach when there is no margin, no room for responding to needs that present themselves at unplanned times."[17] A good mentor is physically and emotionally available in a way that may push our comfort zones. Particularly in the case of substance abuse or dysfunctional family systems, mentors must be prepared to love their mentees through multiple cycles of rebellion, relapse, brokenness, and recovery. Walking with people through the "valley of the shadow of death" (Ps. 23:4 NIV) can be risky. There is the danger that people in desperate times might take advantage of you, rob you, even harm you or your family. As Christians, we draw on the boundless wellspring of the Holy Spirit to stick it out when other mentors might pack it in due to exasperation or exhaustion.

Unconditional love and commitment make all the difference in sharing the gospel with people whose needs result at least in part from sinful choices. Phil Ryken, pastor of Tenth Presbyterian Church, notes that in the church's experience of working with homosexual AIDS sufferers, most often "the people that will stay with them until the ugly, unpleasant end will be people from the ministry. That gives a lot of credibility to what the church is trying to say about the issue" of homosexuality. A church that both speaks out on lifestyle issues and has loving, long-term mentoring relationships with the people involved can have far greater evangelistic impact on the community than a church that simply issues moral judgments.

Conclusion

Thomas Nees writes, "To evangelize is to proclaim that a compassionate God has offered grace (undeserved love) and is calling followers to help fulfill the promises of a better life in this world through the coming of the Kingdom, 'on earth as it is in heaven' (Matt. 6:10)."[18] The coming of God's kingdom on earth and in human hearts is good news for all people, at all times, in all places, in all situations.

The gospel is good news for the person trapped in prostitution or homelessness. It's good news for the person enslaved by unjust economic structures or unfair labor practices. It's good news for immigrants and migrants. It's good news for tax collectors and tax cheaters. It's good news for lottery players and casino operators. It's good news for moms on welfare and absentee fathers. It's good news for racists and terrorists. It's good news for convicted killers and drug-cartel kingpins. It's good news for pornographers and hazardous waste dumpers. It's good news for Africans and Americans. It's good news for persons engulfed in poverty or in riches. Some people (as Bonhoeffer asserted) may not initially receive the gospel as good news, and some may need to hear the bad news before they can hear the good news. But no person or need is beyond the reach of God's amazing grace. This is why we can share the gospel with confidence and with joy in the midst of the world's brokenness.

No wonder the angels celebrate in heaven when a sinner repents and receives eternal life (Luke 15:10)! Through holistic evangelism, we too share in the inexpressible blessing of seeing someone come into a loving relationship with the Savior, join the family of faith, and begin to experience and share the wholeness intended by the Creator.

chapter four

Embracing Social Action— from Relief to Public Policy

> The Church must minister salve to the open sores while challenging and changing the factors that caused them.[1]

Facing emergency needs, Dedra, a struggling single mother of three, approached the Germantown Avenue Crisis Ministry for help. This ministry was born two and a half years after the passage of welfare reform, when a dozen churches in the community realized that they could not keep up with the steadily increasing requests for emergency assistance. They pooled their resources to hire a part-time social worker and set up a system of referrals. The ministry serves roughly one hundred people each month, far more than the churches could do working by themselves. For Dedra, the ministry provided food vouchers, subsidies for her children to attend church camp, and a paid internship at one of the churches while she attended Temple University. The internship led to a job paying $30,000. Dedra plans to volunteer for the ministry's support group for women. "I just want people in my situation to know that with prayer and support, they can make it too," she says. "This has helped me realize that with faith, God will provide."[2]

Thirteen-year-old Talea works intently at a computer, typing notes for an article she is writing about careers for a special insert in the community paper. Talea is on the Journalism Team in New Creation Lutheran Church's Pre-Work program. The oldest of seven children, Talea likes being able to help out at home by earning her own spending money. Through the program she is developing basic skills such as being on time and following directions. The program also emphasizes relational skills, such as dealing with stress, showing respect for others, and resolving conflicts. Devotional times are showing her how the Bible applies to the challenges of daily life. Her horizons have expanded as she has discovered the range of careers open to her. In a community lacking in economic opportunities and role models for stable employment, the Pre-Work program is cultivating the habits, values, attitudes, and skills necessary for success at work and at school.

Rev. Richard Kyerematen of Germantown Church of the Brethren helped found the South Mount Airy Task Force (SMATF) to work on five main issues: crime and safety, seniors' health care, children's educational programs, economic development, and "spiritual bonds" as the glue holding together the community. With $10,000 in grants from the state, SMATF launched a local market that sells healthy, inexpensive produce. Community residents, especially seniors, logged over two thousand volunteer hours to get the open-air market going on rented property across the street from the church. Two years later, another grant allowed SMATF to buy a trailer to house the market. The market has had several side benefits: Senior volunteers supplement their fixed income by bringing in homemade baked goods or jewelry to sell. Littering and vandalism around the market area have diminished. Murals have spruced up neighboring businesses. Now there are plans to expand the market, says the SMATF director, an associate member of Church of the Brethren. "We will expand our economic base into all things that are good and nurturing in our community."

In 1990, Central Baptist Church offered a Learning Community (Sunday school) series on racism. The class attracted Arnelia, an African American. "I had never been in a place where this discussion was taking place among white people," she says. "Most people thought this problem was solved in the 1960s." At the end of the series, the group decided that the subject was too important to let drop, and so they formed a committee. Their purpose, says Arnelia, a co-leader of the committee, is to "undo racism among ourselves and ultimately in the larger community" by confronting racial issues in a positive manner. They undertake this on several fronts. At election time, they work with the League of Women Voters to organize candidate forums around issues relating to racism. After several racial intimidation incidents in their community, two Central Baptist members developed a training program to help churches respond to racism. Another project works with the Valley Forge Visitors Center to acknowledge the role of African American patriots in its exhibits. As they work to change society, they are also examining racism within the congregation and within their own lives.

Micah 6:8 is one of hundreds of passages in the Bible that make our calling to social action clear: "What does the LORD require of you but to do justice, and to love kindness, and to walk humbly with your God?" Each of the ministries above fulfills this mandate in a different way. For some, the words "social action" bring to mind typical church ministries, such as feeding the hungry or aiding children and the elderly. For others, the term connotes the church's involvement with broader social issues, such as the pro-life movement or living wage campaigns. This chapter examines the range of ways that churches can meet the social needs of their communities, with a special focus on ministries of structural change. A church that takes up this calling can become known in its community, like Tenth Memorial Baptist Church has been described, as "a beacon of hope, a symbol of access to resources and assistance and possibilities, a symbol of caring."

Types of Social Ministries

Social ministries fall into four basic categories: relief, individual development, community development, and structural change.

1. *Relief* (giving a hungry person a fish) involves directly supplying food, clothing, or housing to someone in urgent need.
2. *Individual development* (teaching a person to fish) includes transformational ministries that empower a person to improve physical, emotional, intellectual, relational, or social status.
3. *Community development* (giving a person fishing equipment) renews the building blocks of a healthy community, such as housing, jobs, health care, and education.
4. *Structural change* (helping everybody get fair access to the fish pond) means transforming unfair political, economic, environmental, or cultural institutions and systems.

The following table illustrates ministries of all four types that address four different social problems: housing, un- and under-employment, family brokenness, and health.

As this table makes clear, each type of social ministry has an important role. If a family has no groceries, they need a food basket—now. But a food basket provides only temporary relief. What will it take for that family not to need groceries next month? They may need information, skills, mentoring, or counseling to help them make changes in their situation. This personal transformation, however, will have limited impact if there are no jobs in the neighborhood, or if the family is spending most of its income on rent because there is no affordable housing. Those problems in turn may be rooted in unjust policies or institutions, such as a school system that fails to prepare people for the

SOCIAL MINISTRY TYPES

	Relief	Individual Development	Community Development	Structural Change
Housing	homeless shelter, emergency housing	home ownership seminar, credit counseling	affordable housing construction and rehabilitation	lobbying against redlining and other unfair lending practices, suing slum lords to improve housing conditions
Un- and Under-employment	food pantry, clothes closet	GED tutoring, job training, budget counseling	day care center and after-school program for children of working parents, training in small business start-up	advocating to raise the minimum wage and Earned Income Tax Credit, promoting tax incentives for job creation in low-income areas
Family Brokenness	family crisis hot-line, family services information, and referral clearinghouse	parenting classes, family counseling, divorce recovery support group	legal aid clinic that offers family services, family mediation court	encouraging employers to adopt "family friendly" policies, promoting pro-marriage legislation
Health	free immunizations, vouchers for medicines	Overeaters Anonymous support group, health seminars	community gymnasium, health clinic with sliding scale fees	lobbying for affordable health insurance, antismoking campaigns

workforce, racist lending practices, or public transportation policies that limit people's ability to get to good-paying jobs.

God wants to renew every area of human society, from moral choices to family relationships to neighborhood associations to community institutions to laws. Holistic ministries, therefore, confront sin and foster transformation at every level.

A Holistic Approach to Social Ministry

What type of social ministry should your church offer? Obviously, it can't do everything. In fact, it *shouldn't* try to do everything. Carey Davis, a ministry leader at Wayne Presbyterian Church in suburban Philadelphia, advises that churches choose one or two areas of ministry focus. "Churches tend to support a million things in a tiny way," she observes. "They spread out money, time, and involvement." Scattering ministry efforts dilutes their impact. Guided by your study of the congregation and community, along with prayerful discernment of God's vision (see part 3), select an area of social concern in which your church seems most poised to have an influence.[3]

At the same time, impact is enhanced by addressing the selected area of social need from several angles. If you provide only relief, you can end up perpetuating dependence by doing things for people without empowering them to change their situation. If you focus narrowly on individual development, you neglect the contextual and systemic factors that keep people from reaching their full potential. An exclusive focus on community development can result in an impersonal ministry that builds institutions but not people. Overemphasis on structural change fails to take seriously people's need for immediate care and inner renewal.

Seeing social ministry as a spectrum from relief to reform helps a church plan creative and strategic responses to community needs. Theologian Harold Dean Trulear suggests that middle-class churches think outside the "social service" box in order to make the wisest investments in a poor community. A church member who drives to the inner city one evening a week for a youth mentoring program, for example, can make a difference in the lives of a few kids. But if this person is a bank vice president, he or she could also significantly impact the whole neighborhood by recognizing his or her job position as a potential resource in creating opportunities for economic development. Youth benefit from the attention of caring, Christian adults—but they also need parents who can provide for their needs via access to mortgages and business loans. This does not mean sacrificing personal relationships for the sake of long-distance advocacy. There should be room in every congregation's ministry for both, because they are mutually reinforcing.

A Multilayered Approach

A multilayered approach to social outreach seeks to meet the surface need *and* dig into the underlying personal and social causes of the need. If you are concerned about education, don't stop with a tutoring program. A comprehensive approach could include sponsoring college scholarships, offering child development seminars for parents, partnering with an inner-city Christian school, "adopting" a local public school, hosting a forum on school board elections, organizing parents to pressure for curriculum changes, and advocating for public policies that guarantee a quality education for every child. Each layer of ministry addresses a different facet of the need.

As your outreach develops, you will discover the ways that one area of social need interacts with others. Caring for seniors, for example, may reveal concerns related to crime and rising housing costs. A mentoring ministry for women on welfare may point you toward meeting needs related to health insurance and child care. Ministering to at-risk youth may lead you to tackle the issue of single-parent families and get you involved with the school district. Social systems are interconnected. Narrowly focusing on a single issue does not do justice to the whole person or to whole communities.

So how do you concentrate on doing one area of ministry well and yet address the multifaceted needs of the whole person? *One key is collaboration.* Your church does not have to develop expertise or programming on every social issue—you just have to find out who has. By pooling resources and ideas with a cluster of churches or organizations, each contributing a different facet of ministry, you can increase your effectiveness. (Chapter 11 discusses partnerships in detail.)

Another key is to keep in mind that holistic ministry is an ongoing, evolving process. You have to start somewhere, but hopefully you won't end there! Each project is a stepping-stone to the next stage of God's plan. Every church in our study was in motion—adding, expanding, and modifying ministries. Researcher Nile Harper observed a pattern in many urban churches. "What begins as isolated acts of charity, individual actions of compassion, or programs of social service can develop under the power of God's spirit through creative leadership into very positive collaborative actions for systemic justice."[4] For Lawndale Community Church, a safe, low-cost laundromat for inner-city Chicago families grew over two decades into a multimillion-dollar complex of programs in health care, counseling, housing, education, and job creation.[5]

Third, a strong relational component helps your ministry adapt to the complexity of people's lives. A member of Church of the Advocate expressed concern about the impersonal nature of many community development strategies.

> There was a guy who came to a community meeting I went to, . . . a city planner. He brought charts about the way they're going to rebuild that area. But it was about houses. It wasn't about people. There was no mention about how many people were retirement age and on fixed incomes, how many single-parent families exist in the area. They are just coming with a bunch of buildings. But nobody asks, "Why?"

As you come to know and love people, not just as "clients" but as whole persons, you will naturally care about their whole situation. You will learn to ask why. You will pay attention as people talk about their struggles and educate yourself about the broader issues that affect their lives. You will empower people to get involved in solving their own community problems. In the process of providing services, your congregation "may have their eyes and ears opened to experience the systems that are unjustly impacting the lives of the people they are serving."[6] And in working toward systemic change, your congregation may discover that persons have internal barriers to development that need to be lovingly challenged and overcome.

An Incarnational Component

Another feature of holistic ministry is that it is incarnational. This means that Christian servants go beyond giving aid to giving themselves. Patrick Cabello Hansel, co-pastor of New Creation Lutheran Church, explains, "The phrase that I hear when someone is grateful for support is this: 'You were there for me.' Not that you gave me this, or you did this for me—but, 'You were *there* for me,' which means, 'You were there where I was, in whatever the situation was. . . . You had enough courage to be there for me and with me.'"

Aid and advocacy are necessary to get people through a rough time and to open doors of opportunity. People need food, clothing, shelter, transportation, skills, legal counsel, a living wage, clean air and water. But giving aid is no substitute for making ourselves available to broken persons, because Christ lives in us, and Christ's love flows through us. This could mean sitting beside a homeless guest at a soup kitchen to share a meal, or inviting kids from your tutoring ministry over for a slumber party, or moving into the inner city to turn clients into neighbors. Incarnational relationships nurture the seeds of hope, confidence, and peace in those who come to your church for assistance.

Sharing the Good News

The core feature of a holistic approach to social ministry is finding ways of sharing the Good News of salvation with those you serve. Holistic ministry treats each individual as a precious, unique, complex creation stamped with the image of God. How can a social ministry claim to love a person while neglecting the spiritual dimension of his or her being? Professional social work has tended to fragment people with more and more specialization. There is also a natural tendency in institutions toward bureaucracy and secularization. In the face of these trends, the church must be intentional about preserving its fundamentally evangelistic character while doing social action. (The next chapter discusses how to do that in more detail.) After all, if the church does not address people's spiritual needs, who will?

First Presbyterian Church

First Presbyterian Church of Mount Holly demonstrates how holistic ministry is a blend of relief, development, and structural reform, infused with evangelism.

At one time, there were eight to ten boarded up homes in a two-block area around First Presbyterian Church. Members gradually became convicted about doing something about the situation. A neighborhood study revealed that the amount of quality affordable housing was dwindling. In 1980, Wes Kennedy, a respected church elder, left a business venture and stepped out in faith to lead First Presbyterian Church's first nonprofit social ministry: Homes of Hope, Inc. The ministry purchases, refurbishes, and manages low-cost rental housing in the community of Mount Holly and surrounding townships. Since its founding, Homes of Hope has rehabilitated or constructed over twenty housing units and provided housing for more than one hundred low-income families.

Wes and others in the ministry came to realize that their residents needed more than an affordable place to live. "It was taught in our home that poor people were poor because they wanted to be poor, and so I had a lot of overcoming to do," admits Wes. A natural first impulse was to write off the people who had problems keeping up the rent or the properties. Getting to know the residents made him more aware of the basic tools of living that he had learned from his parents and taken for granted. "We're dealing with second-, third-, fourth-generation people who have never had any instruction on how to live." To address this gap, the board of Homes of Hope began matching struggling tenants with a church volunteer who could teach them to budget and balance a checkbook or help them find better employment.

The emotional and spiritual needs of Homes of Hope tenants helped provide the impetus for the founding of a new counseling program called The Well. The program has a clear Christian character and invites (but does not require) clients to incorporate a spiritual dimension into their counseling, such as prayer and reference to the Bible. Homes of Hope and the other social ministries of First Presbyterian Church refer people with emotional or spiritual problems to The Well. The Well likewise refers people with housing needs to Homes of Hope. Tenants are also referred to other appropriate First Presbyterian ministries, such as the feeding ministries and various support groups, as well as to other helping agencies in the Burlington County area. This arrangement ensures that the needs of the whole person are met, while allowing each ministry to focus on its particular area of service.

First Presbyterian Church's concern for housing has led the church to look beyond the needs of individual families to the larger patterns affecting housing needs, such as the lack of cooperation among neighboring townships and restrictive zoning ordinances. In one instance, the zoning board denied Homes of Hope's plans to construct a multifamily housing unit. With the aid of a First Presbyterian member who was a lawyer, Homes of Hope sued the town of Mount Holly to win a zoning variance. The action was controversial but successful. The result was a State Supreme Court decision that has been used by housing advocates not only for affordable housing for homeless and low-income people but for disabled and other special needs people as well.

Then there was the time a group of community activists decided to protest the county's failure to provide effective short-term housing assistance by setting up a "tent city" on the courthouse lawn. In response, the county threatened to arrest the protestors. Rev. Jim Kraft took a public stand with the activists. While Rev. Kraft did not agree with the protesters' tactics, he believed that the issue demanded attention. He attended daily court hearings and spoke out about local housing needs. As the confrontation heated up, he and several other local pastors stood on the courthouse lawn, waiting to be arrested. As it turned out, before arrests could be made, a compromise was reached in the courts.

To increase their impact, First Presbyterian Church helped to organize the Affordable Housing Coalition of Burlington County. Besides sharing information and helping agencies access development resources, the Coalition helps to hold local government and banks accountable to their responsibilities for fair housing policies and community reinvestment. First Presbyterian Church has also lobbied to change people's attitudes about having the "wrong kinds of people" as neighbors: For example, they've been involved with Continuing the Dream, an interfaith racial reconciliation ministry of the Rancocas Valley Clergy Association.

The pastoral leadership is ahead of the congregation in understanding the role of structural causes of poverty alongside personal, spiritual causes. But exposure to people in need through Homes of Hope and other social ministries has enlarged members' understanding of the structural side of social issues and even influenced their political views, as a member of the pastoral staff explains:

> An awful lot of folks in this congregation, when we first started doing some of this stuff, said, "I don't notice any poor people in Mount Holly." But then they came and volunteered. . . . Not only do they see [poor people], but they hear the stories and they begin to become friends—and now it's not just "that poor bum on the street." It's "this guy I know." . . . Then somebody who has voted against any social thing that's ever come along suddenly says, "Wait a minute, that's going to hurt my friend," and they change their vote.

First Presbyterian Church's ministry recognizes that people's housing needs stem from multiple sources and thus require a multilayered response. A basic source of the problem is a shortage of quality low-income housing. On another level, destructive lifestyles and inadequate life skills keep people from financial stability. Counseling, mentoring, and support group ministries help meet these needs. On a broader level, public policies that limit affordable housing stock and people's economic opportunities call for education and activism.

Why Get Involved with Structural Change?

Most churches easily accept the need for providing relief. Individual development also seems to be a natural direction for church ministry. More and more congregations are supporting ministries of community development. Many evangelical churches, however, draw the line at structural change and political advocacy.

"Why bother with political action?" you may ask. "My church and our partners lead scores of broken people to Christ. Our social services meet people's needs. Activism would just be a distraction and create controversy. Why waste precious time on the messy, complicated world of structural reform?"

As explained in chapter 2, people are body-soul unities made for community. We can, to be sure, enjoy a living relationship with Christ no matter how evil and unfair our social setting. But we cannot enjoy the wholeness the Creator intended if we must live in oppressive structures that deny our humanity—whether under totalitarian governments that repress freedom or economic systems that thwart justice. Therefore, one of the crucial ways we love our neighbor is to promote the structural arrangements that nurture the goodness and wholeness of social life intended by the Creator.

Because so many Christians reject structural change as part of the church's mission, the rest of this chapter examines a holistic perspective on justice ministries.[7]

The church must pursue justice ministries for five important reasons:

1. *Systemic social conditions and public policy affect the outcome of ministry to individuals.* Imagine that your church's holistic ministries enjoy stunning success. They convert hundreds of broken people who now seek to reverse tragic decisions about work, education, and marriage that had so corroded their lives. With Christ in their hearts, biblical principles shaping their choices, and your job training program sharpening their skills, they are eager to work responsibly. Unfortunately, no job training program, however excellent, can propel people with little work experience into instant financial success. At the beginning, at least, low-skill jobs may be the only possibility. If the minimum wage and Earned Income Tax Credit are so low that your born-again, hardworking friends with full-time jobs cannot escape poverty or have health insurance, they are still in big trouble. Different policies could change their situation.

Consider another example. Knowing that strong two-parent families are crucial to overcoming urban brokenness, your ministries nurture wholesome family life. But if the politicians and the judges they appoint decide that the schools must teach that all "alternative family lifestyles" are equally legitimate, and they also deny educational choice for the poor, your neighborhood's children will be stuck with public schools that teach values that undermine your work. Again, different political decisions are possible.

An Indian bishop once told a story that underlines the importance of public policy. There used to be a mental institution in India, he said, that had a fascinating way of deciding whether inmates were well enough to go home. They would take a person over to a water tap, place a large water bucket under the tap, and fill the bucket with water. Then, leaving the tap on, they would give the person a spoon and say, "Please empty the bucket." If the person started dipping the water out one spoonful at a time and never turned the tap off, they knew the person still had mental disabilities!

Too often Christians work at social problems one spoonful at a time. Too often we fail to ask how we can turn off the tap by changing legal systems and economic policies that hurt people. Of course we must lead individuals to Christ one person at a time. But understanding the power of politics helps us see more clearly how we can also improve people's lives by reforming unfair laws and socioeconomic structures. This is why Robert Linthicum says, "If the church does not deal with the systems and structures in the city, then it will not effectively transform the lives of that city's individuals."[8]

2. *Sin is structural as well as personal.* A major theme in evangelical teaching is that Jesus delivers people from the ravaging effects of sin. But evangelicals have often defined sin narrowly in terms of individual, moral choices. We have not understood that sin also has a systemic dimension. Wrongful choices become embedded in twisted, unfair policies and social systems. As Ray Bakke puts it, "Some sins have been written into law."[9] That means that the conversion of individuals, while absolutely crucial and essential, is not enough. By dealing only with personal sin, we limit the scope of the transformation God desires. If we believe that God cares about whole persons, not just their "souls," we cannot ignore the impact of sinful social systems. The social dimension of sin must be corrected through structural change.

Because sin is social, advocating for social justice in Jesus' name has significant spiritual implications. Until Christ's return, the world is locked in a spiritual battle. Satan uses governments and social institutions to keep people in bondage. Structural reform is one way that the church testifies to Christ's ultimate victory "against the rulers, against the authorities, against the cosmic powers of this present darkness" (Eph. 6:12).[10]

As the saying goes, "If you're not part of the solution, you're part of the problem." It is impossible to be neutral on political issues. A church that does nothing about institutions and systems in the grip of sin reinforces the status quo. If God's people do not become informed and involved out of love for the community, they leave political and economic decisions to people who do not have the community's best interests at heart. David Apple, director of mercy ministries at Tenth Presbyterian Church, issues this warning: "Silence is more than a lost opportunity. It means becoming a part of the system of injustice, a part of that movement in history which is diametrically opposed to what God is doing."[11]

3. *Biblical teachings call the church to pursue justice.* The third reason for doing justice is that biblical faith demands it. The Mosaic law lays down a framework for the kind of social and economic relationships that please God. Again and again in Scripture, God's faithful people are politically engaged: Moses, Gideon, Joshua, David, Esther, Daniel, and Nehemiah, to name a few. The psalms and proverbs interweave expressions of personal spiritual devotion with prayers and principles for wise rulers and a just society. The prophets charged the people of Israel to confront the systemic evils in their society. Scripture repeatedly describes God as one who "executes justice for the oppressed" (Ps. 146:7).

The biblical record consistently demonstrates that God is concerned about political and economic systems and that God requires his people to work to correct those laws and structures that do not conform to his will. If the church focuses exclusively on biblical teachings that pertain to individuals, a crucial dimension of scriptural truth is ignored.

4. *Jesus is Lord over all.* We know that "all authority in heaven and on earth" has been given to Christ Jesus (Matt. 28:18). The risen Savior we worship is *now* "ruler of the kings of the earth" (Rev. 1:5). It was because the early church embraced the awesome truth that Jesus was "far above all rule and authority and power and dominion" (Eph. 1:21) that they challenged and defied human rulers when their laws and commands contradicted Jesus' way. Since Jesus is sovereign over every realm—from bedroom to boardroom to ballot box—Jesus' followers must seek to submit every area of their lives to him, including their political views and economic choices.

It is important that we fulfill our political obligations under the lordship of Christ as individual citizens, but that is not enough. The church, as the corporate body of Christ, serves as the model and agent of Christ's kingdom on earth. Jesus wants his people to join him in working for the wholeness, justice, and peace that he taught and modeled during his life on earth and promises to complete at his return. The church engages in social reform, says Ray Bakke, "in the name of our risen and reigning Lord whose kingdom has come, but not in its fullness."[12]

Some may argue that because Jesus did not organize a political movement to lobby the Roman Senate, the church should not engage in politics. That is to misunderstand Jesus' unique calling and situation.[13] In his years on earth, Jesus was sent to the Jews, not to the Romans. Furthermore, the Jews were a tiny, oppressed colonial group in a vast totalitarian empire. Consequently, the political options in first-century Palestine were very limited. In our democratic society, political engagement is possible, indeed welcomed, in a way it was not in Jesus' time. It is silly to argue that just because Jesus did not use television and the Internet to preach the Good News we also should not. Nor should the fact that his political options were fewer than ours lead us to conclude that we should not use the political process to work for justice whenever circumstances make that possible.

5. *Structural reform is a witness to the God of justice and love.* Social activism seeks to shape a world consistent with the evangelistic message that Christ is the risen Lord and coming King. Like the testimony of the Hebrew prophets, our efforts to shape a more just society bear witness to God's character over against the values of the world.

A church can strive mightily for justice and hardly seem to make a dent in all the ills of our world. But this does not mean that structural reform is a waste of time. Regardless of apparent results, Christian social action is a declaration of faith in the ultimate triumph of creation's Redeemer. It is "a reminder to a cynical and indifferent humanity that suffering and exclusion are not the final word of the universe."[14] The uncertainty of structural reform points to God as humanity's only source of hope, as Central Baptist pastor Marcia Bailey shared in a sermon:

> Economic justice may just be some far-off dream, some wishful vision. But it's God's dream. It's God's vision. And with God's love and God's power and God's promise it will happen. . . . If we love God, if we walk in God's ways, and if we hold fast to God, then the little we do will be increased beyond anything that we can dream or imagine.

Moreover, God wants to use Christians not only to challenge unjust laws and economic policies but also to serve as witnesses to those who make them. "One of the greatest barriers to evangelism," writes Stephen Mott, "is the failure of Christians to have significant relationships with non-Christians. Social action frequently places the Christian in the midst of non-believers in a situation in which the question of one's motivation comes to the fore. A common struggle for justice establishes vital links and a kinship that facilitates evangelism."[15] The arenas of government, media, and corporate finance are dominated by secularism. Like Daniel in the court of King Darius (Daniel 6), your church's advocacy may become the instrument for converting persons in positions of power.

For all the above reasons, the church must embrace structural change as part of its holistic mission. Theologian and activist Jim Wallis issues this passionate call:

"Let justice roll" [Amos 5:24] into a church made lukewarm by its conformity and isolated by its lack of compassion. "Let justice roll" and set free all the captives—those under bondage to poverty's chains and those under bondage to money's desires. "Let justice roll"—and let faith come alive again to all those whose eyes long to see a new day.[16]

Pursuing Structural Change in the Ministry of the Church

Congregational ministries of structural change can take basically three forms.[17]

1. *Educating and influencing the political choices of individuals, both in the congregation and the larger society.* In a democracy, the king whom the Bible summons to do justice is finally every citizen with the right to vote. Church members should be made aware of how their economic and environmental actions affect the lives of others—such as purchasing items produced in sweatshops, driving cars that have higher pollution emissions and lower gas mileage, or investing in companies that profit from tobacco sales. As Dennis Jacobsen notes, "The Christians who are so generous with food baskets at Christmas often vote into office politicians whose policies ignore or crush those living in poverty."[18]

2. *Advocacy, or working to influence the decisions of those in power.* "Speak out, judge righteously, defend the rights of the poor and needy" (Prov. 31:9). Advocacy does this by bringing the concerns of those who are vulnerable or victims of injustice before those with the power to change the system. This involves "being informed, articulating testimony in public and political arenas, understanding who is responsible for affecting change in relationship to an issue, writing letters and communicating with policy makers and their staff."[19]

3. *Intervention, or direct involvement in the political and social change process—* whether by supporting political candidates or legislation, pressuring institutions to change their practices, or sponsoring reform initiatives. Tactics may be confrontational, such as boycotts and marches, or they may be more behind the scenes, such as attending court hearings to make sure people from the community are treated fairly. A key component of successful intervention is community organization, which urban activist and theologian Robert Linthicum defines as "a process of mobilizing the people in a troubled neighborhood to take action together to identify and defeat the social and spiritual forces destroying that neighborhood."[20]

Normally the pastor, congregation, or denominational assembly should not endorse particular political candidates or legislative proposals. Church leaders must beware of abusing their positions of authority to direct the political choices of individual citizens. Timothy Keller warns, "Churches that are too heavily invested in the political agenda of a particular party or candidate can appear to be captive to an ideology instead of the lordship of Christ."[21] Further, a politicized congregation cannot nurture all its members or offer a winsome evangelistic ministry to all its neighbors, because it excludes those who take a different stand.

How then *should* a holistic congregation work toward structural change? Churches can:

- preach and teach in a way that helps members develop a passion for justice and a wise, biblical framework for political engagement. Leaders should also teach and model the difficult task of disagreeing politically in a way that is civil, respectful, and honest.

- bring social issues to the congregation's attention, particularly those bearing on the church's community of ministry. Without telling people how to vote, church leaders can help the congregation examine their values and become educated on the facts.

- issue or endorse pronouncements on broad social issues (such as abortion, nuclear disarmament, or environmental conservation) that communicate a biblical normative perspective on the issue to political leaders.

- form small groups in which individual members can develop a political philosophy or apply it to a particular social issue. These same small groups provide an organizational base for taking joint action, guided by their analysis and the leading of God's Spirit.

- provide people with opportunities for social activism, whether by sharing information about events in the community (such as school board elections or zoning board hearings) or by organizing church members who share convictions on an issue (such as by busing a group to the state capitol or by distributing a petition for signatures among the congregation).

- start a ministry that organizes people in the community to take action on issues affecting their quality of life, or partner with a local community organizing agency.

- organize persons in the congregation and community to transform specific local unjust institutions and systems (e.g., pornographic video stores, corrupt courts, or check-cashing places that charge exorbitant interest) through prayer, information campaigns, advocacy (e.g., lobbying elected officials), and nonviolent activism (e.g., boycotts).

- contribute funds to local or national organizations that reflect their biblical and social values and analyze and take action on public policy issues.

- offer their space for events of a political nature such as town meetings, elections, or community planning sessions.
- lead a voter registration drive and hold (nonpartisan!) seminars about civic participation.

A congregation that nurtures political discussion and social engagement empowers its members to engage in today's critical political debates in a wise, biblical way. Such a congregation promotes justice and expands the space and opportunity for effective holistic ministry.[22]

Keeping Social Action in Perspective

When it comes to social ministry, American Christians seem to swing wildly from one extreme to the other. Forty or fifty years ago, many evangelicals argued that good Christians should ignore social activism and focus on evangelism. Slowly a better balance emerged. Unfortunately, as evangelicals in recent years increasingly embraced the task of structural reform, they sometimes exaggerated its importance, were seduced by power, and failed to let biblical principles guide their political activity. In wisely warning against these mistakes, some recent voices seem to want to return to an earlier one-sided preoccupation with evangelism.[23] How can we maintain a sane, balanced, biblical approach to social action?

Social action is one God-given tool for loving our neighbors as whole persons. We must view it as important—but not all-important. Biblical people will never fall into the modern illusion of supposing that we can create a brave new world merely through restructuring society. Not even healthy communities, a growing economy, and good government can take the place of spiritual conversion, strong families, and thriving churches.

Holistic congregations understand that evangelism, social service, and structural reform are to complement rather than compete with one another. They never become so preoccupied with social action that they neglect evangelism and discipleship. Rather, they are inspired by the glorious examples of evangelical leaders such as William Wilberforce and Charles Finney. Wilberforce was deeply engaged in evangelism, but his primary calling was politics. God used him to end the slave trade and slavery in the British Empire. As the Billy Graham of the mid-nineteenth century, Charles Finney was primarily called to evangelism, but he also worked politically for the abolition of slavery. Holistic congregations embrace this biblical balance.

Life in Christ Cathedral of Faith

Life in Christ Cathedral of Faith in Chester, Pennsylvania, illustrates a balanced, holistic approach to social action. Voted one of the ten most corrupt cities in America, Chester has no shortage of arenas for social ministry. Nearly three-quarters of households have annual incomes under $10,000. The school district ranked dead last in the state of Pennsylvania. The city is a dumping ground for the rest of the (suburban, mostly Anglo) county, with waste treatment facilities almost literally in (mostly African American) residents' backyards. The child mortality rate is the highest in the state. Businesses have fled Chester for the more friendly tax policies "across the river" in New Jersey. Unemployment, substance abuse, single parenthood, welfare dependency, and violence plague the lives of many residents.

The vision of Life in Christ is "to reach out to the poor and disenfranchised of Chester with a love and hope that only comes from the gospel," as founding pastor Dickie Robbins describes it. From the beginning, the church has taken a holistic, multifaceted approach, from relief to reform. In response to the complex, interlocking problems presented by the community, Life in Christ's outreach contributes to the revitalization of the community "at every level—the spiritual, the economic, the educational, and the social."

Life in Christ is concerned with meeting people's immediate needs. The congregation regularly responds to requests for emergency assistance from people in crisis—people needing groceries or help paying a utility bill, families faced with eviction notices, parents of a teenage shooting victim. Another important way that the church provides relief is through the L.I.F.E. (Love In Feeding Everyone) ministry. L.I.F.E. provides weekly meals for up to seventy-five people at selected open-air sites. Before the meal, an elder in the church shares the plan of salvation and invites people to Christ. Volunteers offer Christian literature and information about church services along with the meal.

To help people move toward long-term transformation, ministries of personal development focus on substance abuse rehabilitation, education, youth mentoring, and financial counseling. In a ravaged city like Chester, personal transformation is a necessary foundation for community development, Bishop Robbins believes. "If you change the people, the people will change the community. If you just change the community and don't change the people, the people will change the community back." Spiritual transformation and character development are thus central to church ministries. Through faith in Christ and participation in a church community, people gain hope, integrity, and perseverance in overcoming brokenness. Without discipleship, Bishop Robbins believes, people can learn new skills but will always struggle to overcome old habits. People do not have to become Christians to get off welfare, for example. But if the goal is to "change their quality of life in every sense, then the power of God is essential."

A key insight of Life in Christ's social ministry is that internal and external needs form a vicious cycle. To stop the cycle, the church complements its ministries of personal development with projects aimed at rebuilding the community. A core ministry is the Life in Christ Economic Development Corporation, which creates opportunities in housing and entrepreneurship. In addition, Life in Christ is active in several local community development collaborations and state-funded projects. Because of the church's reputation, the state invited their involvement in a major initiative to clean up the community and spark economic development.

Life in Christ's ministry does not stop with development. Bishop Robbins also sees political involvement as crucial to fostering community revitalization. "Our people are citizens as well as Christians," he explains. "I don't think that we are expected as Christians to avoid the political arena. In fact I think we have to influence it. I am not certain that ministers like myself should be a part of the political structure. But I certainly believe that I need to be a part of influencing what happens in the political structure." He points to the model of the prophets who advised Israel's kings on creating a righteous government.

One way that he seeks to influence that structure is by participating in governmental and nonprofit committees that develop local policies and implement social programs. These include a government-funded "work first" program that helps people leave welfare, the Chester Education Foundation, the Delaware County Drug and Alcohol Commission, and an environmental action committee. "I can't wait until the wagon's fixed," Bishop Robbins says of his activism. "I should be a part of fixing it."

The church's Political Involvement Ministry (in the process of being separately incorporated in order not to jeopardize the church's tax exempt status) informs and organizes congregational action on local, state, and national social issues affecting the community. The ministry consists of three components: political education, voter registration, and political participation. Because voter turnout in Chester is so low, Bishop Robbins realizes that their congregation has the potential to influence local political decisions. His goal is that members understand the issues from a biblical and practical perspective, know how the political system works, and take a bold and timely stand on issues on which they can make a difference. The ministry also encourages those with "political gifting" in the congregation to become involved in local positions.

Bishop Robbins introduced the ministry at its first meeting:

> I'm tired of things happening around us that affect us that the congregation has no say about. . . . People make unjust laws which impose on us, and by the time we know it, it's too late. The first thing the church needs to do is to monitor everything going on at the local and state level. As soon as it hears about legislation affecting the community, the church can mobilize a drive to affect it.

Political change does not mean becoming disruptive or boisterous, Bishop Robbins says. By working quietly, persistently, and faithfully, the church pursues an ambitious vision: "We'll put an end to evil government in the city."

Conclusion

Rev. Lou Centeno, co-pastor of Bethel Temple Community Bible Church, grew up in the so-called Badlands of Philadelphia. "Worse than the violence and the alcohol and the drugs and the trash," he recalls, "was the hopelessness." A pervasive sense of despair drove him and many young men like him to crime and gangs. "People are angry in our city," Rev. Centeno observes. "They're angry because they feel that nobody cares—nobody cares about me, nobody cares about what's happening to my neighborhood, nobody cares about what's happening to the city, nobody cares about what's happening to the world. They end up becoming a part of the problem." The result is "a cycle of deterioration and disconnectedness, . . . rising despair and violence and crime and anger."

This is why the third arm of Bethel Temple's mission statement, following "discipling our members and evangelizing our community," is "revitalizing our neighborhood in the name of Jesus Christ." Ministries of revitalization give community residents hope: "Somebody cares, and I can be part of the solution." By pouring love, time, skills, and resources into the community, ministry staff at Bethel Temple not only meet pressing needs but also give people a new vision for their future, breaking the cycle of despair. Through the blending of word and deed, many in the community have come to know the Lord as the source of this hope and power for transformation.

Those who work patiently at the hard and often thankless task of social renewal draw on this same source to sustain their efforts. Yes, the needs can be overwhelming. Remembering that Christ is already victorious over sin and death helps us keep perspective and sustain hope that someday God's kingdom *will* come on earth as it is in heaven. By faith, we claim that "the future will see the establishment of the social system reflective of His divine nature, characterized by peace, love, unity, equality, and justice."[24] Through social ministries the church proclaims the coming reign of God in its fullness, helps people to taste the goodness of God's reign, shows people how to live as the Creator intended, and invites people to enter the kingdom.

chapter five

Integrating Evangelism and Social Outreach

The proper model is not (1) to see mercy as the means to evangelism, or (2) to see mercy and evangelism as independent ends, but (3) to see both word and deed, evangelism and mercy, as means to the single end of the spread of the kingdom of God. . . . Our goal is not individual "decisions," but the bringing of all life and creation under the lordship of Christ, the kingdom of God.[1]

If you believe that Christian faith offers hope and strength to people in desperate circumstances, your church's social ministry should provide people in crisis with opportunities to embrace or deepen their faith in Jesus Christ.

If you believe that the forgiveness that Jesus offers frees people from bondage to shame and gives them a new identity as a child of God, your social ministry should share this message with people who struggle with low self-esteem or a troubled past.

If you believe that the Holy Spirit endows people with a divine power greater than themselves to heal emotional wounds and break destructive habits, your social ministry should offer to pray with people to invite God to do this work of supernatural transformation.

If you believe that persons are both material and spiritual beings, then your social ministry should combine spiritual and material aid.

If you believe that a biblical view of persons and the world sheds new light on social issues and provides guidance for making wise choices, then your social ministry should share biblical truth and provide opportunities for Bible study.

If you believe that a loving, supportive Christian community makes it easier to say no to destructive behavior and yes to responsible behavior, then you should be actively recruiting people to join a Christian church.

If you believe the above, but your social ministry does not actively integrate prayer, evangelism, and dependence on the Holy Spirit, then you need to ask, "Why not?" and explore how your social outreach can more effectively and honestly incorporate evangelism. (If, on the other hand, you think that good social behavior is dependent only on a good socioeconomic environment, we encourage you to go back and reread the first few chapters!)

This chapter looks more specifically at how evangelism and social action intersect in community ministries. Because many ministries historically have been conducted in a one-sided manner, new conceptual tools and models are needed to help church leaders grasp how word and deed effectively work together in holistic mission.

Five Ways of Incorporating a Religious Dimension into Social Service

While the term "faith-based social services" has become popular, this single term actually covers a wide variety of programs—some more, and some less, holistic. The "faith" in faith-based programs can range from the presence of Christian symbols (such as a crucifix or posters with religious messages on the walls), to the involvement of Christian staff and volunteers, to the inclusion of prayer and references to the Bible in the program, to invitations to church services, to explicit teachings about Christ and the call to conversion.

As we researched churches and faith-based organizations, we found five basic ways that a social ministry can include a spiritual dimension, including an evangelistic component. (These are not mutually exclusive; a church or organization may combine various elements.)

1. *Passive:* Spiritual truths are largely modeled rather than expressed verbally. The program may be located in a religious environment (such as a church), but evangelistic materials or religious counseling are available only to clients who seek it out.

Example: The Advocate Community Development Corporation (ACDC) was incorporated in 1968 as "the outlet for some of the non-spiritual, nonreligious programs" of the Church of the Advocate, according to the assistant director. ACDC has provided over three hundred new or rehabilitated units of housing over the years, along with sponsoring other community development projects. Founded by the wife of the rector of the Church of the Advocate, ACDC originally operated out of the church building and is still often associated in the community with the church. Many staff are motivated by faith. However, its programs involve no specifically religious activities or content.

2. *Invitational:* Clients are invited to attend (optional) church services or events at which an evangelistic message is presented. The services may be regular church services or special programs for clients.

Example: While the curriculum for the welfare-to-work program affiliated with Greater Exodus Baptist Church is not explicitly Christian, the congregation makes a conscious effort to welcome and include the clients in regular church activities. The church informs the women in the program about youth groups, mentoring programs, and other church ministries relevant to their needs and encourages them to attend worship services. In particular, they are invited to a special lunchtime Bible study (lunch included) with the pastor.

3. *Relational:* In the context of relationships formed with clients beyond the structured programmatic activities, program staff/volunteers share their faith and address clients' spiritual concerns informally, one-on-one.

Example: Throughout its history, Bethel Temple has found various ways to cultivate relationships with kids in the junior high school across the street— for example, by hosting before- and after-school programs, connecting with students informally during their lunch hour, and offering vocational training in the church's graphic arts and media center. Although the members cannot proselytize directly on school time or grounds, the outreach fits the church's style of relational evangelism. A staff member explains, "Kids need to know that you care about them and that you're willing to go where they are." The relationships formed at the school lead to opportunities outside the classroom for mentoring and discipleship.

4. *Integrated-optional:* In this type of ministry, explicitly religious content is woven into the delivery of social services, and staff may give explicit invitations to conversion. However, clients may opt out of any activity that calls for them to interact with or respond to explicitly religious teachings.

Example: For almost fifty years, Tenth Church has been reaching out to Philadelphia's large international student population. The International Students Christian Fellowship (ISCF) offers conversational classes in English, matching small groups of students with volunteer tutors. The discussions help with acculturation as well as language skills and counter the loneliness and alienation felt by many internationals. Though the main focus is not Christianity, tutors may ask students about their religious backgrounds and talk about their own beliefs in return. After an hour of conversation, the students form Bible discussion groups. Students are "strongly encouraged but not required to attend," says the handbook. More than 90 percent of the students choose to stay—some out of politeness, others for the extra English practice, and some out of genuine spiritual interest. The handbook tells tutors, "Whatever the initial motive of your student, you have a tremendous opportunity to share the gospel and Biblical Christianity with an interested learner."

Some tutors take the additional step of becoming a "friendship partner" to students, inviting students for a home-cooked meal or fun activity each month. Friendship partners also help students with personal needs, such as finding an apartment, getting medical care, or learning how to open a bank account. The handbook stresses the optional nature of the ministry's evangelistic potential: "Being a friendship partner provides an irreplaceable foundation for sharing the Gospel with internationals. However, the friendships that are built . . . must not be conditional. Acceptance of Christianity cannot be a requirement for continuing a friendship partner relationship."

5. *Integrated-mandatory:* Spiritual development is at the heart of this type of program. Full participation is considered essential to the desired social benefit and therefore required.

Example: The Men's Redirection Center of Faith Assembly of God provides up to six men with food, shelter, and discipleship training as they recover from substance abuse and put their lives back together. In phase 1, the program teaches basic living skills such as cleaning, cooking, getting a license, and time management. Days are highly structured, with devotional time in the morning, several worship services during the week, odd jobs or volunteer work for various church ministries, and discipleship classes. Twice a week, the men are required to fast until dinner time, and once a week they participate in evangelistic street outreach on drug corners. After six to nine months, graduates move on to the phase 2 home and work at an outside job. While their time is less structured, they are expected to maintain an accountable relationship with their supervisors, an active personal devotional life, and involvement in church ministries. The church is very clear with the men that participation in discipling activities in both phases is a condition of living in the home. Nearly all the men who stay with the program make a faith commitment or rededicate themselves to Christ.

The characteristics of these five forms are summarized in the following table.

When is it appropriate to make religious components of a service program mandatory, and when should they be optional? Of course, a ministry cannot force someone to have faith, but a ministry can require someone to participate in activities of a spiritual nature, such as sitting through a prayer or evangelistic presentation. In many ministries that address deep-seated negative patterns, such as drug dependency or chronic homelessness, spiritual nurture is at the heart of the program. If someone came to Life in Christ's Drug Free ministry but refused to participate in the prayers, sermons, and Bible-based counseling, they would get very little out of the program. In these types of ministries, the key is to inform prospective beneficiaries in advance about the

Is the spiritual dimension of the program . . .	Explicitly verbal?	Part of the planned program design?	Mandatory?
Passive	No	No	No
Invitational	No in the program; yes in other activities to which clients are invited	No	No
Relational	No in the program; yes in informal conversations with staff	No in the program; yes in intentionally cultivated relationships	No
Integrated-optional	Yes, unless clients decline to participate in religious activities	Yes	No
Integrated-mandatory	Yes	Yes	Yes

program's religious nature and not force people to enter the program against their will.

Another case in which a mandatory religious activity is appropriate is when a church offers a onetime benefit, such as a concert or a meal, in conjunction with an evangelistic activity, such as a devotional or Christian video. Germantown Church of the Brethren annually distributes about one hundred Thanksgiving food baskets to needy neighborhood residents. One year, they decided to require people to attend a worship service before receiving their turkeys, so that they "would also realize that worship is a vital part of their existence, so that they would like to do it on a regular basis," explains a staff member. In such ministries the focus is the evangelism, and the social benefit is an accompanying "perk" that tangibly represents the church's message of God's love. The church must be careful, though, that the benefit is offered as a blessing and not a bribe. And again, it should give people advance notice of the evangelistic activity so that they do not feel tricked into hearing a "sales pitch."

Another type of program in which mandatory religious activity is appropriate is children's ministries, such as day care and after-school programs, where part of the purpose of the program is to teach children Bible lessons and Christian values. Children may be expected to sing Christian songs, memorize Scripture, participate in times of prayer, and listen to Bible stories. However, the director of Germantown Church of the Brethren's summer youth camp cautions against exposing children to altar calls, which can pressure them prematurely to make a decision for Christ.

> Children often are easy to persuade. . . . So I tend to try not to force children into a decision but to help them realize that that is a choice they need to make

How Not to Be Holistic

How to Violate Someone's Right to Freedom of Religion

One woman's testimony, posted on a secular welfare-to-work web site, provides a lamentable example of covert religious coercion:

> The job I work on is run by a Christian organization. Some of the people who work there belong to the owner's church. I am not a Christian but I do have respect for all religions. These people do not. . . . Some of the names I have been called [by Christian coworkers] are devil spirit, nonbeliever, and welfare recipient. My job is always threatened by the management. Each week I go to work wondering whether I'll be fired. . . . I have never stated my religion to any of my coworkers; however, I have declined requests to come to their church. . . . This job is over for me, I know.

How to Quench the Spirit

While observing a faith-based homeless shelter one evening, Heidi asked to interview one of the guests. Before long, Katerina (not her real name) was pouring out her life story. When she had become homeless, she had gone to her church for help. Her pastor had told her that God was punishing her because she had not been tithing enough. Since then, she had struggled with doubts whether God could really love and accept her. Now she thought she was pregnant again, and the shelter director (hired for her professional social work credentials, not her faith) was threatening to kick her out unless she got an abortion.

Putting aside her notepad, Heidi asked Katerina if she would like to pray. Katerina eagerly agreed, and they joined hands and came before the Lord. Midsentence, the door opened, and the overnight monitor, a volunteer from an area church, interrupted. "It's almost 9:00, and Katerina should be getting ready for bed," she said, addressing Heidi as if Katerina were not in the room. "She has to leave early for work tomorrow, and if she stays up too late it will be hard to get going in the morning." Katerina's expression and posture slumped as the door closed again. They quickly finished their prayer, as flat now as a punctured tire, and Katerina left to go to bed.

. . . when they understand it to the point where it means that they will make a lifetime commitment. . . . They're welcome to do it or to talk to us individually. But we do not give them a group opportunity to express their decision.

In some situations, mandatory religious elements are clearly *not* appropriate. One example is when you are serving a population that largely belongs to another religion, such as Muslim immigrants. Another example is when you are working in partnership with secular or interfaith agencies, or when your ministry receives government grants. Mandatory religious elements may in fact be counterproductive in ministry with clients who feel powerless or have been abused by authority figures in the past, such as mothers on welfare or victims of domestic violence. Vulnerable people may go along with religious activities and mouth faith statements out of fear or guilt without experiencing real inner transformation. This demoralizing experience can lead to resentment against the church.

Whether mandatory or optional, what matters most is that the spiritual component is presented in a loving, sensitive, and relevant way. There is nothing wrong with an honest, respectful attempt at persuading someone to accept a different system of belief. On the other hand, psychological manipulation, or trying to bribe, threaten, or shame people into a religious response, is never appropriate. "In a way we're like midwives, carefully assisting in a new birth. . . . To try to force premature delivery by high-pressure tactics and insistence on a decision only produces hostility, sometimes even rejection. It can create lasting wounds that close people's minds to the gospel."[2] We must serve people whether or not they accept the gospel, care about their whole being whether or not they recognize the spiritual dimension of their needs, and love them whether or not they understand that God loves them through us. This is the standard set by the God of grace, who "sends rain on the righteous and on the unrighteous" (Matt. 5:45).

Further, the spiritual dimension of a social service ministry will always have a greater impact if a personal relationship is involved. An example comes from the tutoring program at Tenth Presbyterian Church. Not all the kids appreciated the Bible studies that began every tutoring session. Several boys—one from a Muslim family—even stopped coming because they thought the program was too evangelistic. But one day the program coordinator took the group out to the New Jersey shore. It was in that more informal setting that the boys began to open up and ask him questions about his faith. "When you do [evangelism] one-on-one in that interpersonal relationship," comments the coordinator, "sometimes that's better than to have it structured where you sit them all down and you teach them a lesson."

Four Basic Church Types in the Relationship between Evangelism and Social Ministry

When it comes to how and why churches integrate sharing faith and meeting social needs, there are four basic types of churches. Which type best describes your church?

1. *Explicit evangelism is not a part of the church's outreach mission.* This type of church is committed to serving the needy and advocating for justice in Christ's name but without making an explicit attempt to bring those they serve to Christ. Faith motivates and shapes their outreach, but the focus of their ministry is meeting social needs, not nurturing faith in others. They may even sense that they get more spiritual inspiration from those they serve than vice versa. The pastor of a historic downtown church described the impact of their ministry to homeless persons in this way: "They convert *us* to Christianity. We have to serve in order to become Christian. They have changed us, and they have changed our church. . . . In many ways they make us the church."

Often this type of church's approach to social action is based on a theological understanding that equates evangelism with doing good works. Their approach may echo a saying of St. Francis: "Preach the gospel at all times; if necessary, use words." Previous negative experiences with pushy, insensitive evangelism sometimes creates this attitude. Some may believe that personal conversion is irrelevant to social change. Or they may consider it inappropriate to invite non-Christians to accept Christ. In some cases, their programs may have religious overtones (in other words, staff may refer to spirituality or God's love in a general way) without being specifically Christocentric.

Of the five ways of incorporating a religious dimension described above, social service programs sponsored by this type of church are likely to take either of the first two forms—passive or invitational.

2. *Evangelism is valued and practiced but not in the context of social ministry.* Many churches have a dual mission focus, with evangelism and social ministry taking place along separate, parallel tracks. Individual programs or church volunteers focus primarily on one or the other, with little overlap in leadership, administration, or volunteer support. Social ministries normally do not include overt or one-on-one faith sharing with recipients; evangelism ministries do not include meeting material needs.

In some cases, the dualism has practical origins. Programs that focus on community and economic development or political advocacy may involve complex institutional negotiations, requiring staff with a specialized set of technical or professional skills. This kind of ministry work is not as likely to bring staff and volunteers into direct contact with the recipients of ministry or to facilitate the development of long-term relationships. In cases in which the ministry is funded by public dollars, the religious dimension may be constrained by the current understanding of the separation of church and state.

Dualism can also result from the way the church defines its mission focus. Churches may interpret the Great Commission and the Great Commandment as distinct mission mandates. Some churches have different ministry aims for different target audiences. For example, a suburban church may send teams to run social ministries in inner-city neighborhoods, while directing evangelism toward its local community. The church's understanding of social mission may also be influenced by the norms of professional social work that stress an "objective," materialistic approach to addressing human needs.

The most likely ways that this type of church may incorporate a religious dimension are invitational or relational.

3. *Evangelism and social ministry are integrated in various ways.* In this type, evangelism and social action are distinguishable but inseparable, like the two sides of a coin. The blending of evangelism and social ministry is based on the understanding that the physical, spiritual, moral, and relational dimensions of human nature are intertwined. Churches of this type encourage faith commitments in the context of social activism. Service recipients may or may not be required to participate in religious activities, but they are given the opportunity to learn about Christian faith in one way or another.

Some social service programs have a built-in spiritual dimension. The feeding ministry of Life in Christ Cathedral of Faith begins with a devotional, for example. Tenth Presbyterian Church's divorce-recovery support group and seminars use Christian books and videos. When people come to Christian Stronghold Baptist Church for donations from the food pantry, says a lay leader, "Before you walk out of here with that brown bag, somebody's gonna share the Lord with you."

Other programs take a less direct, more informal approach. Participants cultivate personal relationships and look for opportunities to initiate a spiritual dialogue with recipients. First Presbyterian Church of Mount Holly follows this path in offering seminars and workshops on topics such as health or parenting that are relevant to people in the community. Nonmembers and members discover what they have in common and develop rapport around nonspiritual matters. This connection can naturally give rise to the evangelistic moment of saying, "This is who Jesus is. Would you like to enter into a relationship with him?"

Ministries of this type may incorporate a religious dimension in several ways: relational, integrated-optional, or integrated-mandatory.

4. *Little conventional social ministry is present.* This type of church cares about healing social ills, but evangelism and discipleship are essentially the only vehicles for outreach. The underlying belief is that social needs are mostly or entirely spiritual in nature. Helping people in need thus requires getting at the root of the problem through a process of conversion and discipleship that bears fruit in fundamental life changes. Social change comes *only* as people personally experience spiritual and moral change. Therefore, the best way to transform society is by reaching one soul at a time with the gospel.[3] Miraculous conver-

Holistic Ministry at the Dinner Table: Corn Bread and the Bread of Life at Koinonia Christian Community Church

The mouthwatering meal was spread on a table at the front of the room, buffet style: barbecued turkey wings and baked chicken, mixed vegetables, potato salad, rice and gravy, corn bread and white bread, donuts, bananas, and juice. Hungry people deserve a good home-cooked meal, says Sadie Simmons, wife of Pastor Jerome Simmons—"something you would feed to people you invited to your home for dinner."

A short worship service preceded the meal. After an opening prayer, a "church mother" led the group in upbeat praise choruses. She read Psalm 121, encouraging her listeners to look to God for help—always! Then Pastor Simmons stood to share his dramatic testimony. "I was born again behind a bar, outside where I used to go to get drunk." He wove his story into a presentation of the gospel message and the universal need for salvation. To his African American audience he emphasized, "Jesus is *not* white!" Many people feel disenfranchised by American Christianity, he acknowledged, but "this isn't religion, this is life." He concluded by affirming Koinonia's commitment to serve the community.

Pastor Simmons then asked if anyone had questions about what he had shared. One man raised his hand. "When I hear the Good News," he explained, "I have a burning in my heart, but it goes away when I leave church. I want to know, how can I keep it with me always?" Stay in church as much as possible, Pastor Simmons encouraged him, and surround yourself with the fellowship of believers. Closing the service with a prayer, Pastor Simmons invited his listeners to join in a prayer for salvation. A few voices could be heard repeating the words.

As the volunteers served the food, Pastor Simmons also stood in line to receive a plate and sat at the table, eating and talking with the other ministry recipients. "Come to church on Sunday!" he urged as they left.

sion and Spirit-filled discipling that remold lifestyle, character, and attitude in accordance with God's will are believed to be the only effective ways to improve people's social circumstances.

Churches of this type may provide charitable relief such as food baskets, particularly as a prelude to evangelism, but do not typically engage in ministries of economic development or political advocacy. Such wide-scale social programs are ineffective, in the words of one lay leader, because they are like "putting a Band-Aid on a severe cut. Evangelism starts at the core. Once you change a person's life you can also change their social position." Only when people are spiritually transformed can conventional social interventions such as substance abuse counseling or job training have lasting effect. Ministries of social aid are thus generally provided not for the broader community but for those who are already Christians or who are willing to consider accepting Christ.

Evangelism in this type of church is likely to take an integrated-mandatory form—or evangelistic programs may stand alone without any social ministry component.

Assessing the Church Types

The first type is clearly not holistic—or biblical! Every church should actively seek to share the gospel with those outside the church. Striving for social renewal is very important, but biblical Christians have an equal passion for spiritual renewal.

Churches of the second type may not be truly holistic if their evangelism and social ministries run on separate tracks. John Cheyne provides a helpful metaphor:

> One may have a whole watch lying on the table, but it has little value until each of the pieces is joined and functioning. . . . It is the complete working together and mutual interdependency of those parts that make it a watch—not just the parts. Without this it is merely a montage of disconnected pieces. Unfortunately, missions can often follow a similar pattern. All the various parts may be present, but they do not necessarily present the whole gospel to the whole person, and, in fact, the various parts may be in tension with one another rather than functioning as vital parts of the whole.[4]

This type of church should ask some tough questions. Do program staff and volunteers actively seek opportunities to pray with clients or share their faith? Are church members given opportunities to serve, or is the community ministry delegated to professional staff who may or may not be Christians? Is the church's mission structure consistent with its theology and vision for the community, or is it unduly influenced by secular norms or pressure from funders? How might the church introduce relational evangelism into its community or economic development ministries? For example, Tenth Memorial Baptist Church hosts a "welcome to the neighborhood" party for new home owners whose homes have been built and financed through the community development corporation affiliated with the church.

Churches of the third type are closest to the vision of holistic ministry outlined in this book. (See the sidebars for examples of ministries that fit this type.) Whether the gospel message is shared formally or relationally, whether it is shared at the point of service delivery or in a separate setting, the desire in these holistic churches is to see the social ministry bear spiritual fruit. For these churches, a key danger is that they will reduce social ministry to a mere "tool" of evangelism, a hook to snag prospective converts. Unless the ministries are founded on genuine love and respect for recipients, recipients may feel manipulated or bribed into a spiritual response. On the other hand, holistic churches that emphasize informal, relational evangelism should check whether the gospel message is actually being communicated as much as they hope or think it is. You cannot assume that just because staff or volunteers say they care about evangelism that they are actually leading persons to faith in Christ.

Churches of the fourth type seem to neglect the fact that persons have bodies as well as souls. They overlook the fact that since God made us for community, our social environment has a profound effect on us. Even Christians suffer from systemic evils. The fact that someone is poor is by no means an automatic indicator of a spiritual problem or character flaw. Leading people to salvation is thus not a substitute for pursuing community development or working to right social injustices. From a biblical perspective, religious ministries that focus only on the soul are just as one-sided as secular programs concerned exclusively with the body.

One final note: However evangelism and social ministry are integrated, a shoddy program will undermine a holistic intent. The quality of Christian outreach is an elemental ingredient of the incarnational holistic message. "That's why I talk about excellence in the organization," exclaims the director of a community development agency that coordinates several church-based after-school programs. "You can preach, but people want to see results when they come into your building, before *they* make a change." If materials are inferior or out-of-date, if staff are ill-informed or unprepared, if the building is dirty or unsafe, clients will rightly question the truth of your words. "Excellence [gives] you a better platform to share the gospel."

Bridging the Gap between the Social Service and the Community of Faith

Beyond sharing the gospel with the people you serve in outreach, a key component of holistic outreach is helping to connect people with a loving church family—whether your own or another congregation. Bringing people to faith in Christ is incomplete if the new or renewed believer does not also become actively involved in a worshiping community. However, socially active churches often face a dilemma: Many people from the community pass through their doors to receive services, but very few return for worship services. Sometimes there are more people in the church on a weekday than on a Sunday!

There are many reasons why people who come to a church for an outreach ministry never return for worship. The most obvious, and the easiest to fix, is that they were never invited! Ministry personnel may assume that people know they are welcome in worship services—but unless the invitation is personal and explicit, it will rarely be accepted. Or people may have actually visited the church once and felt overlooked or out of place. If you invite people from the ministry to your church, be sure that your church is ready to receive them (see chapter 7). A less negative reason is that a person may already have a different church home or may be looking for a church in a different denomination or neighborhood. In that case, your church should affirm and support his or her active participation in another congregation. Your church may even want to prepare a list of holistic churches that are ready to welcome people from your ministries.

Often, however, the problem lies with resistance to church attendance in general. People may fear the church will condemn them for their past sins or current lifestyle choices; perhaps they experienced previous rejection by "church people." Many think they cannot come to church if they lack dressy clothes. Persons from non-Christian households may be afraid of offending their family by going to church. Single people dread walking into a room of strangers alone. Parents worry about their kids' behavior. Low-skilled wage earners may have to work Sundays or late-night shifts on Saturdays.

The most difficult barrier may be the perceived stigma attached to being the beneficiary of a church ministry. A visitor wants to be received by church members as an equal, not as "the single mother in our welfare-to-work program." As one church member commented, social ministries can create an awkward dynamic between the servers and those served: "It becomes a class thing . . . from 'down here' to 'up there.'" Kathryn Mowry notes the consequences of this kind of fracture:

> One trend for (some) urban congregations is that the "mission" becomes social involvement while the "church" remains limited to a fellowship of urban missionaries. . . . Churches provide food distribution, and housing and employment programs to reach out to the stranger, but the church continues to struggle at the point of extending community to the stranger.[5]

How do you transform "strangers" into members of your family of faith?

At a seminar, a pastor asked Rev. Patrick Hansel of New Creation Lutheran Church, "How do you get people to come to your church from out of your social ministry?" He answered:

> We become their friends. I wouldn't join a church if I had only gone there to receive some benevolent aid, because I would still be labeled as "that person with a need." There's no mutually edifying relationship there. But people stay with us because this is where they not only found Christ, but they found friendships, they found support, they found community, and they found a home.

As Rev. Hansel indicates, the key is to nurture community with people in your church's social ministries. Friendships become the bridge between the social program and the fellowship of the church. Honest, caring relationships not only give people a sense of belonging and equal status, but they help overcome a natural human "fear of the unknown." A leader at New Covenant explains that most people approach a new church with the apprehension, "'I don't know this church. I don't know these people.' This is why we try to build relationships, so they can get to know us," she continues. "And once you have that trust established, then it is easier for someone to say, 'Come on with me, come to my service.'"

There are four main strategies you can follow in building relational bridges between beneficiaries of outreach ministries and members of your congregation.

1. *Create opportunities for members of your church (not just staff) to get to know the beneficiaries of social ministries.* Build relational time into volunteer assignments, or create relationally focused volunteer jobs. For example, schedule enough volunteers for a soup kitchen so that the people preparing and serving the meal have time to take turns sitting down to eat with the guests. Or if not everyone is comfortable interacting with strangers, follow the example of Tenth Presbyterian Church and recruit volunteers specifically to serve as "hosts" at each table. Identify volunteer positions with potential for relationship-building, such as receptionist or child care worker, and look for people with strong interpersonal skills and a heart for friendship evangelism to fill them. For example, the van driver in Germantown Church of the Brethren's outreach to homeless shelter residents does more than just bring people to church activities. The driver often gives informal Christian counseling, shares his personal testimony, prays with guests at pick-up and drop-off points, and invites guests to other church activities.

At Cookman United Methodist Church, the bridge between the church's educational and job-training ministry and worship service attendance was not built by staff or volunteers. During the first two years of the welfare-to-work program, many students came to a deeper faith in Christ, but none joined Cookman. The third year, however, students started visiting the church, and four became members. What made the difference? In the third year, Cookman opened the program to church members who needed the services. Over time these members developed relationships with the people they sat beside in their classes. They invited their classmates to church, and their new friends accepted the invitation. Whenever church members participate in a service or event alongside people from the community, you have the building blocks for welcoming people into church fellowship.

Holistic Ministry in a Government-Funded Program: Helping Welfare Recipients Make a Transitional Journey

After learning about Charitable Choice, Rev. Donna Jones decided to develop an explicitly Christian ministry for welfare recipients, which would address not only job readiness but the "spiritual issues that keep people from full empowerment." The State of Pennsylvania shocked her tiny inner-city church, Cookman United Methodist Church, by awarding it a $150,000 welfare-to-work contract for Transitional Journey Ministries (TJM).

The TJM handbook proclaims to participants, "We want you healed in your spirit, mind and body. We want you self confident and self assured. We want you totally prepared for, and able to participate in the world of work. We know with God's help and your determination, you will succeed." To achieve these goals, students are provided both job skills and spiritual resources. Students learn computer skills, study to pass their GED tests, and are matched with employment opportunities. The church's food and clothing closet are available to meet immediate needs. Classes on such topics as life skills, budgeting, and self-esteem develop confidence and work readiness and address emotional barriers to progress.

The program also includes several explicitly religious elements: weekly worship services, group and individual prayer, and a spiritual development class ("Sisters of Faith") that explains the gospel and invites students to make a faith commitment. It is only the inner strength that comes from faith, Rev. Jones explains, "that is going to sustain them when the kid is sick, the boss is calling, they have to work overtime, and they have to take the third shift." As required by the state, the spiritual components of the program are privately funded and optional—students may choose a nonreligious educational activity instead. Students entering TJM sign waivers stating that they are aware of its Christ-centered nature and of their right to opt out of religious activities.

TJM also addresses spiritual and emotional needs in an informal, relational way. The handbook assures students: "If you have any special needs or problems and you need prayer, . . . if you need someone to talk to or you just need a hug, we are here and we want to help you." Students note that TJM feels different than other programs whose staff have demoralizing, condescending attitudes. At TJM, the availability and caring of the staff, almost all of whom are Christians, are a key reason for students' openness to the religious message.

Shawna (not her real name) came to TJM with ten children, an eighteen-year history of substance abuse, and a fourth-grade education. Her life was in turmoil, and the five-year limit on her welfare clock was ticking. The program's therapist helped her set goals and develop an action plan, but Shawna was simply unable to cope. She became suicidal. The therapist asked Shawna if she wanted to meet with Pastor Jones (whose salary is wholly paid by the church) for spiritual counseling. In Rev. Jones's office, Shawna reaffirmed her faith in Christ and from that point started attending services at Cookman. Eventually she graduated from TJM with a job. To mark the start of her new life, Shawna was baptized at Cookman along with three other students from her TJM class.

TJM has succeeded in helping many people like Shawna achieve both financial and spiritual liberty. If it were not for their ability under Charitable Choice to follow a holistic approach, Rev. Jones doubts their efforts would be as worthwhile. "Before, I never considered federal money because I felt it meant we couldn't maintain our religious integrity," she explains. "The gospel is liberating, and we're dealing with people who need to experience that freedom and hope."

For more on TJM, see Jill Witmer Sinha, "Cookman United Methodist Church and Transitional Journey: A Case Study in Charitable Choice" (Washington, D.C.: Center for Public Justice, August 2000).

2. *Include service beneficiaries in social events outside of worship services, which provide more informal, nonthreatening soil for nurturing relationships.* One way Life in Christ Cathedral of Faith does this is by inviting participants in their drug rehabilitation and feeding ministries to an all-day church picnic in the summer, with lots of games, music, and free food. They post flyers advertising the event at the local homeless shelters and pick up dozens of guests from the shelters in church vans. Church members are also encouraged to invite their neighbors and families. The entire congregation is exhorted to make guests feel welcome—but particular church members are assigned and prepared to interact with people who look as though they might be feeling left out. While the picnic includes a time of worship and a short devotional, the focus is on interaction. Socializing helps guests feel more comfortable accepting an invitation to attend the church. They know they will at least recognize the people who played softball with them! Bishop Dickie Robbins explains:

You establish the relationship outside of the church. . . . You don't expect a fish to just come and jump into the boat! So you throw out a net. We look at the outreach as casting a net. Once we get people into the net we gently draw them in to the local church, the lifeboat. . . . If we use [social ministry] to build right relationship, they will keep coming. If they keep coming then we will have the opportunity in a more traditional worship setting to both share the gospel and give the altar call.

3. *Create an alternative service for people served by outreach ministries who hunger for a worshiping community but just cannot bring themselves to walk into a Sunday morning service.* This may mean starting an informal evening or after-

noon service, perhaps in a different setting, such as a member's home. Some churches offer a worship service in conjunction with a meal, like the Bread and Bible Ministry of First Presbyterian Church. Bread and Bible was founded mainly for evangelistic purposes, but some regular attenders have come to think of it as their church. Services may also be tailored to ministries for particular populations often uncomfortable in traditional church settings, such as a worship service/support group for recovering substance abusers, or a service by and for teenagers following a sports recreational program.

If a church offers these worship services simply because members struggle to accept and integrate people on the social margins into their fellowship, and alternative services keep such people "out of sight, out of mind," then church leaders have more discipling work to do. Attenders in alternative services should be made to feel like part of the congregation. "Seed" these services with regular church attenders. Encourage alternative attenders to continue taking steps toward full membership. This may mean gently prodding attenders to join the main body of the congregation, or it may mean making the alternative service an "official" part of the church. Either way, the gap between service ministry and church fellowship has been bridged.

4. *Involve service recipients in serving alongside church members.* God promised Abraham, "I will bless you . . . so that you will be a blessing" (Gen. 12:2). Accordingly, churches should value and recruit the ministry potential of those whom they bless in ministry. "The implications of calling forth the gifts of others may startle churches with established ministries that tend to do things 'for' people. But if we truly extend community to strangers by calling forth their gifts, we will become recipients of their ministries in our midst."[6] Being seen as the object of charity is dehumanizing. But people will be drawn to a church that recognizes their inherent worth and inspires them with a vision of how they can bless others. Says Bishop Robbins, "You can't wait until they are healthy to start saying, 'Now give back.' You tell them the whole time so that part of the motivation becomes that they can use their experience to help somebody else."

A Holistic Ministry Checklist

When everything comes together, what does a holistic program look like? A ministry that embodies the church's mission and thoroughly integrates evangelism and social change incorporates the following components:

- *Ministry leaders* with passion for both spiritual and social transformation, love for both the congregation and the community, and commitment to the church's overall ministry vision.

- *Staff* who are selected on the basis of their character and spiritual maturity as well as their professional skills, with a commitment to excellence and a longing to pray and share the gospel with those they serve.
- *Holistic program content* that effectively integrates the best insights of the medical and social sciences and community development practice with significant opportunities for spiritual transformation and discipleship, including biblical material, worship, Christian counseling, and prayer.
- The teaching of a *holistic worldview* that understands that personal and societal brokenness result from a complex interplay of both sinful personal choices and unjust social structures, and therefore seeks wholeness in the area of ministry at the spiritual and material, personal and societal levels.
- *Evangelism training* that prepares staff and volunteers to integrate word and deed in ways that are sensitive, relational, clear, and effective.
- An emphasis on *prayer and dependence on the Holy Spirit,* leading staff and volunteers to pray regularly for the healing of those they serve in every dimension of their lives—spiritual, physical, relational, financial, and psychological. (A prayer partner for each staff and volunteer or a special prayer team can be helpful.)
- Opportunities for building *relationships* of caring and trust with the people served, as a basis for faith-sharing, mentoring, holistic support services and referrals, and invitations to join a Christian community (whether your own church or another congregation).

Holistic Ministry in Action: Christian Stronghold Baptist Church

Christian Stronghold provides an excellent example of a "type 3" holistic church that interweaves word and deed in a variety of integrated-optional ministries. Senior pastor and founder Rev. Willie Richardson laments that so many churches get hung up on the question of providing services versus saving souls. "We who are ministering in the city cannot afford to engage in that debate," he says, "because our people are dying."[7] In response to urgent spiritual and social needs, the church blends multiple evangelism strategies with a dedication to serving the community.

At Christian Stronghold Baptist Church, says Rev. Richardson, "Everything we do is an evangelistic outreach in nature. Every opportunity we have, we witness to people." Diverse service ministries connect people to the church around various "felt needs," ranging from the need for food and health to the desire to do better in school to the aspiration to own a home. While there is inherent merit in meeting material needs in the name of Jesus, says Rev. Richardson, feeding and healing are only part of what Jesus modeled. People who have their physical needs met without an explicit evangelistic encounter "came to eat the appetizer and never got the rest of the menu." This does not mean that every person who comes to the church for help is forced to listen to a sermon. Ideally, however, the act of providing the service is part of a larger process in which relationships are formed, church members have the opportunity to verbalize the gospel, and the recipient makes the connection between the social need that was met, their underlying spiritual need, and the promise of the gospel for a better life.

The youth group, for example, sponsored a free car wash. While some youth washed the cars, others talked to the owners about Christ. In a program that helps new home owners obtain a mortgage, recipients hear about God's plan for their lives as part of the process of financial counseling. Counselors encourage new home owners to give God the credit for this life-changing blessing. At church-sponsored health fairs, doctors integrate spiritual and medical advice, telling hypertension patients not only about exercise and proper nutrition but also "that your body is the temple of the Holy Spirit and that you have a responsibility to be a steward of it," explains an associate pastor. "We don't want [doctors] to bombard the participants with Scripture, but we want them to know that they do have accountability to the Lord in how they treat and respond to their bodies."

Another example of a holistic service ministry is a GED preparation program, started as a response to welfare reform. The director of outreach and evangelism describes how the ministry incorporates a spiritual dimension:

> When they step in the door, we give them the gospel. . . . We open up with prayer, and every opportunity we have we witness to people. . . . Our purpose is to help them with their education. With that in mind, when the opportunity arises, we turn the conversation to Christ. . . . We have opportunities within the lesson plan to discuss the way God would have them handle the situation. . . . You have to rely on the Holy Spirit to bring back into remembrance all you have studied. If you rely on God to help you, it makes it much easier.

About half of the GED students are not from the church; some were recruited for the class through the ad placed in the church-published community newspaper. Students are invited but not required to attend church services. One year about one-third of the nonmembers in the class ended up joining the church.

Not every social ministry has an overt evangelistic component. In some ministries, the faith-sharing occurs through informal witnessing by church staff and volunteers. The church's Youth Self-Esteem Ministry, for example, works with at-risk boys from the local elementary school. The program is not explicitly Christian because of its connection with the public school, but God's love is displayed in the caring relationships staff develop with the boys. "I take them to my home on weekends, and I ask them, 'Why do you think I do this?'" recounts the ministry director. "I tell them, 'I do this because I love you.' They don't know what that means, so I have to demonstrate it."

Christian Stronghold believes that spiritual transformation is the cornerstone to developing the capacity of individuals and that empowered individuals then become the key to transforming the community. Reaching African American males with the message of salvation is a particular mission focus. An associate pastor describes the vision for ministering to "people that are burdened and beat down":

> To give them hope; to give them direction for their lives. To help them to understand that God wants them to be all that he created them to be, and that . . . because they're of a lower economic standard does not mean that they have to remain there; that there's pride in being black; that they're supposed to have a positive self-esteem in Jesus Christ because they're a new creation in him; and that as they submit their lives to God and as he shows them their gifts, talents, and abilities, they're going to rise above that economic condition they are in.

Noting that men are in the minority in many African American churches, Christian Stronghold launched a "Win 1,000 Men to Christ" campaign that brought many men into the kingdom of God—and increased the number of female church members as well! A core component of this outreach is the "Glory and Honor Groups," or care groups for men, which mingle church members and spiritual seekers. The format combines fellowship, Bible study, and education, giving particular attention to social and health issues pertinent to African American men. The care groups encourage network evangelism and offer a friendly environment where men can receive support and counsel.

While its social ministries focus on individuals and families, Christian Stronghold has also invested in community development. Christian Stronghold helped organize and support the Nehemiah project, a coalition of churches that built or refurbished 128 homes, and launched the collaborative Phoenix Project to renovate three hundred abandoned city-owned homes for resale to lower- and moderate-income families. Other projects have involved negotiations to bring a supermarket into the neighborhood, a job placement collaborative, and plans for a new recreational center. The church also created a Community Action Council "to be the salt and light from a biblical perspective" in response to moral and political issues affecting its membership. The council has undertaken a wide range of actions, including planning a health fair, "adopting" the local elementary school, lobbying to upgrade a public bus stop near the church, and blocking the liquor license of a nearby business. Such initiatives respond to the disconnect between neighborhood conditions and what God desires for the people of West Philadelphia.

Holistic Ministry in a Mall: Sharing Faith in a Cathedral of Consumption

Burlington County Mall Ministry sees itself as a mission outpost station in a jungle of materialism. The goal is not to usurp the place of the local church but to encourage people who would never set foot in a church to develop a relationship with God. The ministry creates an inviting atmosphere with living room furniture, free literature and lollipops that proclaim "Jesus loves you," a box for prayer requests, an electronic sign announcing current programming, and a friendly host who models God's hospitality.

BCMM offers a variety of programs for all ages and interests. These include seminars on useful and appealing topics, from job-seeking skills to overcoming loneliness to knowing health care options. The ministry also sponsors special events, such as concerts, dramas, puppet shows, and a gymnastics exhibition. A seasonal highlight is a living nativity, giving costumed actors the chance to tell their reason for being at the mall. Support groups for overcoming self-destructive behavior, conquering grief and stress, and managing weight problems attract regular guests. A basic beginners Bible study provides an introduction to Christianity.

When the ministry first opened, volunteers were eager to lead evangelistic activities. They soon learned that anything blatantly Christian rarely attracts the ministry's target audience, the unchurched. Some mall visitors are even put off by the neon sign proclaiming "ministry" and keep their distance. BCMM developed a strategy of offering programs that reach out to people at their points of need, weaving in the gospel message in varying degrees according to people's openness. The ministry continually searches for creative, nonthreatening ways to let people know God loves them and to encourage people to examine their spiritual needs. One avenue is the window display, which creates visual representations of Scripture and Bible stories. For example, one display featured streamers inscribed with 1 Corinthians 13, along with pictures of different aspects of love.

Perhaps the most important elements of the ministry are the informal interactions. People stop by to chat with volunteers for various reasons—some out of curiosity or interest in a particular program, some out of loneliness, some out of an unrecognized spiritual hunger. One man came looking for help with a nosebleed and then opened up about his struggles as a widower. When homeless people ask for aid, they receive donated certificates from food court vendors. As the ministry became established, people increasingly revealed their questions and deep hurts. Volunteers make themselves available to listen, to show God's love, and to pray for those who stop by. A designated "Prayer Zone" provides privacy for people who request prayer or who want a quiet space for meditation.

Regular visitors, says Elsie, often tend to be "loners" or people on the social margins. One woman who was nearly blind was drawn repeatedly to talk with volunteers, who kept encouraging her to develop a relationship with God. Finally, the woman decided to take their advice and attend church. There she accepted Christ. She returned to BCMM and told Elsie, "I want to help." With new-found self-confidence, she greeted visitors with a smile and cheerfully kept the place neat. When Elsie tried to thank her, she replied, "No, thank *you* for help-ing me!" Soon afterward, she told BCMM volunteers she was moving to Ten-nessee, where she planned to serve God as a "missionary," as they were doing.

Elsie Nicolette (Burlington Center Mall Ministry Director) contributed to this write-up, as well as the case study of the Burlington Center Mall Ministry in chapter 13.

Christian Stronghold views community development as a way to overcome the obstacles of racism and poverty that prevent people from full empower-ment, as well as the spiritual forces that keep people in despair. As a testimony to God's goodness, community development and advocacy also have evange-listic implications. Hosting Town Watch meetings and other community events creates evangelistic opportunities by bringing nonmembers into the church and facilitating interactions with church members. Speaking out on political issues from a biblical perspective offers a moral and spiritual example to pub-lic officials. Just as meeting a felt need makes it more likely that a needy per-son will be open to an evangelistic message, displaying a commitment to com-munity development helps to create openness on the part of those who share a concern for the community. Church leaders can point to members who have joined Christian Stronghold because they appreciated the church's involve-ment in the community.

How does Christian Stronghold sustain its commitment to holistic ministry? Three factors are key: emphasis on the responsibility of every church member to fulfill the Great Commandment and the Great Commission, thorough train-ing to carry out that calling, and a strong focus on biblical discipleship.

Evangelism, discipleship, and social ministry are linked in the expectation that as members grow spiritually, they will minister to the outside community. "We're a serving church," affirms the coordinator of New Member Ministries. "We are here to serve, not just to get saved." Through new member classes, sermons, Sunday school, and small groups, Christian Stronghold calls believ-ers to participate in ministry to the body of Christ and to society. One woman describes what led her to become a church member: "When you walked in there, you met Christ. When you walked out, you were equipped to serve."

Members are equipped through rigorous training. As a staff member explains, training is essential because "most people don't join the church because of the minister, they join the church because of the people." Christian Stronghold's Church Bible Institute (attended by Christians throughout the Philadelphia area) offers courses in various areas of ministry, including sharing one's faith. An annual "Concentrated Weekend" offers intensive training. Many members begin their evangelistic involvement through this weekend, following up with courses from the Church Bible Institute. Ministry leaders go through extra training on evangelism, discipleship, and leadership skills. Evangelism is also stressed right from the start in the new members class. Says Rev. Richardson, "Nothing matches the joy of new converts enthusiastically experiencing the joy of the Lord and sharing their faith with other people!"[8]

The goal of evangelism, Rev. Richardson teaches, is active discipleship. Christian Stronghold stresses the necessity of living in accordance with biblical teachings in order to participate in God's design for a wholesome life. The Community Action Council coordinator describes coming to a new understanding of salvation after attending Christian Stronghold: "I called myself a Christian, but I wasn't saved. There's a complete difference in being saved . . . not just going to church on Sunday but living your life as a Christian every day." Most altar calls in the church include an invitation to rededication for people whose faith in Christ or church membership have lapsed. Those who make a profession of faith are given Christian literature, matched with a mature "spiritual sister or brother" from the congregation, and channeled into an extensive discipleship process.

This emphasis on personal spiritual growth fuels members' commitment to holistic ministry. Bible study and prayer are cornerstones for the church's outreach. Believing that prayer is a powerful influencer of people and events, many ministry activities—even routine staff meetings—incorporate intercessory prayer. Volunteers gain confidence by drawing on a power source beyond themselves, as one of the counselors testified:

> I don't have to walk away [from a counseling session] thinking, "Did I say the right thing?" . . . No, I know I gave them the Word, and I know that the Word is not going to go out void. . . . I'm not so wrapped up in my own skills and my own ability to counsel. I'm more wrapped up in the power of the Word and how the Holy Spirit will be used in the life of that person.

With this combination of consistent calling, training, and discipling for ministry, Christian Stronghold has had stunning success in engaging members in holistic outreach. About half of the congregation is involved in a church outreach ministry. But members go beyond involvement in programs to make sharing the Good News a way of life. According to our member survey, 90 percent of respondents said they often or sometimes talked about their Christian beliefs or testimony with non-Christians in the last year, and 70 percent invited people to church. And 82 percent of respondents said they helped lead someone to Christ! Christian Stronghold members are equally committed to demonstrating God's love with caring actions in their daily lives: 95 percent of respondents reported providing someone in need with food, clothing, or money in the last year; 83 percent helped someone find a job; and 82 percent took care of someone who was sick or handicapped.

Members' personal dedication to a holistic lifestyle is one major factor behind the church's explosive growth. Average adult Sunday morning attendance is about seventeen hundred—and roughly half of these people had never belonged to a church before Christian Stronghold.

Conclusion

Christian Stronghold's example shows that when mature disciples of Christ are taught and trained to blend word and deed, the result is transformed lives, renewal of a hurting community, and the growth of a dynamic congregation. Imagine the impact if there were ten thousand holistic congregations like Christian Stronghold in America's one hundred largest cities. And imagine the impact on your own community if your church were to embrace this vision.

Part 2

The Essential Elements of Holistic Ministry

chapter six

Divine Love and Power for Outreach Ministry

The closer we get to God, the closer we get to the people of the world. We find the world at the heart of God.[1]

Worship and Mission

The church in Jerusalem was suffering from famine and persecution. The first-century Christian leaders decided to organize the churches to do something about it. In Paul's second letter to the church in Corinth, he prepared the church to take up a love offering for needy people in Jerusalem. To inspire them to greater giving, he wrote them a glowing report about the contribution of the churches in Macedonia. The Macedonians had limited resources and were facing persecution, yet their generosity overflowed. What was their secret?

> They voluntarily gave according to their means, and even beyond their means, begging us earnestly for the privilege of sharing in this ministry to the saints— and this, not merely as we expected; they gave themselves first to the Lord and, by the will of God, to us.

> 2 Corinthians 8:3–5

The Macedonians gave sacrificially. But their most important act of self-giving was not to those in need but first of all to the Lord.

For our service to become truly holistic, we must first offer our lives to God. In the Great Commandment, the part about loving your neighbor as yourself is the second half. It depends on the first half: "You shall love the Lord your God with all your heart, and with all your soul, and with all your mind, and with all your strength" (Mark 12:30). God does not just want our time or our money. God is looking for Christians who will dedicate their whole selves to the love of the Lord.

Without this passionate love affair with God at the root of our service, we may do good deeds, but their ultimate value, both to others and to ourselves, will be limited. "If we lose our 'first love,'" warns Amy Sherman, "quickly our service to others becomes mechanical, our touch efficient but cold."[2] Our spiritual witness is likely to feel artificial and forced, sapped of spontaneity and joy. We may find ourselves questioning whether it is all really worth it.

There's nothing wrong with motivating people to ministry by telling them how much it can make a difference, or how good it will make them feel, or how it will introduce them to new friends and new skills. No doubt about it, involvement in service ministry is rewarding. But there comes a time when every ministry worker will feel alone, exhausted, discouraged, even disgusted. Acts of compassion will seem useless; advocacy for justice will feel ineffective and dry. Only spiritual devotion can breathe new energy and meaning into service. Rev. Donna Jones's ministry offers a striking illustration. "We don't have custodial support at Cookman," explains Rev. Jones, "so when the toilets overflow, I'm often the one cleaning up. . . . And I think, 'All right, Jesus, this is for you.'" The desire to look Jesus humbly in the face and say, "This one's for you" transforms even menial acts of service into gifts fit for a king.

Mother Teresa was once asked, "How did you receive your call to serve the poor?" She answered, "My call is not to serve the poor. My call is to follow Jesus. I have followed him to the poor." Jesus' story of the sheep and the goats in Matthew 25:31–46 assures us that Christ is present in those who hunger and thirst, in those who feel lonely and sick and rejected. When we reach out to others in need, we touch Jesus. When our lives are wrapped up in love for Jesus, we rejoice to meet him in "the least of these." We don't put poor persons on a pedestal, but we dedicate our hearts and hands in worship of the God of the poor. "Our love and compassion for people is in direct relationship with our love for God," Rev. Bill Borror says of Media Presbyterian Church's ministries. "We see Christ in their eyes, and hopefully they see Christ in our eyes as well."

In the wilderness of the world's needs, our cry can echo the passionate longing of the psalmist: "O God, you are my God, I seek you, my soul thirsts for you; my flesh faints for you, as in a dry and weary land where there is no water"

(Ps. 63:1). Our quest for the living water of Christ merges with our act of giving a cup of water in Christ's name.

Love for God produces obedience to God. True worship means offering ourselves to God as living sacrifices, to do God's will and to be conformed to God's likeness (Rom. 12:1–2). We grow to desire the things God desires, to hate the things God hates, to imitate God's character, and to pursue God's priorities. "Out of the . . . heart the mouth speaks" (Matt. 12:34). If our hearts and minds are set on Jesus, our faith will spill out onto those we serve as a matter of course, rather than out of guilt or a desire to please others.

When we dedicate ourselves to the God "who forgiveth all thine iniquities; who healeth all thy diseases; who redeemeth thy life from destruction; who crowneth thee with lovingkindness and tender mercies; who satisfieth thy mouth with good things" (Ps. 103:3–5 KJV), we thereby dedicate ourselves to proclaiming God's forgiveness, healing diseases, showing mercy, and filling the mouths of the hungry. "The LORD executeth righteousness and judgment for all that are oppressed" (Ps. 103:6 KJV), and so we too make this our business. Even as God "made known his ways unto Moses, his acts unto the children of Israel" (Ps. 103:7 KJV), we also seek to teach people how to live according to God's will. As "the LORD is merciful and gracious, slow to anger, and plenteous in mercy" (Ps. 103:8 KJV), followers of Christ must exhibit these attributes in their ministry. Through these expressions of ministry, our lives proclaim, "Bless the LORD, O my soul; and all that is within me, bless his holy name" (Ps. 103:1 KJV).

Holistic ministry is thus a form of the "sacrifice of praise" (Jer. 33:11) in which God delights. We acknowledge that any good thing that we have to share—our resources, our skills, our life in Christ, even our desire to serve— does not come from us but is ultimately God's gift to and through us. We praise God for the grace of giving and give out of gratitude for God's grace. The more we serve, the more we can see and appreciate God's love, grace, and mercy toward us and others. The deeper our gratitude, the more passionate our worship, the more motivated will be our service.

Love God, Love Your Neighbor . . .

Holistic ministry is not only a natural outflowing of our love for God; it is essential in order to develop a right relationship with God. At the heart of holistic ministry is this paradox: You can't truly love and serve people unless you love God. And you can't truly love God without loving others. As Rev. Patrick Hansel of New Creation Lutheran Church puts it, "When we love God, we must love our brothers and sisters, because God loves them through us." Our relationship with the Lord and our relationships with other people are inseparable (Mark 12:29–31).

Christlike love is the cornerstone of holistic ministry. "Above all," writes St. Paul, "clothe yourselves with love, which binds everything together in perfect harmony" (Col. 3:14). It is possible to meet people's needs without loving them. Here are some symptoms of a loveless ministry: condescending do-goodism; inflexible, task-oriented busyness; "doing for" rather than "doing with"; self-lauding (or self-pitying) self-sacrifice. St. Paul warned against charity in word and deed without the true "charity" of love: "Though I speak with the tongues of men and of angels, but have not love, I have become as sounding brass or a clanging cymbal. . . . And though I bestow all my goods to feed the poor, and though I give my body to be burned, but have not love, it profits me nothing" (1 Cor. 13:1, 3 NKJV). But take heart, because "love never fails" (1 Cor. 13:8 NKJV).

Where does this unfailing, overcoming love come from? It is relatively easy to be moved by compassion, or even to drum up affection, but Christlike love comes only from the Father. Recognizing our debt to God for his boundless love for us, we rely on God's grace to share in his boundless love for others—particularly those who are unloving, unloved, and unlovable. We are the pipeline for God's refreshing, living waters to regenerate parched lives.

The coordinator of a food ministry at Faith Assembly of God depends on God each time she volunteers to open her eyes and heart to love people in Christ's name. "When we pray in a circle [before the food distribution], we pray to God to let us see through his eyes," she says. "We have to look and know that God loves that person the exact same amount that he loves us." Just as Christ became like one of us in order to become our Servant (Phil. 2:5–11), holistic ministry involves identification and solidarity with those we serve. This solidarity does not mean we try to become something we're not (or shouldn't be); it means viewing all people as our equals, created precious in God's image.

. . . as You Love Yourself

"We love because he first loved us" (1 John 4:19). The most important way we love ourselves is to receive God's generous, gracious, unconditional, and unmatchable love for us. The Spirit calls us to stay still and enjoy God's love. When we rest in God's love for us, we can't help but radiate that love to others.

Activists often neglect themselves. We may feel that we matter to God only to the extent that we are useful to him. In contrast, "Jesus' kind of servanthood flows from a powerful awareness of our dignity and worth based in the knowledge that the Creator of the universe made us in the divine image and redeemed us at the cross."[3]

To be involved with holistic ministry, we must respect ourselves and stay healthy as whole persons. How can we fulfill the Great Commandment, "Love your neighbor as you love yourself," unless we love ourselves? Does it make sense to care for other people's bodies and neglect our own? Can we reach out in relational ministry to the community with integrity if our own family relationships are fractured? What message does it send if we encourage others to come to Jesus but never take time to be with him ourselves? God desires our holistic well-being as much as that of anyone we serve.

Jesus sometimes pushed himself so hard that his family thought he had lost his mind. He skipped meals and went without sleep, when his mission demanded it. But he also slept when he needed to sleep, even if a storm raged outside (Matt. 8:24), and he ate when his body needed food, even if it offended religious legalists (Mark 2:23–28). Those who find themselves consistently running ragged, on the edge of physical or emotional collapse, may be driven not by holistic mission but by a false estimation of their own importance. Such frenetic activity reflects a lack of trust that God is really in control. Because we are to love the Lord with our *whole* selves, getting a good night's sleep at the right time can be just as spiritual an act as attending an all-night prayer service.

Immersed in Prayer, Empowered by the Spirit

When it comes to holistic ministry, prayer is not optional. Prayer is not a seasoning to be sprinkled over social service to give it a pious flavor. Prayer must bathe the entire process of development and implementation; it is not just a step in the process. Prayer is at the heart of holistic ministry. The apostle Paul enjoins us to "pray without ceasing" (1 Thess. 5:17). This means, pray, pray, pray, and pray some more. For God's sake. For your sake. For the kingdom's sake. For the world's sake.

Sometimes a one-sided dualism creeps into a church's prayer life: There is a tendency to pray about people's "spiritual" needs and organize action steps to meet their social needs. It is far more common to soak an evangelistic rally with prayer than a housing construction project. But prayer and action are both/and, not either/or. Holistic ministry includes:

> both praying vigorously to bind the demonic powers and also working hard to reduce sex and violence in the media and reform unfair economic patterns. . . . We change history, both by our prayers and by our actions. . . . Prayer is not incidental to evangelism or peacemaking. Prayer is not peripheral to empowering the poor, protecting the unborn, and restoring the environment. Prayer is a central part of how we do those things.[4]

Many churches have found ways to merge prayer and social action, beyond starting committee meetings with a perfunctory prayer. Central Baptist Church, for example, has a "Prayer and Care Circle" that supports each of its social justice mission groups. Germantown Church of the Brethren lifts up the prayer concerns of a different church ministry in its prayer meeting each month. Faith Assembly of God includes the various social ministries of the church in the prayer calendar distributed to the congregation. A group of volunteers gathers for prayer the hour before the weekly Bible study for homeless guests at Tenth Presbyterian Church. These churches look to God in prayer to empower their good works.

Prayer is also the key to a reliance on God's Spirit to guide ministry decisions. A single church simply can't do all things for all people, so holistic ministry entails making difficult decisions. Which neighborhood to focus on? What needs take highest priority? How much time and money to invest? When to get started? Different leaders have different ways of making decisions and discerning God's will, but the bottom line is the leading of the Holy Spirit. Pray "that you may be filled with the knowledge of God's will in all spiritual wisdom and understanding, so that you may lead lives worthy of the Lord, fully pleasing to him, as you bear fruit in every good work" (Col. 1:9–10). The assurance of "all spiritual wisdom and understanding" is particularly critical when the leader's decisions are unpopular with the congregation or community, or when the Spirit-led path seemingly runs counter to common sense.

Jerome Simmons, pastor of Koinonia Christian Community Church, is one who has been emboldened by the Spirit's guidance to take risks. If you ask Rev. Simmons how he manages a full-time social work job on top of his church work in a gritty inner-city neighborhood, his answer is immediate and simple: only through prayer. Pastor Simmons relates the story of how the church came to own its building:

> The owner of the property approached me and asked, "Reverend Simmons, why don't you buy the building?" I said, "Well, let me go back and talk to the church." Actually I meant that I was going back to talk to God. . . . The Lord said to me in that time of prayer and devotion, "I'm going to give you from Germantown Avenue to 11th Street, from the basement to the roof. I've already done it!" I went back and told the owner, "Yeah, we'll buy it." He said, "All right, give me $105,000. Give me $50,000 down," and the balance in a certain amount of time. . . . I said, "Okay." We didn't have any money, we didn't have a dime. . . . I began to seek the Lord. I said, "Lord, you started this, now I have faith to go to the next step with you, but that's all I have. I don't have any money." He said, "That's all you need. That's more than money."

The owner agreed to hold the mortgage, and Koinonia has slowly been making its payments. The small congregation soon opened a thrift store and feeding ministry in the building next door. Pastor Simmons is still claiming by faith the corner property, a bar known for drug dealing and prostitution. A banner that hangs over the church boldly proclaims God's promise to the community:

"This block belongs to God, from Germantown Avenue to 11th Street, from the basement to the roof!"

The Holy Spirit also provides specific guidance in the practice of holistic ministry. For instance, there is sometimes a fine line between meeting a legitimate need and enabling a destructive habit. When people come to church with requests for emergency assistance, church staff often have to make quick decisions about what resources to offer. Getting to the root of a person's problems sometimes requires seeing past the obvious presenting need to a deeper issue, such as a history of sexual abuse. Professional social work skills are important, but sensitivity to the Spirit in each particular situation is also essential. A staff person in Christian Stronghold's counseling ministry put it this way: "When you're sitting in a case, . . . and quite frankly you don't know where to go with it, it's at that moment—even while you're listening to them—you just start praying for the Holy Spirit to give you wisdom in what to do in the next second." Her counseling team prays over their case notes at home, asking for wisdom and guidance for their next counseling session.

The Spirit also gives ministry practitioners the vision to discern underlying spiritual realities. While Jesus walked the earth, he rebuked evil spirits and healed people of demonic possession. When Jesus sent out his disciples to heal diseases and preach the gospel, he also gave them authority over evil spirits in his name (Mark 3:14–15). The Spirit continues to empower the church to confront the spiritual forces affecting the individuals and communities it serves. "Our struggle is not against enemies of blood and flesh," Ephesians 6:12 cautions us, "but against the rulers, against the authorities, against the cosmic powers of this present darkness, against the spiritual forces of evil in the heavenly places." These spiritual forces of evil work to destroy human lives—through corrupt and exploitive social systems, twisted cultural values, corrosive addictions, and distorted relationships. Their enmity is not finally with humans but with God. Those who proclaim and demonstrate the Good News of God's kingdom can expect to encounter spiritual resistance, manifested in many forms—"for all who do evil hate the light" (John 3:20). If we put on the protective armor of the Spirit (Eph. 6:10–19) and draw on "divine power to destroy strongholds" of the enemy of Christ (2 Cor. 10:4), we can minister boldly in the assurance that Christ is Lord over all things, visible and invisible (Col. 1:16).

The staff of the Peacekeepers program of Faith Assembly of God know they are immersed in a spiritual battle. Peacekeepers was founded in response to several violent incidents involving local youth. The grant-funded program trains kids in conflict resolution, safety, and self-respect. Although the program has secular funding, the staff members lay an unobtrusive spiritual foundation through occasional group prayers, informal one-on-one sharing, and invitations to church activities. One of the program's coordinators explains that the ministry is one way the church wages spiritual warfare against the violence plaguing their community. "I believe the devil is using our children," she says from her personal experience working with the youth. "And they can't cope, because the parents are not there—if not physically, then emotionally." When they begin to feel overwhelmed, the staff will stop what they are doing to pray together. "I believe in this program, and I believe in the church doing it, because our children are weary and they gotta get strong," she asserts. "You think we are in spiritual warfare now? When this generation becomes adults—man! So they need to know the Lord and how to fight this."

Those in holistic ministry face twin temptations. The first is to succumb to despair because the problems are so much greater than we can handle. The apostle Paul often faced the specter of discouragement in the face of persecution and conflict in the early church. In Ephesians 1:18–21, Paul prays that the eyes of his readers' hearts might be enlightened to know their hope, their inheritance in Christ, and "the immeasurable greatness of his power for us who believe, according to the working of his great power" (v. 19). God's power in us, Paul says, is the same as that which raised Jesus Christ from the dead and set him "far above all rule and authority and power and dominion" (v. 21).

In the days of Elisha, a great army of Arameans surrounded his city by night. In the light of dawn, Elisha's servant saw the army and came running in to Elisha to warn him of their danger. Elisha's response was to pray: "O LORD, please open his eyes that he may see." Suddenly, "the LORD opened the eyes of the servant, and he saw; the mountain was full of horses and chariots of fire all around" (2 Kings 6:17). In the same way, when we pray and seek divine power for ministry, we realize our access to far greater resources than we ourselves possess. We may be surrounded by corruption and perversions, by decay and death—but the same power that breathed back life into the crucified Christ is also with us! The perspective that comes when our spiritual eyes are opened through prayer imparts new hope and courage for ministry.

If the first temptation is to despair of our ability to cope with the demands of ministry, the second temptation is to think that we are capable of handling all the problems on our own. We have a natural tendency "to fall back on human energy when responding to human need," says Mary Thiessen, a missionary theologian. But, she warns, "Moving ahead of the Spirit's timing and responding with human solutions where only the power of the Spirit can perform healing quenches receptivity to the Spirit. Innumerable human efforts cannot accomplish what the Spirit's power is able to do."[5] This does not mean that we wait limply for God to act. No real tension exists between human effort and supernatural empowerment, between careful planning and divine intervention. When we submit ourselves to God as instruments of his will in our community, we should be equally prepared for hard work and for surprising miracles.

A Tenth Presbyterian Church member who leads a Bible study at an AIDS hospice reflects on how this ministry has changed his life. The outreach has "forced me to rely on God in a continual way that I never had to before." He adds simply, "I recognize that without the Holy Spirit, I'm clueless." When we admit we are "clueless" before the stark, overwhelming realities of evil in our world, we are free to admit our dependence on God and to allow him to equip us for the work of ministry. In Christ we are "strengthened in our inner being with power through his Spirit," so that God "by the power at work within us is able to accomplish abundantly far more than all we can ask or imagine" (Eph. 3:16, 20).

Social work bureaucracies strive to maintain an illusion of being in control in order to project an image of power. In contrast, "Prayer is the demonstration of our contrition, humility and utter dependence upon God to do what only he is capable of achieving and what we are totally incapable of accomplishing ourselves."[6] When we in the church make our weaknesses transparent to the community, our posture of dependence on God adds to our evangelistic witness. As Paul writes in 2 Corinthians 4:7, "We have this treasure in clay jars, so that it may be made clear that this extraordinary power belongs to God and does not come from us."

"Let the Same Mind Be in You That Was in Christ Jesus" (Phil. 2:5)

"As the Father has sent me, so I send you" (John 20:21). We are the inheritors of Jesus' amazing charge to his disciples to adopt his mantle of mission. At the center of holistic ministry is Christ—our Lord who commands ministry, the Suffering Servant who modeled ministry, our Friend and Shepherd who leads us forth in ministry. We present to the world a "unique and profound combination of Jesus as *message* and Jesus as *model*," as Ray Bakke points out.[7]

Jesus was himself the message, in a way that we are not. But there is a sense in which the same is true for us. We cannot separate our ministry deeds from our character as doers of ministry. Both in our outreach programs and in our daily lives, we are the ambassadors of Christ to the world. The reputation of Christianity has been grievously tarnished over the centuries and around the world by "missionaries who went in Christ's name, yet without his nature."[8]

What is the character of Christ we are to imitate? Four attributes are essential to holistic ministry: incarnational servanthood, abiding submission, visionary compassion, and grateful joy.

Incarnational Servanthood

Christ, "being in very nature God, did not consider equality with God something to be grasped, but made himself nothing, taking the very nature of a servant, being made in human likeness" (Phil. 2:6–7 NIV). God incarnate took his place among humans. As a human who identified fully with human needs (Heb. 4:15), Jesus served not with resentful obligation or condescending pity but in gracious love for those whose lives he willingly intertwined with his own.

> Jesus insisted that he "did not come to be served, but to serve" (Mark 10:45). Both in life and death, he acted that way. He spent vast amounts of time tenderly ministering to the physical needs of hurting people. He went out of his way to bring love and dignity to socially marginalized groups like lepers, tax collectors, bleeding women, blind beggars, and even a guilty adulteress.[9]

As we stoop to wash another's feet—whether by serving a hot meal, teaching computer skills, or lobbying for Third World debt relief—we imitate Christ. It is no good to proclaim the gospel of Christ the risen Lord unless we are willing to live like Jesus the humble servant.

Abiding Submission

Christ was one with God, yet obedient to his Father—"obedient to the point of death" (Phil. 2:8). In John 5:19, Jesus declared that he did only what he saw and heard from the Father. In John 15:1–7, Jesus tells his disciples that they likewise can do nothing unless they abide continually in him. To abide in Christ means to trust him, to draw strength and sustenance from him, to center our lives around him. The goal is not to develop our ministries to the point where we can say, "Thanks, God, we'll take it from here!" Jesus depended daily on God for direction and did not hesitate to pause in his activities to pray and prepare himself spiritually for what lay ahead. His power flowed from his intimate relationship with his Father. If we abide in Christ, we too have the promise that we shall bear much fruit (John 15:5).

Abiding in Christ also saves us from "the tyranny of the urgent." The need around us is not our primary call to holistic ministry; it is the love of Christ that urges us on (2 Cor. 5:14). "If we are need-driven," cautions Ray Bakke, "we can become manipulated, even co-dependent on our ministries for identity, for security, and not the least of all, for funds."[10] Jesus could easily have become overwhelmed by the sheer volume of needs around him. People tried to manipulate Jesus for their own ends and to coerce him into performing miracles on demand. But his bond with the Father gave him a solid grasp on his purpose. He recognized that "his mission was not to touch and heal every person, but to be obedient to his Father," as Jude Tiersma puts it.[11] In the same way, God does not hold us accountable to meet every need that crosses our path but to be faithful to the mission he entrusts to us.

Visionary Compassion

Compassion means, literally, to "suffer with." We enter into another's pain in order to bring comfort and healing. The natural human inclination is to get past the "suffering with" part and on to the fixing part as quickly as possible. Like the Good Samaritan, compassion moves us to take action to help the traveler lying bleeding on the road. But to some extent, our desire to rescue the needy also reflects a deep-seated "denial of death and pain."[12] Americans are naturally can-do optimists who want to believe that with enough resources and hard work, no one need suffer.

Jesus came to rescue humanity from sin and suffering, but even as the embodiment of Good News, he allowed himself to grieve. He wept at his friend Lazarus's grave. He wept over Jerusalem. He did not stop the woman who washed his feet with her tears, preparing them for his burial. But Jesus also knew the difference between mourning and despair. Our sorrow is like the pain of a woman in labor (John 16:21)—we grieve in the expectation of joy, we mourn with the assurance of comfort. Tony Campolo captured this tension in his now-famous line: "It's Friday . . . but Sunday's coming!"

Christians who confront the evils and sorrows of the world must be prepared to follow Jesus into the space between Friday and Sunday. Jude Tiersma asks those in ministry to consider, "How do we truly embrace the suffering of the cross and still live in the hope of the resurrection? How do we live in resurrection hope without denying the intense pain in our world?"[13] One way we follow in Jesus' footsteps of compassion is through prayer. Through the Spirit who "intercedes with sighs too deep for words," we not only claim Christ's victory but share his groans over a broken world (Rom. 8:26). In prayer, "We *suffer with* God in Christ for the salvation of the world, for freedom for the oppressed, for the cessation of war, for the healing of sickness, for the comfort of the anxious and sorrowing."[14]

Jesus was not afraid to look suffering in the face. But his compassion was also visionary in the sense that it transcended the immediate or obvious need in a given situation. Jesus saw to the heart of human need. He looked at the paralytic man lying on his mat and surprised everyone with his first words: not "Rise and walk" (that came next), but "Take heart, son; your sins are forgiven" (Matt. 9:2). He did not let the pressing physical needs divert him from taking a holistic approach. Jesus also saw the potential lying beyond the need. He did not just heal a demon-possessed man; he made him an evangelist (Luke 8:27–39). He treated individual women with dignity, giving them unprecedented attention for Jewish rabbis of his day, while at the same time planting seeds for a revolutionary new equality between women and men to unfurl in the early church (Gal. 3:28).

Grateful Joy

Jesus faced all the challenges, frustrations, and weariness of holistic ministry, but without growing discouraged. Not only did he deal with having other people's problems thrust at him all day long, he lived with foreknowledge of the terrible things to be done to him and his disciples—and yet that didn't stop him from being branded as a party-lover by his critics (Matt. 11:19). Rather, "for the sake of the joy that was set before him [he] endured the cross, disregarding its shame, and has taken his seat at the right hand of the throne of God" (Heb. 12:2). Jesus was sustained by a source of joy that nothing in the world could drain.

Like the father who rejoiced at the return of the prodigal son in Jesus' parable, Christians are called to celebrate the grace of God at work in the world. Rev. Patrick Hansel was once asked how New Creation attracts people from the community to become involved in the church. His answer: parties! The church uses any excuse to host a potluck meal, and in the midst of all their hard work tries to maintain a fiesta attitude. "Celebration" is the first of their four core mission words. Church services are called "celebrations." The bright flowers and butterflies painted by children on the sidewalls of the church sing of the joy and freedom of life in Christ. In a community in which life is often a series of disappointed dreams, the church's spirit of celebration is contagious.

Effective holistic ministry also depends on cultivating, as Teen Challenge counselors like to say, an "attitude of gratitude." Ten lepers came to Jesus begging to be healed, and all ten had their desire fulfilled—but only one turned back to fall at Jesus' feet with loud expressions of praise. "Was none of them found to return and give praise to God?" Jesus asked of the other nine (Luke 17:18). The ultimate purpose of human generosity, according to 2 Corinthians 9:11, is to "produce thanksgiving to God." It is easy for holistic ministry to become so problem-centered that it loses sight of victories won in the past, or of God's quiet mercies that grace each day. Cynicism, burnout, and despair often threaten to overshadow Christlike compassion. But if you follow the exhortation of Philippians 4:6–7, "in everything by prayer and supplication with thanksgiving let your requests be made known to God," then the promise follows: "The peace of God, which surpasses all understanding, will guard your hearts and your minds in Christ Jesus." With gratitude for what has gone before, and rejoicing in anticipation of the harvest ahead, God desires those in holistic ministry to sustain the joy of Christ.

Avoid the Messiah Syndrome

While the previous paragraphs stressed the importance of following Christ's example in ministry, there is one more point to keep in mind: We follow Christ, but we are not Christ. "One of the greatest dangers we face," warns Jude Tiersma, "is that we create dependencies not on God but on ourselves and our programs. We must never forget: There is only *one* Messiah."[15] Our physical limitations, fallibility, and sinfulness will invariably bring us up short of hoped-for outcomes. Accepting that we can't meet every need, we must trust that God is sufficient—not as an excuse for inaction but as the foundation for peace and hope in the midst of action. If we expect our church's ministry to wipe out the problems of our community, we will be disappointed and so will the community. The church is not the hope of the world; Christ is.

At a time when the media and social scientists trumpet the good works of churches (note: we're not complaining!), this distinction is important to remember. A good test of holistic ministry is whether the church consistently points to Christ, or whether the glory goes to the church. Henri Nouwen says that we must be *showing* the way or else we will be *in* the way.[16] Thus, our prayer should be, in the words of the hymn, "May his beauty rest upon us as we seek the lost to win, that they might forget the vessel, seeing only him."

This is why Richard Foster says that "more than any other single way, the grace of *humility* is worked into our lives through the discipline of service."[17] Holistic ministry requires us to cultivate a humble, teachable, vulnerable spirit and to live in a continual process of renewal. Like Paul, we must acknowledge ourselves to be chief of sinners (1 Tim. 1:15). Rev. Patrick Hansel paraphrases this for his own church's mission:

> God's power gives us the ability to say yes to two things. One is: Yes, I'm a sinner. I'm not perfect. I have made big mistakes. I have caused a lot of pain, and I'm part of the pain in the world. But also: Yes, God through Jesus not only forgives me but sends me out to bring the new life to other people.

Holistic ministry does not allow a false hierarchy between the "us" who have it all together and the "them" who need help. Christ died for all and invites all equally into his service.

A humble spirit thus allows the act of service to be mutually transforming. Christians who become immersed in holistic ministry can expect to be changed by the experience. Involvement in ministry often confronts people with areas within themselves that call for repentance—prejudice, lack of faith, materialism, hardness of heart. Sometimes ministry participants come to realize they have unworthy motives for service, such as the need to be powerful or the desire to gain "brownie points" with God. The theologian Thomas Merton asserts, "Whoever attempts to act and do things for others or for the world without deepening their own self-understanding, freedom, integrity and capacity for love, will not have anything to give others."[18] But to those who continually submit themselves to God in the service of others, God promises to "increase the harvest of your righteousness. You will be enriched in every way for your great generosity" (2 Cor. 9:10–11).

Personal Transformation for Mission

The goal of the church's holistic outreach is the transformation of people, communities, and society for the glory of God. For God to work through us in this mission requires that we first, and continually, allow him to transform us. "Daily life becomes a discipline of asking how one may move more squarely into the realm of God's reign and how one may welcome and receive it into the fabric of one's life this day more than ever before."[19] Each church member comes to holistic ministry from a different starting point, but we all need to "grow up in every way into him who is the head, into Christ" (Eph. 4:15). Some Christians need to be transformed in order to venture out from self-centered comfort zones. Others discover a need to be immersed in and renewed by God's healing love. Others seek to change from being mere activists to becoming ambassadors of the Good News. Whatever our need, the transforming Spirit of Christ takes root in our lives through the practice of personal and corporate spiritual disciplines, including prayer, Bible study, and meditation.

Prayer

Earlier in this chapter we talked about the importance of prayer in guiding and empowering holistic ministry. "Prayer changes things" as the popular saying goes, but it also changes the pray-er. Prayer puts us on the potter's wheel, reshaping us to be God's vessels. As we beg that God's will be done on earth as it is in heaven, we present ourselves to God to do it. Prayer strengthens resolve in the face of discouragement and danger, nurtures trust and patience to wait on God's timing, and knits Christian hearts together in unity of purpose. The prayer of repentance and intercession is particularly powerful in combination with fasting, as the stories of Nehemiah (1:4–11) and Daniel (9:3–19) demonstrate.

Prayer also "transforms our vision of the world,"[20] helping us keep a godly perspective on our work in the world. Henri Nouwen wrote beautifully about the critical need for social activists to engage in the discipline of prayer:

> As long as ministry only means that we worry a lot about people and their problems; as long as it means an endless number of activities which we can hardly coordinate, we are still very much dependent on our own narrow and anxious heart. But when our worries are led to the heart of God and there become prayer,

then ministry and prayer become two manifestations of the same all-embracing love of God.[21]

Bible Study

Another transforming spiritual discipline is the study of Scripture. The Word of God, "powerful and active," is given that the Christian "may be complete, thoroughly equipped for every good work" (2 Tim. 3:17 NKJV). Scripture provides a necessary corrective to the culture's distorted views of money and power. Ron Sider collected all the passages in the Bible pertaining to hunger, justice, and poverty for the book *For They Shall Be Fed*.[22] It is two hundred pages long! If more evangelicals were as diligent about reading and obeying the *whole* Bible as they are about revering its authority, their ministry priorities would be radically revised.

Meditation

Scripture repeatedly calls us to meditate on God's actions (e.g., Ps. 64:9). The biblical record of God's salvation history, and our personal and congregational histories of God's presence, inspire faith in God's faithfulness. As we reflect on what God has done throughout history and in our own lives, we can sense more clearly where God is leading us in the present. Meditation cultivates an attitude of hopeful expectancy for ministry, because we can trust God to continue working in and through us in a way that is consistent with his actions and character in the past. Introspection and outreach should be complementary. Richard Foster (inspired by Karl Barth) suggests combining reflection on God's actions with exercises in awareness of the community and the global situation: "This form of meditation is best accomplished with the Bible in one hand and the newspaper in the other!"[23] Many find a spiritual journal a helpful tool in recording their reflections.

These spiritual disciplines take time. We must allow sufficient time for the work of transformation in our lives, just as we must be patient with the slow but steady growth of the fruits of our holistic ministry. But if we do not invest time in our spiritual development, we will find our busyness becoming a waste of time. Mary Thiessen writes:

Awareness of the deep inner work of the Spirit is difficult when running from job to project, from program to crisis, from family to neighborhood. When we no longer enjoy God's intimate presence in our souls, we merely tend to respond to others' wounds with cold action. . . . How we need the Spirit's life-giving breath to blow through the dryness of our souls![24]

Conclusion

Ron Sider wrote in *Living like Jesus:*

I dream of a new movement of Christians who immerse all their activity—not just their worship and evangelism but also their political analysis and cultural engagement—in all-night prayer meetings. I dream of a movement that thinks as it prays; that plans careful strategies as it surrenders to the Spirit; that prays for both miraculous signs and wonders and also effective social reform; that knows in its heart that nothing important will happen unless the Spirit blows through its plans.[25]

This dynamic holistic movement begins as Christians submit their whole lives to God as instruments of his love by the power of the Spirit.

chapter seven

A Commitment to Community Outreach

Identifying with a specific neighborhood helps a congregation make concrete its willingness to be for the city—rather than being a church against the city, disdaining its evils; a church above the city, caring only about heavenly and not earthly realities; or a church in the city, so accommodating to its values as to be indistinguishable from it.[1]

Some churches have a lopsided emphasis on social ministry. Other churches have a one-sided focus on evangelism. But most churches simply do too little of both. A church cannot have holistic outreach ministry if it has no outreach! Thus, a key place to start growing a holistic congregation is to cultivate a commitment to reaching out beyond the walls of the church, as a central expression of the congregation's faith and worship.

Despite the overall movement toward a holistic understanding of the gospel in the last few decades, too many American churches still neglect outreach mission. From observing where many churches spend their energy, money, and time, said Christian activist Harold Fray, one would think that John 3:16 read: "God so loved the *church* that he gave his only Son." What does the text really say? "God so loved the *world* that he gave his only Son." Church leaders do have a significant responsibility toward the members of the church, but one key dimension of this responsibility "is to lead them into their vocation (mission) in the world, which God loves, and for which Christ died."[2]

What does it take to become a mission-oriented church—a church that shares God's self-sacrificial love for the lost, lonely, and broken and cultivates a commitment toward outreach as an expression of worship? There are two main hurdles to be overcome. First is an inward focus that keeps the church from reaching out to the community. Second are the barriers (of geography, demographics, race, class, and culture) that keep the church from being inclusive of the community.

Before we go on, we need to clarify what we mean by "community." Churches on the same city block may come up with different answers to the question, What is your ministry community? Amy Sherman identifies three types of churches in terms of the way they define their community of ministry. *Settlers* concentrate on the neighborhoods where their churches are physically located and "work for the transformation of these neighborhoods from the inside out." *Gardeners* develop ministry ties with neighborhoods outside their immediate area, which they view "as extensions of their own churches (spiritual homes), in the same way that home owners view their gardens as an extension of their houses." For instance, a suburban church might reach out to cultivate a particular inner-city neighborhood. *Shepherds* "primarily serve one targeted population . . . rather than a specific geographic neighborhood." A church with a commitment to Haitian immigrants, for example, might have ministries spanning several neighborhoods.[3] Any one of the three types is valid.

By "community," therefore, we mean the particular area where the church concentrates its ministry, whether that means the neighborhood where the church is located, where members live, and/or where outreach is targeted. In this book, we are referring primarily to a geographic neighborhood, but in most instances "community" could be understood as a particular people group as well.

We caution, however, against defining different "neighbors" for different aspects of ministry—in other words, meeting needs *here* while targeting evangelistic ministry *there*. This sends a mixed message to each community: "God cares about your needs, but you're not good enough for our church," and "God loves you but is only interested in your spirit." A holistic approach ministers across the spectrum of needs in a community.

We further want to note that while the focus of this chapter (and this book) is *local* community outreach, that does not diminish the importance of *global* missions as well. American churches must not be blind to the needs of the rest of the world, particularly desperately poor Third World countries and totalitarian societies that are closed to the gospel.[4] On the other hand, some churches dedicate all their missional energies to other lands while neglecting God's children in their own backyard. Holistic ministry calls for a balance of local and global mission.

The Mission of the Church

Despite an outreach activity here and there, many churches are not really outreach-focused churches. They might give out holiday gift baskets to needy families, or sponsor an annual Bring-a-Friend-to-Church day, or raise money to support the local homeless shelter. But their ministries flow more from skin-deep compassion ("Those poor homeless people") or superficial obligation ("There, that takes care of that!") than a genuine longing to see God's will done in their community as it is in heaven. The dominant understanding is that the church exists to serve the needs—spiritual, social, and relational—of the membership.

Rev. Tom Theriault is mission pastor at a wonderful holistic congregation, Solana Beach Presbyterian Church. He writes about the tension between "inreach" and "outreach":

> I've gotten a lot of mileage from my M & M soap box . . . the "More and More for Me and Mine Syndrome," the "What-can-you-do-for-me-today,-God gospel." As in the time of Jesus, many are looking for an M & M Messiah, a savior who will deliver us from all manner of oppressions (and depressions and repressions and dysfunctions). As with Jesus' contemporaries, we are frustrated, if not infuriated (Luke 4:30f), by a savior who is for the world. When He turns the "M & M's" right-side-up and into "W-W's" . . . a "We are for the World" gospel, we have trouble.
>
> To be sure, ours is a delivering God. But He delivers for a purpose. He delivers us out of our dead-end obsession with self and into the mainstream of His life-giving water that is destined for the nations (Rev. 22:2). We want a "sit-and-soak Savior," One who fills our little hot tubs up with all kinds of soothing blessings. What we really have is a "Get up and GO God," One who soothes and saves so that He can launch us out (the root of the word for "mission" is the same as for "missile") into His Kingdom purposes to soothe and save the world. Hot tubs are great, but if you spend too much time in one you shrivel up and get sick. Same is true for the bath of blessings that our wonderful Savior provides for us. The blessings are meant to be fuel in our little rockets, rockets that have a trajectory set by the Word of God (Luke 4). If we stop with merely basking in the blessings of salvation, we, our families, our churches, will shrivel up and get sick. A body needs exercise, and so does the Body of Christ. The mission of Christ is the exercise regimen prescribed by the Ultimate Personal Trainer.[5]

Continuing Tom's metaphor, to prescribe the proper exercise for a human body, trainers have to know what the body is designed to do. Internally focused churches are busily doing an incomplete set of exercises, because they have a flawed understanding of what the church body is designed to do. An inward-focused congregation must be led to examine the questions, What is the church designed to do? What is the church's mission?

Say "mission," and many think of what some Christians do "over there." The word has come to be identified with special projects and trips. But mission has more to do with the church's purpose than its programs. As David Bosch explains, "Mission is not primarily an activity of the church, but an attribute of God. God is a missionary God. . . . Mission is thereby seen as a movement from God to the world: the church is viewed as an instrument of that mission. . . . There is church because there is mission, not vice versa."[6] Holistic ministry, when it is placed within the context of mission, answers the question, How are God's character and saving actions expressed through our church in the world?

The church's mission has three basic components: The church is to be a witness to God's kingdom, an agent of God's kingdom, and the sign of God's kingdom.

1. *The church witnesses to God's kingdom by proclaiming the Good News of Christ.* With lips and lives, the body of believers offers testimony to the redemptive power of salvation by faith. To moral relativists and skeptics, the church preaches Jesus as the way, truth, and life; to poor and oppressed persons, the church announces the coming of the Savior; to oppressors and offenders, the church speaks out on behalf of God's justice and righteousness; to those ensnared by violence and prejudice, the church tells of the reconciling work of the cross. Sometimes our proclamation is directed toward those outside the church, in evangelism; sometimes proclamation is directed toward the church body, in preaching and teaching; sometimes it is directed toward God, in worship.

2. *The church not only points to God's coming kingdom but is an agent of its inception.* Paul addresses Christians as "co-workers for the kingdom of God" (Col. 4:11). The church shares God's compassion for those in need, God's righteous indignation at injustice, and God's holy wrath over violations of moral law—and the church follows God's example of active intervention in response. The church is God's instrument for bringing about his desired changes in individuals and in society as a whole (the church is not God's *only* instrument, but it is a crucial one). Though not presuming to bring about the kingdom by its own efforts or to establish a "Christian nation," the church prepares the way for the full reign of Christ by continuing the ministry of Christ and doing the work of the kingdom. The church's deeds of love and power anticipate the coming final restoration of the cosmos.

3. *The church serves as a sign of God's kingdom by modeling the Good News in the community of faith.* In his earthly ministry, Christ planted the seeds of a

new Spirit-filled community who would continue to live out the kingdom principles that he proclaimed and demonstrated. As it modeled redeemed socioeconomic relations, this new community began to challenge the status quo of the larger society at many points. The early Christians showed they were different in their attitude toward material things; in their hope and courage in the face of persecution; in their compassion for poor, disabled, and other marginalized people; in the way they treated their enemies; and above all in the way they cared for one another. While waiting for Jesus' full reign to be inaugurated, the church is to give the world a foretaste of its glory. "Whoever has seen me has seen the Father," Jesus said (John 14:9). In the same way, comments Bishop Dickie Robbins, "The only God many people are going to see will be the church. So we consecrate ourselves to be the representation of who God is in this locality." Another church member put it simply, "Before people read the Bible, they will read you first."

The three dimensions of mission are interrelated. The church engages in ministries of service and advocacy as an instrument of God's kingdom, giving people a taste of the promise of shalom that we proclaim as well as embody in our fellowship. Through our outreach we invite people to enter God's kingdom and join a faith community dedicated to living out kingdom values. As "the human community that experiences and communicates the saving intention of God," the church becomes the agency by which God brings blessing to all human communities (Gen. 12:1–3).[7] The various aspects of church life are to be integrated around this holistic mission. Witness and service, fellowship and worship, preaching and advocacy all flow together through the heart of the congregation out into the lives of others.

"Missional church" is the shorthand term for this vision used by some theologians.[8] A missional understanding of the church challenges some commonly accepted indicators of church health. A church may be growing—but has proclamation about the gospel resulted in new believers, or has PR about the church resulted in church transfers? A church may be fiscally sound—but is it funding ministries that are instruments of shalom? A church may have beautiful buildings and the latest equipment—but do its assets show the world what the kingdom of God is like? Some church and denominational leaders may need to redefine what it means to be a "successful" church in light of a missional church focus. Yes, in most cases, churches that engage in dynamic holistic outreach will grow numerically! But growth and wealth alone are not signs that the church is fulfilling God's mission.

Overcoming an inward focus means changing members' perception from "going to church" to "being the church." "Going to church" is only part of the purpose for the church's existence. A church cannot be a witness, agent, and sign of the gospel if its pews are full on Sunday but it sits empty the rest of the week. A lay ministry leader at Cookman United Methodist Church put it this way:

> Being a place where people can just come and worship on Sunday does not make you a church. You have to be in service to one another to be a servant to our Lord and Savior Jesus Christ. So that means church doors need to be open during the week, not just Sunday. . . . You need to just be there for the people. . . . A lighthouse isn't just out there sometimes. It's always out there. The light is always on. And that's what we need to do as a church.

Cookman United Methodist Church struggles to keep its lights literally on, the staff paid, and the building standing in one piece. The group that gathers for worship on Sunday morning is small, and the tithes from members' modest incomes are meager. But every day, Cookman is a lighthouse reaching people in the neighborhood with the Good News in word and deed. Women and men in the church's welfare-to-work ministry learn work and computer skills, pursue their GED, study the Bible, and participate in a weekly worship service. Overcomers, a Christ-centered twelve-step support group for recovering addicts, leads a worship service for people who feel uncomfortable in a traditional church service. The Kids Café offers youth a nutritious meal, Bible study, and fun activities. Women rebuilding their lives in a transitional housing program in the parsonage meet in the pastor's study for Bible study and Christian counseling. People in crisis drop by the church for groceries, clothes, a prayer, and a hug. A group of members occasionally takes prayer walks through the neighborhood, interceding for their neighbors and the urban evils that hold them in bondage. Churches like Cookman are beacons of hope and healing, attracting people to God's kingdom. The harvest is slow but steady.

Rev. William Moore of Tenth Memorial Baptist Church reflects on the nature of the church: "The Jordan River feeds into the Dead Sea, and there's no outlet. Nothing lives. They call it the Dead Sea because it takes in but it does not give out. The church is the same way. If you take in and don't give out, you die." Sometimes churches literally die for lack of mission. They are like the Dead Sea: full of water but unable to support life. Throughout the history of the church, writes theologian John Driver, Christians have wrestled with "a perception of the church as a self-concerned community of salvation— an end in itself. This has led to a clear separation between its own church life and its calling to mission. . . . The church has existed without mission, and mission has been carried on outside the church, resulting in the impoverishment of the church and the deformation of mission."[9]

Unless a church embraces its calling to holistic mission, it will fall short of the extravagant biblical vision for the body of Christ—to be a visible sign of the dawning of God's kingdom, a preview of heaven, living salt and light that transform the world.

Boundaries and Barriers between Church and Community

"When we try to 'put feet' to what we have learned about loving others, we often collide with various obstacles," writes Amy Sherman in *Restorers of Hope.*[10] Church leaders who have gotten started in outreach mission often experience "hitting the wall." The church members have embraced a holistic theology and are geared up to love their community in word and deed—but then, once they actually start relating to needy neighbors, things begin to fall apart. Effective holistic ministry has been blocked by the boundaries between church and community.

Boundaries are not all negative. In some ways, the church is to be distinct from the world around it. We are to "be holy, for I the LORD your God am holy" (Lev. 19:2). In other ways, we overlap. We are "in the world" even as we are "not of the world" (John 17:11, 14). So what makes the church "us," and what makes the community we are called to serve "them"?

Spiritual Boundaries

Spiritual boundaries probably spring first to mind. Paul thanks God for having "rescued us from the power of darkness and transferred us into the kingdom of his beloved son" (Col. 1:13). There is a substantive spiritual difference between those who abide in Christ's kingdom and those who do not acknowledge Christ as Lord. Of course, this does not mean that God loves the church more than the world—it was for love of the world that God created the church! But we do expect the church to reflect a different set of priorities, values, and lifestyles than the surrounding society. This is one of the signs of the kingdom of God.

One question to consider, however, is whether your church assumes that anyone from the community who is not in your church is automatically "of the world." Do you take it for granted that if someone is poor, he or she must not be a Christian? Do you search for God's presence in the neighborhood through other churches and faith-based ministries, or do they automatically fall under doctrinal suspicion? Are you willing to embrace anyone who follows Jesus Christ as "us"?

Geographic Boundaries

How far your congregation has to commute to the community of ministry is an important dynamic.[11] In what sense are the people whom you want to serve your congregation's "neighbors"—in the sense that you see them over backyard fences, at PTA meetings, in the grocery store? Or are they neighbors only in the sense of the parable of the Good Samaritan—strangers whom God has brought into your path and called you to serve? Or are they a mixture of both?

Neighborhood churches, where most of the members live around the church, have a natural advantage when it comes to developing an outreach focus. They have an existing network of relationships, a cultural affinity, and built-in incentives for community development. Members know their neighbors from "real-life" settings, not just Sunday mornings. Helping members of neighborhood churches become outreach-focused is sometimes just a matter of helping them realize their personal stake in what happens to the neighborhood. When people on their block come to Christ, when the schools improve, that benefits them as well.

On the other hand, it is human nature to love the neighbor on the other side of the city and dislike the person who lives next door. Members may need to be confronted about a prideful attitude that sets church people above "those people" (single moms, gang members, Muslims, and so on) in the community. On the flip side, sometimes church members in distressed communities have an inferiority complex that keeps them from reaching out. They may be struggling with needs themselves and do not want to expend the church's resources on outsiders. They need to be encouraged to see themselves, and the church as a whole, as vital community assets. Leaders can help members dream of how collaboration, community organizing, and evangelism could expand the church's resources for both internal and external ministry.

Commuter churches face particular challenges in overcoming an internal focus. Members' lives are already spread out; they resist participating in one more thing they have to drive to. The ability to distance themselves, literally, from the pain and problems of a needy community dilutes commuting members' motivation to address the needs. Members may also wrestle with prejudices and fears about going into certain kinds of communities. Their status as an "outsider" to the community may be a barrier to forming relationships of affinity and trust.

But commuter churches have their own advantages too. Commuting churches can draw on a broader network of human and financial resources to support their ministries. They can build bridges between communities, providing a hedge against the stagnation and sense of isolation that plagues many distressed neighborhoods. The exposure to a different culture or socioeconomic class can be mutually transforming and can form the foundation for authentic racial reconciliation.

Demographic and Cultural Boundaries

Boundaries of demographics and culture proclaim, "This is who fits in here (and who doesn't belong)." The church's identity can become a barrier to community acceptance. Single moms often feel uncomfortable in a church full of two-parent families. A gray-haired congregation may feel out of place in a neighborhood where half the residents are under eighteen. A church with a penchant for loud music and aggressive evangelistic programs will clash with a quiet, reserved community.

A congregation can make an intentional effort to define its cultural boundaries in a way that includes the community of ministry. For example, Life in Christ was once known as "the little drug church on Third Street," because it reached so many people struggling with addictions. New Creation Lutheran Church honors its community's Latino heritage through celebrations such as the popular Latino festival called Three Kings Day. Circle of Hope in Philadelphia has shaped its worship, message, and activities to meet the spiritual needs of Gen-Xers. Church consultant Jack Dennison writes that as a church identifies the various people groups in its community, "Each group must be treated as unique and approached with a level of integrity that says we understand you and will adapt our methods in an appropriate manner to who *you* are rather than expecting you to become what *we* are."[12]

Boundaries of Class and Race

Sadly, many churches also still struggle with barriers of class and race. This is especially tragic where demographic change has swept through a neighborhood, and people of different races who find themselves living next door still cannot bring themselves to worship together at the church on the corner. Peter Wagner calls this ungodly syndrome "ethnicitis."[13] Even congregations that include people of more than one color can suffer from this syndrome. If the music, preaching style, and leadership all reflect one dominant ethnic group, the church sends a message to the community that minorities are welcome to attend—*if* they are willing to conform. A church must embrace diversity in every area of church life if it is to overcome ethnic barriers.

Middle-class churches—particularly those located in distressed neighborhoods—encounter significant barriers in reaching out to people who feel socially marginalized. Differences in the way people dress, talk, behave, or smell create mutual discomfort. A warm welcome, genuine friendliness, and social interaction outside the church service can help people who struggle to fit in.

Boundaries of "Church Culture"

Another type of boundary can keep the community at arm's length: the "church culture." In a church service, try counting the number of "church lingoisms," references, or rituals that would make no sense to an unchurched person. Seen through their eyes, a church service can look pretty strange—people suddenly stand up, sit down, kneel, sing, or recite something in unison from memory. Rev. Bill Moore remarks from his long experience as pastor of Tenth Memorial Baptist Church: "There was a time you could just assume that everybody knew who Jesus was, everybody knew how to find Matthew, Mark, Luke, and John. . . . They knew what the church was about. That day is long gone."

On top of this, each church has its own "in-crowd" references and routines: which door to use to enter the church, what kind of clothes are appropriate, how loud to sing, how children are expected to behave, where to go for coffee and doughnuts after the service. Whether all these distinctives create boundaries between your church and the community depends on how much exposure people in the community have had to church culture and how intentional your church is about becoming culturally adaptive and "user friendly." Do members value people above in-house church rules, or do they look on naive newcomers as a nuisance? "The *belief system* of the church may not have changed. The pastor may still be preaching 'you all come to Jesus!' But the *behavior system* of the congregation can be communicating an intent to screen those who join."[14]

Physical Boundaries

Finally, boundaries can take physical form. Buildings that stand empty most of the week signal that the church's commitment to the community is part-time. Aspects of the church's physical layout can send the community mixed messages about the extent of their welcome. One church, for example, installed large glass doors as a symbol of its openness to the neighborhood. However, the doors stay locked. People enter the church through conventional doors off to the side, so that they won't smudge the glass. And there are even churches with "No Trespassing" signs on their buildings!

Fences, locked gates, or a lack of handicap accessibility can also convey a double meaning. Sometimes these physical barriers are necessary to protect people and property, or they are the product of an earlier era that the congregation cannot afford to fix. Sometimes, however, fences make a symbolic statement about "the rights of the members to worship without being joined by anyone who might make them feel uncomfortable" and "reflect a profound resistance to change that is often subconscious."[15] This does not mean that churches must keep every door unlocked and abandon all standards for decent, safe conduct. But consider the signals your church sends about what kinds of people are decent and safe.

Building Bridges between Church and Community

Overcoming the barriers to holistic ministry requires an intentional effort both to welcome the community into the church and to bring the church out into the community. Chapter 13 addresses in more detail how to rally a congregation around the church's holistic ministry vision. Following are seven suggestions for cultivating an outreach-minded congregation.

1. *Welcome whoever walks through the door.* A good place to start cultivating the congregation's commitment to reach out to the community is by loving the people in the community who come to you. "We need a theology of welcome to tear down the fences that have come to separate 'church' and 'mission,'" writes Kathryn Mowry. "Welcome becomes a transformational process, initiating and extending the community of the kingdom."[16]

A friendly face can go a long way in a person's evangelistic journey. An elder at Life in Christ Cathedral of Faith gives this testimony of the power of a welcoming congregation: "One of the things that made me want to stay here is that when I first came to the door, before I was delivered from drugs, there was a guy there who greeted me with this great, huge smile. . . . I was down to 130 pounds, I really looked a mess. . . . He greeted me with a hug. That made me think, 'Man, I like this place. I want to stay here.'" A welcoming congregation looks past the barriers to see each person as a potential bride of Christ.

Being a truly welcoming congregation involves the whole church, not just the greeters at worship services. In our daily lives, we often tend to view encounters with people in need as annoying interruptions. Encourage the congregation to welcome opportunities to minister informally to the needs that present themselves. Examples of this kind of everyday compassion abounded in our case studies. One day at First Presbyterian Church a woman came to the office looking for a volunteer who had told her about a business that was hiring, to ask for more information. When the receptionist found out the woman didn't have a car, she put down the envelopes she was stuffing and drove her to the site.

Welcome should extend beyond the walls of the church to members' homes. A member of New Covenant literally welcomed the homeless woman with two children who knocked on her door. Over the weeks of the woman's stay, the member led her to the Lord. The guest began attending New Covenant and was hired to help with the job of painting the church building, though she had never painted before. Now she is a self-supporting master painter. Bishop Robbins and his wife welcomed two at-risk children from the community into their home and raised them as their own, and they have encouraged others at Life in Christ to do the same. Such acts of loving hospitality may be overlooked by news crews and grant givers—but they form the warp and woof of a church's transforming presence in a community.

2. *Network in the community.* Networking is the exchange of information, ideas, and resources. The goal of networking is not to accomplish any partic-

Networking as a Foundation for Outreach Ministry

Half a block from New Creation Lutheran Church is an elementary school with eleven hundred children. On weekday afternoons, Rev. Patrick Cabello Hansel often walks over from the church to make contact with the children and their parents as school gets out. The low curbside wall around the school yard boasts a colorful mural of cheerful pictures and positive slogans, painted through New Creation Community Center's youth employment program. Tulips blossom in the school yard, thanks to another church-sponsored project.

Rev. Hansel initiated contact with the school during the church-planting process. For six months, before starting regular church services, Rev. Hansel networked with area residents and institutions. "I was looking to build allies in relationships with potential members and also with leaders in the community," he explains.

> The first thing we did was to go out and knock on doors and go to as many community meetings as possible, and to meet many of the players in the community. . . . I would go to people and ask them what they wanted to see in their community, what they would like a new church to do. . . . Out of that came the focuses of our ministry since then.

One of the first people Rev. Hansel met was the principal of the elementary school. She invited him to speak at a parents' meeting, where he shared his hopes that the new church could support the school. New Creation has fulfilled that promise by providing space for parents' advisory meetings, by serving on the school improvement team, by sponsoring special events for students around holidays, and by hosting a thank-you breakfast for the staff and teachers of the school each spring. When parents ask for academic help, school staff refer them without hesitation to the after-school program at the church's community center.

New Creation's openness to the community makes it stand out. "Some churches are just there for Sunday," says the principal, "but New Creation glorifies God through its activities Monday through Saturday."

ular task but to build relationships as we gather information, scout out potential allies, and let others know about our church. "A community network that knows the pastor's concerns and commitments," write Ray Bakke and Sam Roberts, "can have extraordinary significance for informing and defining the local church's priorities as it seeks to shape its mission in that community."[17] Another benefit of networking is that it builds the church's reputation in the community, says Carl Dudley. "Others will see your church as a concerned neighborhood institution. The people you contact begin to think of the church as a potential partner in the area of shared concerns. They will treat the church differently and include the church in community meetings it has not been invited to before."[18]

Get to know the executives and staff of key community institutions. Offer to take people out to lunch, arrange to meet for coffee, or ask for a tour of their facilities—and leave a packet of information about your church. Institutions to target for networking include other churches (and non-Christian houses of worship), social service agencies, schools, police departments, social security and welfare offices, businesses, health clinics, and foundations. Bakke and Roberts suggest a useful conversation starter when networking with pastors of other congregations: "What is the most important lesson you have learned about being a pastor in this community since you have begun?"[19] Every church leader should network in the community in the area of his or her ministry—for example, the youth leader should sit down with public school principals and teachers, the director of the local Boys and Girls Club, and people associated with the juvenile court system.

3. *Cultivate a sense of belonging to the community.* "Your people shall be my people," said Ruth to Naomi (Ruth 1:16). In the same way, help the congregation to think about the residents of the community as "our people."

Cultivating a sense of belonging is a transformational process that takes place through many small steps. Help the congregation become familiar with the community by leading "field trips" to cultural events and restaurants. Invite community leaders to your church's Christmas party and attend the dedication for the new elementary school. Provide the congregation with a list of community restaurants and leave waiters the church's business card along with your tip. Host town meetings, AA meetings, community theater productions. Become a sponsor for the community's Little League team. Display artwork in the sanctuary that reflects the community's ethnic heritage. Print church bulletins, clean the carpet, and purchase office supplies using local businesses. Write letters to the editor about issues affecting the community.

Be a presence in times of tragedy or outrage. For example, while Phil was mission pastor at First Presbyterian Church, a home for the developmentally disabled was vandalized. Phil wrote an editorial to the local newspapers and organized members from various congregations for an overnight prayer vigil at the home. Find ways of identifying with the struggles of those in the community (Heb. 13:3) and express your sorrow over the things that cause God and your neighbors grief. But do not focus exclusively on what is different or dysfunctional about the community. Encourage the congregation to identify with everything in the community that is delightful. Give thanks for all its assets—from block captains to children's smiles—as gifts from God (1 Thess. 5:18).

Such involvement contributes to the process of becoming friends with the community. The more a congregation knows and likes the community, the better it will be able to express love for the community in ministry. Moreover, these small steps also encourage the community to think of the church as its friend. In the beginning stages of holistic ministry, invest in later initiatives by building up the congregation's visibility and reputation in the community. Recognition is the first step toward trust. Developing a profile as a community-oriented church, for example, through wise use of media contacts to publicize church events or by consistently sending representatives to community meetings, increases the likelihood of winning support from the community for new ministry projects. Becoming known as the church that gets involved in local issues will help open doors to resources and collaboration.

4. *Incorporate a commitment to the community and outreach mission into church life.* Church members will consider outreach mission unimportant if it is invisible to them. How much does a concern for community outreach enter into the life of your church? Here are some self-examining questions:

- Do the songs sung in worship services mostly talk about our personal relationship with Jesus? Or do they also reinforce a message about God's love for the rest of the world and the church's calling to serve and reach out to others?
- What do the art and religious symbols in your church communicate? Is there anything that reflects the biblical themes of service, evangelism, restoration, and transformation?
- Do the needs of people outside the church and the issues faced by the community or other lands around the world regularly find their way into congregational prayers and bulletin announcements? Is there anything visible inside the church—newspaper articles or flyers about community events posted on the bulletin board, for example—that reminds congregants of the presence of the world outside the church?
- Do the books in the church library or the literature in the foyer address issues of mission, or are they solely directed at the spiritual and personal development of Christians?
- Is the concept of "mission" used in such a way as to imply that it applies only to *foreign* missions? For example, if you have a missions bulletin board, are the pictures and letters all from overseas missionaries?

Consider ways to enfold a loving awareness of the community of ministry into "ordinary" aspects of church life. This communicates to the congregation that what happens inside the church walls is meant to be lived out in mission to the world outside. The church should be a refuge for members from the bruising realities of the world but not a fortress where people go to shut out the world.

5. *Interweave the interests of church and community.* A Christian speaker told of the time God convicted him of not taking seriously Christ's command to love his neighbor as himself. Sure, he occasionally did nice things for people in need—but did he love others *as himself?* So he set up a jar in his home marked "For the Neighbor." Whenever he bought something nonessential for himself, like a soda, he put an equivalent amount of money in the jar. His family got used to saying, "Here's one for me, and one for the neighbor!" When a crisis arose in a neighbor's life, he went right to the jar, dumped out the money, and was able to help meet the need.

In a similar spirit, a church might link its internal care to outreach. When the church raises funds for new carpeting, raise an extra "tithe" of the amount to donate to a local housing organization. When the youth group plans a ski trip, invite (and pay for) youth from a homeless shelter to go along. Hold a congregational meeting in the local community center and afterward repaint it. Offer a series of evening seminars on parenting and post notices in the local YMCA where parents can see it when they drop off their kids for activities. These kinds of actions signal that the congregation is serious about loving community neighbors. They also help develop the habit of talking about inward ministries and outreach ministries in the same breath as all part of the church's essential work.

6. *Take the church out into the community.* A congregation cannot hope to build loving relationships with the community, particularly those who are most needy and vulnerable, by "sitting in the four walls of the church. You've actually got to get out in the community," says Bishop Dickie Robbins. Instead of always waiting for the community to come to the church, the church can "take its show on the road," moving out into the community.

This does not entail starting a new ministry program—just relocating some of the existing ones. One of the simplest things to do is to hold a regular weekend worship service outdoors in the summertime. (Just make sure you don't annoy the neighbors by blasting your music into their windows early on a Sunday morning!) Tenth Presbyterian Church's Sunday school classes overflow their building, spilling out into the community—meeting in the American Jewish Congress, a community theater, and restaurants. "I love the idea of being outside of the building," says the Sunday school coordinator. "Everybody says, 'But we want to be in the building!' And I say, 'The building is not the church.'"

A success story of ministry relocation comes from New Covenant Church of Philadelphia. Rather than holding the traditional Vacation Bible School at the church, New Covenant one year decided to tell families, "We will meet you right where you are." In the summer of 1997, 120 VBS groups met in homes, public facilities, and community nonprofit agencies. While the decentralized format required a higher level of congregational participation, it also allowed the church to reach far more children than if it had held a single VBS at the church's facility. That summer, over five hundred children made decisions for Christ! Another impact of moving the program out of the church and into members' homes, explains a church leader, is that now "families in that community see those homes as places of refuge." People in the community who would not dream of calling the pastor to ask for prayer feel more free to ask at the home where their child went to VBS.

Members also take the church into the community when they adopt the incarnational understanding that wherever they go, they *are* the church. Routine interactions and chance meetings provide opportunities for members to represent the church to those outside the congregation. One day Rev. Richard Smith, pastor of Faith Assembly of God, was walking with a lay leader through the neighborhood around the church. A little girl who did not attend the church passed by, and Rev. Smith greeted her. She stopped, because she did not recognize them. "Who are you?" she asked. Rev. Smith answered her, "I'm your pastor!" Holistic congregations embody this attitude. They communicate through the way they relate to others in the community, "We're your church, even if you don't know it yet. We care about you. You might not feel you're ready to come to church, but through this encounter you can glimpse what our community of faith is like."

7. *Support the relocation of church members into the community.* If your church is not located in the community of ministry, encourage members to consider a calling to relocate there. The ministry of relocation is essential to breaking down barriers and developing a healthy sense of belonging to the community.

The pastors at Central Baptist Church once preached a series on the theme of "windows." One sermon made the point that what we see out our windows every day shapes us in subtle but profound ways: whether we are used to seeing paved roads and streetlights, "for sale" and "help wanted" signs, cement or trees, horizons or high-rises. This is why John Perkins, the founder of the Christian Community Development Association, calls passionately for relocation—because you can fully identify with the people you serve only if you greet the same scene out the window each morning. "Relocation transforms 'you, them, and theirs' to 'we, us, and ours.'"[20]

The Book of Nehemiah provides a wonderful model for relocation. The Israelites had completed the rebuilding of the walls of Jerusalem, but the city was still in ruins and the local economy was a shambles. Few residents remained in the city to complete the work of restoration (7:4). Those who had fled the city were naturally reluctant to return to such an unstable, unsafe environment. So the people of the outlying area came up with an innovative solution: They "cast lots to bring one out of ten to dwell in the holy city Jerusalem" (11:1). In other words, they tithed their population to relocate to the city! The Nehemiah model encourages congregations to anoint those who dedicate themselves to living in the neighborhood as the church's ministry representatives (11:2). Those who have relocated become community liaisons who help others in the congregation understand and connect with the community.

Besides nurturing an affinity between the church and the community, relocation also lays an important foundation for effective community ministry. Bob Lupton writes of the importance of "achieving neighbor-leaders" who "bring living, personal modes of hope back into a disheartened environment. Achieving neighbors bring resources and skills into a depleted neighborhood, along with fresh energy to deploy them."[21] Seeding a community with strong Christian families strengthens the fabric of community life.

On the other hand, without a strong community presence, a church's success in transformational ministry can actually undermine the overall quality of life in a distressed community. As maturing Christians get their lives together, as they get better jobs and higher incomes, and as they develop healthy family lives, they often move out of the community. By empowering persons, the church might be helping to drain the community of its best assets—stable Christian families. Encouraging church members to relocate helps to counter that trend. It sends a strong message to residents of the church's long-term commitment and serves as a symbol of hope. If the church is consistently cultivating a sense of belonging to the community, incorporating an emphasis on reaching out to the community, stressing its hopeful vision for the community, and modeling its dedication to the community through relocation, it is better able to attract and keep Christian families in the community who share the church's mission.

These seven measures can help strengthen a congregation's commitment to outreach and ties to the community of ministry. Ultimately, however, the congregation must choose whether it wants "More and More for Me and Mine" or more and more of God's boundless, self-sacrificial love for the world on its doorstep. Without love, outreach ultimately amounts to busywork (1 Cor. 13:3). Bridge-building activities and relationships can easily become just means to an end, a kind of community public relations, if love is not the heart of the matter. The more a congregation loves God, the more God can love a community through the congregation. The more a congregation yields to God's will and relies on the Spirit's power, the more it will identify with God's mission in the community. The more a congregation enters into the life of the community, the more the life-giving Spirit can flow through them to their neighbors.

Germantown Church of the Brethren

The following story is about a congregation that has become a church in, of, and for its community.

In 1723, the first Brethren church in America was founded by a small group of German religious refugees. For over two hundred years this congregation thrived. But in the 1960s, the church sadly discontinued Sunday worship services, sapped by the dispersion of its white members to the suburbs. Then in 1989, a denominational officer met Richard Kyerematen, and together they agreed to give the church another chance.

A visionary, energetic native of Ghana, Rev. Kyerematen came to Germantown Church of the Brethren and he heralded a change in the church's relationship with the community. The church already had a legacy of providing social services, including a day care, a feeding ministry for homeless people, and a food and clothing bank. People in the community viewed the church as a place that cared about their needs. However, according to a long-standing church member, the pastor prior to Rev. Kyerematen "never invited people to come into the church." Rev. Kyerematen invited everyone he met. He wanted to see the church provide its neighbors not only with services but with a spiritual home. He preached the gospel on the street, in housing projects, and at homeless shelters. Within roughly six months, the church had grown from fifteen church members to almost seventy-five in attendance—about one-third of these the fruit of outreach encounters.

Despite the commitment to outreach, inherited barriers between church and community have impeded the church's ministry. "The church is perceived by the community as a rich congregation," observes Rev. Kyerematen, in part because the church manages through partnerships and grants to carry out far more ministry than is warranted by its actual budget. Rev. Kyerematen adds that residents have also tended to think of the church "as a white church, because when most black people moved into this neighborhood, they didn't feel welcomed here." The church has made significant progress in dispelling these myths in recent years, particularly through its combination of social ministries, persistent but patient witness, and warm fellowship. A church member affirms, "The outreach programs and the open doors, it's like a big welcome sign on the outside. And people get a lot of love when they come here."

The church's answering machine greets callers, "Welcome to Germantown Church of the Brethren, where our family can be your family." The congregation's reputation has been growing as a family that welcomes all cultures and economic backgrounds. The church serves as a bridge between a predominantly white, middle-class, rural denomination and a predominantly African American, struggling urban neighborhood. As an African transplanted in America, Rev. Kyerematen says, "I try to take a stand for the issues that I believe are germane to African Americans." The style of worship and special events such as an annual "Celebration of Life" gospel concert affirm the community's cultural heritage. The congregation's socioeconomic diversity also helps people feel welcome. Germantown Church of the Brethren is home to single mothers and two-parent families, recovering substance abusers and social workers, home owners and homeless people.

"When I came here," Rev. Kyerematen recalls, "the church was just going downtown and feeding people, which I call 'Sandwich Evangelism.' Our desire has been to take people into the life of the church." The church embraces homeless shelter residents, for example, by organizing other Church of the Brethren congregations in providing a meal and devotional at a shelter, teaching occasional Bible studies, and transporting residents weekly to church services.

Arthur (not his real name) was one of the shelter residents who accepted a ride to the church. He felt drawn to the congregation but was sucked back into a life of addiction and homelessness. Many years later, after he had recommitted his life to Christ in a rehab program, he came looking for the church that had first shown him Christian love. He felt anxious whether he would be accepted, but he sensed in his spirit that this was the place he was supposed to be. The church welcomed him back, and his confidence grew. He found a job, remarried his wife, and bought a home and a car. Now he coordinates the church's homeless ministry. When he tells other homeless guests, "I've been there," he means it literally. His life embodies the church's message of hope.

Integrating people on the socioeconomic margins into the life of the congregation is rewarding, as Arthur's story illustrates, but also challenging. There are barriers to be overcome on both sides. Rev. Kyerematen describes one little girl from a homeless shelter who wanted to join the praise team. When they started to sing, she asked, "Is this the choir for the shelter people or is this the choir for the church?" Her question reminded him of how isolated people in distress can feel. The testimony sharing time, a regular feature of worship services, helps to build bridges. As church members share their struggles and praise God for having brought them through, newcomers from the community see that their stories are not so different.

Rev. Kyerematen continually encourages the congregation to look beyond the walls of the church and to feel a sense of responsibility for the community as a whole. "I have a big problem when people go to church and say, 'I'm just in this church because it meets the needs of my family, because this church has these programs,'" he says. "What about the other children who don't have that opportunity?" The church is reminded of its outreach mission in sermons, prayer times, and announcements of volunteer opportunities. Information on community programs, issues, and resources are posted on a bulletin board near the entrance, alongside flyers for such church ministries as the summer camp, after-school program, youth activities, counseling ministry, and discipleship class.

Germantown Church of the Brethren also makes itself visible and available to the community. Outdoor worship services, tent revivals, and door-to-door distribution of church flyers proclaim to the neighborhood, "We're here!" At the start of their youth ministry, they held an outreach crusade on a street crowded with kids. The crusade led to a Bible club in the home of one of the parents. After six weeks, they invited the kids to a Friday youth service at the church, and seventy youth came—far more than if they had not first gone to where the kids were. In many ways the church has signaled its intentions not just to serve but to identify with the community. The leader of a community nonprofit organization describes how this has helped to change the church's reputation: "In the past, I don't know if it was a neighborhood church; it was really more a mission church. It's made that transition. . . . It's not just open on Sunday and people come in from outside the neighborhood. It's part of the community now."

Rev. Kyerematen invests significant time in community networking. He is well known at local social service agencies, both for recruiting their participation in the church's ministries and for offering his support. "When the community has a problem, [Germantown Church of the Brethren] backs the community and gets that problem solved," says a woman active with a grassroots organization that has collaborated with Germantown Church of the Brethren. "This church is a blessing to the community. . . . We work together to get things done." Significantly, the church has been willing to work collaboratively on community development projects without insisting on taking charge or getting the credit.

One creative way that the church draws in neighborhood leaders while promoting the congregation's awareness of the community is its annual "Church/Community Award Sunday." The award honors persons from the community who have worked hard to make it a better place for its residents. In 1999, for example, the award went to two people who were involved in starting a low-cost community market. Rev. Kyerematen asks other churches and community groups to nominate the names of people for the award, then selects the recipients. The awardees usually bring their families, and often others from the nominating agencies attend as well—giving the congregation an opportunity to build a relationship with people who might not otherwise attend church.

The church's mission statement, printed weekly in the bulletin, includes a call "to be a beacon of Light, Love, Hope, Peace, and Service in our homes, church, community, and world." The community service and revitalization projects give concrete expression to this mission. But the church's relationship with the community is more than the sum of its many activities. Rev. Kyerematen explains that the church is "a spiritual, living community. Our influence has also come through just being here, being one of the neighborhood institutions that people could rely on and trust." As the church has become invested—financially, relationally, and spiritually—in the holistic well-being of its neighbors, its very presence has become a beacon of God's Good News to the community.

Conclusion

Rev. Lou Centeno observes that many churches have become "a kind of incubator, a safe zone for themselves, but there's no connectedness to the community. . . . They are pursuing protection and purity, but they have neglected the command of the Lord to help your neighbor." Is your church too comfortable? Chip away at the walls that keep the community at arm's length. Embrace the upside down values of God's kingdom to become a church that proclaims, "We are for the world." Then your church can fulfill its calling to be a witness to God's kingdom, an agent of God's kingdom, and a sign of God's kingdom, to the glory of God.

chapter eight

A Healthy Congregational Base for Ministry

The first mission is always the internal mission.[1]

Once church members begin to catch the holistic vision, it's natural for them to want to jump right into the "how" of community ministry. It's easy to get caught up in the technical, programmatic aspects of ministry: forming boards, generating resources, designing curriculum. But there are dangers in losing the focus on the "church" in "church-based outreach." A church that is good at community-serving ministries but loses sight of being the church may start prioritizing programs over people, sacrificing integrity and grace for efficiency and efficacy. It may become driven by numbers rather than relationships. Its outreach may actually undermine the spiritual life and fellowship of the congregation by draining resources and heightening unresolved conflict.

A holistic church is not a social service agency.[2] Though this distinction sounds obvious, it can easily get lost in all the talk these days about the role of the church in caring for community needs. Churches don't exist primarily to provide services; outreach programs are not the only important activities of the church. A church is more than a mission agency. It has a purpose beyond replicating itself in new believers. It is a tragic situation when the church's entire focus is on bringing people into the church, but nothing of significance happens once they get there. Therefore, whatever the church does to reach and serve those outside the church—soup kitchen, after-school tutoring, street evangelism, lobbying city hall—must be considered in the context of the church's complete identity.

This chapter encourages churches to take a step back from the *task* of developing outreach ministries to look at *who they are* as a body of believers. We must not lose sight of how outreach relates to the church as a whole. Holistic ministry requires not just outreach programs but a Christian community, a group of loving people committed to the Lord and to one another, as well as to service. It is this body of believers that provides the setting for helping people, empowering social change, and telling the world about Christ.

Holistic Mission and Congregational Ministry

When Phil was a mission pastor at the First Presbyterian Church of Mount Holly, he brought new energy and ideas to the church's local mission. He helped organize new initiatives, raise funds and recruit church volunteers for service projects, and develop partnerships with other churches and community agencies. Then came the day a church member vented: "You care more about *them* than you do about *us!*" In a way, she was right. As mission pastor, outreach *was* Phil's job. Yet the incident confirmed for Phil that providing pastoral care, nurturing and mentoring people in their faith, bringing congregants together in worship, and serving in Christ's name in the community must all fit together in mutual support.

One of the key challenges churches face in the development of holistic mission is crafting the delicate balance between nurture and outreach. If a congregation becomes overly focused on its own needs, it becomes a social club that never gets around to carrying out the work of the kingdom for others. On the other hand, the people of God cannot reach out effectively if they're hurting, visionless, ill-equipped, or divided. The church cannot help new converts grow if it lacks strong ministries of discipleship and fellowship. As Bishop Dickie Robbins puts it, "If you don't have healthy people, then you don't have a healthy approach to ministry."

How can church leaders build a healthy congregational base for community ministry? Sometimes a commitment to outreach competes with other church priorities, such as nurturing the spiritual life of members. Sometimes the outreach arm of the church tries to stake out its territory and carry out its business independent of the other parts. To function as the organic whole envisioned by Paul's "body" metaphor (1 Corinthians 12), the many functions of a church must be unified by a vision of its overall nature. This chapter examines the relationship between the church's external mission of holistic ministry and several key internal functions—worship, the sacraments, tithing, small group discipleship, youth ministry, and *koinonia*—revealing the ways that "outreach" and "in-reach" are mutually supportive.

Worship

"One of the things that worship does, aside from honoring God, [is] it recharges the troops," says Rev. Bill Moore, pastor of Tenth Memorial Baptist Church. "It's a part of the joy of the journey to come and get recharged, and to go back again. . . . That's what worship ought to do—it ought to inspire people, it ought to challenge people through the Word to go out there and get 'em."

Rev. Moore's words illuminate the natural rhythms of holistic ministry. We gather together before God to receive grace, instruction, and empowerment. We go out from God's presence to share what we have received, serving singly or in groups. We come back together to celebrate what God has done and to be renewed for the next round. Holistic outreach can (if it is done right!) be exhausting, frustrating, and costly. When members of a congregation encounter the Lord in worship, either in jubilant celebration of God's sovereignty or in quiet moments of adoring intimacy, they are reminded why it is all worthwhile.

Worship nurtures the spiritual gifts and passion needed for ministry. God promises each individual spiritual gifts, and those gifts are to be developed and exercised in the congregation (1 Cor. 14:12). The Holy Spirit can move uniquely and powerfully in a body of believers when it is gathered in the unity of worship (Acts 2:1–4). Training programs are necessary to teach the principles and skills of holistic ministry, but the congregation also needs the spiritual preparation that happens only through the corporate experience of God's grace. Nile Harper's study of churches around the country with dynamic community outreach found that one common denominator was "worship [that] is spiritually powerful, culturally diverse, and directly related to mission." Such worship prepares and moves people "to act from faith, hope, and love in order to bring compassion, new life, and justice into neighborhoods."[3]

Vibrant worship also solidifies the fruit of holistic ministry. As people come to a worship service for the first time as a result of a church outreach, they are "hooked" by an authentic, exciting, culturally relevant worship service. On the other hand, if spiritual seekers or new converts hear from ministry staff about the joyous blessings of following God, and then they visit the church and everyone looks bored or distracted, which message are they likely to believe?

No one is bored during worship at Faith Assembly of God. A lay leader describes their church services: "God is here. That's the bottom line, and that's what I tell people when they come and say, 'Wow, I've never been to a church like this.' . . . You've been in the presence of God. . . . It's not just a ritual and somebody speaking across the pulpit while you're yawning—no! There's a lot of life here." At Faith, that life takes a very charismatic form: people dancing, praying in tongues, shouting ecstatic praise to God. But churches don't have to be "charismatic" to enjoy lively, contagious worship.

Finally, worship helps the church keep everything else in perspective. The final destination of every Christian is to bow in adoration before the throne of the Lamb (Rev. 7:9–12). "Our ultimate purpose" in holistic ministry, Amy Sherman reminds us, is "to bring about a restoration that leads us, and those we serve, to praise and worship King Jesus from atop the wall of rebuilt lives."[4] That praise continues forever!

Sacraments

Properly understood and practiced, the sacraments of baptism and the Lord's Supper unite the inward and outward tasks of the church. The historic rituals of the church are not only intensely spiritual acts, communicating the mysteries at the heart of the divine-human relationship. Sacramental acts also involve a horizontal dimension. As Darrell Guder writes:

> They have communal and missional meaning from the outset: by their very nature they are social, visible, practical, and public. . . . These practices not only form and guide the internal life of the community but also define the church's action within the world.[5]

The Lord's Supper, for example, has its roots in the celebration of Passover, a Hebrew feast marking the deliverance of the Israelites from the oppression of Egyptian slavery. As they partook of the Passover feast down through the years, the Israelites were to remember what it was like to be slaves and to renew their commitment to treat poor persons and "aliens" (those without legal standing in the community) with compassion and dignity.

During the Last Supper with his disciples, Jesus reinterpreted the Passover feast in terms of the grander scheme of the liberation of all people from bondage to sin, bought with his broken body and shed blood. Just as the Hebrews were to remember how God delivered them from Egypt, Jesus instructed his disciples, "Whenever you do this, remember me." The Lord's Supper, then, should make us mindful anew of the holistic teachings and ministry of Jesus. The Israelites were to show mercy to the vulnerable because God had showed them mercy. Likewise, the celebration of our salvation in the taking of communion should reinvigorate our personal and congregational commitment to share sacrificially with our neighbors.

Paul made it clear that the meaning of the Lord's Supper is distorted when celebrants participate only for their own benefit, while ignoring the material needs of other members (1 Cor. 11:21–22). The taking of communion is both a private event, in which we examine our conscience and rejoice in our personal salvation, and an expression of our public mission to love others as we ourselves have been loved. In this way, Guder writes, "The practice of breaking bread together is to cultivate communities of gratitude and generosity in solidarity with the hungry, dispossessed, and marginalized."[6]

Church leaders will need to spell out for the congregation the implications of the sacraments for the church's "social, visible, practical, and public" ministry. We have been so ingrained to think of everything that happens in a church service in terms of "me and Jesus" that making connections with the church's broader holistic mission will not come naturally. Members need to see how bringing a holistic perspective to sacred rituals can both expand their understanding of holistic ministry and strengthen their commitment to it.

Tithing

Tithes and offerings are critical to holistic ministry, not only because they pay the bills but because they represent members' support of the mission. At Christian Stronghold Baptist Church, for example, the congregation applauds when the tithes and offering time is announced, signifying their gratitude for all that they have received from God through the church, and their excitement about the opportunity to participate in the ministry of the church by giving.

Hebrew law emphasized the connection between tithing and aid to poor households.

> Every third year you shall bring out the full tithe of your produce for that year, and store it within your towns; the Levites, . . . as well as the resident aliens, the orphans, and the widows in your towns, may come and eat their fill so that the LORD your God may bless you in all the work that you undertake.
>
> Deuteronomy 14:28–29

The tithe does not belong to the church. As Malachi 3 makes clear, it belongs to God. Malachi 3:10 directs the people of God to "bring the full tithe into the storehouse." The church, as a "storehouse," gathers in the tithes and offerings, but they are not all to stay there. In God's plan, the church is not a sponge soaking up handouts or a spiritual investment bank where people make deposits to be cashed in later. Rather, Deuteronomy 14 portrays the congregation as a distribution center, collecting the money that rightfully belongs to God and apportioning resources to those who do the work of the congregation and to those on the economic and social margins. Christians are to give individually to charity, but it is also part of God's design for the church as a collective body to pool its resources for the sake of people in need (Acts 2:45).

Malachi further shows the connection between the failure of God's people to tithe fully, or in the right spirit, and the lack of justice and moral integrity in the land (2:13–17; 3:8–9). In the first place, stinginess with God can be an indicator of the church's need to "clean house" in other areas. It does no good to urge members to write a check on Sunday if the rest of the week they make money fraudulently and cheat others of their due. This passage helps us to see the tithe as a spiritual discipline in a more holistic light. Second, the church serves as the sign or firstfruits of shalom in society, revealing a spiritual link between the health of the church and the well-being of the community. When we do not bring the tithe to the storehouse, we not only rob God, but we rob our society of God's blessing. The act of dedicating the firstfruits of our income to God is part and parcel of the church's transformational mission.

New Creation Lutheran Church has found a creative way to fulfill Deuteronomy's call to use the tithe to aid those in need. Every month the church "tithes" its tithes. It donates 10 percent of all that members give to the church to a particular charity or mission. The recipients of this tithe range from denominational ministries to missionaries to local nonprofit organizations. The recipient agency is announced in the bulletin. New Creation is by no means a wealthy church. It can barely meet its own budget. Yet the church sets an example to its members, most of whom also struggle to meet expenses from week to week, by giving sacrificially to help others.

Holistic Mission and Discipleship

A key purpose of church leadership, according to Ephesians 4:12, is to "equip the saints for the work of ministry, for building up the body of Christ." The church is to nurture Christians in the way of Christ, increasing their knowledge of the Word of God and strengthening their commitment to the Lord. Many internal church activities—sermons, Bible study, pastoral counseling, accountability groups, Sunday school, men's/women's fellowship, and so on—have discipleship as their aim.

Holistic ministry must stand on a firm biblical foundation. The more that Christians are solidly grounded in the Word, the greater their openness to the voice of the Holy Spirit calling them into mission. Activism is most fruitful when rooted in a growing understanding of who God is, how God has been working salvation in human history and individual lives, and the mission of the church. The congregation should understand not only the theological basis for holistic ministry but also the connection between outreach and the rest of the church's work.

A holistic approach to discipleship sees spiritual growth and service as an interlocking spiral. Study and devotion should foster active obedience, and the experience of carrying out God's mission in the world deepens our desire to know God better. The more we know about who God is and what he is doing in the world, the more we act on our knowledge; the more we follow God's will, the more insights we gain into God's character and the closer we grow to

Christ (Matt. 12:50). If we do the works of Christ without *knowing* Christ, ultimately our good deeds will prove meaningless (Matt. 7:22). But if we walk away from our Bible study rejoicing that we understand God better but then we do not put the Word into practice, Jesus says we are like a foolish builder who constructs a house on a foundation of sand (Matt. 7:26). David Apple of Tenth Presbyterian Church summarizes the relationship between study and action: "Christians need to know what they're doing. And Christians need to do what they know."[7]

Many churches, however, approach discipleship as a two-stage process: First, you study and learn the disciplines of a vigorous personal spiritual life; then, after you have achieved a sufficient level of spiritual maturity, you may graduate to active ministry duty. Jesus' teachings and example, however, indicate that even for fledgling believers, engaging in acts of ministry should go hand in hand with instruction in the faith. A wealthy young ruler approached Jesus with the classic seeker question, "Good Teacher, what must I do to inherit eternal life?" Jesus first answered with basic spiritual principles. Then, knowing that this "head knowledge" of the way to God was not enough, Jesus gave the man some startling instructions: "Sell all that you own and distribute the money to the poor, and you will have treasure in heaven; then come, follow me" (Luke 18:22).

Setting new believers to work in obedience to the mandate for holistic ministry makes the teachings about the kingdom come alive and tests their commitment to a life of discipleship. "The initial ministry assignment should follow close on the heels of conversion," advise urban ministry specialists Edgar Elliston and Timothy Kauffman. "Passive, unattached, uncommitted believers risk being stunted in their spiritual formation and ministry maturity."[8] Church leaders must be prudent about the kinds of assignments and levels of responsibility given to new or immature Christians (e.g., not putting a recently converted child abuser in charge of youth outreach!). However, the supervision and mentoring that takes place within a ministry project as new believers work alongside more mature Christians can be a vital component of discipleship.

"The best way to disciple in the way of Jesus Christ," asserts Rev. Bill Borror, "is to have Christians involved in hands-on ministry." Many church members credit participation in service projects with making their faith more meaningful and alive. Bob, for example, transferred to Media from another church, where his spiritual life had grown stagnant. At Media, Bob was soon put to work in the Carpenter's Club ministry. As he built handicap ramps and did home repairs for low-income home owners, his faith grew by leaps and bounds; he became active in other areas of church life, and within a few years, was elected deacon. The Sunday after about 150 members returned from an annual trip to build a Habitat home for a poor family in North Carolina, participants gave testimonies about their experiences. People stood up, one after another, to share how they had gone expecting to help someone else, but to their surprise, in the process they discovered new spiritual truths and reached new depths in their relationship with God.

Help the congregation make the connection between holistic outreach and personal spiritual growth. How does hands-on ministry enrich our discipleship?

- It allows us to enter into God's heart of mourning for sin and brokenness. "Seeing the needs firsthand softens our hearts and makes them 'break for the things that break God's heart.'"[9] We realize in greater depth the deadly power of evil and the even mightier power of the cross.
- It confronts us with areas in our own lives where we need to repent and seek God's transforming grace: for example, lack of faith, materialism, all forms of prejudice, hardness of heart, laziness, the idolatry of comfort, a shame to confess the gospel.
- It yields new insights into Scripture, as we see it brought to life in the course of ministry. We can study about God's compassion and love, but until we encounter the man wounded on the road to Jericho, bathe his wounds, and pay for his care, we can't know fully what it means to be a good neighbor.
- It brings us closer to God's passion for justice. When we minister to people who lack access to quality, affordable health care, housing, or education, we join with Jesus and the prophets in the cry to release the oppressed (Luke 4:18).
- It strengthens our faith by giving us tangible evidence of God's hand at work, while at the same time demanding a deeper level of trust.
- It leads to greater dependence on God's grace and wisdom. As one volunteer confessed, working with people with HIV has "forced me to rely on God in a continual way that I never had to before. I recognize that without the Holy Spirit, I'm clueless."
- It drives us to draw closer to Christ. "Many times, when we go out," says Rev. Kyerematen of Germantown Church of the Brethren, "we find out how unprepared we are, and we need to come back and study some more and to pray some more. Jesus sent his disciples out and let them see what they needed, and when they . . . came back, he did more teaching."
- It helps us discover and develop spiritual gifts we might not otherwise have known about: compassion, hospitality, evangelism, intercessory prayer, administration, healing.
- It expands our understanding of God's providence, particularly in congregations that are insulated from social pain. "In a white, middle class church, we learn how God intervenes, equips, provides and graces us for

the trials of white, middle class life," writes Amy Sherman. "Our spiritual lives are diminished in some measure because we are exposed primarily to our own experiences with God—and the experiences of those like us."[10] When we are exposed to new contexts for God's saving work, we gain new perspectives on God's character.

- It deepens our appreciation for our own salvation. A lay leader at Life in Christ put it this way: "Sharing the gospel increases your faith. It draws you closer to God. It keeps you constantly reminded of what Christ has done in your own life. . . . It keeps your heart humble and grateful to God."

- When we encounter Christians among those served, we learn "important lessons from economically poor but spiritually rich fellow believers"—such as contentment, joy in adversity, hope, and faith in receiving "this day our daily bread."[11]

Members of holistic churches believe, as Amy Sherman reminds us, that "outreach to the poor and needy is not only a matter of obedience to Scripture, but also a necessary component of spiritual growth. In other words, they believe they need the poor as much as the poor need them: They assert that their own spiritual health is impoverished if they are not entangling their lives with the lives of others different from themselves."[12] When the path of discipleship focuses exclusively on our personal relationship with God, our Christianity tends to become self-centered and narrow. We forget that a central purpose for our salvation is to reach and serve others—that we were "created in Christ Jesus for good works" (Eph. 2:10).

Another cost when discipleship is divorced from active involvement in holistic ministry is that spiritual truths can become just so many words. To believe in Christ is something that you *do,* not just a mental process. The Bible includes only two instances of the passive word *belief*—and 173 instances of the active form *believe* (New Revised Standard Version). Just as our witness in the world is hurt when we do not integrate word and deed, so our discipleship suffers when it is reduced to propositional learning without the complementary experience of Christlike engagement with a suffering world.

The flip side is equally important. For holistic outreach ministry to be effective, the church must have a strong program of discipleship. A ministry leader at Life in Christ Cathedral of Faith explains:

> There are many churches that call themselves community oriented that have a lot of outreach ministries, but the essential part of an outreach ministry is having a good follow-up discipleship component that keeps the people. I could reach out all day long, and tell people about Christ all day long, but if I have nothing to help them grow and to deal with their problems besides Sunday and Wednesday night, then I'm going to lose them.

Discipleship is the process that turns a person with needs to be met by the church into a person with gifts to be shared through the church. Thus, discipleship is essential to sustain holistic ministry over the long haul. (See appendix B for recommended materials on discipleship that make the connection with holistic ministry.)

Small Group Discipleship and Outreach

The church must have a structure in place for bringing people together face-to-face beyond a superficial level for the purpose of discipleship and mutual support. In our fast-paced, mobile culture, this does not happen accidentally—especially in larger churches where individuals easily get lost in the crowd. One member of Christian Stronghold expressed the value of small groups this way: "Even though a lot of things are happening here, you don't ever have to feel as though you're just one in a number, that you're going to get lost, that nobody is going to know you're here. That's what attracted me to this church."

Small groups can blend discipleship and outreach in several ways.[13] Outreach can be part of a small group's purpose, one of its planned activities. For example, First Presbyterian Church's S-Groups bring members together for "Sharing, Service, Support, and Study." A church with a strong small group system has a key asset in place for organizing members for volunteer ministry. Small groups also strengthen network evangelism, providing a good entry point for people who are not ready or willing to accept an invitation to a church service. This is particularly the case for affinity groups, organized around a shared characteristic such as gender or age, and support groups, which bring people together around specific life situations or problems such as substance abuse, divorce recovery, or single parenting. In these kinds of small groups, unchurched guests immediately have something in common with church members. Mentoring groups or pairs, matching new Christians with mature members of the congregation, are helpful as a follow-up to evangelism.

One remarkably effective discipleship model is the NetCare small group system of New Covenant Church. After completing the new members class, members are encouraged to join NetCare—small groups of eight to twenty that meet twice a month in members' homes for fellowship, worship, prayer, and Bible study. All the groups share a common format and study curriculum written by the pastor, so that Sunday services can build on what each group has studied the previous week. Most groups are intended to be inclusive, but some "specialty" groups have emerged—Mothers' Care groups, NetWork groups that meet in a place of employment, morning groups in coffee shops, even a group that meets in a prison.

Saundra, a NetCare leader, explains that the purpose of NetCare groups is to empower members for service: "God touches us, and we touch others." Each

NetCare group is expected to minister to the social and emotional needs of its members and to serve as the first line of defense in times of crisis. Group members assist one another with financial needs, food, transportation and car repairs, youth mentoring, job searches, furniture, and funeral costs. "I have seen people come into a small group broken and hurting," testified Saundra. "Now we have seen the 'after.' It's such a blessing to know our ministry has made such a difference in their lives."

In one dramatic example, when a church family's home burned to the ground, they called their NetCare group leader. The leader went to the scene immediately to assess their needs and then called the Zone Minister to organize a strategy for response. Within four hours, the family had clothes and food. Within a week, they had to tell the congregation to stop giving because they had all the furniture and supplies they needed. The church helped the family recover financially as well. In such a large church, the pastors cannot possibly take care of every crisis; the NetCare system ensures that the congregation's needs are met without overwhelming the leaders.

Besides caring for members, the NetCare groups are the primary way that New Covenant "reaches out to the lost, evangelizing those the Lord brings to us," particularly the people in members' relational networks. "One of my personal testimonies is my husband," says a NetCare group member. During the meetings at their home, her husband "wouldn't come downstairs, but he was upstairs and he heard the prayers being prayed for him. As a result of that he was saved." As New Covenant became involved in the Lighthouses of Prayer movement (see appendix B), the NetCare groups provided a natural organizing basis for ministries of intercessory, evangelistic prayer.

Youth Ministry and Outreach

Media Presbyterian Church printed T-shirts for its youth group to wear on a mission trip to Mexico. The front of the shirts read, "We Are the Church." This slogan is a valuable reminder that young people in the church are disciples of Christ too. Discipling youth to share in the church's mission is a vital task of holistic congregations.

Many youth groups are one-sided. Some groups emphasize the conversion experience and moral teaching while providing few opportunities for mission and service. Other groups emphasize social development and community involvement while minimizing "God talk," assuming that kids are not yet ready for serious discipleship. Whichever side they fall on, many groups also fall into the trap of endorsing our culture's idolatry of entertainment, fearful that if they do not provide constant activities and stimulation, the youth will get bored and leave. Such an approach sees youth exclusively as "users" of ministry, rather than potential ministry assets.

In contrast, a holistic approach to youth ministry treats youth as whole persons, touching every area of their lives; sets high expectations for youth as disciples of Christ and members of the body of Christ; fosters meaningful relationships between adults and youth, as the foundation for discipleship; invites youth to be participants in, not just passive observers or recipients of, outreach ministry; and, of course, provides fun in the process!

Bethel Temple Community Bible Church provides an example of a holistic youth program. "We're not an entertainment ministry," says Rev. Joel Van Dyke. "We've gotta be about something different." The difference at Bethel is that youth are challenged on many levels to grow in discipleship and participate in ministry, as Rev. Van Dyke describes:

> They're expected to talk to their friends and to introduce them to the Lord. . . . We train them to do it, but they have to be the ones to do it. They're also challenged when they get an idea for some kind of ministry. I used to come up with all the ideas myself, and I've realized why no one really got excited about it. If they come up with them themselves, then they're much more invested. In missions projects, they're challenged to do things that are way beyond what anyone would say is possible. . . . And the whole area of holding them accountable—sexual choices, getting in their faces about what kind of choices they're making—that's a challenge; no one else is doing that in their lives. . . . We are one place in the community that challenges them to live above mediocrity, which is what the world is offering them.

It would be easy for Bethel to lower its expectations because of the significant needs of its youth. Most come from poor and broken families. Many have academic difficulties and behavioral problems. Some, like Hector, have a background of drug sales and substance abuse. Friends in high school told him he should try Bethel's youth group, and there he learned about Jesus Christ. Now Hector volunteers on youth nights, leading a room full of squirming young children in games and Bible stories. "Three years ago, I wouldn't have even thought that I would be at this point, working with the youth ministry," he reflects. "It's great to be able to teach the kids what I've learned." At Bethel the focus is not just on youths' needs but on helping them become part of the solution.

Along with a passionate focus on evangelism and discipleship, ministry staff are also concerned with youths' practical, "this-worldly" needs. When Rev. Van Dyke made a follow-up visit to a girl who had recently accepted Christ, for example, he discovered that the family had just been evicted from their apartment. He brought them food and invited the family to stay in a church-owned building that was unused at the time. The whole family joined the church.

Like Bethel Temple, Media Presbyterian Church has made service an important ingredient of their youth program. By ministering alongside adults, youth learn that Christianity means reaching out to others in word and deed. Service projects broaden middle-class kids' horizons, exposing them to multicultural and cross-class settings and relationships. Including youth in community outreach helps them find meaning and self-worth in serving others. It also develops future ministry leaders. For example, as a result of taking their youth group on a Habitat for Humanity work trip, the church ended up adding youth representatives to their Faith in Action outreach committee. Service projects also give unchurched youth a nonthreatening way to connect with the congregation. Activities such as housing rehab and visiting the elderly have attracted many nonchurched youth, thanks to church youth who invite their friends. The youth minister notes wryly, "They're probably better evangelists than we are as adults."

Holistic Mission and Koinonia

Koinonia—the Greek word for Christian fellowship—is an essential quality of a holistic congregation. Loving, welcoming, reconciling, accountable, joyous fellowship is a foundation for other church activities (Col. 3:14). The essence of the gospel is uniquely embodied in the way members of a congregation treat one another.

In its first few years, Koinonia Christian Community Church learned an important lesson about the biblical principle that gave the church its name. From the beginning, Koinonia had emphasized active outreach. The church's founding couple, Jerome and Sadie Simmons, led neighborhood witnessing teams, provided food bags and hot meals to the community, opened a thrift store, and had begun building renovations to start a day care as the planned cornerstone of a comprehensive community development center. Rev. Simmons spent a great deal of time out on the streets, telling people about Jesus and inviting them to church. The church grew slowly. But Rev. Simmons had a hard time recruiting congregants for active participation in the church's vision, and many new believers were slipping out the church's "back door."

A series of special services surrounding the celebration of their fifth anniversary brought the small congregation together in a new way. It was then that Rev. Simmons realized that they needed to take a step back from their outreach to focus on developing loving relationships within the church. When new or renewed Christians came to Koinonia, he did not want them to find an atmosphere of indifference, stubborn pride, or contention. "You don't want to bring people into a place that's not that different from the world," he notes. The quality of a congregation's relationships says to the community, "Something new is happening here." As Jesus told his followers, "By this everyone will know that you are my disciples, if you have love for one another" (John 13:35).

The kinds of Christians who "love one another deeply from the heart" (1 Peter 1:22) are those whom God can use to share his love with others. Thus, by helping your congregation to cultivate a spirit of *koinonia,* you are also preparing your congregation for holistic ministry. A church's lasting impact is not only in its structured programs of outreach but also (and sometimes especially) in the informal relationships and ordinary, day-to-day acts of compassion and fellowship among its members. "Hope comes from a community that reflects Jesus, a community that calls forth the reaction, 'See how they love each other!'"[14]

What are the characteristics of *koinonia* that mark a holistic congregation?

Meeting Internal Needs

One concrete way that a church expresses love is by striving to meet the material and emotional needs of its members. Galatians 6:10 urges us, "Whenever we have an opportunity, let us work for the good of all, and *especially* for those of the family of faith" (emphasis added). The needs are not just "out there." Many Christians are ashamed to admit their problems to their church. Sadly, people often encounter more compassion from a nonprofit agency than from their own church. If a congregation does not care for members who are struggling with hunger, unemployment, or domestic abuse, how can the church authentically say it wants to help others? If a church provides people with all kinds of aid when it is "wooing" them, but then neglects them once they join the congregation, won't people see through this hypocrisy?

If members do not feel secure that the church cares about them, they are less motivated to reach out to others. A member of an active congregation wrote to the pastor: "While I applaud and support our growing involvement in social action issues, . . . sometimes I think we are perceived only in terms of outreach to others while our own needs are overlooked. I would like to be a person and not just a resource tool." Nurturing the holistic health of members is an investment in the church's holistic ministry.

Churches should adopt the standard of Deuteronomy 15:4: "There will . . . be no one in need among you." This is not an unrealistic goal. The early church actually achieved it, as the Book of Acts records: "All who believed were together and had all things in common; they would sell their possessions and goods and distribute the proceeds to all, as any had need" (Acts 2:44–45). The result? "There was not a needy person among them" (4:34). Further, the story in Acts illustrates the connection between caring relationships and evangelism: "And day by day the Lord added to their number those who were being saved" (2:47). A caring church fellowship is not a substitute for intentional, explicit evangelism (the apostles didn't stop preaching!), but it offers a living demonstration of the Good News we share. True *koinonia* makes the world sit up and take notice.

While churches today need not necessarily imitate the early church's specific methods, all must find ways of addressing members' needs. At Life in Christ Cathedral of Faith, aid flows through a Blessings and Needs ministry that provides emergency relief and links members' extra goods (such as clothing or furniture) with other members' or neighborhood residents' needs. The shepherding ministry of First Presbyterian Church ensures that each family in attendance has a trained "shepherd" looking out for them and addressing their needs. New Covenant Church of Philadelphia fights unemployment in its midst by asking members to report any open positions in their place of employment and printing a help wanted list, among other strategies.

During one New Covenant church service, a man asked for prayer because he was unemployed. He had been saved while in prison. After his release he joined New Covenant Church and reunited with his family, but he could not support them because employers would not hire a man with a prison record. Bishop Grannum turned to another member of the congregation and asked him to stand up. He announced, "This brother right here, Stan, he's a former policeman. Stan, I want you to take this man under your wing and help him find a job." From that day on, the ex-convict had a job laying cinder blocks. He ended up working for the subcontractor who was constructing the new sanctuary at New Covenant. The church helped him rebuild his life—and in turn he literally helped build the church!

A formal benevolence committee is helpful, but more important is the willingness of people in the congregation to look out for each other. "If you are here in this community of faith, and it hits the fan for you," assures Rev. Marcus Pomeroy of Central Baptist Church, "there is a group of people who are going to be there for you"—providing child care for parents of twins, house cleaning for disabled persons, food for families with a member in the hospital. The congregation takes it for granted that they ought to share financial assistance, goods, services, and time with one another as a routine way of life.

Reconciliation

Another critical feature of *koinonia* is racial, class, and gender reconciliation. The church must carry on Christ's work of breaking down the barriers between God's children. In the early church, the miracle of Jews and Gentiles, men and women, slave and free, Pharisees and tax collectors, breaking bread together in the name of Christ was an electrifying sign of the truth and power of the gospel. The reconciled, unified church is not just a part of our witness to the community; it bears testimony in the spiritual realms as well. According to Ephesians 3:6–10, humankind is united in Christ "so that through the church the wisdom of God in its rich variety might now be made known to the rulers and authorities in the heavenly places" (v. 10).

Welcoming diversity within the congregation is an important feature (though not the sum total) of reconciliation, especially when the church is located in or serves a diverse neighborhood. It's tough for the group that has traditionally dominated the congregation to break free from old patterns and share power. It's tough for Christians of a minority group to feel at home on someone else's turf. But when people truly love the Lord, the Bible promises that the obstacles to unity can be overcome. "There is one body and one Spirit, just as you were called to the one hope" (Eph. 4:4). Become sensitive to anything in the church that contradicts this fundamental truth of Christian unity by conveying an unscriptural exclusivity. For example, images of a "white" Christ on stained glass windows or children's Sunday school materials, an expensive dress code, or the use of exclusively male pronouns for humanity can be practical or symbolic barriers to reconciliation.

Welcoming the Stranger

Effective holistic congregations embrace those who are "different." Jesus consistently attracted followers who had been marginalized by poverty, disabilities, or sinful lifestyles, yet without condoning sin. Congregations who are likewise welcoming will hear Jesus say in praise, "I was a stranger and you welcomed me" (Matt. 25:35). The "strangers" among us include those with handicaps, physical and mental; divorcees and single parents; homosexuals; homeless people; and immigrants. Such individuals are often ignored at best, ostracized at worst. If your congregation rarely has to deal with "strangers," it may be because they no longer feel comfortable coming to your church. But the apostle Paul helps us understand that we should actually value those who are "foolish" and "weak" as assets to the body of Christ (1 Cor. 1:26–29).

Media Presbyterian Church's Ministry to Special Friends supports people in the church who might need extra attention. For example, kids of single moms can be matched with a male mentor from the congregation, who takes them to soccer games and other activities. Other volunteers befriend handicapped persons in the church, meeting occasionally to play cards or go out for dinner. The ministry coordinator knows how it feels on the church margins, because she herself has a family member who is mentally challenged. "One reason I'm here in this church today is because we were greeted with open arms over twenty years ago," she reflects, "and that's not always typical. If you're looking for help and support, and you have a special need, there's no better feeling than to come to a church and have them open their arms to you."

Interruption or Opportunity?

During the time of sharing one Sunday at Cookman United Methodist Church, a man came forward who was new to the church. In a low and shaking voice, he shared that he is a believer in Jesus Christ as his personal Lord and Savior. But, he told them, "I need help." The congregation listened attentively as he poured out his heart for about fifteen minutes, nodding their heads or murmuring agreement from time to time. When he mentioned being in prison for five years, a man from the back called out, "Amen."

Then the man broke down crying. At this point, the worship leader who had been standing beside him put her hand on his shoulder and said something quietly. Rev. Donna Jones came down from the pulpit area and led the man to kneel at the altar. As she prayed aloud for the man, an elder of the church anointed the man's head with oil from a small glass jar. Then the man sat down.

The worship leader took the microphone. "The church is the place to get the kind of help that you need," she told the man. She assured him that the congregation would be there for him—"to love you to wholeness."

Some churches might have viewed the man's impromptu sharing as an intrusion on their worship service. But the congregation of Cookman United Methodist Church embraced it as an act of worship.

Joyous Fellowship

"The kingdom of God is a party," says Tony Campolo.[15] Contagious worship has a festive dimension, as people experience the joy of coming before God as well as the joy of being in one another's company. Descriptions of the early church give the impression that the first Christians had a great time just being with one another: "Day by day, as they spent much time together in the temple, they broke bread at home and ate their food with glad and generous hearts" (Acts 2:46).

A holistic church is a busy church. Members can easily be swept up in the ministry maelstrom and lose the joy of simple fellowship. Just as busy households have to guard precious family time, churches must set aside "family time" where there is no agenda other than enjoying one another's company. This is the lesson Bethel Temple Community Bible Church learned when leaders became too worn down by the pace of ministry to fellowship with church attenders. The message the congregation got from the leaders' example, according to co-pastor Joel Van Dyke, was that "you have to run very fast, you have to run very hard, and you need to keep up. And no one can keep up." The church's leaders realized they needed a more balanced focus. They planned the first annual church picnic to represent the church's movement toward being more nurturing of its membership. A caravan of church attenders drove to a beautiful park, removed from the pressures of their church's inner-city setting. While children ran around the playground and played soccer, adults sat on blankets and chatted about the morning's sermon, last night's community violence, and their spiritual journeys. For once they were not looking for newcomers to greet or planning ministry tasks. The congregation was simply resting and rediscovering the joys of being a church family.

To sustain a commitment to holistic ministry, people must share a sense of humor and a spirit of gratifying companionship. People have to know how to have fun together. That is almost impossible if they do not know one another well, or worse, just don't get along. At the same time, doing ministry together can also strengthen members' bonds with one another. Leaders can promote holistic ministry as an opportunity for people to "let down their hair" outside a more formal worship setting and to get to know one another on a deeper level in a "real-world" context. "In a Sunday morning relationship, you can choose to be involved with people as much or as little as you want," says Bishop Dickie Robbins. "But when you're forced to work with people hand-to-hand and heart-to-heart, there's a prolonged time where you're exposed to one another."

Mutual Accountability

The final characteristic of *koinonia* considered here is accountable fellowship. "People today desperately need a church that functions as the church— a body of believers who accept liability for one another, are available to one another, and make themselves accountable to one another," wrote Ron Sider in *Rich Christians in an Age of Hunger.*[16] If church members are not able or willing to hold one another accountable, they cannot imitate Christ in ministry. An essential way to mature in Christ, according to Ephesians 4:15, is by "speaking the truth in love." For holistic ministry to take root in a congregation, it must be a place where members can challenge and correct one another in love. Sin must be confronted in a loving way, without rancor, coercion, or self-righteous condemnation. As Paul says in Galatians 6:1–2, "My friends, if anyone is detected in a transgression, you who have received the Spirit should restore such a one in a spirit of gentleness. . . . Bear one another's burdens, and in this way you will fulfill the law of Christ." The purpose of accountability and discipline within the church is not to weed out sinners (there would be no one left in the pews!) but to help the congregation grow together in holiness and righteousness.

Believers must hold one another accountable when there are blatant, grievous sins that infect the church body (1 Corinthians 5). No less important is holding one another accountable for the "smaller" or hidden sins that hinder personal spiritual growth. People who are involved in outreach ministry, in particular, need help in discerning whether their lives match the message of God's holy love that they preach and model. A focus on effective outcomes must never obscure the imperative of personal and institutional integrity. Without accountability, ministries may be tempted to gain results at the expense of moral compromise. Moreover, a church that has healthy internal accountability is better able to walk alongside people from the community who are struggling to make better moral choices—for example, by helping an ex-convict to reconcile with his family, develop productive work habits, and avoid slipping back into substance abuse.

As the church grows in holistic ministry, members should also gently help one another overcome the personal obstacles that conflict with the church's mission, such as a crippling fear of evangelism or degrading stereotypes about poor persons. "In good relationships, priorities get challenged," writes David Mann. "One may need to challenge an apparently too-busy person to invest some time in action about something in which he or she believes. A cynical person may need to be encouraged to persevere as an agent of change."[17] David Apple notes that part of his ministry at economically diverse Tenth Presbyterian Church has been to "convert" well-off Christians to a new perspective on social action. "The affluent must desire a change of attitude, to come to a point in their spiritual pilgrimages where they understand that the heart of God goes out in a special way to the widow, the orphan, the beggar, and the sojourner and that God desperately wants these church members to share that concern."[18]

Churches should hold members accountable for their economic choices as well. "Imagine how it would transform the lives of Christians today if we truly believed Paul's warning that economic greed is just as terrible as sexual sin."[19] For most American Christians, truly letting Christ be Lord of our pocketbooks does not come naturally. Central Baptist Church offered a series of classes called "Your Money or Your Life." The classes used a biblically based study guide on economic justice and simple living. Almost a third of the congregation attended. People in the class shared openly about the implications of materialism and consumerism for their lives. One of the fruits of the class has been the creation of a directory of items belonging to households in the church that are available for others to borrow.

The church's leadership has a special responsibility for dealing with sin in the body of Christ. However, members have a role in holding one another accountable as well. Often this is best done through small fellowship groups in which members can be transparent with one another. In a small group setting, members can encourage, challenge, and guide one another about lifestyle choices, ministry struggles, evangelism, theological questions, and responses to social issues.

Conclusion

Effective holistic ministry depends on vibrant worship, sound discipleship, and loving fellowship within the congregation. When Christians truly love one another and meet one another's needs, when they experience growth and unity in Christ, and when their lives display the wonders of the Spirit, then congregations become powerfully attractive and transformational communities. Again and again, in our interviews with pastors, we heard them say that without strong nurture ministries, their churches could not sustain community outreach. But a healthy church becomes a vessel through which God can pour the Good News of salvation into the world.

chapter nine

Church Leadership
for Holistic Ministry

Leadership begins when a God-revealed mission captures a person. . . . Leadership turns to service when the leader equips those recruited to carry out the now-shared mission. . . . Simply put, servant leadership is passionate service to the mission and to those who join the leader on that mission.[1]

The first time Rev. Herb Lusk preached at Greater Exodus Baptist Church, there were eight buckets catching rainwater in the sanctuary, and seven people sitting in the pews. The one-hundred-year-old inner-city Philadelphia church needed extensive repairs, and the forty-member congregation was $200,000 in debt. When offered the pastorate, his response was, "No way!" But as he left, he was struck by the sight of a line of men waiting for food outside a Salvation Army. On his drive home, he ended up in a nearby housing project. "As I sat there, staring," recalls Rev. Lusk, "I thought, 'What better place to work than where there's such great need?'" He returned to the church and accepted the position.

Today Rev. Lusk, called one of Philadelphia's "most charismatic preacher-entrepreneurs," leads a church of roughly two thousand members and a thriving nonprofit organization called People for People (PFP). From its Christmas food basket program, PFP's outreach has grown to include Youth Enrichment mentoring, drug prevention, after-school and summer camp programs, a state-of-the-art computer lab, substance abuse support groups, a well-stocked recreation center, a charter school, and a credit union. PFP runs a state-funded job training program for 250 welfare recipients (with a placement rate of 82 percent!) and jointly with a private company sponsors a worker-owned apparel factory to employ welfare recipients. Program participants are invited to the church's lunchtime Bible studies, youth groups, and other discipling ministries, and many have joined the church.

How has Greater Exodus transformed itself from an empty, leaky sanctuary to a church bursting at the seams with dynamic ministry? Certainly, Rev. Lusk's connections as a former Philadelphia Eagles football star have helped with fund-raising and publicity! But his vision, energy, compassion, spiritual discernment, and management skills have also been essential ingredients. Where there was great need, Rev. Lusk saw great opportunities to lead his church in becoming an agent of God's love and power. God uses called and gifted leaders like Herb Lusk as instruments to fulfill his purposes.

Thanks to consultants and organizations like Bill Easum, Tom Bandy, Lyle Schaller, and the Leadership Network, a wealth of material now exists for cultivating church leadership (see suggested resources in appendix B). While this material is quite useful, much of it leaves open the question of just *where* the leader is taking the congregation. This chapter focuses on becoming a better leader for holistic ministry.

Qualities of Leadership for Holistic Ministry

Effective holistic ministry leaders share certain characteristics. As with every aspect of holistic ministry, developing these qualities is a mysterious process that blends divine grace and human response. As leaders respond in faith to God's calling, the Holy Spirit "superintends, empowers, equips, gifts, guides, directs, disciplines, provides insight and delegates the authority to lead."[2] Following are ten essential qualities of a holistic ministry leader. The first six have to do with the leader's character, the last four with the leader's capabilities.

This list of critical qualities does not apply just to pastors. Often it is the pastor who is responsible for guiding and empowering the congregation's journey into holistic ministry, but in larger churches, or in churches with prominent lay leaders, someone else may play that role. Church leadership for ministry can include clergy, lay professional staff, program directors, chairs of boards, committees, task forces and ministry teams, and behind-the-scenes congregational leaders—those unofficial lay leaders whom other members emulate and whose approval is required before anything can move forward (they don't have a title, but everyone knows who they are!).

Committed Discipleship

Before people are leaders, they are disciples of Christ. To lead people in loving their neighbors, leaders must love God with their whole heart, soul, mind, and strength (Mark 12:30–31). They must have a growing faith, sound doctrine, and an earnest prayer life. And they must be able to discern the Holy Spirit's leading. Following Jesus' example, good leaders carve out time to spend alone with God, renewing their commitment and listening for the still, small voice of the Spirit. For "God does not shout His best vision through hassled Christian living. It is in the quiet that He gives the most delivering visions of life."[3] Personal spiritual renewal is the pillar upholding a leader's public ministry.

"The spiritual health of the pastor and other key leaders is intimately intertwined with that of the congregation. A congregation will rarely grow beyond the health of its pastor and key leaders."[4] If leaders lack a healthy spiritual life, the ministry of the entire congregation suffers. On the other hand, the spiritual vitality of a leader is contagious. Others will be drawn to drink from the same life-giving well that sustains a leader's compassion, witness, and enthusiasm for the church's mission.

"The tree is known by its fruit," says Matthew 12:33. One core fruit of discipleship in a leader's life is integrity and strength of character (1 Tim. 3:2–10). People will not follow leaders they do not respect and trust. Congregants can forgive a leader who makes an honest mistake, but deception, hypocrisy, and gross moral failings destroy credibility. On the other hand, a leader's vulnerability and transparency can reinforce the congregation's confidence. People need to know their leaders share the struggles, temptations, and heartaches of ministry. Trust in a leader's character, motives, spiritual maturity, and obedience to God's leading eases a congregation's natural resistance to change. David Heney writes in *Motivating Your Parish to Change*, "When a leader must present a really bold vision, people will follow even if they find the vision incredible, because they find the leader credible."[5]

A Costly, Contagious Love

Holistic ministry leaders can easily become frustrated with the church, even critical of the church—but the bottom line must be love for God's people. The ideal for leaders is Christ's love for the church, which Ephesians 5:25 compares with the faithful, self-giving love between husband and wife. Only a loving servant leader can navigate the difficult balance between nurture and outreach, displaying deep concern for the congregation's welfare without pandering to self-indulgence. When a leader pushes people to leave their comfort zones, they can tell if the leader has their best interests at heart, or if they are being used to fulfill the leader's personal agenda.

Good leaders also share God's love for the world outside the church. One pastor of a Philadelphia church, for example, found a homeless person on the church steps one Sunday morning. She stopped to help the person, even though it made the service start late (and she is usually very punctual!), because she wanted to demonstrate to the congregation that helping the needy neighbor in their midst is more important than keeping to a schedule. Godly leaders do more than just preach about love as an abstract theological ideal. In word and deed, in ways lofty and menial, they display the heart of the Good Samaritan.

Love for God and people come together in a leader's deep, long-term commitment to the theology and practice of holistic ministry. How does Life in Christ's ministry continue to flourish, despite many obstacles? A church elder attributes it to Bishop Dickie Robbins's infectious passion for reaching people with the incarnational gospel. "I've never been around someone," he says, "who had such a tremendous heart for evangelism and for hurting people. And he pours that heart into us. Even if he's not teaching on it, [it is in] his whole attitude, the way he deals with people." Discipling drug addicts, lobbying for educational reform, providing housing for low-income families, and teaching an evangelism training series are all ways that Bishop Robbins seeks to embrace his community with the love of God. Through the pastor's consistent example and persistent teachings, the congregation understands that evangelism and social ministry are both indispensable expressions of God's love.

Christlike love often entails great personal risk and sacrifice. The leaders in our study gave up many things to be in holistic ministry: a comfortable and safe living environment, a good school system for their children, more prestigious careers, leisure time, financial security. Tina, Bishop Robbins's wife and cofounder of Life in Christ, recalls her family's hardships in the early days of their ministry.

> We'd lost the house, we'd lost our car, we had to file bankruptcy. . . . [I was] sitting on the couch with my feet pulled up crying, with my Bible in my lap, saying, "Lord, please give me something to read because I can't sleep. I need a nice psalm to read." And so he told me to turn to Ezekiel 2. . . . That was when God said to Ezekiel, "I'm sending you to some people who are hard, and they're that way because their parents were that way. And I don't want you to be afraid of them." . . . [God told me], "The reason you had to give up those things was because the community's perception is that you are wealthy. And in order to reach these people, you can't have much. I want you to start where they're at and I'll bring you up." . . . That was the peace I needed to sleep.

Many holistic ministry leaders choose to relocate into their community of ministry. Rev. Richard Smith's family lives next door to a housing project near

Faith Assembly of God Church. Their presence and availability have made an impact on the community. A neighborhood resident who coordinates the church's food ministries exclaims, "Look at our pastor and his wife. His wife is a doctor! They do not have to live behind the projects. Pastor Smith is among the people, as Christ was among the people. That's what you need to be—not, 'Oh, let me give you a pair of shoes . . .' and then run to the suburbs."

Church leaders (and their families) who love the community with everything they've got are like "the good shepherd [who] lays down his life for the sheep" (John 10:11). When they proclaim the Good News, the sheep listen to their voices (John 10:16).

Faith

"Be strong and courageous!" The Lord repeated this instruction three times as he prepared Joshua to lead the Israelites into the Promised Land (Josh. 1:6, 7, 9). Faith in God's presence, power, and promises gives holistic ministry leaders the confidence to march boldly into unknown territory. Holistic ministry is an ever-changing quest that stretches leaders as well as congregants. It puts faith to the test. Often church leaders have to lead people where they do not want to go or are afraid to tread. Strong faith, not in oneself but in God and in the ministry vision from God, is what helps leaders keep the flock moving forward through seasons of doubt and discouragement. Faith-filled leaders trust in the Holy Spirit's leading yet remain open to the Spirit's correction. They act with authority, make decisions with confidence, and take risks with bold courage.

Faith also goes hand in hand with patience. It takes faith for a sower of seed to water and tend a seemingly empty field for weeks, waiting until the gardener's efforts "bear fruit with patient endurance" (Luke 8:15). Leaders are perceptive of *kairos* time, or "God's time of favor, fulfillment, and purpose."[6] A lack of trust in God's timetable can induce ministry leaders to thrust volunteers into ministry without the proper training in holistic evangelism or social work skills, to accept staff or funding sources not consistent with the church's mission, to adopt overly aggressive evangelistic methods, to settle for quick-fix emergency aid over deep-rooted development, or to give up on those who initially resist the gospel.

It takes faith to slog through the hard parts of developing holistic outreach and avoid the lure of "microwave" ministry: Triple your outreach budget with a big grant! See thousands saved by subscribing to this new program! Double your church attendance in six months or your money back! Jesus withstood Satan's temptations to pursue instant gratification, the grand spectacle, the painless shortcut. Then he went on to perform miraculous healings and preach to thousands—but in his Father's way and according to his Father's timetable.

Jesus' patient obedience showed that he trusted God to secure the fruit of his ministry. At the end of Jesus' earthly life, it didn't look as though he had much to show for his efforts. Had Jesus been interested in a show of power and flashy results, he could have built an empire for himself. But he was more interested in producing fruit that would last. Leaders who follow Jesus' example of trusting obedience are encouraged by the promise of Galatians 6:9: "Let us not grow weary in doing what is right, for we will reap at harvesttime, if we do not give up." The test of holistic ministry leadership is faithfulness to God's calling despite obstacles from inside and outside the church and—at times—limited results.

Humility

Leaders must beware of the temptation to think that "they, and they alone, really know what is best for everyone; only they can set the course, only they can sail the ship. These leaders will soon be alone."[7] Egotistical, power-hungry leaders do not last long in holistic ministry. Leaders who crave approval and many followers are generally reluctant to give risky or unpopular orders. Effective leaders do give marching orders—but in the spirit of Christlike humility, as a servant to those who follow them. Jesus' words turn the world's notion of leadership upside down: "Whoever wishes to become great among you must be your servant" (Mark 10:43). The paradox of leadership is that authority rests in submission, greatness resides in servitude, and glory lies in exalting God's glory alone.

Confidence and humility are not contradictory qualities. As Moses rallied the Israelites to follow him to the Promised Land, he humbly acknowledged that his authority and guidance came solely from God. When Pastor Jerome Simmons was complimented on his leadership in the ministry of Jobs Partnership, he laughed and said that his confidence in the program's success rests not in his leadership ability but in the assurance that God wants it to happen. Humble leaders allow themselves and others the freedom and grace to make mistakes, particularly when it comes to new ministry ventures. They grow by learning from trial and error. The words "I was wrong" do not undermine a leader's authority. Leaders are not threatened by critical feedback, because they accept the necessity of divine pruning.

Rev. Bill Borror of Media Presbyterian Church says one of the main qualities he looks for in prospective leaders is teachability. "Are you willing to be led? Are you willing to grow in the faith if you're not where you're supposed to be?" Teachable leaders have the posture of a learner, particularly when cross-cultural ministry is involved. Joel Van Dyke, co-pastor of Bethel Temple Community Bible Church, learned this from his mentor, theologian Manny Ortiz. "One of his constant sayings was that you need to sit at the foot of the culture in which you are ministering and serving . . . being a student as opposed to being the teacher." As an Anglo ministering in a predominantly Latino community, Rev. Van Dyke says, "I see myself as the student of what's happening around me." Eagerness to learn from others keeps leaders in holistic ministry from becoming condescending and paternalistic toward those they serve and helps the growth of relationships that can lead to evangelism.

One sign that a leader is a learner is having an ongoing relationship with a mentor. Leaders never grow out of the need for a personal mentor to provide spiritual wisdom, guidance, correction, and advice. Without a mentoring relationship, leaders and their ministries risk stagnation, elitism, and myopic vision.

Flexibility

If you like safety, well-laid long-range plans, goals, strategies and objectives, decency and order, i's dotted and t's crossed, then stay out of holistic ministry. It's too messy, mysterious, open-ended, confounding, and confusing. Why? Because holistic ministry centers on people. And human beings are gloriously, maddeningly complex. They refuse to be categorized, standardized, stereotyped, or normalized. While patterns and social trends are often evident, at root each person and life situation are unique. That is why it is such a challenge to respond to the variety and volume of problems that come as God's opportunity for us to use our spiritual gifts and skills.

How do agents of spiritual and social transformation minister in the new millennium? By cultivating leadership for change. Cutting-edge ministry leaders are able to tolerate seasons of ambiguity and weather storms of change. They think outside the box in creative problem solving. They welcome diversity of cultures, ages, classes, and abilities, and they learn the best way of communicating to each group. They accept that it is impossible to discern God's direction fully, either in the details of the moment or in the future big picture, for as the apostle Paul said, "Now we see through a glass, darkly" (1 Cor. 13:12 KJV). They expect the unexpected and roll with the punches. Even after the church has established a trajectory of sharing the Good News in word and deed, good leaders remain open to redirection and adjustments in the church's mission. Effective holistic ministry leaders take their cue from

> a God of surprises, indeed, a God who works by irony, who can use even opponents of the mission to move the divine purpose forward. The mission must work within limits, but God repeatedly breaks out of these limits in ways that surprise both the church and its critics. Faithfully serving in mission while trusting in a God whose exact moves cannot be anticipated is a part of the ongoing struggle of faith.[8]

Moreover, if leaders would be transformation agents in the world, they must remain open to radical change within. Radical personal change is triggered by an event or idea that shakes us, as leaders and disciples, to the core of our being. In his book *Taking Discipleship Seriously,* Tom Sine calls for "whole life conversion," including personal life, ethics, family life, career, stewardship, and ministry. The process of conversion is ongoing, with peaks and valleys, but it is always taking us somewhere new. "Walk in newness of life," urges Paul in Romans 6:4. Ongoing personal transformation is the ground for radical holistic ministry. Followers will not move forward in holistic ministry unless their leaders—challenged, guided, and empowered by God's Spirit—are flexible enough to model the way.

Vision

An essential quality of leadership for ministry is the capacity to generate, communicate, and sustain the ownership of vision in the congregation. A congregation's vision shapes its ministry in response to the questions, Who are we? What is our purpose? What is God calling us to do? A vision is born out of a sense of dissonance between God's ideals and the present reality. Leaders are able to bring the congregation under the guidance of the vision. "The visionary leader is someone who assumes responsibility for transforming reality and practices the art of getting others to want to contribute to the transformation."[9] Vision does not originate solely from the upper levels of leadership, but the congregation looks to its leaders to embody, communicate, and advocate for the vision.

Visionary leaders move from a perception of a need to a plan of action. Rev. Moore tells the story of how Tenth Memorial Baptist Church developed a senior housing complex providing safe, affordable shelter for sixty seniors. "The vision came out of an experience with an older member of the congregation. She was living in substandard housing. One morning her house caught on fire and the woman died. At that point, I vowed that no senior citizen should have to live in substandard housing."

Leaders must be farsighted, able to look past the demands, delays, and disappointments of the moment to the promise of the future goal. As the vision becomes reality, leaders use success stories to strengthen the vision in others and galvanize further action. Despite initial difficulties in obtaining the needed funding for the project, Rev. Moore persisted. And in the end, the vision bore much fruit. He recalls:

> The story that stands out in my mind is an elderly lady who was living in a drug-infested apartment. She spent most of her money on rent, and never was able to go to sleep at night. I'll never forget the day that she moved into the senior

citizens' home. The next morning, she literally kissed the floor and said, "This is the first full night's sleep that I've had in ten years."

A good leader is not possessive of the vision. Ideally, each member whom a leader recruits into ministry "feels a sense of leadership, of ownership, and of responsibility to teach others to understand and follow the mission."[10] A leader of Acts 29, a nonprofit ministry that partners with Faith Assembly of God, observes, "One special quality about Faith Assembly is that the vision started with Pastor Smith, but now it is obvious that others share the vision, that the love for people and for the lost is really in other people's hearts as well now." This sense of shared vision is the goal.

Part 3 explains more about the process of developing, communicating, and implementing a congregational vision for ministry.

Ability to Build Up People

"The best leaders have never merely pointed the way. They have said, 'C'mon, let's go!'"[11] As effective holistic ministry leaders help the congregation take ownership of the vision, they also recruit and empower the congregation to participate in the ministry vision. A leader reminds the congregation that each person has a valuable piece of the ministry puzzle, and they help members discern where their pieces fit. "No one we lead should ever wonder, 'What should I be doing around here?'"[12] Leaders do not wait for members to step forward to help them explore their contribution.

One church member at Life in Christ gave the analogy of quiet, unobtrusive church members being like cells that the body does not know are important, until something goes wrong with them. At her previous church, she felt like one of those cells. She did not want to call attention to herself, but she wanted to have a role. One of the things that drew her to Life in Christ was the way Bishop Robbins stressed participation in ministry as a condition of membership. This teaching helped her to connect her work with the Social Security Administration with a call to join the church's new political action ministry.

An elder at Life in Christ preached a sermon at the Drug Free ministry that ended with this definition of grace: "The empowering ability of God to enable you to be what you're called to be and do what you're called to do." Leadership is to be a vehicle of this empowering grace. Leadership "exists for the express purpose of serving the church, equipping the saints, and enabling their ministry to the world."[13] Leaders equip people on several levels: developing skills, strengthening spiritual vitality, exploring capacity for leadership. Carl Dudley also points to the leader's role as "theological coach"—"the one with a megaphone who unites the voices of believers with new energy to play the game."[14] Leaders can employ a variety of means to empower members for ministry: through mentoring relationships, training programs, supervision of hands-on ministry opportunities, and preaching and teaching on ministry.

A key point is that holistic ministry leaders do not use people to get ministry done—rather, they develop people through ministry. They see participation in ministry as a maturation process aimed at helping church members become more Christlike. A Faith Assembly of God volunteer described Rev. Richard Smith in the following way: "Our pastor puts us in positions where we have to grow."

Ability to Serve as a Catalyst

"Dynamic," is how one Tenth Memorial Church member described Rev. William Moore. "He's a real motivator. . . . He believes that it's going to get better, that the church can make a difference in the community. He doesn't sit back—he just does things." In other words, Rev. Moore is a catalyst.

A catalyst is something that sparks an active response. Many alleged leaders can spin grand visions—but somehow, little seems to come of them. Real leaders make things happen. They are not just satisfied with dreaming dreams; they work to bridge the gap between dreams and reality. They turn ideas into action. Holistic ministry leaders often have entrepreneurial, charismatic personalities that magnetically sweep people and events along behind them. Others are behind-the-scenes leaders who quietly and efficiently accomplish their goals. Leaders function with different styles at different paces, but they are driven by an energy that does not rest until they see the desired changes. They are strategists with a grasp of the steps needed to achieve a plan, and when faced with obstacles, they construct alternate routes.

The image of a visionary is someone with his or her head in the clouds, but holistic leaders are also grounded in the nitty-gritty of ministry operations. Granted, not every leader is a natural organizer or administrator. Some leaders in the churches we studied had exceptional organizational skills. Others were conspicuously disorganized. So to be effective, they rallied others with administrative gifts to perform those functions.

A catalyst by its nature is not a one-person show. Catalysts are not remarkable for the amount of work they get done but for the accomplishments of others that they inspire and coordinate. They bring "the power of ethical, inspiring influence and enablement" to bear in getting others to join in working toward their vision.[15] Leaders must be comfortable with delegating. For many this may involve a paradigm shift in their understanding of the function of a leader—from doing ministry to preparing others to do ministry. Carl Dudley's research on church-based social ministries found that pastors were twice as likely to be doers than delegators, but that ministry projects were twice as likely to succeed if the pastor was an effective delegator.[16] Catalysts foster a climate where delegated efforts can succeed. They tap into the needed resources, create training and support systems, and set multiple wheels in motion to bring ministry visions to fruition.

Ability to Connect People

The previous characteristic suggests that holistic ministry leaders must be consummate networkers. They continually look for ways to connect resources with needs, partners with programs, people with opportunities to serve. This quality is particularly essential in churches with few resources. Effective ministry leaders multiply their church's impact by building bridges to outside resources. Their radar is always alert for potential ministry assets and allies. For example, Heidi was talking with Pastor Jerome Simmons outside Koinonia Christian Community Church one day when a horse went by. Pastor Simmons stopped the horse's rider to introduce himself, saying, "Tell your boss I'm interested in pony rides for our summer kid's camp, and let's see what we can work out." Connectors are good at "sniffing out" people's skills and spiritual gifts, finding out where their interests intersect with the church's goals. They are also effective at translating the church's mission to outsiders in a way that motivates people to share in the vision.

Like other small churches we studied, Germantown Church of the Brethren has an astonishing amount of ministry for a church of its size and budget. A key factor is Rev. Kyerematen's ability to recognize and recruit the ministry gifts of the people who cross his path. Rev. Kyerematen first met the man who became the counselor at the church's family center in a supermarket! Their wives had stopped to talk, and Rev. Kyerematen and Elijah were introduced. Rev. Kyerematen learned that Elijah needed to build up hours of practical counseling experience for his degree and immediately invited him to work with the many recovering drug addicts and homeless persons who regularly came through the church. This win-win proposal led to the founding of the counseling program and a ten-year collaboration. In another instance, the then-director of planning for the Philadelphia Housing Department was researching development projects in the church's neighborhood. When she interviewed Rev. Kyerematen for her report, he learned that she had experience in grant writing. He arranged for her to write several proposals that have helped fund the family center.

Within the congregation, leaders must also be able to help people connect the dots between their skills and spiritual gifts, their ministry calling, and the needs and opportunities at hand. When we asked ministry participants how they came to be involved, they typically answered that the pastor or ministry leader had personally invited them. Good leaders prayerfully select and persistently recruit people for ministry, not leaving it up to the members to plug themselves in. People may not recognize their own talents, or it may not occur to them to apply their "secular" skills to ministry. They may think they don't have the time. They may think the church already has all the help it needs. They may be a "Jonah," hiding from a calling they are reluctant to follow. Leaders must discern the setting where people's gifts can blossom and gently but persuasively draw them into it.

Ability to Maintain Perspective

The final essential quality for leaders of holistic ministry is the ability to keep the big picture of a holistic vision in perspective. Keeping the church's mission in focus helps a leader avoid getting sidetracked by nonessentials, discouraged by minor setbacks, or overwhelmed by details. As always, the model for keeping the course is Jesus—"who for the sake of the joy that was set before him endured the cross, disregarding its shame, and has taken his seat at the right hand of the throne of God. Consider him . . . so that you may not grow weary or lose heart" (Heb. 12:2–3). The crisis of the moment can never compare with the glory of seeing the Father's kingdom come in a community.

Leadership is a continual balancing act. Leading a church or ministry program involves navigating multiple, sometimes competing, elements: the personal (nurturing the needs of individuals); the group (developing healthy organizational dynamics); and the task (performing the job to be done). The leader must be "able to keep all three focused at the same time, carefully balancing and assigning proper weight and attention to each, never sacrificing one in order to achieve the other."[17] In making ministry decisions, leaders have to weigh short-term against long-term goals, opportunities against costs. A leader also has to be able to step back and assess the church's balance of evangelism and social ministry against the holistic paradigm. Only by maintaining a big-picture perspective can leaders make wise decisions while keeping all the requisite balls in the air.

Mission perspective is also essential to the leadership task of setting appropriate boundaries. The demands and possibilities of ministry are unending. Thus, churches need leaders like Rev. James Kraft, described by a First Presbyterian Church staff member as "the standard bearer, the sea anchor who keeps us from going after every idea that comes to our heads." Leaders have to know when to say no. "Personal and corporate opportunity does not mean calling," warn Mark Gornik and Noel Castellanos in *Restoring At-Risk Communities*. "Be willing and ready to turn down everything from speaking requests to program dollars if it will not help you fulfill your ministry goals. Guard carefully your time and energy."[18] Leaders who plan in terms of the church's core purpose will not feel guilty about passing up a grant to start a senior center if the church's vision calls for developing holistic youth ministries. When lay leaders come to Bishop Dickie Robbins with suggestions for new ministries, he asks them, "Will it take you from the primary focus that God has given you? Is it good or is it God? . . . Because you can find yourself involved in too many good things, and you miss the primary call that God has for you."

These ten qualities are basic to effective holistic ministry leadership, but no two leaders "wear" them in the same way. Leaders wear a variety of styles: Some leaders are up-front and directive, while others exert a more subtle influence from behind the scenes; some are very verbal, while others lead primarily by example; some play a central role in developing and implementing the church's ministry vision, while others see their role in terms of guiding, empowering, and coordinating individual members to carry out the vision. Cultivating the most appropriate style of leadership is a matter of prayer, observation, and self-reflection. Wise leaders also take into consideration the church's "personality," ethnic and denominational heritage, and stage of ministry development—the extent to which the congregation shares a common vision, is spiritually mature, and has ministry experience, for example. Changing seasons of ministry call for an evolving style of leadership.

Team Ministry

Although this chapter has referred to "the leader," the reality is that a healthy congregation has a team of interdependent leaders. "Leadership is always complementary. Ministry happens when clergy and laity mesh their strengths and compensate for their weaknesses in working toward a common end within the culture of the congregation."[19] A leadership team may be formalized in the church's structure (as in a co-pastorate or an elder board with the pastor as one among equals), or it may take shape more informally, as when a pastor and group of lay leaders develop a close working relationship. The important thing is that the collective leadership contains the blend of skills and styles necessary to grow holistic ministry in the congregation.

A leadership team in which each member uses his or her unique gifts in complementary ways flows from the biblical image of the church as one body with many parts (1 Corinthians 12). The "people person" on the leadership team needs the strategic planner. The fund-raiser needs the theologian. The entrepreneurial leader who launches new enterprises needs the steady leader who is gifted at holding the course. In particular, visionary leaders often need the complement of nuts-and-bolts managers, as Barbara Williams Skinner explains:

> Leaders are those who inspire others toward a vision of the way things should be. Yet, vision and inspiration alone are not enough to make things happen. . . .
> It takes leaders to dream about creating a school that motivates children to learn
> . . . but it takes managers to run the school with efficiency and excellence once

it is created. It takes leaders to shape a vision for an urban youth center . . . but it takes managers to develop the curriculum, the schedule, the funding and the staffing to run the program effectively.[20]

A team is built not only around strengths and weaknesses but also around differences in leaders' sense of calling. Bethel Temple's Rev. Lou Centeno, for example, has a passion for evangelism and discipleship, particularly among recovering substance abusers. He preaches regularly at revivals and open-air services. Co-pastor Joel Van Dyke recognizes the importance of evangelism, but he acknowledges, "Evangelism that way is not my heart. That's not my driving passion. I don't get up in the morning excited about going on the street corners. I go out in the morning excited about training leaders." Their relationship frees each to focus on what they feel called to do.

Teamwork of a different sort has developed between Pastor Donna Jones and church board chair Wilhelmina at Cookman United Methodist Church. A former welfare recipient with a vision disability, Wilhelmina connects with the congregation with greater ease than Rev. Jones, a seminary-trained former corporate professional. "Even though she and I share a similar viewpoint," comments Wilhelmina about her relationship with Rev. Jones, "she can never sit amongst the congregation like I do." Wilhelmina helps "translate" the congregation's culture and relay members' feedback to Rev. Jones, and vice versa. When Wilhelmina encourages hurting women in the church's welfare-to-work program by reminding them, "You are a precious child of the King!" it has a different impact than when Rev. Jones says it—because, as Wilhelmina notes, "She's *supposed* to say it. That's her job." Of course, Rev. Jones is not just mouthing the words; she truly has a heart for comforting and empowering women. As a lay leader, however, Wilhelmina has a different rapport with the women that brings her unique ministry opportunities.

Unity of purpose in a diversity of gifts characterizes an effective leadership team. A firm foundation of healthy relationships—characterized by accountability, openness, mutual trust, and respect—supports long-term commitment to mission. Personality differences, squabbles over "turf" or theological minutia, and competing ministry visions in the leadership team will undercut the church's outreach. On the other hand, affirms a New Covenant lay leader, God can accomplish great things through "a group of people who are united, who have vision, who are committed, who have effective communications, and who are also in God's will."

Reproductive Leadership

Moses sat as judge for the people, while the people stood around him from morning until evening. . . . Moses' father-in-law said to him, "What you are doing is not good. You will surely wear yourself out, both you and these people with you. For the task is too heavy for you; you cannot do it alone."

Exodus 18:13, 17–18

This story from Exodus illustrates that religious leaders have always been prone to "Atlasitis"—allowing the full burden of ministry to rest on their shoulders. Leaders can be so overwhelmed by the press of immediate tasks that they fail to recognize the potential under their noses for sharing their load and multiplying their impact. For holistic ministry to be effective both in the short and the long term, church leaders must engage in "reproductive leadership,"[21] that is, leadership that reproduces leadership qualities and capabilities in others.

The exchange between Moses and Jethro suggests several benefits of new leadership development. First, it saved Moses from burnout. The tendency in many churches is to install good leaders and work them to death. The pressure on existing leaders can be relieved by expanding the workforce and by preparing substitutes for times of staff turnover, leaves of absence, and ministry sabbaticals. Second, it helps to ensure continuity of vision. Would your church's holistic mission carry on without you? "Every leader's role is to prepare each ministry to be an equipping link to the next generation of leaders."[22] Third, leadership development strengthens the process of helping the congregation take ownership of the vision. "When the leader shares power with other people, those people in turn feel more strongly attached to the leader and more committed to effectively carrying out their responsibilities."[23] The judges Moses trained gained new knowledge and reverence for God's law, as well as a better appreciation for Moses' leadership. Fourth, expanding the pool of skilled, committed leaders better serves the community. It improves the quality and quantity of social services and creates more opportunities for unchurched people to interact with mature Christians.

Leadership development is part of God's plan for the church. The gifts of leadership are to be used "to equip the saints for the work of ministry" (Eph. 4:12). If existing leaders fail to recognize and nurture God's call in an emerging leader, they thwart the work of the Holy Spirit in that person's life and in the life of the congregation. Moreover, because leadership development brings out the best of God's design in people, it is another way that a church loves and nurtures its members. "The more we train people to lead, the more they are blessed in their 'secular' jobs," observes a New Covenant leadership trainer. "If you can be a leader in a church, you can be a leader anywhere." New Covenant has found that developing people's leadership skills has often improved their overall quality of life. Leadership development in the church is particularly important among populations who have typically been disempowered by society—such as minorities, people with disabilities, or people without access to quality education.

For busy church leaders, new leadership development may feel like an inefficient distraction from the press of urgent ministry demands. Showing someone how to do something usually takes twice as long as doing it yourself. But Jesus' ministry demonstrated the priority of leadership development over short-term efficiency. He could have organized his ministry in assembly-line fashion, to teach and heal the greatest number in the shortest amount of time. Some days, in fact, that was what Jesus did. But he invested significant amounts of his limited time on earth developing a close mentoring relationship with his disciples. This investment laid the foundation for the explosive growth of the church after Jesus' ascension.

What should you look for in prospective ministry leaders? Clearly, signs of the ten qualities listed above indicate leadership material. Look for someone who consistently serves and witnesses to others in low-key, spontaneous ways, as a holistic servant leader in the making; someone who takes initiative and tends to attract a crowd, as a budding catalyst; someone who has had an experience of stepping out on a limb of faith or weathering a period of ambiguity and change, as an ally in helping the congregation develop new holistic outreach.

When considering a person's qualifications for leadership, don't overlook people who have experienced transformation relevant to the church's area of ministry. Consider the "success stories" among those served by your church's outreach to see if they may be potential ministry leaders. Most of the current leadership of Life in Christ, for example, began as converts in the church's Drug Free ministry. Bishop Dickie Robbins personally discipled the men who eventually became the elders of the church. He stuck with them through their addiction because he recognized the potential power of their testimony. They in turn responded to his love and commitment and eventually dedicated their lives in service to a holistic vision.[24]

Most importantly, select people who are willing to share the vision and mission of your church. You don't want lay leaders who are automatons, submitting in lockstep fashion. But there has to be some consensus of purpose, says a lay leader at New Covenant, else you end up with "leadership with their own agenda, with the vision of the church going one direction and their vision going another direction." If leaders do not buy into the vision, they will wander off by themselves, or worse, wander away with some of the sheep from the fold.

Tools such as temperament and personality indicators (e.g., Myers-Briggs) can help assess an individual's potential place in the leadership team. But no matter how much information you gather, there remains an element of art and mystique to identifying and developing leaders. Discerning God's guidance for current and prospective ministry leaders is rooted in prayer (Matt. 9:37–38; 2 Cor. 1:11). Jesus prayed before selecting his disciples, prayed for his disciples, and then prayed for future generations of their disciples (Luke 6:12–13; John 17:9–20).

New Covenant Church: A Crucible of Leadership Development

New Covenant Church of Philadelphia has thirty-five hundred members. About four hundred of the members are in positions of leadership or leadership-in-training, with fifty-six of these on staff. How does the church generate this remarkable level of leadership?

In the mid-1990s, about a dozen years after its founding, the leadership of New Covenant felt the church had become static. In 1996, they accepted a new visionary challenge based on Isaiah 54:2–3: to rebuild communities all around Philadelphia. Developing strong lay leaders, they saw, was the necessary foundation for a period of expansion. In a leadership retreat, they were guided by the Holy Spirit to develop a system of leadership development based on small groups. New Covenant's small groups, called NetCare (introduced in the previous chapter), for years had been primarily oriented toward church members. With the church's growing emphasis on outreach, the focus shifted to "how to empower people to go forth to take the Good News of the gospel to those they meet," says Saundra, a NetCare Zone Minister.

NetCare has proven an excellent vehicle for leadership development. The small groups provide opportunities for skill development in a structured, supervised context. Within each NetCare group, leadership is shared by a team with clearly defined roles, which helps establish accountability. The positions carry different levels of responsibility so that people with minimal leadership experience can start their involvement by taking on very basic assignments, such as being in charge of the music or the refreshments. Each leader has an assistant, chosen by the leadership team, so that when the group gets large enough to multiply, they already have leaders in place.

A well-defined leadership ladder encourages people to advance in degrees of responsibility and supervision. The structure of authority flows from the pastors, to four directors of NetCare (two married couples), to eight Zone Ministers, to NetCare group leadership. Most leadership positions at the upper levels are occupied by a married couple, which strengthens the family as well as the position. NetCare leaders meet with their overseeing minister at least once a month. Supervisors adjust their oversight based on the lay leaders' experience and competence.

NetCare leaders and the hundreds of other church leaders are also supported by monthly leadership breakfasts and Bible studies, led by the pastoral staff. Prospective ministry leaders must attend at least two of these meetings before taking on solo responsibilities. Bishop Milton Grannum also teaches a ministry of management class and periodic leadership seminars, which not only impart leadership skills but shape a consensus of purpose. An annual retreat gives leaders a break from their day-to-day tasks to refocus on the big picture of mission.

Along with the formal training opportunities, Bishop Grannum stresses personal mentoring as a leadership development tool. Emerging leaders need not only *information* about the theology and skills for ministry but also *formation* as disciples and whole persons through mentoring relationships with other leaders. Existing leaders serve as a living textbook for the church's mission. Ten years ago, Bishop Grannum invited a select group of men in his church to meet with him for a Bible study twice a week, at 5:30 A.M.—a sure test of commitment! He selected the men based on "what I saw they could become." The purpose of these meetings, says Bishop Grannum, was to give prospective leaders a chance to "get to know my mind," and he theirs. Out of this close-knit group came a core team of elders and ministry leaders.

As senior pastor, Bishop Grannum sees his role in leadership development as twofold: to articulate the vision of the church and to empower people to accomplish it. The church's strategy, he explains, is to help people find "their area of call, the things that are burning in their spirits, and commit themselves to it. . . . What we do as a corporate body is raise the level of competence, confidence, and skills so that [leaders] can function better." A ministry leader at New Covenant Church praises Bishop Grannum for keeping a healthy balance between holding leaders accountable and helping them grow into positions of authority. "He gives you all the freedom you need," she says, "but when you call him to get involved, he comes."

Saundra's story is typical of New Covenant leadership. After she and her husband began attending the church, a ministry leader encouraged them to pursue more active involvement. They started serving with NetCare as assistant group leaders and "worked their way up," becoming coordinators and eventually Zone Ministers as supervisors recognized their gifts of leadership. Saundra's zeal for the church's holistic vision sustains her commitment despite living forty-five minutes from the church and working full-time at another job. "We have found our passion at New Covenant," she says.

The fundamental role of NetCare leaders, Saundra explains, is to "build relationships that will edify and will change lives for the glory of God." New Covenant's deliberate, disciplined system for leadership development equips people with both the skills and the passion to fulfill this mission.

Conclusion

What does a church need to make a difference? Leaders with a growing relationship with God and passion for sharing Christ's love with the lost and broken. Leaders who minister with bold faith, gracious humility, risk-taking flexibility, and a balanced perspective on life and ministry. Leaders who are connectors, catalysts, and agents of change in their church and community. Leaders who encourage and equip people to share in the church's vision and who recognize and cultivate the strengths of others on the leadership team and in the congregation.

But what if your church's leadership is not there yet? What if, as a church leader, *you* are not there yet? Does this mean your congregation has no hope of cultivating dynamic holistic outreach? Not at all—but it does mean the congregation will need to dig in with prayer and take a longer view of the process.

Dr. David Apple reflects on the lesson in prayerful patience he learned in his decade of developing mercy ministries at Tenth Presbyterian Church:

> We're dealing with a three-mile-an-hour God, and I'm in the fast lane. It takes a long time for God to act, from my way of seeing things. This is the same God who could have gotten Moses the nine miles to the Promised Land pretty quickly—but it had to take forty years in order to build up a leadership, and a community, and a servant heart, and a respect for God's perfect timetable.

In his early years at Tenth Church, Dr. Apple was impatient to start ministries and sometimes used the Bible to bludgeon people with his ideas about what needed to happen. But he gradually learned "the discipline of active waiting" and came to put his trust in the transformational power of the Spirit instead. In time, God raised up other mission-minded leaders, and Tenth Church now supports a spectrum of fruitful holistic ministries.

It is God's design to supply the church with gifted leadership (1 Cor. 12:28). God will accomplish great things in the kingdom through leaders and the congregants they serve who are faithful in taking the first steps toward holistic ministry (Matt. 25:21).

chapter ten

A Ministry-Centered Organizational Structure

Organization puts ideas on wheels, translates faith into action, and enables our vision or ministry to become a tangible reality.[1]

If holistic mission is the soul of the church, a solid organizational structure is the body, giving it bone and muscle. Systems for planning and implementation provide the skeletal framework for getting things done. Communications systems circulate information and ideas, heading off stagnation and conflict. The church gathers resources from members, partner agencies, and the community and uses them to fuel kingdom work. People power—time and talents—is the muscle implementing the church's ministry. And through it all throbs the life-giving Holy Spirit, holding body and soul together.

Warning Signs of an Unhealthy Organization

Without a healthy body, the soul loses its spark. Setting up an effective structure and keeping it running smoothly may not be glamorous, but both are essential if the church is to fulfill its high calling. How healthy are your church's organizational systems? Three warning signs indicate a need to renovate a church's structure.

1. *A lack of organization.* Disorganization is no more a sign of spirituality than messiness is a sign of genius. There are several classic excuses for disorganization. The laid-back version: "We just go with the flow and leave things up to the Holy Spirit." The harried version: "Who has time to get organized? We're too busy doing God's work." The intense version: "We're on the cutting edge of community ministry. Organization is a luxury we can't afford."

Do not confuse disorganization with Spirit-led spontaneity. There is nothing super-spiritual about chaos. God desires order in the church (1 Cor. 14:40). While organization takes time and energy, the cost of disorganization is even higher: missed deadlines for proposals, late fees on bills, lost time spent looking for buried files, frazzled staff, mismatched or unsupervised volunteers, repair costs for equipment not maintained properly. A well-run system is flexible enough to adjust to the disorderly and unpredictable realities of daily life but structured enough not to be at their mercy. The goal of organization is for the right people to focus on the right tasks at the right time with the right tools, instead of scrambling to cover for what should have been done by someone else last week.

2. *An overemphasis on structure and efficiency as the goal, rather than a means to an end.* If a church does not keep the higher purposes for its existence in clear view, it may "fall subject to the illusion that managing the organization is equivalent to being the church."[2] Such a church is likely to resist innovation, because the cry "We've never done it that way before!" drowns out the voices calling for change. In churches that place too high a premium on order and traditional ways of doing things, ministries become as rigidly bureaucratic as government programs, and the gifts of those who think outside the box are lost.

When religious organizations "lose their vitality, when programs and projects replace relationships, when structures leave no room for the Holy Spirit, and when control squelches growth," Mary Thiessen warns, "sometimes God intervenes with crises."[3] Leaders who pursue holistic ministry must be prepared for God to break the mold, to "reorder priorities and reorganize schedules." It's an uncomfortable process, but out of the uncertainty can come a liberating openness to the movement of the Spirit.

3. *The church is efficiently organized to serve a purpose—but it is the wrong purpose.* There is a mismatch between what God is calling the church to do and what its systems and routines are set up to do. The church may be organized primarily to satisfy the needs of its own members, for example, or to perpetuate its endowment or to enhance its status and reputation in the community. As a congregation strengthens its commitment to holistic mission, it needs to examine whether its structures help or hinder the goal of reaching out in word and deed. "The shape of the church must be determined by its mission.

Often the reverse is true," notes Tom Nees, administrative director of Nazarene Compassionate Ministries. "Creating appropriate organizational structures to carry out the mission of the church is in itself of theological importance."[4]

"The bottom line," writes Amy Sherman, "is whether we're being faithful stewards of the resources, time and talents God has given us for the purpose of loving our neighbors. If the old ways aren't working, it may be time for us to start pouring our love out of new wineskins."[5] Is it time for your church to create some new wineskins? Restructuring the church is not a substitute for revival—it will not make people more loving or more self-sacrificially dedicated to Christ—but it can define and ease the path that you are asking the congregation to take.

Organizing for Holistic Ministry

Six critical organizational tasks of the church have direct bearing on holistic ministry. (In addition, of course, churches must have the usual behind-the-scenes administrative functions that are basic to the operation of any institution: accounting, handling bills and payroll, maintaining facilities, keeping records, and so on). What must church structures accomplish for the church's holistic mission to succeed?

Make and Implement Ministry-Related Decisions

During the process of developing holistic ministry, expect your church to be inundated with new questions and choices. Should the church revise its mission statement? Which ministries should you start, and in what order? Will you accept government grants? What qualifications should you require of prospective program staff? Should ministry beneficiaries be expected to contribute anything in return for services? Ministry decisions relate to three basic categories: the church's overall vision; ministry life cycles (creating, expanding, altering, or discontinuing); and day-to-day administration.

Every church has a different process for making decisions, reflected in the structure of the church's central governing body and the broader organizational flowchart (committees, boards, etc.). The process of making decisions is less important, however, than the values and theological principles that guide the process. Try to anticipate how your system of governance is likely to handle the kinds of questions that the holistic ministry journey will generate. Is the system designed to protect the church from the world or to equip the church to go out into the world? To serve its members or to empower its members to serve? To preserve the status quo or to adapt to the ever-changing context for ministry? Examine the last five major decisions your governing body faced.

What core values were reflected in the deliberation process and the outcomes? Developing holistic ministry is a process of aligning the core values of the decision-making body with the church's mission.

Good leaders work within the system whenever possible and gently push for changes as they go. For example, a pastor might begin working with the board of deacons to help them understand and restructure their role in light of Acts 6, where "the diaconate represents that body of persons whose major function is that of managing the Church's benevolence, charity, and relief programs."[6] In a church that has a lopsided focus on evangelism, the evangelism committee could launch a "service evangelism campaign" charged with training members to carry out holistic service projects.

But good leaders also know when they have to work around the system or even dismantle existing structures to create new pathways for making wise decisions and getting things done. Consider, for example, a congregation that commissions the building and maintenance committee to explore the possibility of renovating a wing of the church for a new youth center. Like most maintenance committees, the members are dedicated to keeping the building in good shape, and they balk at intentionally exposing the facilities to the ravages of children. Committee meetings focus on issues of cost and liability, without much reference to the church's mission or to the community's need. The committee deliberates for six months and at the end votes not to start a center but to send a check to the denomination's youth ministry fund instead.

Now consider an alternative organizational approach. The governing body of the congregation appoints a new ministry group to explore the youth center, which includes representation from the building committee and the finance committee but also from parents, youth likely to be served by the new youth center, and the volunteers/staff who will operate it. This new committee is chaired by a mature member of the congregation who enthusiastically embraces the church's vision for holistic outreach and who meets regularly with the pastor and other church leadership. Once a month, the ministry group joins the members of all the other church committees for a Bible study on the church's mission, led by the pastor. This gathering includes time for sharing and prayer, giving the "old guard" a chance to rub shoulders with new ministry recruits and to air suggestions and concerns. It takes time to clear up all the questions and conflicts that arise, but gradually the ministry group completes a strategic plan for the youth center, backed by the key leaders in the congregation.

Decisions are valid only if they can be implemented. Bringing a vision into reality requires the discipline, as Barbara Skinner calls it, of "planning the work and working the plan."[7] Without getting bogged down in minutiae, every ministry decision should indicate *what* action steps are required to carry it out, *who* will do the work, *when* it should be completed, and *how* the leadership will follow up on the progress of the plan. Excellent resources are available to help churches develop an action plan or set up committees to carry them out. (See Carl Dudley's *Basic Steps toward Community Ministry* and Timothy Keller's *Ministries of Mercy: The Call of the Jericho Road*.) While time-tested organizational strategies can help, there is no one right way to move from vision to plan to ministry. "The task of organizing is a puzzle to be solved, not a blueprint to be followed," writes Dudley.[8] Flexibility within a structured, accountable framework is a key to implementation.

The church's leadership team must be able to see how all the church's systems fit together as a whole to make ministry work. A GED program, for example, may involve the finance committee in fund-raising and accounting, the office support staff in answering calls and photocopying materials, the media or public relations committee in placing an ad in the local paper, the evangelism committee in ordering Christian literature to distribute in the program, and the maintenance committee in making sure there is extra toilet paper in the bathrooms. Effective implementation requires organizational foresight, but it also depends on an attitude of teamwork. The director of operations at New Covenant exemplifies this attitude, as his team carries out the behind-the-scenes work necessary for the church's ministries to thrive. "We're not here to be a stumbling block for the ministries," he says. "We're here to make the programs better."

A creative approach to organization that blends empowering structures, focus on the church's mission, and supportive relationships can liberate the church to embrace the new opportunities—and weather the risks—of holistic ministry.

Facilitate Communication

Communication is vital to the health of any organization. For churches in the midst of change and activity, the need for the open exchange of information, ideas, and concerns is multiplied. Communication must flow in multiple directions: among the leadership, from the leadership to the congregation, and from the congregation to the leadership. An organizational system must allow for sharing and accountability among vision makers (those who influence the church's theology and mission), vision managers (those who make the decisions regarding how the vision will be fleshed out in ministry), and vision implementers (those who carry out or financially support ministry decisions).

Among busy church staff, avenues of communication must become a priority and a habit. Regular staff meetings are essential for announcing information, making plans, brainstorming new ideas, tackling problems, sharing prayer requests and personal needs, and rekindling dedication to holistic mission. Planning special events outside routine meeting times, such as staff retreats and the occasional pizza night, encourages sharing on a more personal level. Bethel Temple staff, for example, were feeling isolated from one another in the press of inner-city ministry, so they began the tradition of celebrating staff birthdays by going out to eat as a group. In addition to group meetings, pastors should plan to meet regularly (at least once a month) with ministry leaders one-on-one. This allows the pastor to give constructive criticism in a private setting and prompts people who feel shy in a group to speak their minds more freely.

Communication among ministry leaders both averts conflicts and generates inspiration for creative collaboration. The fitness class should plan its workouts so they do not conflict with the after-school program, and the evangelism team might want to use the educational ministry's new discipleship curriculum. A basic organizational necessity is a communication flowchart that shows ministry leaders whom they should contact with problems and ideas that arise in the field. Another structured way to promote collaboration is to invite representation from each ministry group to a central committee. At Central Baptist Church, for example, a board of outreach coordinates and supports the work of largely autonomous mission groups. The pastor who attends (but does not chair) board of outreach meetings brings information and ideas from the rest of the congregation to the board.

In addition to keeping one another informed, church leaders must create avenues and habits of communicating with the congregation about ministry. If this communication consists only of asking for things (donations or volunteers), however, people will become adept at tuning it out. You can relay "free" information in a way that draws people in and makes them feel like part of the action. Tell stories, distribute newspaper articles, ask for prayer, share your dreams and your struggles related to holistic ministry. Don't wait until you hit a major milestone or success to let people know how things are going—update them about the bumps in the road. If you keep the congregation informed about the zoning board hearing that threatens the church's affordable housing project, they can more fully share in the joy when it is approved—or rise up in righteous indignation if it is shut down.

Leaders—especially church leaders—are more used to talking than to listening. But communication is a two-way street. The congregation needs opportunities to share with leaders and with one another about ministry, beyond the regular congregational meeting. Most church members are not used to sharing their thoughts with church leaders (because they are so rarely asked) and may be insecure about volunteering their ideas. If leaders do not actively solicit input, all they are likely to hear are the complaints of the most negative, outspoken members. Thus, an explicit invitation and clear process for gathering feedback from the congregation—positive as well as negative—is critical to bringing a congregation along on the journey toward holistic ministry.

This can take many forms. A congregational survey is one common tool. This can be as simple as distributing a sheet of paper at a worship service with one or two open-ended questions at the top, such as, What does holistic ministry mean to you? What fears and hopes do you have about our new mission statement? Another method is to set up listening groups in which church members discuss open-ended questions as a group. If the church has established small groups, they might dedicate a session to giving feedback on the church's ministry. Or how about an email discussion list? Or a ministry journal, a blank book in which members are invited to write notes to the pastoral staff? Whatever system you establish should include a method for periodically summarizing and reporting the congregation's input. This does not mean that leaders must agree with or take action on everything that is said. The idea is to create a safe space for constructive dialogue that fosters learning and growth toward holistic ministry.

When you feel enthusiastic about a ministry, it is difficult to hear negative comments about it. But you cannot stop complaints and concerns by ignoring them. If not provided a proper channel, they will spread by improper channels and cause dissension or apathy. (See chapter 14 for more on how to handle opposition sparked by holistic ministry.) Another reason for seeking feedback is that people are more motivated to participate in something they have had a hand in shaping and more apt to listen to leaders when they feel they have been heard. But the most important reason for soliciting the congregation's ideas is that the Spirit gives every member of the body essential gifts for holistic ministry. Members may well have information that the pastoral staff lacks or see challenges from a uniquely helpful perspective. Good communication between the leaders and the congregation unlocks this valuable resource.

Generate Ministry Resources

"God's work done in God's way will never lack God's supply" is a reassuring promise for leaders who stretch the ministry capacity of their congregation. But God's supply does not come without human planning, effort, and wise management.

Some churches are able to sustain their programs entirely with in-house funds. Most, however, rely on some form of outside funding: grants, loans, donations, fund-raisers. Hiring the services of a professional grant writer and fund-raiser can be a good investment if church leaders or ministry partners lack experience in writing proposals. As you look at expanding your financial base for new projects, your leadership team should prayerfully consider criteria for accepting funds. Decide what "strings" will be acceptable and where you will draw the line—such as rejecting secular funding sources with strings attached that would secularize your ministry. (The next chapter addresses further the issues surrounding government funding.)

While grants or donations might cover certain projects, outside resources should never wholly replace internal support for ministry. Holistic outreach should be a regular part of your church budget, because it is a basic task of the church. People naturally are more interested in and feel more responsible for the things they pay for. Churches should have a generous benevolence fund for meeting emergency needs in the congregation and community, as well as line items in the budget for particular outreach programs.

Money is not the only or even the greatest resource a church has for holistic ministry. Our study included churches on shoestring budgets, churches that struggled to keep up with utility bills and even staff payroll. But these congregations engage in ministry far beyond what their own financial resources can support, because they capitalize on other assets. Church buildings are the most obvious asset. Most programs take space—for activities, training, meetings, storage. Facilities can also be leased to generate income for ministry. They can be offered at no cost to another organization doing ministry in partnership with the church. Or they can be made available for community meetings such as Neighborhood Watch. Dr. Ram Cnaan of the University of Pennsylvania led a study of church-based community outreach in Philadelphia and found that the value of churches' contributions of space and utilities to service programs averaged over $23,000 per year.[9]

Other material assets of the church may provide raw ingredients for ministry: Computers can be used in tutoring; audiovisual equipment can be used in youth outreach; the bookstore can stock material relevant to holistic ministry; a kitchen can make a hot meal program possible; vans can transport seniors to the doctor and grocery store; the sound system can be used for a Christian concert. Consider, as well, the church's *intangible* ministry assets, such as a positive reputation in the community, a proven track record with funders, or a spirit of can-do optimism and energy.

Also encourage members to take stock of personal assets that could be used for ministry—not only money and time but also such intangibles as power, access, personal connections, and media savvy. "Many of the CEOs and decision makers of large companies are members of suburban churches," points out Rev. Herb Lusk, pastor of an inner-city Philadelphia congregation. Rev. Lusk has been helping organize a network of suburban churches to match job openings in members' businesses with graduates from the church's welfare-to-work training program.

Interns from local colleges, seminaries, or ministry training and placement programs such as KingdomWorks and Here's Life Inner City can be a valuable and low-cost supplemental human resource for a church. While interns often lack the expertise and commitment of paid staff, they can be particularly helpful in short-term ministries such as summer youth programs or in a program's start-up phase. New Creation Lutheran Church, for example, used a grant-funded intern to conduct a community study in preparation for a new ministry. Interns can also strengthen the church's connections with educational and professional institutions.

A system for raising and allocating resources must remain accountable to the church's mission, so that you do not find yourself chasing resources in ways that compromise your identity or integrity, accepting funds and personnel for projects not in line with your ministry vision, or holding too tightly to assets that could be used in ministry. Financial decisions in a mission-centered organization are guided by a proper understanding of stewardship. Stewardship and servanthood must go hand in hand. The servant says, "I belong to God." The steward says, "All I have belongs to God." Too often churches equate stewardship merely with fiscal prudence, which can easily mask self-interest. The servant-steward asks, "How can we use what God has entrusted to us to carry out God's work in our congregation and community?"

Manage Volunteers

Perhaps the greatest wealth of many churches, particularly in poor communities, is their people power—persons who are dedicated to the church's ministry vision and are willing to sacrifice time and financial gain to serve the community through the church. Most outreach ministries rely on the skills, experience, commitment, energy, and ideas of volunteers. There are many good books available on volunteer management. Following are the key organizational elements involved in the effective use of volunteers in holistic ministry:

Recruitment: Getting people to work for free takes work! It's not enough simply to post an announcement, "We need volunteers for . . ." Recruitment includes "advertising" in multiple church venues, initial contact, and follow-up. Getting commitments usually takes proactive invitations, because waiting lists of eager volunteers are rare. Skill and ministry interest inventories can help target recruitment efforts.

Assignment: Volunteer managers must play matchmaker between the right volunteer and the right job. This means screening volunteers. Another aspect of assignment is stating clearly (preferably in writing) what the duties and time commitment are and what performance standards are expected.

Training: Some volunteer ministries call for a preliminary class; others require only on-the-job training. Training not only relates to skills but also to theology and attitudes. In particular, antiracist and anticlassist training is recommended for any ministry that crosses ethnic or class boundaries.

Supervision: Once volunteers are identified and put to work, they mustn't be abandoned. Supervisors need to check to see that the work is being accomplished. Supervisors should also manage the distribution of tasks so that vol-

Organizing Human Resources: First Presbyterian Church

In its welcome letter to first-time visitors, First Presbyterian Church of Mount Holly underscores its commitment to holistic mission:

> Another element of our shared life together as a congregation is our work together for the cause of Christ. Besides our concern to share faith in Christ with our neighbors, we're very active in trying to meet some of the social concerns of the needy and hurting in our community. . . . We invite everyone to find a place where they can find fulfillment through serving.

The church backs up this invitation with an impressive system for matching members with ministries, starting with the new members discovery class, which dedicates several weeks to spiritual gift discernment. Interviews with new members probe what skills, experiences, and interests they bring to service. The church maintains a database of this information along with each member's service record, as an aid to volunteer recruitment. The database is updated through an annual Time and Talent Survey. Periodic workshops on discovering spiritual gifts also help to keep the topic before the congregation.

The director of Servant Development posts information about volunteer opportunities on the church's bulletin boards and in the newsletter. She keeps the other staff informed about open volunteer positions, so that they can be on the lookout for people to recruit. For people who want to take the initiative, a brochure lists the names of staff "available to equip, encourage, and engage you" in community ministry. The director of Servant Development tries to stay in touch with volunteers, not waiting for them to come to her with problems. Otherwise, in her experience, "You just don't know if they are struggling or hating the job they are doing, until all of a sudden somebody quits." Her job also includes being an "all-around encourager of those who are volunteering."

First Presbyterian leaves members no room to doubt that they are a valuable resource to the church and to the kingdom. They also leave members no excuse for not participating!

unteers are not overworked, under-worked, or inefficiently spinning their wheels.

Evaluation and feedback: Volunteers need continual inspiration and encouragement to sustain their motivation. Tell volunteers how they are doing (privately when it's criticism, publicly when it's praise). People like to be told they're doing a good job, but they also need to know how they can do it even better. Clear, written goals and guidelines for performance help workers feel less defensive. Evaluation also means reassessing whether the volunteer is in the right position or needs a fresh assignment.

Recognition: Volunteers do not expect payment, but they deserve to be appreciated and commended for their work. "As a staff leader, see yourself as God's agent. Learn to say, 'Well done, thou good and faithful servant.'"[10] Recognition should include both the informal pat on the back, and formal ceremonies hosted at least annually.

Running through all these organizing tasks is the importance of facilitating communication and relationships, as discussed above. The most effective program of volunteer management not only gets people to do a task but keeps them informed of how their work fits into the big picture, seeks their input for ministry decisions, and nurtures their personal and spiritual growth in relationship with others who share their ministry commitments.

Plan for Growth

Holistic ministry means planting seeds of faith. Expect a harvest! New faces will start walking through your church doors. Look for people who have come to new or renewed faith through evangelistic or social outreach, Christians looking for a new church home where they can use their gifts to make a difference in the world, community residents who want to be part of a church that is making a difference in their neighborhood, people who feel unwanted and unwelcome in other churches. How will they be integrated into your congregation? Managing growth positively means more than just adding chairs and doing the same things with more people.

First, the church needs a plan for greeting and following up with first-time guests. At the very least, prepare guest packets that include information about the church and its programs. Guests at New Covenant Church receive a packet that includes a short welcome on cassette tape by the pastor, describing the church's history, vision, and ministries. Don't instruct guests to sign a guest registry unless you intend to use the information to contact them afterward. Many churches send letters or cards welcoming guests. Media Presbyterian Church's cookie ministry delivers fresh-baked cookies on Sunday evenings to their first-time guests, along with a church brochure.

Second, managing growth requires systems that anticipate newcomers' needs and ways to channel them into church life: Sunday school classes or small groups for seekers and new Christians, new members classes, spiritual gift and ministry interest inventories, mentoring programs matching new and mature believers, meet the pastor social events, brochures introducing church staff and describing ministry opportunities, calendars listing church activities, a ministry fair with booths for all the church's nurture and outreach programs. Ask people in your congregation with the spiritual gift of hospitality to give special attention to newcomers from the social margins (e.g., people from a different economic class or ethnic group than the majority of the congregation, or people with disabilities).

Growth also stretches the church's infrastructure. Your budgeting should anticipate the need for new staff, training, internships, and equipment. You may need to consider changes to the facilities, such as expanding the sanctuary or making the building handicap accessible. Monitor whether staff and volunteers are feeling burdened by new responsibilities.

Finally, prepare for growing pains in church leadership. As congregations grow, the role of the pastor changes. Acts 6 describes a crisis that erupted in a period of rapid church growth. The apostles were overwhelmed with the demands of day-to-day church operations, and people were becoming frustrated that their needs were not being met. The apostles appointed a new group of leaders and delegated a specific set of tasks. As a congregation grows, senior pastors need to prepare a new flank of leaders to handle particular areas of responsibility, which will vary from church to church. Word of Life's Bishop Dickie Robbins trained church elders to handle most of the visitation and counseling; New Covenant's Bishop Milton Grannum works with ministry leaders to develop their administrative skills. Leaders also need to cultivate the art of saying no to guard against filling their calendar with extraneous activities.

Respond to Requests for Emergency Assistance

Once word spread about Jesus' miracles, he couldn't go anywhere without being approached by crowds of sick, lame, and demon-possessed people. Once word gets out that your church helps people in need, don't be surprised when many people in need (including some from your own congregation) start calling on you for help. Unless your church has a system to handle requests for emergency assistance, you may quickly become overwhelmed and tempted to close your doors. Your church should have a plan in place for responding to people in crisis, before they throw you into a crisis. There are no hard and fast rules, but here are some guidelines.

Prepare your staff. Create an "emergency squad" of individuals from the congregation who are trained and ready to respond to specific crisis situations when they arise: one person who can handle emergency hospital visits and funerals; another person who knows how to work with needs related to child welfare and domestic abuse; another who knows the contacts for arranging emergency shelter and transitional housing. This more efficiently utilizes the skills and experiences of the church body and relieves the pastor from having to deal with every situation. Also, prepare the church receptionists, who are most often the frontline people for responding to people in need. Provide them with training, communicate the value of their roles as the church's representatives, pay attention to their safety concerns, and regularly express your appreciation and support.

Coordinate your efforts with other local agencies that provide emergency assistance. By doing so, your church can identify people who are just "working the system" and help the people who are caught in a cycle of crisis and who could benefit from more intensive intervention. Don't replicate what others are already doing well; rather, try to fill in the holes in the support network and refer the rest to credible agencies.

Develop intake, interview, and follow-up procedures. It is a good idea (for case management and legal reasons) to create a paper trail that tracks the need and your response. But don't go overboard—keep the focus on the person, not the filing system. A brief interview format should acquaint you with the person's background and needs without being overly intrusive or humiliating. In the interview, also take time to share a little about your church and the reason that you care about this person's needs. Also develop a system for follow-up contacts. Follow-up can make the difference between a month's rent and a life-changing encounter. Some aid recipients will not want any further contact (out of shame or busyness or distrust), but others may be eager for spiritual encouragement, personal counseling, budget management training, or a simple cup of coffee with a friendly listener. Decide what your church can offer and who will be responsible for making the follow-up arrangements.

Decide on your criteria for giving aid and what form the aid will take. If you can only help so many, will you give priority to families, to homeless persons, or . . . ? Are other sources of aid available—such as family members (offer to mediate the reconciliation, if necessary) or a home church? A wise policy is to avoid giving cash whenever possible: Pay the utility bill or rent directly, give grocery and clothing gift certificates, buy the bus ticket. This prevents contributing to potential problems such as substance abuse, gambling, or poor budgeting. Put the criteria and giving guidelines in writing so that applicants can see that you are not being arbitrary or selective. Of course, you can always make exceptions at your discretion (and the Holy Spirit's prompting).

Prepare the church for the inevitable occasional abuse to the system: the sad story that turns out to be an utter lie, the person who "makes the rounds" of relief agencies under various names, emergency housing that is trashed and quickly abandoned, the car that is sold for drugs just after the church pays for repairs. "Sometimes people will make you angry," warns the coordinator of Faith Assembly's food ministry. "We get the needy here but we also get the greedy."

Some churches are so wary of being duped that they set up a hyper-detailed screening system that intimidates people in a genuine crisis; at the other extreme, churches that give too uncritically can end up burning themselves out and cheating those who really need the help. Take prudent precautions (such as calling the landlord to check requests for rent assistance) but also be willing to absorb some losses. Don't take it personally when people abuse your charity. Remember that God desires their spiritual and physical wholeness just as much as the wholeness of those who are more "deserving" of aid. When you discover that someone is abusing your help, seek other ways to show unconditional love for the person.

Finding the Right Relationship between the Church and Ministry Program

When a church starts a new ministry program, it must decide how to structure that ministry in relationship to the church. There are three basic possibilities. A ministry program may be:

1. a dependent ministry of the church, administered by church staff
2. a quasi-independent program sponsored by the church but having its own staff and a separately funded budget
3. a separately incorporated 501(c)(3) nonprofit organization, affiliated to the church to a greater or lesser degree and having a separate board and budget

The challenge is to develop a program structure that is appropriate to the congregation's context and culture (including denominational factors), that maximizes cost-efficient administration and effective outcomes, and that keeps the "faith factor" central to social ministry.

Each setup has its own advantages and risks. On the one hand, separate incorporation may open new doors for partnerships and funding, as many government funders and foundations only give to entities with a 501(c)(3) nonprofit status. It affords the church legal and financial protection, should the ministry run into problems. It can also draw in people with skills and commitment from outside the congregation to serve on the program's governing board. On the other hand, spin-off programs run the risk of drifting too far. Separate incorporation may weaken the congregation's sense of ownership of the ministry, as well as the community's sense of the ministry's connection to the church. "If Christian community development ministries maintain an all-too-typical parachurch stance that is apart from the church," says Glen Kehrein, "we can spiritually cripple new converts, giving the impression that [their] participation in the church is optional."[11] Whatever the governing structure, the crucial issue is to make sure that the program remains holistic.

If you set up a separately incorporated nonprofit organization, you must decide how tight to draw the strings between it and the church. Must a certain percentage of board members also be church members? Will the pastor or governing body of the congregation have any leadership role in the organization? What level of accountability will the organization have to the church?

In the beginning, the ties between church and para-church programs are often informal and personal. The church's leaders trust that the program leaders share the same vision, and the program staff are naturally recruited from the congregation. Over time, however, the link to the church's mission may drift with changes in staff, funding opportunities, ministry context, and external pressures (such as laws requiring professional certification). A board member of a church-sponsored community center describes this process of drift: "In my time on the board we debated whether to serve alcohol at a fund-raiser, and then whether to remove the 'churchy-type' banners from the walls when someone found them offensive, and someone else worried about funding. Then we wondered whether to reserve a place for a pastor on the board. . . . We determined that it didn't have to."[12]

One way to prevent this loss of vision is to build in the requirement that board members and key staff embrace your church's faith and mission. After an extensive study of how faith-based organizations respond to government funding, Charles Glenn concluded, "The most crucial aspect of maintaining the integrity of any organization with a mission is to control with great care the hiring and discipline of staff. Without such controls, the organization is likely to lose its focus with or without government interference."[13] A common strategy is to stipulate that a percentage of nonprofit board members must also be members of the church, and/or that the pastor also functions as chair of the nonprofit board. A Salvation Army social service director describes how they recruit staff who share their mission:

> When we advertise to hire professional staff [we] always . . . bill ourselves as a "Christian social service agency." As part of the hiring process we hand candidates a copy of our mission statement and ask them to describe in writing how they would integrate it into their daily work. These two perfectly legal practices result in our being able to hire a professional staff almost all of whom support the Army's professional mission.[14]

You can also create informal links between the nonprofit organization and other church ministries, such as by jointly sponsoring an evangelistic concert or seminar, or by requiring students in the church's evangelism training class to volunteer with the organization. No structure can anticipate every future problem, but you can put policies in place that are likely to sustain holistic ministry.

One point to remember: Just because a ministry becomes a separately incorporated nonprofit organization does not mean it must be drained of religious content. Although some programs do secularize once removed from direct sponsorship by a church, many para-church organizations retain a dynamic spiritual character. Moreover, having a ministry run directly by the church (even staffed by the pastor) does not guarantee a significant spiritual component. Holistic witness can flourish in any of the three program organizational structures. But it will not happen in any of them unless it remains a high priority and gets regular attention.

Under Construction: Churches in Transition

Whatever the structure, the dynamic nature of holistic ministry demands that it be flexible. Programs and staff will come and go; new opportunities will arise; funding streams will dry up; institutional partnerships will evolve. The key is to keep the structure in service to the mission. A great temptation for churches, once they have achieved a level of success in holistic ministry, is to set the system in stone and resist further development. Mountaintops soon become plateaus if churches are not prepared to modify the way they do things in order to do new things, or to do the old things even better.

Most of the churches we studied were undergoing some kind of structural transition directly related to their outreach ministry. Being in a state of flux did not weaken their commitment or capacity, for the most part; rather, it freed them to incorporate new people and try new ideas. Three examples follow of churches that experienced organizational evolution during the course of our study.

Bethel Temple Community Bible Church

When our study began, most of the church's organized ministries were carried out under the auspices of a separately incorporated ministry, Proclaimers of Hope, which predated the church's founding. However, a great deal of "unorganized" ministry had sprouted in response to immediate needs or opportunities. Little documentation existed to guide the administration of ministry activities: no job descriptions for staff or board members; no written policies or procedures for the allocation of emergency food, clothing, and housing; no guidelines for acceptance into the Addictions Discipleship program. Organizational challenges were exacerbated by explosive church growth, an expanding staff and volunteer pool, and changing community needs.

Over about eighteen months, the leadership of Bethel Temple and Proclaimers of Hope engaged in a visioning process. The prayerful discussions of the church's mission began with the two pastors and elders, then expanded to include the staff. This process yielded a new mission statement, introduced at the annual congregational meeting: "Discipling our members, evangelizing our community and revitalizing our neighborhood in the name of Jesus Christ."

Leaders recognized the need for a new administrative structure to serve this refocused mission. This gave rise to a plan to merge church and para-church organization under one leadership body called Bethel Ministries.

"Having the overarching mission and building everything under one ministry umbrella is crucial to where our vision and values lie," explains Rev. Joel Van Dyke. "We wanted to have the church in the driver's seat of all that happens, so the outreach . . . is directed by the spiritual leadership." Proclaimers of Hope retained its separate incorporation (largely for legal and funding reasons), but the church's board of elders now serves as the governing body for the whole entity. Under the board of elders are ministry directors who are responsible for the administration of specific programs. An advisory board assists with fund-raising, networking, and informal guidance, without decision-making authority.

As part of implementing the new structure, Bethel's leadership has given priority to addressing the "growing pains" of the congregation (e.g., visitor and new believer follow-up, membership classes, youth programming, and cell groups) and staff (creating job descriptions for volunteer and paid staff positions, and expanding opportunities for personal nurture, spiritual growth, and fellowship). These steps strengthen the foundation for a new strategic plan for community outreach also birthed during the visioning process.

Life in Christ Cathedral of Faith

"I had people coming to me in the middle of the winter, women with children, saying, 'We don't have a place to stay and the shelters are full,'" says Bishop Dickie Robbins. "So occasionally we put people up in a hotel overnight or for a couple of days until we could seek out more permanent arrangements for them. We decided that we needed to begin to develop some housing alternatives ourselves." The church purchased seven apartments to use for housing needs. Later, the church added another six apartments, two houses, and vacant land for building new homes. Besides having properties available for emergency needs, several apartments are rented at a discount (one, for example, to a young man on work release from prison), and one is provided for a church staff member in place of a salary. The church expects people receiving emergency housing to attend church services and Bible study. Bishop Robbins also developed a relationship with an apartment complex owner to make additional housing available. The owner knows that the church holds these people accountable: If someone is late paying rent, he calls the church, and the church works with the tenant.

When we studied the church, Bishop Dickie Robbins was in the process of pursuing 501(c)(3) status for the Life in Christ Economic Development Corporation, which would take over ownership of the properties from the church and pursue funding for other community development projects. Because the board of the Economic Development Corporation is currently the same as the church board, with Bishop Robbins as chair, the distinction is primarily administrative. One reason for separate incorporation is that a separate nonprofit organization would be eligible to participate in government-funded economic development initiatives. Second, separate incorporation ensures that the church would not be held liable for any debts or (in a worst-case scenario) lawsuits incurred by the nonprofit organization. A third reason is that the owner of the properties must play the role of landlord. Bishop Robbins explains, "It is more consistent with the mission of the Economic Development Corporation than it is with the church itself to own investment properties." Several apartments are reserved as rental units to pay for maintenance costs and to generate funds to finance other church ministries. The Economic Development Corporation will be set up to return its profits to the church.

The goals of the Economic Development Corporation are consistent with Life in Christ's holistic mission but concentrated in a single area: to develop the total economic health of the community. In addition to providing housing, the ministry has sponsored various events involving small business development, job training, home ownership, and healthy personal finances, open to both the congregation and the community. In addition, the ministry has fostered entrepreneurship by providing space and administrative support for a dozen locally owned new businesses. While the program is not overtly evangelistic, its close ties with the church create a bridge between nonchurched community residents and the congregation. "This is not an evangelistic arm," Bishop Robbins explains. "This is a social justice arm because we need to improve the economy of the community. Evangelism takes place in many other areas of our ministry. . . . The strategy is to establish a relationship [with non-Christians]. The relationship will usher them into the local church setting."

Germantown Church of the Brethren

Until a few years ago, the church's structure followed the traditional denominational pattern. The leadership team consisted of the pastor plus nine members on three ministry commissions: witness, nurture, and stewardship. It was a tidy system, but it wasn't working from a ministry perspective. "We experimented," Rev. Kyerematen recalls, "because we thought that the old structure limited leadership potential. There was always a struggle to find people to serve on the commissions, and . . . they always turned out to be more like administrative committees as opposed to our church going out and *doing* something."

The church suspended its bylaws to try a new system, which divided the three committees into twelve congregational ministries. "The congregational ministries are the building blocks of the congregation. They make the entire

ministry of the church function well and help us to be effective in our outreach," explains Rev. Kyerematen. The twelve ministry coordinators comprise
the church board. One of the twelve congregational ministries is outreach/fol-
low-up. This in turn is made up of six ministry teams representing a holistic
range of outreach programs (with room to expand as more ministries develop).
These ministry team leaders also meet monthly for planning and prayer.

"It's one thing having an outreach committee," says Rev. Kyerematen. "It's
another thing moving the whole congregation to be in outreach." In two years,
the new structure doubled the number of people involved in church leadership. Since leaders then recruit other volunteers from the congregation, the
new structure advances the pastor's ultimate goal of having ministry participation be a requirement of membership. A more decentralized structure is also
more efficient, the pastor believes, because each leader is responsible for making something happen within a narrower frame. As a result, they spend more
time on action than on talking.

The main challenge of this transition has been providing sufficient training
and support. The pastor has been stretched to follow up with so many new
leaders. During an initial adjustment period, while leaders were still clarifying
their roles and expectations, some ministry activities were put on hold. But the
congregation has been willing to live with some ambiguity, and overall the
change has enhanced leaders' motivation while helping them feel less burdened.
"Our leadership team is made up of people who are very gifted, talented, have
a desire, have a lot of zeal," says Rev. Kyerematen. "They are doing this out of
joy. In fact, many times they are really thinking, 'We could do more if we can
make more effective use of our time.'"

Conclusion

"Without structure and a plan," writes Calvin Miller, "there exists no form
to direct the vision. The vision is then only a powerful locomotive without
rails."[15] With a mission-centered organization that plans and implements ministry decisions, facilitates communication among staff and members, generates and stewards ministry resources, harnesses the church's people power, grows
gracefully, is prepared to help people in crisis, and sets up ministry programs
with a faithful and flexible structure, a holistic vision will stay on track.

chapter eleven

Ministry Partnerships

We recognize that we can't do the entire job that God has called us to do alone, and we believe that God has ordained partners for us. . . . Successful holistic ministry involves finding out who our partners are supposed to be.

Bishop Dickie Robbins, Life in Christ Cathedral of Faith

Partnerships are risky. Partnerships take energy and time. It is not easy to look past the challenges of organizing your own congregation for ministry to see the potential in collaborating with others. Nor is it easy to adjust to a partnering agency's different methods and priorities. Is the effort worth it?

Why Partner?

A recent study found that congregations best serve their communities "by weaving together a network of money, volunteers, and other supports." The average congregation collaborates with a total of six community outreach organizations.[1] Churches seeking to engage in effective holistic ministry should work through partnerships for seven practical reasons and four theological reasons.

Practical Reasons

1. *Few churches have the resources to carry out their vision by themselves.* Partners bring funds, volunteers, facilities, ideas, information, expertise, contacts, and enthusiasm to ministry projects. In addition, some foundations give preference to collaborative projects over independent church programs. Thus, teaming up with other agencies enables churches to accomplish more.

2. *Partnerships expand a church's opportunities to form evangelistic relationships.* After a measles epidemic took the lives of nine Philadelphia children in 1992, Tenth Presbyterian Church partnered with Esperanza Health Clinic, a nonprofit Christian clinic in a Latino inner-city neighborhood, to found the Summer Medical Institute (SMI). SMI recruits medical students from around the country to provide door-to-door immunizations and other medical services, as well as prayer and a presentation of the gospel. A team of neighborhood churches linked to Esperanza cooperates with the program, providing input to the planning process, translators, and spiritual homes for those who come to Christ through SMI. Since its first year, more than 275 students from 45 medical schools around the country have served with SMI. These medical volunteers gain training in medical evangelism as well as a powerful cross-cultural and spiritual experience as they see God's love and power transform lives in an impoverished community. They return to their medical schools with a new zeal for sharing the gospel with their peers. Thus, a web of partnerships allows Tenth Church's evangelistic reach to extend from inner-city children to Ivy League professionals.

Besides expanding opportunities to share Christ with the people served in social ministry, partnerships also offer a unique avenue of reaching co-laborers in social action with the gospel. As Robert Linthicum points out, when church members participate in community collaborations, they tend to develop "intense relationships of trust and respect" with fellow activists. "In such relationships, sharing about Jesus is natural. People who would normally be unreceptive to the gospel willingly hear it from their community partners because they trust them—and the Christians likewise respect them."[2]

3. *Partnerships prevent duplicating services and thus focus the church's resources where they are most needed.* In downtown Philadelphia, there are many agencies that help homeless people with food, shelter, and substance abuse. Networking with these resources frees Tenth Presbyterian Church to offer what secular agencies cannot—Bible studies and worship services designed to meet the spiritual and relational needs of homeless people.

4. *Church ministries are more effective when they cooperate, rather than compete, with local efforts.* Partnerships with local agencies give people in the com-

munity a greater sense of ownership and responsibility for local needs and prevent the community from developing an unhealthy dependence on the church. A principle of community development is, Never do for people what they can do for themselves. As long as the partnership does not lead the church to water down its faith, the church should come alongside agencies organized by residents to meet their own needs.

5. *Partnerships expose people to social issues and needs outside their usual context.* Partnerships allow church members to work alongside people from outside their neighborhood. A woman whose suburban, Anglo congregation is a "sister church" with urban, African American Tenth Memorial Baptist Church expresses her appreciation for this aspect of partnering: "When you hear in the news that something happened, that there's a fire in North Philadelphia, then it means something. . . . You want to call and say, 'Is everything okay?' . . . It's more now than just a place that you drive through."

6. *Partnerships with established agencies smooth the way for churches new to holistic ministry.* Through partnerships, churches can learn from successful program models, develop internal organizational structures, and build a volunteer base. Such low-risk "internships" in holistic ministry can help a skeptical congregation get its feet wet.

7. *The current social and political context for church-based ministry creates new opportunities and incentives for collaboration.* Businesses and secular foundations are increasingly willing to work with churches. Federal and local governments are turning more often to private agencies rather than public bureaucracies to carry out social policy. Developments such as Charitable Choice (see sidebar) and the Presidential Office on Faith-Based and Community Initiatives have created unprecedented opportunities for religious organizations, including churches, to receive public funds for social services without losing their religious character. At the same time, because the social welfare arena has grown so large and complex, it is difficult for churches to become significantly involved in providing social services without bumping into other public and private agencies.

Theological Reasons

Churches should also choose to work through partnerships for four theological reasons.

1. *The holistic ministry of each congregation is only part of the larger work being done in God's kingdom.* "We do not bring God's reign into the city. God is

Charitable Choice

The 1996 federal welfare reform law included an encouragement to government to reach out to community-based organizations, including congregations and faith-based nonprofits, to devise ways of working together to serve poor and needy people. The Charitable Choice provisions . . . establish new rules for such collaboration. . . . Charitable Choice creates a level playing field between secular, and faith-based, organizations that want to compete for government contracts to underwrite their community service efforts. . . .

Before Charitable Choice, faith-based groups that accepted public money sometimes felt secularizing pressures from government. Charitable Choice . . . protects the religious integrity and character of faith-based organizations accepting government dollars. Under Charitable Choice, religious groups contracting with government:

- retain authority over their mission, governing board, and prophetic voice
- have the right to maintain a religious atmosphere in their facilities
- retain the right to use religious criteria in employment decisions

. . . [Charitable Choice] also seeks to protect the civil liberties of individuals who receive social services from faith-based ministries and congregations collaborating with government. Religious groups must offer their services to all eligible participants regardless of their religious affiliation (or lack of affiliation). In addition, if a client objects to receiving social services from a faith-based provider . . . the government must ensure that he/she obtains assistance from another organization. Moreover, faith-based organizations must not use governmental funds for purposes of "sectarian worship, instruction, or proselytization," and they must not require service recipients to participate in religious practices. Inherently religious activities like prayer, evangelism, Bible studies, or discipleship training have to be clearly voluntary. . . . (Of course, faith communities remain free to use *private* funds for inherently religious activities such as evangelism and discipleship.)

Excerpted from Amy L. Sherman, *The Charitable Choice Handbook for Ministry Leaders* (Washington, D.C.: Hudson Institute and the Center for Public Justice, 2001).

For more information, see *A Guide to Charitable Choice: The Rules of Section 104 of the 1996 Federal Welfare Law Governing State Cooperation with Faith-based Social-Service Providers* (Center for Public Justice, 1997), <http://www.cpjustice.org/charitablechoice/guide/>.

already there. He invites us to join Him in His activity," writes Jude Tiersma. "The ministry belongs to God, not to us."[3] A church that works on its own may not see how its efforts fit into a broader plan for the transformation of the community. This is why Bethel Temple Community Bible Church helped organize a network of all the Christian organizations ministering in the community. "We are all a part of this solution. We're not out there isolated," explains Rev. Lou Centeno. "We have to say, 'Come let us hear what God has laid upon your heart, and let us learn from each other.'" In the book *City Reaching*, Jack Dennison describes the radical, expansive vision for urban transformation that becomes possible when individual congregations come together to function as the one body of Christ.[4]

2. *God created people to live in community, and a healthy community is made up of diverse institutions.* Government, businesses, banks, schools, nonprofit organizations, and hospitals all play an important role in promoting God's intended shalom. Sometimes churches must step in when a particular institution is absent or dysfunctional in a community (for example, by opening a private school when the public schools are failing). Ideally, however, the church should come alongside local institutions and strengthen them to do their part with justice, integrity, and effectiveness.

3. *Through partnerships, the church embodies Christlike servanthood to the community.* Churches must not avoid collaboration because of competition ("How dare the community center offer a new tutoring program just as *our* after-school ministry is getting started!"), condescension ("Why should we coordinate our health education program with the local clinic? Their services are lousy!"), or pride ("We're the only ones who can do the job right!"). Such attitudes not only give the church a bad name, but they rob community institutions of the church's transforming influence.

An example of an empowering collaboration comes from Christian Stronghold Baptist Church's relationship with Rosenbluth International, Inc. When the company asked to purchase a plot of land from the city to build a computer processing plant, Christian Stronghold Baptist Church saw an opportunity to secure more jobs for its economically depressed community. The church became the liaison between the community and the corporation. Christian Stronghold negotiated with Rosenbluth to set aside two hundred jobs for local residents and to build a community center. In return, Christian Stronghold agreed to provide the screening for the job applicants and the administration of the center. Originally Christian Stronghold had been interested in purchasing the land itself to expand its church facilities. But Rev. Richardson recognized that the church could best advance its mission through collaboration rather than competition.

4. *Partnerships among Christian churches and agencies strengthen evangelistic witness.* Jesus prayed that the loving unity of his one body would convince the world that he came from the Father (John 17:21). When Christians of different denominations, races, and socioeconomic backgrounds come together around the banner of holistic ministry, people take notice. Such ministry partnerships are a living testimony to the reconciling power of the gospel. As Bishop Dickie Robbins believes, "This probably is the greatest witness to the world, that the body of Christ comes together in cooperation."

Qualities of Good Partnerships

Most partnerships are organized around a shared commitment to address a need. A common concern is not enough by itself, however, to make a collaboration work. Healthy partnerships have the following six qualities:[5]

1. *Healthy partnerships have a compatible core mission.* "Whenever you partner with anybody, make sure that their mission and their objective complement yours, so that you don't get absorbed or sidetracked by what somebody else wants to do," advises Rev. Bill Moore. A strong, shared commitment to ministry goals is what sustains partnerships despite differences in leadership style, clashes in organizational culture, and imbalances of power. The church's ministry vision must guide all partnership decisions. Opportunities for collaboration that lie outside the church's mission are tempting but ultimately will set back the church's progress.

2. *Healthy partnerships do not hinder the faith or evangelistic witness of the church.* In deciding whether to partner with secular agencies, churches must weigh the benefits of access to resources and ministry opportunities against the costs of the limitations to a holistic approach. Partnering with a secular or interfaith agency is not in itself unbiblical. Special caution is needed, however, when such partnerships impose restrictions on the religious nature of a program. One example involves the law against using public funds for evangelism, religious teachings, or worship. Churches must distinguish carefully between rules that limit the spiritual components of a particular program and requirements that would lead the church to contradict biblical teachings, compromise its values, hide its Christian identity, or secularize its programs outside the collaborative project.[6] To protect a church's independent witness, it may be prudent to set up a separate 501(c)(3) nonprofit arm affiliated with the church to manage programs involving partnerships with secular entities.

Challenges to a church's witness can be indirect. Cookman United Methodist Church's state-funded welfare-to-work program has a holistic program design (see the sidebar in chapter 5), but the partnership threatened the church's integrity in other ways. "The state is an abstract entity that looks at people as numbers," comments Pastor Donna Jones. The amount of paperwork required by the state cuts into the staff's availability to spend time relating with clients. The church resisted being associated with the welfare system's bureaucratic and restrictive rules. One policy in particular caused friction: The welfare department requires programs to drop clients who miss a particular number of days, even in cases of illness or family crisis. Staff felt that complying with this rule would violate their relationships with clients. They decided on a compromise: They would follow the rule but then immediately reenroll the expelled client. This cost the program thousands of dollars in penalties, but it was worth it to Cookman to maintain a consistent Christian witness.

3. *Healthy partnerships are founded on mutual trust and respect.* Bishop Robbins says of partnerships, "Very little is sustained unless it is based on relationships." Trust emerges as partners work through conflicts and challenges over time. Respect develops from seeking to understand the partner's point of view and building on the partner's strengths. Each partner must value what the other brings to the relationship. This respect is particularly important in partnerships that cross racial or economic lines. Dr. Harold Dean Trulear writes that urban-suburban partnerships must be conducted in "a spirit of mutuality and not paternalism. . . . In relationships of mutuality, the middle class must be willing to *learn* from the underclass. There must be dialogue among equals, celebration of our commonality and appreciation of all resources brought to the table."[7]

A church can expect respect from others only if it first respects others. Unequal partnerships can reinforce a pattern of dependency. For small, poor churches used to seeing themselves on the "receiving" end of relationships, healthy partnerships require a change of mind-set. Any church should be wary of entering a partnership in which it feels intimidated or overpowered. In particular, one of the risks of church-state collaboration is that churches will be reduced to an arm of the government, stripped of autonomy and integrity. Churches must insist on being treated as a valued asset. As Amy Sherman puts it, "Healthy cooperation means that the church will not allow itself to be the weaker partner."[8]

4. *Healthy partnerships involve a sense of ownership on both sides.* Loss of ownership means feeling out of control, disconnected from the aims and rewards of the ministry. Churches with limited financial resources are particularly vulnerable. Church of the Advocate provides space for several programs funded and run by other agencies. Because the congregation does not fund the programs, the question of ownership creates tension. "When we have to depend on a lot of outside places for resources, we take a risk and lose a lot because

we're involved in a balancing act," comments a church member. "You're at the mercy of someone else's discretion. . . . Since they're holding the purse strings, you have to juggle."

Investing other kinds of resources in the program, such as volunteers or prayer support, can help restore the balance. Church of the Advocate, for example, brings a trusted reputation and decades of networking with the community to its partnerships. The director of an organization that works with Advocate says she relies on the church's leaders for insights into community problems and personal connections with neighborhood residents. Knowing they make a unique contribution strengthens Advocate's commitment to its partnerships. Regularly reminding the congregation of the importance of the shared mission and celebrating the outcomes in a worship service setting also help the congregation retain a sense of ownership of the ministry.

5. *Healthy partnerships do not substitute for the gifts and resources of the congregation.* One of the advantages of partners is that they fill in gaps in the congregation's resources or abilities. This can become a weakness, however, if the congregation becomes dependent on the partner and takes no steps to develop its own capacity. A church should never use a partnership to subcontract its evangelism or social ministry. For example, turning over its youth evangelism program to a para-church agency may hinder a congregation from developing its own passion for evangelism. An effective partnership is an investment that multiplies the congregation's gifts, not a crutch for its inadequacies.

Ray Bakke warns that pastors eager to begin new programs too often recruit outsiders "first to supplement, and then to replace local people who cannot measure up to the requirements and expectations of the program."[9] Bethel Temple learned this lesson. At first, they relied heavily on Bible college students and visiting youth groups to staff their youth programs, expanding their capacity and impact. Gradually, however, church leaders realized that their dependence on people from outside the community sent the wrong message—especially since most of the visiting staff were Caucasian, and most youth were Hispanic or African American. Church leaders began preparing local youth who were maturing in their faith for positions of ministry leadership. Bethel still hosts interns and visiting volunteer groups, but their focus is on mentoring local youth to minister to the community.

6. *Healthy partnerships involve clear communication and accountability.* Collaborations cannot last when misunderstandings cloud the relationship or when one partner fails consistently to live up to its responsibilities. Be explicit about goals, roles, and standards, whether the agreement is set down formally in a document or discussed informally in person. Regular communication between the partners is vital, particularly if there is no institutional bridge such as shared

board membership. Ongoing collaborative projects, such as a bimonthly leadership breakfast, provide opportunities for feedback and conflict resolution.

Churches that partner with government entities should expect a high level of scrutiny and strict financial accountability. Sometimes this external check is just what a church may need to get its house in order! However, the accountability need not flow all in one direction. Government also needs to hear from ministry leaders how it can improve its policies and implementation.

Types of Partnerships

Partnerships come in many forms and reflect a variety of relationships between the church and the partner entity. Here we highlight five types of cooperative relationships, with illustrations from partnerships between churches and nonprofit agencies.

1. *The partner comes alongside a church with the resources the church needs to flesh out its vision for holistic ministry.* Rev. Jerome Simmons found out about Love Links, a ministry that distributes clothes and food to needy families and nonprofit organizations in Philadelphia, at a city-wide prayer meeting. His church, Koinonia, paid $150 to become a Love Links cosponsor. On a spring day, two eighteen-wheel trailer trucks pulled up in front of the church, full of goods to donate. Rev. Simmons had distributed flyers to block captains and needy families in the neighborhood about the giveaway, and church volunteers handed out evangelistic tracts to residents along with the food and clothing. Various nonprofit organizations and churches picked up their shares of the goods, and Koinonia kept the leftovers to stock its food pantry and soup kitchen. Rev. Simmons sees their involvement with Love Links both as an opportunity "to fulfill the Scriptures to feed the hungry" and as "a tool for evangelism."

Another example of this kind of effective partnership is the informal affiliation between Acts 29, an incorporated music ministry, and Faith Assembly of God. Their relationship began over fifteen years ago, when the Acts 29 leader helped provide music for the church's annual revival. Acts 29 travels to the church several times a month to lead worship, teach music lessons to the youth, and work with the Say Yes (youth self-esteem club) singing group, the Faith Wonders. Acts 29 has also led music for the noontime outreach service connected with Faith's food ministry. The partnership is successful because the two groups share a similar theology, a commitment to evangelism, and a vision for the church's transforming impact on the community. "We want to support the pastor's vision and the church's work in any way we can," says the ministry's director.

2. *The church supplies the partner with volunteers or funding, and in return the partner provides the church with a ministry outlet that does not require much*

administrative effort. Such is the case with Central Baptist's longtime participation as a covenant member of Habitat for Humanity. Habitat, an international organization dedicated to ending homelessness, provides a structure that makes it simple for church volunteers to make a significant difference in the life of a poor family. This simplicity is one of the selling points for Central's busy congregation. Once a month, a group from Central Baptist joins volunteers from other churches and the prospective home owner (putting in "sweat equity") on a work site. All the work details are coordinated by the local Habitat chapter. Through this steady commitment, Central Baptist has helped six families over the years to become home owners. The experience brings hope not only to the families but to their entire neighborhood, says one of Central's volunteer construction workers. "It's like sowing seeds in the desert—the effect is subtle at first, but can be profound."

3. *The church allows the partner to use its space.* In this mutually beneficial arrangement, the partner gets the use of the church's facilities, for free or at a discount, and its clients often gain access to the host church's other programs. The church gets an on-site ministry, which adds to its reputation in the community as a service provider, and often provides an additional ministry resource to its own congregation. Hosting a program can also bring unchurched people into relationships with members of the congregation.

Cookman United Methodist Church has rented space to Senior Wheels East, a nonreligious day shelter for the elderly, for about a quarter of a century. The agency provides a wide variety of activities and programs, including meals, legal counseling, crafts, computer training, recreational activities, and emergency assistance. The location has posed some drawbacks for the agency. There have been some quibbles about property upkeep and turf boundaries between the church and the organization; Cookman does not have a strong security system, and computers and other items have been stolen. On the other hand, the church's location in the heart of a high-poverty area makes the agency accessible to its senior clients. The church opens its clothing and food pantry to the seniors and at times provides pastoral care.

4. *A partnership develops when the church is the parent of a ministry program that spins off to become its own entity.* "We want to be intentionally open for the Spirit to move someone in our congregation to ministry, and we will assist them," says one of the pastors of Tenth Presbyterian Church. Some outreach ministries birthed with the church's assistance have remained under the church's umbrella. Other programs—such as a crisis pregnancy center, a ministry reaching out to homosexuals and other sexually broken people, and an agency serving people and congregations struggling with HIV/AIDS—have become independent. While Tenth Church does not formally oversee these ministries, the

church is linked through members who serve on their staffs, a steady stream of volunteers, financial support, and newsletters distributed to the congregation. The agencies refer the people they serve to appropriate Tenth Church outreach ministries, and vice versa. In addition, the agencies are highlighted in the church's annual urban ministry conference and other special ministry-related events. The congregation feels a sense of ownership of these ministries, even though they are not part of the church's organizational structure.

   5. *A partnership develops through a history of cooperation and joint project sponsorship, based on personal relationships and shared ministry goals.* Often this type of collaboration arises when a church member is on staff with a nonprofit agency. An example is the Church of the Advocate's relationship with the Village of the Arts and Humanities, which engages inner-city residents in the arts. A long-standing member and lay leader at Advocate heads the drama program at the Village. The church and the nonprofit organization cooperate in several ways. The church gives the Village space to hold productions and rehearsals and recruits volunteers for Village projects. In return, the Village helps the church plan special events and offered a performance workshop as part of Advocate's outreach to lapsed members and community residents. Rev. Isaac Miller says the Church of the Advocate makes a conscious effort to "develop relationships with places like the Village, which we must support and respect. There are too many turf problems in the city. Advocate cannot do what it wants to do alone, and neither can the Village."

Examples of Partnerships

   The rest of the chapter describes examples of church partnerships with various entities to illustrate the benefits (and, in some cases, the risks) of collaboration.

Partnerships with Denominational Programs

   Episcopal Community Services began an art program for preteens in an inner-city neighborhood. Soon they realized that the children were struggling with reading and writing. They approached Church of the Advocate (one of the few Episcopal churches remaining in North Philadelphia) about a partnership. The program expanded to an after-school program and summer camp for roughly eighty children called Learning Is Fun and Exciting (LIFE), with homework help, arts education, enrichment field trips, and a rite of passage program for preteen girls. LIFE is housed in the church and funded through Episcopal Community Services and the Children's Aid Society. Episcopal Community Services also funds a social worker who coordinates Advocate's youth programs.

The relationship between LIFE and the church poses advantages and drawbacks to both sides. Episcopal Community Services benefits from Advocate's trusted reputation in the community as a service provider. Families in LIFE have access to the church's other programs, such as the Grandparents As Parents support group (partially funded by Episcopal Community Services), the soup kitchen (which serves 1,250 hot meals per week), and the Food Cupboard/Clothes Closet. Setting the after-school program in a church also gives the participants a heightened sense of safety and propriety. On the other hand, the building needs repairs, the space was not designed for children, and the small congregation cannot provide as many consistent volunteers as are needed.

From Church of the Advocate's perspective, the after-school program is an extension of the church's mission to care for neighborhood children and families. For many years, Advocate had an active youth ministry, but the children grew up and left the neighborhood, and few new young families have joined the church. Through the partnership with Episcopal Community Services, a new generation of children has connected with Church of the Advocate. On the other hand, since Episcopal Community Services receives government funds, its programs have no overt religious component. To address this lack of spiritual care, Advocate invited KingdomWorks, an evangelical para-church agency, to help with the summer camp.

Partnerships with Businesses

Jobs Partnership of Philadelphia, modeled after successful Jobs Partnership programs in other cities, brings together churches and businesses "to befriend, equip, and employ some of Philadelphia's neediest residents, empowering them towards becoming productive community members and experiencing wholeness through relationship with Jesus Christ," according to its mission statement. The program has five main components: (1) a twelve-week Human Resource Development class that teaches practical life and work skills such as resumé writing; (2) a twelve-week "Keys to Work" Bible study, covering such topics as "God and Work," "Resolving Conflict," and "Stewardship of Time and Money"; (3) an assurance of employment with partner businesses after students graduate from the training classes; (4) a Christian mentor who walks alongside a participant for at least a year during job training, placement, and career advancement; and (5) a prayer team assigned to each student. The biblically based curriculum and prayer support address the internal barriers to long-term employment, while the mentors and employers help overcome the external barriers. This holistic approach, combined with the commitment of the partners, is what makes the program effective. Says the director, "Even though it is common sense, it is amazing to see what can happen when we pool our resources."

Partnerships with Public Schools

A framed certificate of "school adoption" hangs in the lobby of Tenth Memorial Baptist Church. To celebrate its adoption of nearby Vaux Middle School in the early 1990s, Tenth Memorial held a special worship service and invited the teachers and some of the students over for a meal. The church helped out at first in small ways—transporting students to the health clinic and to chess tournaments, providing funds for graduation gowns. When the heat went out in the school, the church opened its classrooms and fellowship hall.

Then the principal of Vaux Middle School called the church to see if they could do anything about the increasing problem of crime and violence among students before and after school. Fights and thefts had become common. Tenth responded by designing the Safe Corridors program, which posted volunteers in orange shirts and hats carrying walkie-talkies on every other corner along the main walking routes to the school. The success of the program caught the attention of President Bill Clinton, who talked about Safe Corridors at the signing of the Brady Bill. Eventually, Safe Corridors so reduced the violence that the church decided it was no longer needed. As an outgrowth of the success of this collaboration, Tenth Memorial's pastor, Rev. Bill Moore, joined the board of the school's Family Life Center, which addresses parenting skills and other family issues.

Community Coalitions

Suburban Wayne Presbyterian Church wanted to invest resources in developing a struggling urban neighborhood. Rather than create a new program, the church helped organize community leaders and organizations in the Kingsessing neighborhood of Philadelphia into a coalition called CityLights. Its mission: "to enhance the good work already happening in the community and to address areas of need not currently being tackled. Joint efforts in Kingsessing are carried out in a spirit of Christian compassion and justice."

About twenty groups, including neighborhood churches as well as nonprofit agencies, participate in CityLights. At monthly meetings, representatives report on progress toward joint projects, such as opening a produce market and renovating a recreation center; share announcements about needs, available services, and upcoming events; brainstorm ways to address community problems; and pray for one another. Wayne Presbyterian Church supplies the administrative backbone to the coalition and contributes consulting, volunteers, funds, and board members to projects initiated by the neighborhood partners. As part of its capital campaign, for example, Wayne Presbyterian Church raised funds for a computer center in a private Christian school in the community.

By bringing neighborhood organizations together, Wayne Presbyterian Church can have a more lasting impact than if it did ministry on its own. The coalition develops leaders and nurtures relationships that help the community solve its own problems. Wayne Presbyterian serves as a bridge between the urban community and outside resources. The slow pace of progress is frustrating, but the experience has educated the suburban residents about the obstacles to community development faced by urban pastors—such as having fewer responsive public officials and fewer full-time church staff, retirees, and stay-at-home moms to do the work.

Ministry Coalitions

Germantown Church of the Brethren's outreach to homeless people brought the church into contact with many people with substance abuse problems. Rev. Richard Kyerematen also received calls from other churches wanting to know how to help addicts. As he made referrals to various Christian rehabilitation programs, he realized that the programs could be more effective if they had closer working relationships. He organized the Christian Anti-Drug Dependency Coalition, a city-wide network of churches and nonprofit organizations that meets monthly for prayer, support, and the sharing of ideas. Many of the programs, Rev. Kyerematen found, were being run by recovered addicts who lacked formal training or adequate administrative skills, and so he arranged for leadership training sessions. The coalition has both strengthened participating programs and simplified the process of making referrals.

Church Coalitions

In the early 1990s, teenagers broke into Central Baptist Church and used the gas stove for heat. This led the church to assess the needs of its community, and in the process it discovered the Main Line Interfaith Hospitality Network (IHN). IHN is a national organization (with affiliates overseas as well). A team of "hosting congregations" provides shelter to several homeless families (screened for drug, alcohol, or mental problems) for one-week stays on a rotating basis. "Supporting congregations" serve meals to the families at the host church and help in other ways, such as with donations of clothing or school supplies. The program transports guests during the day to work, job training, or school. Each participating church contributes money for the salaries of an executive director and a van driver. A coordinator from each church recruits and supervises the twenty-five to thirty volunteers needed for the week. Some volunteers work behind the scenes, setting up partitions for the temporary bedrooms or doing laundry; others spend time visiting with the guests in the evenings, eating meals together, and helping kids with homework; others spend the night with the guests.

IHN illustrates the way that interfaith partnerships often restrict the possibility of evangelism. IHN, which involves synagogues as well as churches, has a spiritual character without being explicitly Christian. Guests are invited to attend services at the host congregation, volunteers lead a prayer before meals, and parenting classes include discussions of faith and values. Some of the volunteers from supporting churches look for opportunities to share their faith informally as they visit with the guests. However, as a host church, Central does not engage in overt evangelism. Instead, says Central Baptist's IHN coordinator, "We show our faith in God through our kindness." Her commitment to the program takes strength from "the biblical mandate . . . to take care of others as Jesus taught us to do" and from her gratitude for the way God has blessed her own family. "I'm just human hands for a program that is God's," she says.

Peter and his family are among the guests for whom IHN has made a difference. He and his family had been evicted from their apartment after their fourth child was born, because the owner said their family was too large. They had been living in IHN shelters for almost three months. Peter worked a second job as the IHN van driver during the day, in addition to his night job as a security guard. His wife worked all day for a supermarket. Finally, they saved up enough to move into a four-bedroom house. "I couldn't save enough money to get another place if the churches weren't here to help me," Peter said. Without IHN, they might have ended up paying daily to stay in a hotel. "I was glad to go to congregations, because they care for you. They help people help themselves."

Clergy Coalitions

Regional or denominational clergy consortiums bring clergy together for networking, emotional and prayer support, and continuing education. These consortiums can also form the foundation for joint ministry projects. For example, the pastoral staff of First Presbyterian Church of Mount Holly participates in the interfaith Rancocas Valley Clergy Association (RVCA). Rev. Kraft brought the idea to RVCA for a racial reconciliation initiative called Continuing the Dream. To celebrate Martin Luther King Day, RVCA sponsors an interfaith service and a leadership breakfast featuring prominent speakers from a minority community. The day's events conclude with a "justice" march through Mount Holly, ending with lunch at First Presbyterian Church's soup kitchen. Continuing the Dream events also include a joint summer picnic and a worship service, bringing churches together across racial lines to celebrate their oneness in Christ.

Another ministry sponsored by RVCA was the Caring Center, which provided emergency food, clothing, and referrals to other human service agencies. First Presbyterian Church founded the Caring Center, then transferred its administration to the Clergy Association in order to expand the pool of volunteers and referral networks and to attract more grant funds. At its peak, the Caring Center served four hundred families a month. But the Clergy Association was unable to generate the solidarity, commitment, and volunteer supervision necessary to sustain work with high-need clients. "People burned out," explains a First Presbyterian staff member. "They just lost the energy and the will." Compounding the problem, conflict surfaced between the Center's board and the Clergy Association over control of program vision and operations. Poor management decisions led to a loss of grant funds. After fifteen years of operation, the Center had to close.

This was a sad loss to First Presbyterian and to the community. But the demise of the program did not destroy the relationships in the Clergy Association or its commitment to help poor people. Slowly, RVCA began organizing again to respond to emergency needs. A new project, for example, is creating a database of all the private and public social services in the county.

Community Organizing Coalitions

Phil Reed, pastor of Voice of Calvary Fellowship in Jackson, Mississippi, calls Christians to influence government and other powerful social institutions through community organizing. "It is important that the voice of believers be heard in those places of power where decisions are being made . . . to be the voice of those who cannot speak for themselves." This task often brings Christians alongside other groups who share the same goals. As Reed continues, "This job is so big that we will need to join with whoever has a genuine concern for justice for the poor."[10] Community organizing coalitions often have an interfaith (or even a non-faith-based) membership. While this limits opportunities for evangelism, participation is not problematic for a congregation that is explicitly sharing the gospel through other aspects of its outreach.

In 1991, Church of the Advocate was a leader in the founding of Philadelphia Interfaith Action, which organizes the faith community to respond to urgent urban issues. Over forty congregations send delegates to organizational meetings and action sessions. By joining many voices, PIA has a more significant impact with public officials than one congregation could alone. Sometimes PIA uses its collaborative influence to undertake major community development projects, such as building 135 new homes in the inner city. In response to welfare reform, PIA established an intensive training program that prepares people for high-paying machinist jobs. Sometimes PIA's actions are confrontational in nature, as when it lobbied the city to clean up environmental damage in an inner-city neighborhood.

"Getting the congregations together has proven to me that [PIA] gives an individual power in the group," says a Church of the Advocate member who resides in the devastated neighborhood around the church. "Even if the improvement is not in your area now . . . you watch your neighbors improving, and you know you will benefit later."

Participation on Public Boards and Committees

The Chester Educational Foundation, a public commission, needed a consultant to help launch a state-funded small business development project. They hired Dickie Robbins, pastor of Life in Christ Cathedral of Faith. Although the project took time from his already overloaded church schedule, he realized that many of his church members could benefit from such an economic development program. Since he already spent roughly five hours each week on economic development-related activities such as financial counseling, he figured some of this time might as well be funded by the government. Through his investment of time, his financially struggling congregation gained another ministry resource that they did not have to pay for.

Over the years, Bishop Robbins has served on several public boards to establish services and public policies beneficial to his community. Does Bishop Robbins feel any tension as a pastor working with the government? "I don't pretend to be other than I am," he says. He does not hide his Christian identity. At the same time, he has become "bilingual" in secular settings—using religiously neutral concepts and terms, such as self-sufficiency and responsibility, to promote principles that are consistent with biblical teachings. While he sees value in secular programs, he believes their effectiveness is limited without the transformation that accompanies personal faith and church attendance. In his secular contacts, he often hints that in a nongovernmental setting he could provide a richer understanding of the Christian approach. His main role, however, is not to persuade his secular colleagues to adopt a Christian perspective. Rather, his role "is to be a voice of sanity in the midst of insanity sometimes, and to keep the focus on issues of justice and fairness. . . . That honors God."

Partnerships with National Organizations

"Most short-term mission/service projects can only be justified when they have a view toward education, recruitment, and servant leadership development," says Mark Baker, director of Koinonia Leadership Mission. KLM is a ministry of Evangelicals for Social Action, a national organization founded by Ronald Sider that provides resources and networking for holistic ministry. "We want to see [participants] return home and get involved in holistic ministries in their church or start them through their church." To this end, KLM organizes mission projects that help Christians, especially young adults, think more Christianly (use their head), demonstrate kingdom values (use their heart), and develop servant leader skills (use their hands).[11]

Historic First Presbyterian Church, a growing multiethnic and bilingual congregation in downtown Phoenix, Arizona, served as the host church for KLM's "Phoenix Project 1.01" during winter break 2000. KLM arranged the schedule for the week and coordinated the logistics. Holistic ministry specialists from the host church and from local agencies led hands-on ministry experiences and gave workshops on relevant theological and social issues. Twenty-four ministry apprentices linked head, heart, and hands in various service projects, such as ministering to kids in Historic First Church's outreach program, landscaping with two Indo-Latino agencies in a Phoenix "ghetto," and serving more than eight hundred meals on New Year's Day at St. Vincent de Paul, a Catholic para-church agency.

The students' work accomplished projects that the church and ministry agencies had little time to do themselves, encouraged and energized the local ministry staff, and enabled one agency to qualify for a matching grant. But the primary outcome of the mission related to the ministry apprentices themselves. Rubbing shoulders with "passionate prophetic voices in action" at the church and nonprofit agencies left a deep impression on the project participants. One participant, who had joined the group as a seeking nonbeliever with an interest in social justice, was moved by the week's living demonstration of the gospel and made a commitment to follow Christ. Another woman was so touched that she decided to return the following summer for an internship with Historic First Church, sponsored by KLM.

Collaborations with Government

Nehemiah rebuilt the walls of Jerusalem using materials supplied by the King of Babylon (Neh. 2:8). Today, churches sometimes provide social services using government resources. In our study, collaboration with government ranged from contracts for hundreds of thousands of dollars for housing projects to grants of under $5,000 for food pantries. Some collaborations are nonfinancial. For example, Penn State University contributes a nutrition instructor and materials for New Creation Lutheran Church's eight-week nutrition education and food distribution program, while the food comes from a nonprofit agency.

Tenth Memorial Baptist Church provides a model for effective large-scale church-state collaboration. In accord with Rev. Bill Moore's belief that "the church is to be a change agent," Tenth Memorial has provided leadership for several extensive community development projects with the support of government funds. "Members of congregations are taxpayers, and so we have fashioned a way to leverage those dollars," says Rev. Moore. "Churches should not be intimidated to do that."

The first major project was Moore Manor, a sixty-unit apartment building for low-income seniors, down the street from the church. In order to work with the federal government on this initiative, the church created the Tenth Memorial Nonprofit Development Corporation. When the church decided to tackle the problem of deteriorating housing in its neighborhood, taking advantage of Empowerment Zone funds (public funds and tax breaks targeted at specific disadvantaged neighborhoods), it launched a second nonprofit agency as the administrative conduit for a construction and first-time home buyers program, with the motto, "Building our future." Though not explicitly religious, the nonprofit organizations are linked to the church through their leadership. Rev. Moore serves as president of both, and the majority of both boards are made up of members of Tenth Memorial. By constitution, the chairs of Tenth's trustee and deacon boards, the church treasurer, and the pastor all have to be nonprofit board members as well. Both boards also include community representatives, such as a minister from another local church.

Says Rev. Moore, "People need to hear the Good News, but they also need to see it." A row of ten new homes across the street from the church, their neat yards contrasting with the crumbling housing stock all around, testifies that the church's investment in church-state collaboration has indeed visibly improved the community.

Urban-Suburban Church Partnerships

For thirteen years, inner-city pastor Dickie Robbins prayed for a cross-cultural partnership. He participated in several joint church projects, but each one fell through. In a suburb only a few miles away, Rev. Bill Borror was also seeking a cross-cultural partnership that would open new doors for Media Presbyterian Church to engage in holistic urban ministry. "As Christians, we need to share with those who haven't been given as much, or who because of sinful structures or their own sinful habits have been prevented from experiencing all that God would have them have," he explains. "We need to be there with our brothers and sisters who are ministering directly in that community." He had found, however, that many African American pastors were reluctant to work with suburban or Anglo churches. He too had experienced a church partnership that had failed.

Then, "by divine appointment," Bishop Robbins and Rev. Borror met and discovered their shared vision. Slowly, they built a partnership that has brought their very different congregations together for work and worship. Media Presbyterian Church sends construction crews to help renovate the homes purchased by Life in Christ's economic development corporation. Volunteers from Life in Christ travel to North Carolina with Media Presbyterian's annual Habitat for Humanity work trip. Professionals from Media provide financial and legal consulting to Life in Christ ministries. Life in Christ hosted the commissioning service for Media's youth group. Pulpit exchanges help bridge their divergent worship styles.

The foundation for all their joint activity is the friendship that has grown between the two senior pastors. "Projects will come and go," says Rev. Borror. "We'll have success, we'll have failure—but to build an accountable relationship, to build a mutual love and respect in Christ, that's powerful." Despite hectic schedules, the pastors meet regularly for prayer. They do not hesitate to speak their mind if problems arise in the relationship or if they see something amiss in the other's ministry. They are "kind but clear," says Bishop Robbins, and do not offend easily. A sense of humor is another essential ingredient in their relationship.

With the imbalance of resources between the churches, the relationship could easily become paternalistic. Recognizing this danger, Bishop Robbins stressed that Life in Christ's track record in holistic ministry preceded their relationship with Media Presbyterian Church. The partnership expanded what they could do but would not make them dependent. For their part, Media participants do not dictate how they will be involved; they plan the work together with leaders at Life in Christ. Media leaders affirmed early on that they wanted not only to give but to receive. They are grateful to Life in Christ for helping them accomplish their goal of discipling their members through hands-on ministry.

Another key to the partnership's success has been having a staff worker dedicated to the collaboration. The first year, Media funded a full-time "urban intern" to live and work in Chester and organize their joint projects. The intern, a Media church member with a love for the city, helped the two churches network with other Christian agencies. She also served as a mediator between the two church's worlds, giving presentations about Chester at Media and "translating" suburban culture to members of Life in Christ. The urban intern quickly ended up with too many projects on her plate, and both churches decided to scale back their expectations and narrow their goals. Media now funds a half-time urban intern who also works half-time with their youth group. This arrangement promotes greater youth involvement with Chester ministries.

The cross-cultural partnership has challenged both congregations. The experience has helped Media confront members' ignorance and prejudices. Some were too fearful at first even to drive through the city of Chester, let alone do volunteer work there. Early in their collaboration, Bishop Robbins spoke at a congregational meeting at Media that straightforwardly addressed racial issues and cultural stereotypes. Bishop Robbins acknowledges that his own congregation at first felt threatened by cultural diversity but has been learning to appreciate it.

Another challenge has been Life in Christ's lack of organization, especially at the start of their collaboration. Three times, a group from Media drove to Chester to help rehab a building, and three times Life in Christ volunteers failed to show up to unlock the building. Robbins "took his flock to task" for not taking the ministry seriously and worked with his church leaders to follow through on delegated projects. At the same time, people from Media had to adapt to the more casual, crisis-oriented urban style of getting things done. Plans suffered from miscommunications, financial arrangements fell prey to misunderstandings, and deadlines came and went without progress.

With all the problems they encountered with the partnership, did either church consider giving up? No, says Rev. Borror. "We're in it for the long haul." He never told his church it would be easy. Bishop Robbins agrees that building relationships is hard work that requires patience. But he is equally confident that their partnership is long-term. "No return trip—this is where I'm called," he says. "If we exalt the Lord and believe in his purpose for his church, we can work together."

Heidi observed firsthand the fruits of this partnership. On a chilly Saturday morning she joined work crews from Media Presbyterian Church and Life in Christ at a skeleton of a house in Chester designated for a low-income family. As Heidi scraped wallpaper, she noticed that the woman working beside her had on a shirt that had the number "5" with a halo over it, and she asked her about it. Mrs. Sanders (not her real name) told Heidi her story.

In the spring of 1999, five high school girls were killed in a terrible car accident. Mrs. Sanders's daughter was one of the casualties. Though it was not their church home, Media reached out with a caring embrace. A friend who attended Media arranged for Rev. Borror to conduct the funeral. Afterward, Rev. Borror continued to visit the Sanders family and provide counseling, and other church members brought meals. As they struggled with their grief, the family began attending services at Media. After a few months, they became members, and Mr. Sanders was baptized.

Like many victims of tragedy, Mrs. Sanders questioned God: "Why did this happen?" What she has learned, she told Heidi, was that God did not cause the accident, but God used it to bring her to Media Presbyterian Church and to a closer relationship with Christ. She doubts the family would have recovered had it not been for the church. In gratitude, she wanted to give something back to Media. But she wanted to do more than write a check; she wanted to be personally involved. When Media asked for volunteers for the joint housing rehab project, the entire family signed up. Working on the house gives her peace, a sense of knowing God better, and a sense of satisfaction in helping another family in need. She thinks her daughter would be pleased to see her family serving together.

Two families were helped that day: An African American urban family in need of a new home, and an Anglo suburban family seeking healing from grief—brought together in mutual blessing by a church partnership.

Part 3

Cultivating and Implementing the Vision

chapter twelve

Developing a Holistic Ministry Vision for Your Context

A crucial task for leaders . . . is helping a congregation gain a realistic picture of itself, its situation, and its possibilities in the present and immediate future. . . . Without such realistic assessments, . . . planners often experience frustration. Either they fail to see new possibilities for the congregation because of an inadequate grasp of the congregation, or they find that their dreams for the congregation do not fit the realities of the situation.[1]

How do the principles of holistic ministry outlined in this book connect with your church's story? How does the theological rubber grip those tough roads of your neighborhood? Holistic ministry will just be an abstract concept, an impossible ideal, unless you can give it "feet" in your own context. It helps to study models of holistic ministry, but you shouldn't simply copy them—because then your church won't become what God is calling *it* to be.

This chapter outlines three steps in the process of developing a plan for your church's holistic mission: identifying your church's unique character, potential, and hurdles related to holistic ministry; studying the community to understand your context for ministry; and cultivating a ministry vision to guide your next steps forward in mission.

249

Studying the Congregation

As a foundation for the changes that lie ahead, your congregation's first step is to take a careful look at where it is now. A congregational study recognizes that holistic ministry is not just something your church *does;* it flows from the essence of who you *are* as the body of Christ.

Why Study the Congregation?

What, concretely, are the goals of a self-assessment process?

1. *To appreciate your church's uniqueness, so that ministry remains grounded in a specific identity, vision, and context.* Holistic ministry must be incarnational—"God's people fleshing out the truth of the gospel in real needs with real people," in the words of Rev. Bill Borror. Being real means remaining true to what God is doing in *your* congregation, not just trying to imitate some other successful church. Though holistic ministry may change your church significantly, the church's essential characteristics will continue to shape the way it "fleshes out" holistic mission. Your church's outreach ministry will reflect the history, style, culture, and priorities of the congregation as a whole.

2. *To identify where God has already been at work in and through your congregation.* No church is a blank slate when it comes to ministry. Successful ministry is a growth process that builds on past experiences, learning from the failures and celebrating the successes. Throughout the Old Testament, God's promise for Israel's future is always linked with the worshipful remembrance of God's past actions in their midst. Recalling afresh how "we've come this far by faith" should lead a congregation to praise God and inspire greater trust in the Lord's leading.

3. *To bring new patterns into focus.* When Phil wore glasses for the first time as a boy, he was shocked to discover that he could see faraway things such as signs, bricks on buildings, and leaves on trees. Similarly, when you look at your church through a self-study lens, aspects of church life may become clearer. You may discover, for example, that your church has a history of hiring detail-oriented, independent-minded ministry staff who come into conflict with the congregation's informal, participatory style. Or that a theological foundation for holistic mission is already present but is not reflected in actual ministry practices. Or that new Christians generally fade out of church life because there are no programs to connect them with discipling opportunities. These discoveries can energize the drive to change.

4. *To help develop a strategy for change.* In the business world, before a company launches a new project, it often conducts a detailed feasibility study that lays out the history, resources, staff, and track record of the organization. This helps planners determine the most efficient and realistic approach to the new project. While churches can't—and shouldn't—try to map their course in too much detail, having a game plan grounded in the facts is an essential ingredient of successful ministry development.

5. *To help anticipate challenges.* Knowing its weaknesses as well as its strengths allows your church to shore up spiritual and material defenses. Conflict, discouragement, and strained resources are inevitable—but they are easier to deal with when they don't catch you off guard.

6. *To take the pulse of your church's commitment to serving Christ and openness to change.* The aim is not to test whether the church has already arrived, or whether it has what it takes to get there, but whether it is willing to be made ready for the journey.

The Congregational Study Process

We suggest that the church commission a small group to gather church documents, talk to representative attenders, and reflect on your congregational life together. The group should reflect the diverse makeup of the congregation and include laypeople as well as staff. So that the members of the study committee will not feel overwhelmed, assure them that their task is to write a brief overview of the key points, not a doctoral dissertation. A "working first draft" report of reasonable length completed by church members in three to four months is far more useful than an extensive, year-long study undertaken by professionals. Encourage the committee to proceed boldly, knowing that their task is just to start the ball rolling.

Below is an overview of five areas of congregational study most relevant to outreach. The questions cover a broad range of topics, because the health of the church's outreach is dependent on the health of the church as a whole (see chapter 8). Don't expect consensus when answering the questions; congregations are (and should be) internally diverse. And don't try to make your church look good. You are not creating a brochure for outsiders but holding up a mirror in order to paint a self-portrait. In any case, there are no "right" answers.

These questions and the self-study process are outlined in more detail in a resource available from Evangelicals for Social Action.[2] You may also want to refer to the handbook *Studying Congregations*,[3] which offers a comprehensive guide to the "disciplined study of the congregation," for more in-depth discussion and additional data-gathering tools.

Five Congregational Self-Images

Which image best describes your church?

The *Pillar* church is anchored in a place, its community, and feels a distinct responsibility for it. The members are pillars of the community, good citizens. Resources of heritage, leadership, facilities, and finances are used to strengthen the community (1 Peter 2:4–5).

The *Pilgrim* church takes care of its own people wherever they are, as distinguished from the Pillar's sense of being rooted in a place. Some Pilgrim congregations have moved with their people, from one dwelling place to another. Their culture and their Christian faith are woven into a single fabric. Other Pilgrim congregations have seen waves of immigrant or racial change, and "old ethnics" and "new ethnics" now share the story (Heb. 11:13–14; 1 Peter 2:9).

Survivor churches live on the edge, always on the verge of being overwhelmed by emergencies. They do not expect to conquer their problems but hang on because "we've made it through worse than this before." They are determined rather than domineering, relentless rather than aggressive. They can be resilient, productive, and loving when leaders learn to make positive use of their orientation to crises (Matt. 7:2–3; 1 Cor. 4:12).

The *Prophet* church understands its calling to challenge the world and may focus on individuals or corporations, communities or nations. These crusades are supported by people who share the church's commitments. Both Prophetic and Survivor churches carry a sense of crisis and expect a high energy response, but the Prophets are proactive while the Survivors are reactive (Great Commandment and Great Commission, Micah 6:8).

The *Servant* church goes about the work of helping people in need with a quiet faithfulness. Whereas Pillars feel responsibility for the entire community and Pilgrims respond to people groups, Servants see individuals in need and reach out to help them in supportive and pastoral ways. Their faith is lived out in service. Prophet and Servant churches are able to recruit nonmembers to join them for a particular ministry program (Mark 9:35; Acts 2:45).

Adapted from Carl S. Dudley and Sally A. Johnson, *Energizing the Congregation: Images That Shape Your Congregation's Ministry* (Louisville: Westminster/John Knox, 1993).

Self-Study Questions

1. *Who are we?* Examine your congregational *identity* and *history.* How would your congregation describe itself and its ministries? What traditions and characteristics make you unique? What problems, questions, or concerns now occupy

the congregation's attention? What major changes or upheavals has the church experienced? What projects or acquisitions have generated the most satisfaction/controversy in recent years, particularly related to outreach ministry? Who in your church's history has played a key role in ministry development?

Also look at *membership*. Who makes up the congregation? Describe the members and regular attenders of your church in terms of key demographic factors such as age, gender, ethnicity, family status, income, education, and occupation. Who is "our kind of people"? Who is most—and least—welcome? Where do members live in relationship to the church: Are they mostly commuters or community residents? How does your congregation recruit new members? Are they coming from conversions or transfers? How has the membership changed over time? Who has been leaving the church and why?

2. *What do we believe?*[4] Examine key areas of your church's *theology* relevant to outreach: What is the Good News? What does it mean to be saved? How is the church to witness to Christ: by telling people about the gospel and/or by demonstrating the gospel (e.g., through lifestyle and service)? Is sin personal and/or structural? In what sense do God's plans for redemption include communities and the world as a whole? What is God's purpose for the church in the world? What Scripture passages are most central to your church's mission? What other sources—such as the denomination, a historical legacy, books, Christian leaders, or other churches—have been influential in your church's theology of mission?

3. *What do we do?* This question has three components. Examine your church's *ministries of congregational nurture*. How does your church help members deepen and apply their spiritual life? How does your church meet material, personal, and relational needs within the congregation (such as helping with rent or transportation, responding to a death in the family, or offering marital counseling)? What programs does your church offer to help members improve their lives (such as support groups or seminars on health or parenting)? What ministries does your church sponsor for children and youth (such as recreation, spiritual development, or mentoring)? To what extent are nurture ministries open to the community?

Also describe your church's *outreach*. What social ministries are in place? Are these primarily aimed at providing goods and services, developing skills or character, promoting economic/community development, and/or reforming politics and social structures? What programs of evangelism and evangelism training are in place? Does the church target a specific geographical area, ethnic group, or type of need for outreach? How are outreach ministries promoted within the congregation? To what extent do evangelism and social care occur informally, through members' everyday lives? What is your process for handling requests for emergency assistance? What have been the observable outcomes of outreach ministries, both quantitative (e.g., numbers of people served or units of assistance provided; numbers who have accepted Christ, rededicated their life to Christ, or joined the church) and qualitative (e.g., improvements in the overall quality of life in the community, transformation in individual lives)?

Additionally, assess your church's *ministry priorities* in terms of staff and volunteer time, resources, attention from the pulpit, and so on. What is the balance:

- between ministries of internal congregational nurture and external outreach to others?
- between evangelism and social outreach? Are they completely separate ministries, interconnected ministries, or integrated within the same ministries?
- between local and global mission?

4. *How do we do what we do?* Examine your church's *leadership*. How would you describe the style of pastor(s) and key ministry leaders: hands-on types or delegators, orderly or spontaneous, independent or team workers, entrepreneurial or managerial, down-to-earth or visionary? What activities take up most of the leaders' time—and what (if anything) would they rather be doing? What education, training, work history, and significant personal experiences have shaped the leaders' approach to outreach ministry? In what sense, if at all, do leaders work as a team? What factors, both within and outside the church, support and/or drain leaders' ability to carry out their roles? How are new church and ministry leaders identified, recruited, and trained?

Consider your church as an *organization*. How are decisions made and implemented, especially those that involve your church's outreach (for example, launching a new ministry or allocating funding)? What values or principles guide these decisions? How do things actually get done? How is information shared about church activities, decisions, and ministry opportunities? To what extent does your church engage in strategic planning? What systems of accountability and evaluation are in place?

What *resources* does your church have to work with? This includes financial resources, including funding sources within and outside the congregation; facilities, equipment, and other material resources; human resources from within and outside the congregation; and intangible resources, such as a positive reputation in the community and connections to influential people or institutions. How are funds raised and managed? How are ministry volunteers recruited and supervised?

5. *What are our relationships like?* Examine the congregation's *relationship with God*. What is the role of the Bible, prayer, and the Holy Spirit in decision making, in outreach activities, and in other aspects of congregational life? Are

people growing spiritually? How are members' spiritual gifts recognized and used to build up the church? Describe a typical worship service. In what ways is a theology of holistic mission or the church's mission/vision statement referred to in worship services?

What are the characteristics of *relationships within the congregation?* Do members of the congregation live within the same neighborhood or see one another outside of church activities? Are there small group opportunities for church members to get together regularly on a more intimate basis? To what extent do members look to one another for spiritual nurture and practical care? How are newcomers welcomed and incorporated into church life? How has your church handled conflicts, particularly pertaining to the church's mission?

Also look at your church's *relationships beyond the congregation.* How would you describe your church's relationship with and reputation in its community of ministry? How has the church been involved in community life, outside of outreach programs? What opportunities exist for people in the congregation to get to know people in the community? What outside groups does your church connect with to carry out ministry goals (e.g., the denomination, foundations, community agencies, government, etc.)? Does the pastor or other church leader represent the church in an official capacity, for example, on a city committee or the board of a nonprofit agency?

Processing the Congregational Self-Study

After the self-study committee turns in its report, the church should appoint a group (not necessarily the same group that created the report) to process its implications for ministry development. A retreat setting is helpful to eliminate distractions and foster an atmosphere of worshipful reflection. The purpose of this group is to explore how your congregation's unique characteristics may affect the shape of its ministry, to assess your church's readiness for holistic ministry, and to discover areas of church life needing to be strengthened, clarified, or changed in order to move forward in ministry. At this stage, the group is not trying to develop a detailed plan for expanded outreach. Rather, it should pray and share ideas for an initial sense of direction.

The following five reflection questions can help the group focus the analysis of your church:

1. *In light of the theology and models presented in this book, how holistic is your church?* There is no simple scale from 1 to 10, but you can identify the areas in which growth is most needed, including:

- *theology* for mission
- *spiritual passion* animating mission

- the congregation's *commitment* to mission
- the *amount* of outreach mission
- the *type* of outreach
- the *integration* of spiritual and social ministry within outreach
- the *balance* of outreach with internal congregational nurture

In particular, look for areas where your church's beliefs and practice are inconsistent. Many churches agree with holistic mission in principle, but their actual ministry says something quite different.

2. *What does your church's identity and history tell you about the likely direction and shape your outreach mission might take?* Every church should do something, but no church can do everything. How does the way you answer the question, Who are we? influence your answer to the question, What kind of ministry should we do? Nor can a church work on everything at once. Holistic mission is a journey that unfolds one step at a time. Does your history cast any light on the direction for your next steps? What stages of the journey have you passed through thus far? What ministry doors have opened and closed, what past problems have been resolved, what themes keep reoccurring? This reflection on your church's unique story is a critical ingredient in strategic planning.

3. *What are the church's strengths and weaknesses for holistic ministry?* Most congregational characteristics can be an asset and/or an obstacle. For example, a large building opens up space for ministry programs, but building maintenance can siphon off funds and energy. Having a strong sense of church as family is healing to people within the church body, but it can also give outsiders the impression that the congregation is a closed circle. A historical legacy of providing an after-school program may rally church members to continued acts of service, but it can also be difficult to break out of the mold if you sense the Lord is calling your church in a new ministry direction.

4. *Are there areas of conflict or confusion related to ministry?* Sometimes church leaders have one set of beliefs and priorities, while the congregation has another. Sometimes different groups within the congregation pull the church's mission in different directions. Congregants may have only a vague sense of what the church's mission is and why they should support it. This may call for further teaching and training or for a demonstration ministry project to educate and unite the church body.

5. *What might hold back the church from moving forward in mission?* Barriers to change may include a sense of inadequacy related to church size, skills,

leadership, or resources; an overly bureaucratic structure that resists change, or an overly loose structure that provides no foothold for change; prejudiced attitudes about people in need; objections from the denomination or from key financial supporters; internal struggles that drain energy from outreach; or negative past experiences with outreach mission. Every change and innovation comes with a price. What will a new emphasis on holistic ministry cost (see chapter 14)? What individuals or groups in the congregation will be most affected by the change?

A careful, honest look at the attributes, strengths, and weaknesses of your congregation will help you avoid fatal mistakes later in the process. Of course, you don't want the self-study to continue forever as an excuse for inaction. Self-assessment should be undertaken with a posture of sober humility and open-minded optimism. A church should take its past and present seriously enough to recognize that its uniqueness is an important clue to what God wants it to do, but not so seriously that it refuses to change in order to participate more fully in God's redeeming mission.

Studying the Community

After or alongside the congregational study, your church should also study its community context. Evangelicalism, notes Ray Bakke, has had "a theology of persons and programs, but it lacked a conscious theology of place."[5] Evangelical theology has traditionally focused on individuals while forgetting that individuals are created to live in community. You can't love the whole person without paying attention to his or her context.

Why Study the Community?

Your church may have a general sense of the needs in the community where God is calling it to serve. But that is not enough. Trying to do holistic ministry without carefully studying the community context is as unwise as interpreting a particular Bible verse out of context, without regard to its setting within the book and the Bible as a whole. Churches must learn to do "exegesis of environments."[6] A church must become a student of a community in order to become its servant.

A thorough community assessment has five main goals:

1. *To guide strategic planning and the development of new ministries.* Tenth Memorial Baptist Church ministers in the heart of North Philadelphia with open eyes and open arms. Hear how Rev. Bill Moore's knowledge of the his-

tory, demographics, and identity of this community flows into his vision for its revitalization:

> North Philadelphia at its height in the 1950s and 1960s . . . [had] some 500,000 people. From the riots on, . . . we lost about a quarter of a million people. That accounts for a lot of the vacant and abandoned houses in North Central Philadelphia. The demographics indicate that the population . . . is primarily senior citizens and single-headed households. . . . We also noticed that for a lot of home owners, when the senior member of the family died, the young people didn't want to live in North Philadelphia—they moved out of the area.
>
> So we had a goal of not only providing safe and affordable housing for seniors but also repopulating the area with home buyers, because this brings a different level of investment and pride into the community. . . . With the revitalization that's going on in the area, there's more and more of a desire on the part of people to come back to the neighborhoods. . . . When we did the marketing for [the new housing], we got calls from people out of the area, people wanting to come back.

Familiarity with his community's past and present conditions motivates and guides Rev. Moore in drawing the blueprints for a new future.

Without a community assessment, ministry designs may be flawed. Effective ministry depends on an accurate diagnosis of the need. Timothy Keller provides a helpful metaphor:

> In some ways, trying to devise a program to help "the poor" is something like asking a doctor to prescribe medicine for "sickness." There is no cure for "sickness," because it is only a general term for many specific conditions. In the same way, *the poor* is really a vast heading for numerous specific conditions. A systematic assessment of the community helps us identify and pinpoint the characteristics of different target groups of people.[7]

While some "target groups" are obvious (homeless persons, nursing home residents, prisoners), some needs lie below the surface. "Every community has people who are ignored, marginalized, or simply out of sight," writes Carl Dudley in his helpful book, *Basic Steps toward Community Ministry.*[8] Seniors making ends meet on meager pensions. Undocumented workers fearful of deportation. Divorcees coping with emotional and financial loss. Parents worn down by caring simultaneously for children and ailing parents. People with mental illness. Low-skilled workers scraping by on low-wage jobs. Latch-key children. Uncovering these pockets of pain and tracing their causes can change a church's ministry priorities.

Since communities are always in flux, a community study also helps anticipate a future trajectory for outreach. Churches often struggle to keep up with entrenched problems. Your church has the opportunity to get ahead of the game by preparing to respond to the needs just beginning to emerge. For example, if demographic trends reveal a large increase in the number of younger married home owners, you can begin planning for day care and after-school programs. Information improves a church's ability to make prudent, strategic investments with its ministry resources.

2. *To help understand the forces that affect the lives of people in the community.* Individuals are profoundly influenced by the demographic, cultural, and organizational dynamics of their community. The community environment not only governs residents' access to basic essentials such as jobs and housing, but it conveys a message about residents' value and worth. A community can either affirm or undermine the image of God in people. This is not to say that the environment *determines* a person's worldview and choices. God gives individuals free will and holds them accountable for their actions, regardless of their context. However, the social context influences what choices people are faced with, the options they perceive are available to them, and the resources they can use in exercising their choices. William Bratton, chief of police in New York City, based his policing strategy on this fact of human nature. His book *Fixing Broken Windows* describes how taking measures to restore order and decency in public spaces helped curb crime of every sort.

Some community dynamics responsible for creating human need are obvious: a shortage of jobs, for example, or neglectful slumlords.

> Other forces can be quiet and nameless, like the slowly declining real wages that create pressure for both parents of very young children to work outside the home in order to make ends meet. . . . Other trends that can creep up on us are those that first affect our children, for example, the expectation that everyone in a classroom is computer-literate.[9]

One of the "quiet and nameless" forces is the availability of "social capital." Social capital "consists, in part, of trust and mutual obligation, in part of information gathered and available, and in part of norms that encourage prosocial and discourage antisocial behaviors."[10] Social capital operates like financial capital, as a building block for accomplishing residents' goals. A healthy civil society shapes the community's moral values, provides crucial social support, and attracts the investment of outside resources into the community. "Community cohesion" is a key factor in preventing violence in a community. A cohesive community is one in which people look out for their neighbors' children and take pride in keeping their streets clean. Another necessity is healthy links between the community and the rest of the world. When a community is cut off from outside resources and cultural influences, it becomes as stagnant as a weed-choked pond. Tools that measure a community's social health can help your church find ways of naming and talking about the "invisible" barriers to community restoration.[11]

The community's history can also provide important clues about the roots of human need. In Wichita, Kansas, for example, Hilltop Urban Church often deals with housing-related crises. Their neighborhood is a by-product of World War II. The "temporary" homes in their neighborhood were hastily built by the U.S. government to accommodate the rush of workers producing fighter planes and weapons. The original designers certainly did not foresee that the homes would continue to house families fifty years later. Today the cracker box homes with their rock bottom rents continue to attract low-income families. When residents come to Hilltop Urban Church for help paying their high utility bills in the winter, or after an electrical fire has destroyed their furniture, the church does not assume that they have poor budgeting skills or were simply careless. The church views each individual crisis in the context of the problems that history has literally built into the community as a whole.

3. *To help understand community factors that influence the effectiveness of church ministries.* New Covenant Church of Philadelphia used to sponsor an outreach to a housing project that had the reputation of being the worst housing project in Philadelphia. Church members brought in food, clothing, and holiday baskets; gave out tracts; led children in games and Bible stories; organized evangelistic musical events; and held regular Bible studies and worship services. Residents began coming to the Lord, and a new church was planted. Then, within a matter of months, the ministry (except for an off-site computer learning center) shut down. Not because the church lost interest or volunteers or because the residents rejected them. Rather, the Philadelphia Housing Authority hired a new director, with a goal of breaking up the larger housing projects. He reduced the number of apartments from 1,300 units to 465, moving out many residents as the buildings were demolished or renovated. The church's community of ministry simply disappeared!

This may be an extreme example, but there are many ways that a community can influence a church's effectiveness and opportunities for ministry. Demographic changes, factory closings, new housing construction, political battles, overly zealous building inspectors, zoning laws—all these can affect (for better or for worse) a church's outreach. Researching community assets (both secular and faith-based) allows a church to connect with other resources, to prevent the duplication of services, and to identify potential allies, such as block captains. The culture of a community is also a factor to be taken into account, particularly when a congregation is from a different ethnic or class background.

If a church is not aware of these external influences, it may too quickly become discouraged or fight the wrong battles. On the flip side, failing to note the contribution of contextual factors to a program's success may leave church members wondering why a program that has succeeded elsewhere does not work when it is replicated in a different setting. Churches are most effective when contextual information shapes their planning and when their ministries are responsive to feedback from the community.

4. *To help understand how the church itself is affected by the community.* We often think about the church as salt and light, as an agent of change in a community. That is, after all, the point of outreach ministry. But the surroundings also affect the church. The relationship between church and community is what sociologists call an "open system," with reciprocal lines of influence. That is why it is important to understand how your church's specific geographic and cultural setting has helped to shape its identity. *Studying Congregations* explains, "The more leaders and members are helped to see and understand the power of the context on their congregation's life and their participation in it, the greater the possibility they have of cultivating a more responsible and effective expression of their faith commitments."[12] As researcher Nancy Ammerman has found, churches that are willing to accept and adapt to changing environmental factors remain more viable than the ones that stubbornly resist all adaptation as "compromise."[13]

The history of Cookman United Methodist Church in North Philadelphia dramatically illustrates this point. Like many urban churches of the post–World War II era, Cookman was built to serve an Anglo working-class population, bolstered by a booming postwar industrial economy. That all changed in the 1960s and 1970s. Cookman's neighborhood like so many others was devastated by the combined impact of "white flight," increasing violence, loss of industry, and the eventual decay of the city's infrastructure. The congregation dwindled to a handful of Anglo church members who continued to commute to Cookman for Sunday worship, driving through what had become a predominantly poor, African American neighborhood. The rest of the week, the large stone edifice stood empty, with locked doors. One Sunday in the 1970s, a black activist group stormed into the service and chained themselves to the altar. They pledged not to leave until the church made itself available to the community. That was the original congregation's last worship service!

Because of that confrontation, however, the denomination allowed a senior services agency to use the property during the week—a relationship that has lasted to this day and that opened the door to other community partnerships. After a gap of several years, the church reopened with eight attenders from the neighborhood, as a new pastor slowly began rebuilding a congregation more open to the community. Rev. Jones, the current pastor, has continued to build this identity. The community's deteriorating physical and social conditions threaten to overwhelm the congregation and contribute to the church's chronic budget shortfalls, maintenance needs, and inconsistent attendance record. Rev. Jones believes, however, that the best response is not to shore up the church's defenses against the community's problems but to identify with them and meet them head-on. The church is vulnerable to the ills of the community, but in return, the community is becoming more responsive to the life-giving, transformational message of the church.

5. *To discern how your church is perceived by the community.* Taking the pulse of the community gives a church the opportunity to see itself from the community's perspective. Churches are sometimes woefully unaware of, or misled about, their reputation in the community. A church may consider itself a model of compassion and integrity—while what leaves an impression on local residents are church members who are rude drivers and youth who sneak out of the service to smoke. Or, more positively, the church may not know that the community still associates the church with the dedicated outreach of a prior generation. The community's point of view is certainly not *the* truth about the congregation. But it can represent a stepping-stone—or a barrier—to building effective ministries. Moreover, hearing what people think about your church and the role of churches in the community in general can make your evangelistic efforts more sensitive to people's hopes and concerns.

Getting to Know Your Community

To build effective ministry, says Carl Dudley, "we must see the world as clearly as possible. Otherwise our familiarity and our prejudices will bind us to the past and blind us to problems, trends, and new possibilities."[14] A church's preconceptions are the colored lens through which it interprets and applies a community study. An important preliminary step in studying a ministry context, therefore, is to check the church's perceptions of the community. "How do you look at your community? Opportunity for or obstacle to change? 'Field white unto harvest' or wasteland? Us vs. Them? Babylon or New Jerusalem? A place to embrace or a plague to avoid?"[15]

Or is the community off the church's radar screen altogether? In the play *Our Town,* the character Emily dies but is granted an opportunity to return home to relive one day of her life. She comes to realize that people live most of the time without truly seeing and hearing the people around them. "So all that was going on and we never noticed," she cries regretfully. Similarly, a church can exist in a community for decades without ever really paying attention to its neighbors. A community study provides a structured process for "noticing" the community in a new way (see sidebar).[16] Not only does this process bring neighborhood dynamics into clearer view, but the disciplines of looking and listening nourish a congregation's sense of belonging and attachment to a community.

Tools for Community Study

Methods your church can use to get to know its community include:

Census data and other published reports: The census (available on the Internet, www.census.gov) provides a wealth of demographic information and tracks changing trends. Other kinds of studies of the community may also be available from a local university, the school board, the chamber of commerce, or another church.

Maps: Get or make a detailed map of your community. Fill in symbols for the key components of community life: owner-occupied homes, rental properties, abandoned buildings, businesses, schools, nonprofit institutions, government agencies (post office, police station, welfare office, etc.), youth-oriented places and hangout spots, churches, and so on. Color code the symbols to indicate which represent key assets, needs, and potential partners.

Surveys: Written or oral questionnaires ask residents to identify local needs, issues, and assets. Surveys are best conducted door-to-door by church members, creating opportunities to develop relationships and name recognition in the process. (Amy Sherman suggests that if church members are not from the community, pair each member on the survey team with a local resident who knows the people in the neighborhood.)

Interviews: Identify leaders and insiders in the community (elected officials, business leaders, other pastors, longtime residents) to interview. Ask questions about their experiences and perceptions of the community, their perceptions of your church, and their suggestions for how the church could contribute to the community's well-being.

Focus groups: Gather a group of community residents to share their insights. Groups can either reflect the diversity of the community or share a common key characteristic (such as being seniors or parents of teenagers). At the start of a community study, it is helpful to ask broad questions about people's opinions and observations of community life. Later, focus groups can target specific questions (such as what kinds of ministries for seniors are needed, or why residents think so many local teens are becoming pregnant).

Observation: Conduct visual surveys by foot and by car ("windshield surveys"). Soak in community life: shop, eat, and take public transportation in the community; hang out in public places such as parks, libraries, and welfare offices; listen in (inconspicuously) on conversations at public events such as a T-ball game or a town meeting; volunteer for local nonprofit agencies. Observation in a spirit of Christian servanthood—as distinct from voyeurish, gawking, "slumming"—is especially important if your community of ministry is geographically, culturally, or economically distant from your own.

To appreciate the marvelously complex realities of a community, a church has to learn to see it from several different perspectives.

The social science perspective: What is the community like? Community analysis from a social science perspective has three layers:

1. *demographics*—characteristics of community residents, such as gender, ethnicity, income, occupation, family size and structure.
2. *culture*—"systems of meaning, values, and practices" that shape how people in the community live, including ethnicity, religion, and social class.
3. *organization*—"systems of roles and relationships that structure the interactions of people in the community." Organizational analysis takes note of institutions such as schools, businesses, and churches; infrastructure such as streets, parks, and telephone lines; and systems such as the criminal justice system and the local economy.[17]

A description of the community should not be limited to the typical question, What are the community's needs? If a church looks only at needs, it will end up defining the community only in terms of its needs. An asset-based analysis leads a church to look beyond quick fixes for the community's problems.[18]

The political perspective: How do things get done here? Consider how decisions are made that affect people's quality of life. Positions of decision-making power within a community are both formal (ward captains) and informal (block "mamas"). Who holds power in the community, and who benefits from their decisions? What are the channels of access to those in power? Also consider the impact of decision makers outside the community. For example, pressure from suburban municipalities may force an urban district with little political influence to accept a new sewer treatment plant. Changes in a bank's lending policies can shrink the investment capital available to a low-income community. Coverage decisions by news media can reinforce negative stereotypes about a community. Who in the community is active in responding to these types of challenges?

The historical perspective: What happened here? "Contexts are in a real sense consequences," writes Ray Bakke, "environmental, economic, and political consequences of historical forces. Context is the residue of the past experienced in the present."[19] As you consider a community's character, needs, and issues, ask, How did the community get to be the way it is today? How have changes in the community impacted residents' lives?

History can also point to past accomplishments that can inspire hope for a community's future. Bethel Temple Community Bible Church ministers in the community of Kensington, known by some as the "badlands." The church is surrounded by the husks of abandoned factories, boarded row houses, and weed-filled lots. Today these are emblems of urban blight—but they also serve as mute reminders of a flourishing past. In 1900, Kensington was distinguished for its abundance of industry and manufacturing. It was a proud neighborhood where families could raise their children in safety and dignity. Knowing this legacy makes it easier for Bethel to sustain faith that the community can once again be a place of shalom.

The spiritual perspective: What is unseen here? In Daniel 10:13, an angel refers to a struggle with "the prince of the kingdom of Persia" that hindered a response to Daniel's prayer for the restoration of his people. Much about this text is mysterious, but it and other texts, such as Paul's reference to principalities and powers (Eph. 6:12), show that evil spiritual powers are intertwined with personal brokenness, societal decay, and unjust systems. Destructive events can leave spiritual scars that affect a community for generations. On the positive side, "lighthouses" of prayer and faithful Christian service can quietly leaven the loaf. By the Spirit we can discern the spiritual realities that lie behind the tangible, visible attributes of our communities.

Processing the Community Study

Many churches conduct the study, write the report, talk about the report, file the report, and *forget* about the report. But a community study is not information for information's sake; it is "harvest field data," gathered with the purpose of equipping the church to sow faith and hope.[20] Keep this goal in mind. If you allow your study committee to get bogged down in statistics or overwhelmed with details, you will end up with "paralysis of analysis." Three questions can guide your church as it processes the community study report.

1. *What aspects of community life need to be transformed by God's holy love in word and deed?* Some things about your community should stir up what David Frenchak calls a "holy discontent."[21] The whole creation groans under its bondage to decay, says Romans 8:21–22, and we too groan in our spirits as we yearn for Christ's complete redemption. This world is not the way the good Creator intended it to be! What about the community grieves you, raises your hackles, fills you with a yearning to see things change? Who in the community is crying out for God's healing touch?

Address these questions from a holistic perspective, tuning in to both spiritual and material needs. Ask God to help you see the community through his eyes, looking past the outward appearance of things to the heart of the matter (1 Sam. 16:7). In more affluent communities, we may be inclined to conclude from the well-kept lawns, expensive cars, and clean streets that all is well and that the church's services are not needed. But polished exteriors can mask many forms of brokenness—family conflict, addictions, the scars of abuse, spiritual emptiness. And in low-income communities, while the eye is naturally drawn to physical evidence of need—graffiti, abandoned buildings, trash blowing along the street—God can redirect our vision to the asset he cares about most: the people.

2. *How is God already at work in the community?* Often churches assume God is only "in here" and is waiting for us Christians to reach out. But God is also "out there" in the community working ahead of us, preparing hearts, cultivating the soil of relationships, planting seeds of common grace. To be effective in the community, we need to get on board with what God is already doing. A community study becomes a treasure hunt for the wheat of God's activity, hidden among the tares (Matt. 13:24–30). This approach is especially essential for distressed neighborhoods that are usually viewed in terms of their problems. With the understanding that "every alley, street, and barrio is under Christ's lordship" (Col. 1:15–17), ask the Lord to show you where his reign is already evident in the community.[22]

While we naturally gravitate toward the movers and shakers, Scripture makes it plain that God also (or even primarily) works among those on the margins. Look for the people who demonstrate God's love and build up the community through the rhythms of ordinary life, people such as teachers, homemakers, and Little League coaches. And don't limit your search to Christians. Remember that God called the idolatrous king Nebuchadnezzar "my servant" (Jer. 27:6). God can work through any person or institution to accomplish his aims.

3. *What does God desire for this community?* In the midst of a violent, oppressive, and idolatrous society, the Hebrew prophets sparked hope with a bold promise of a new age for their people. As theology professor Cornelius Plantinga Jr. describes, they spoke of a time when:

> weeping would cease, and people could sleep without weapons on their laps. People could work in peace and work to fruitful effect. Lambs could lay down with lions. All nature would be fruitful, benign, and filled with wonder upon wonder; all humans would be knit together in brotherhood and sisterhood; and all nature and all humans would look to God, walk with God, lean toward God, and delight in God. . . . The webbing together of God, humans, and all creation in justice, fulfillment, and delight is what the Hebrew prophets call *shalom*.[23]

What would shalom look like in your community? This is the time for exercising the sanctified imagination, for holy wishing. Draw on the hopes and dreams of the community residents you have talked to, as well as the extravagant stock of biblical promises. What could this community be like if people embraced God's transforming redemption, if neighbors loved one another, if the natural environment was flourishing, if social institutions treated people as responsible, valued creations made in the image of God?

These three questions should naturally lead your church to a fourth: *So what are we going to do about it?* How is your church, as Christ's hands and feet in this community, called to participate in God's redemptive plan? This brings us to the process of crystalizing the church's holistic ministry vision.

Developing a Holistic Ministry Vision

A vision is a portrait of the future that a church is called to help bring about. A vision points to a church's unique potential to help bring about "another reality beyond what is immediately visible," through the transforming power of Christ.[24] While the hopes and dreams sparked by a community study may be quite broad, a vision focuses a church's attention on a particular area of ministry. This focus is necessary to establish priorities and form a strategic plan. A holistic ministry vision builds on a congregational identity to respond in a specific way to the needs and opportunities in the community context, out of a desire to share the love of God in word and deed.

Sometimes a leader already has a clear sense of where the church should go. God often speaks first to leaders. However, a ministry vision is strongest when it is not imposed from the top down but is allowed to percolate through the prayers and reflections of a group. A group discernment process may end up confirming and refining the leader's vision—or it may alter the leader's sense of direction. Involving other members increases the congregation's sense of ownership and its willingness to work to make the vision a reality. As Bishop Milton Grannum puts it, "People will commit 80 percent to the things that concern them, whereas they commit 20 percent to the things that concern you." The more people you involve in the planning and visioning process, and the more they sense that the ministry touches their concerns, the closer people will get to committing 100 percent to the vision.

To make the process collaborative, form a group with a cross section of clergy and laypeople (including representation from major church ministries and from the groups that conducted the church and community studies). The helpful book *Leading Congregational Change* calls this a "vision path committee."[25] These people must be mature Christians, dedicated to the congregation, and open to the Spirit's leading (1 Tim. 3:1–13). Everyone in the group should have read the reports from the church and community studies. This group can then seek God's direction through a baker's dozen steps:

1. *Pray.* Prayer is central to the process, not just an agenda item at the beginning or end of meetings. Thank God for all the unique and wonderful attributes of your congregation. Pray about the areas of church life that

need strengthening and the obstacles to holistic ministry. Pray over what you've discovered about the needs and God's activity in your community. Thank God for all that you see in the community that brings glory to God. Ask God to give you a burden for the things that grieve the Spirit and for courage and openness to receive God's direction. Pray to be guided by love.

2. *Read.* Study passages of Scripture that shed light on the church's mission in the world. Read your local newspaper, with spectacles that seek God's activity and God's perspective on current events. Draw from the many great books and articles on the mission of the church: case studies to enlarge your vision and theological tomes to stretch your thinking. Read classics from authors who challenge us in ministry: Jacques Ellul's *Presence of the Kingdom,* Dietrich Bonhoeffer's *Cost of Discipleship,* or John Howard Yoder's *Politics of Jesus.* Read books by futurists such as Tom Sine, Len Sweet, Peter Senge, or Peter Drucker. Don't stick exclusively to Christian literature. Not everyone needs to read the same materials; expose the group to as many ideas as possible.

3. *Pray.* Ask the Lord for insights from your reading. Where is God directing your group's attention? What does God want to say through these resources? How might God be challenging the church's ministry beliefs or practices? Thank God for the examples and teachings of other faithful servants.

4. *Discuss.* What issues are raised by the reports and the readings? Which ministry models seem most applicable to your context? What action steps seem possible? What seems so impossible that it just might be from God?

5. *Pray.* Be still. Quiet yourselves. Spend more time listening to God than talking. Allow God's Spirit to speak to your spirits.

6. *Brainstorm.* List what you've learned and new ideas—on laptop, overhead, flip chart, or notepad. At this stage, no idea is too insignificant or implausible. Some items may stand out as immediately useful, while you may want to store others in a backup file. Do any common themes emerge?

7. *Pray.* In preparation to apply what you've learned, submit yourselves and your congregation to God. "Lord, we don't want to run ahead of you. Help us to move boldly, courageously, and confidently forward at your pace. We want to do your will in your way. Please remove any obstacles that exist in our thoughts and deeds."

8. *Discern.* Are you sensing a direction? Can you narrow down all the wonderful potential holistic ministries and opportunities for service to a few that you could do and sense you should do? In what areas do you need

to trust God that some other entity will take on what your congregation is not called to do?

9. *Pray.* Talk to God about your emerging sense of vision. Lay before God the many decisions to be made—leadership, budgets, location, logistics. "God, how should we proceed? What do you want us to learn in this process?"

10. *Plan.* Spell out a concrete plan and examine the action steps this new direction will require. Who is God raising up to lead these new endeavors? What partners, resources, and new organizational structures may be needed? At this stage, prepare to communicate your tentative vision to a larger circle.

11. *Pray.* Ask God to transform your lives and the entire congregation. Ask for humility, boldness, and above all, love. Ask that the church's leaders will have open minds and hearts. "We want to bring honor and glory to you in all that we say and do, so check our egos and make us one in the Spirit."

12. *Confirm.* By whatever process is appropriate in your church, share the new vision with those in a position to make decisions regarding the church's direction, such as the governing board or the entire membership. Also confirm the vision with those outside the congregation who know the church, such as a sister church or denominational leaders. If you have cultivated relationships with congregations, agencies, or individuals within the community of ministry, ask for their feedback as well.

13. *Pray.* Give God the glory! Offer praise and thanksgiving. Request power, diligence, endurance, and faith to press on. Ask for "a second touch" (Mark 8:23–25) so that you can see more clearly what lies ahead. Pray for church leaders and for all the saints. Pray for those whom you will reach with the Good News and good works of Christ.

Whether or not a pastor chairs the vision path committee, pastors should be deeply involved in this process to ensure that the developing vision meets several criteria:

- Is the vision consistent with holistic ministry theology? Will it be truly holistic when put into practice?
- Is it born out of love for the community, or does it primarily serve the interests of the congregation?
- Does it take input from the community into account, or is it based on the church's assumptions about what the community needs?
- Does it take the church's specific identity and context into account, without being a slave to "the way we've always done things around here"?

A ministry vision is not static; it grows and evolves as it is implemented. Calvin Miller supplies this metaphor: "No ship ever sails in a straight line. It moves between corrected settings of port and starboard to zigzag its way along what appears to be a straight course. A thousand corrections of rudder and sail make the right course possible."[26] Pastors play a key role in discerning the corrections needed to keep the vision alive.

Conclusion

When the Hebrews approached the Promised Land after their escape from Egypt, they knew they faced a challenge. They sent spies to survey the terrain and to assess their strengths and weaknesses in relation to the goal. The spies came back with good news and bad news. The good news was that the land was as pleasant as God had promised; the bad news was that its current residents liked it too, and they were bigger than the Israelites. Their report concluded with a self-assessment: "To ourselves we seemed like grasshoppers!" (Num. 13:33). Some in your church might feel this way after you survey your congregation and community. It takes visionary church leaders, like Joshua, to keep a church focused on the goal, urging the people forward in mission.

After forty years of wilderness wandering, God gave the Hebrews a second chance to claim their land. Again, they sent spies ahead. This time, the spies came back glowing with confidence. The land was theirs for the taking! Their size and strength had not changed, nor had that of the Canaanites. But their perspective on their ability to tackle the challenge ahead was different, because their purpose was resolved. They were no longer questioning *whether* to proceed but were gathering information to help them determine *how* to proceed. Informed by the spies' report, inspired by a new sense of vision, and guided by their spiritual leaders, the people of Israel prepared to take action. They crossed the Jordan River, set foot in the Promised Land, and then went on to a miraculous victory at Jericho.

Holistic ministry is God's plan and promise for every church and every community. Whatever the challenges in your community, whatever your church's portrait looks like now, the Lord has promised "to equip the saints for the work of ministry" (Eph. 4:12). In God's eyes, "we are what he has made us, created in Christ Jesus for good works, which God prepared beforehand to be our way of life" (Eph. 2:10). Embrace this assurance as you seek to catch a vision of the wonderful works of ministry God has already ordained for your church. Every church starts in a different place and goes through a different process of working toward the goal, and so it is important to know the lay of your unique "land." But the most important question is whether your church trusts the Spirit to be its guide and to bring down the walls.

chapter thirteen

Rallying Support for the Vision

One special quality about Faith Assembly of God is that the vision started with Pastor Smith, but now it is obvious that others [in the congregation] share the vision, that the love for people and for the lost is really in other people's hearts as well now.

Leader of a ministry that partners with Faith Assembly of God

The building blocks for holistic ministry are in place. Your church is passionate about proclaiming to its neighbors the Good News of salvation while serving them in Jesus' name. The leadership team has invested time in nurturing a healthy congregation that has loving internal relationships, vital worship, a deepening spiritual maturity, growing ties to its community, and an emerging commitment to outreach mission. The church is prepared to renovate dysfunctional or stale organizational systems that might hinder the development of effective mission. The studies of your congregation and community have provided a portrait of your church's ministry context and have pointed out the relevant needs, obstacles, and resources for holistic ministry. A vision for holistic ministry that makes a difference in your community has emerged through a process of prayerful discernment. Your congregation is not perfect, of course (and neither are its leaders), but you are ready to get started.

So—now what? How does the vision begin to take form? Certainly, implementing a ministry idea requires important organizational steps: developing action plans, forming committees, raising support, and so on.[1] These action steps have a better chance of producing sustainable, growing, effective holistic outreach, however, if the congregation stands behind the vision. This chapter explores ways to rally the support of the leadership team and the congregation around the holistic ministry vision.

Nurturing the Vision among the Leadership Team

Once the vision path committee has done the work of developing a tentative ministry plan, the next critical step is to bring it to the leadership team. A leader with a passion for reaching the community with Good News and good works may be eager to take the ball and run with it. But bypassing others who are "gatekeepers" for the larger congregation's support (whether the pastoral team, staff, or influential lay leaders) multiplies the chances of conflict, ineffectiveness, and burnout down the road. David Heney points out that when God gave Moses the charge of delivering the Israelites from slavery, his "first act of communication was to talk to the elders (Exod. 4:29). By getting the already accepted elders onboard, Moses greatly shortened the time needed to spread his message with good credibility."[2]

How do you encourage the leadership team to embrace and implement a holistic ministry vision? The most effective way is to expose them to what others are doing in holistic ministry. Seeing and experiencing transformative ministries in action help people develop a taste for holistic mission that cannot be generated through words alone. The following discussion suggests ways of rallying the existing leadership and also training an expanding base of new ministry leaders.

As is done in the corporate world, send out venture teams or scout squads to check out the playing field. Send leaders to sample effective holistic church-based models. These encounters can last for a few hours, such as observing another church's housing rehab project. Jesus Day/March for Jesus offers a one-day adventure in holistic ministry. For a more intense experience, take a weekend plunge at an innovative rural or inner-city congregation; this affords the opportunity to experience worship that is the heart and soul of holistic ministry. Get involved in short-term mission trips sponsored by groups such as Network 9:35 and its partners (see appendix B).

Leaders should process a ministry experience by gathering afterward for reflection and prayer. Sabbaticals allow staff time to really dig in. When Phil was missions pastor at First Presbyterian Church, he and his family used their sabbatical to visit effective ministries across North America and to take a course on urban church planting with holistic practitioner Michael Green. His sabbatical brought a breath of fresh ideas, inspiration, enthusiasm, and vision to his church.

There are also many ways to nurture a contagious vision among leaders and ministry staff at your church home:

- Sponsor "witness weekends." Invite a group (including laypeople, not just clergy or staff) from another congregation more experienced in holistic ministry to visit your church. This group can join you in a mission tour of your community, share stories and experiences with leadership and congregants, and answer questions. The weekend might include a service project that allows you to work side by side.[3]
- Provide leaders with more substantial fare by hosting a holistic ministry expert-in-residence—that is, offer housing to an experienced practitioner in exchange for sharing his or her expertise (teaching leadership development classes, leading small groups, helping launch a targeted ministry, and so on).
- Bring seminary, college, or church training institute professors to your church. Enrolling every leader in a course may be financially prohibitive, but the church may be able to afford to pay a professor to teach a course on site, either as an intensive weekend or as several weekly classes. Leaders can study topics such as the theology of mission, economic justice in the Bible, dealing with other religions and cults in evangelism, or a Christian perspective on social work.
- Similarly, invite seasoned veterans from the field of community ministry to teach classes on practical topics such as grant writing, starting a microenterprise, youth outreach, or political advocacy.
- Staff exchanges—from a month to a year—with churches more experienced in holistic ministry provide a dual benefit. During the exchange, your congregation gains the abilities and insights of an experienced ministry leader, along with an "outsider's" critique of your church's foundation for ministry. Your staff member brings home a wealth of new ideas and skills to pass on to others. An exchange might strengthen a growing relationship between churches that could lead to additional exchanges of ideas, people, and programs for years to come.

Nurturing the Vision in the Congregation

With the support of the leadership team, the next vital step is to cultivate the congregation's ownership of the holistic ministry vision. "Ownership" means that the congregation understands the vision, identifies with the vision, is excited about the vision, and acts according to the vision.

Getting the people of God to move forward requires a compelling cause that motivates members to participate. "Effective leaders never bring others to submission. . . . Saints are made by gaining their partnership, not their obeisance."[4] Churches are voluntary associations; people choose whether to be in a church, which church to join, and how they will participate in the life of that church.

Unless leaders are extremely authoritarian or manipulative, they will rarely succeed in trying to move the congregation against its will.

A holistic ministry vision, however, calls people to do things they normally would not choose to do and often takes them, literally, where they would not normally choose to go. It asks people to set aside their comfortable routines for the sake of others. It exposes people to the hurts and wrongs of society. It pushes the boundaries of class and race. It puts people out on a spiritual limb. So to bring members into partnership with a holistic vision, leaders must tap into something deeper than self-interest. They must trust that holistic mission resonates with the reason we have been created and re-created. God places in every Christian a yearning for the shalom of God's kingdom, born of God's abounding love for the world, which is not satisfied by "church as usual." As leaders cultivate the holistic ministry vision, they kindle this yearning and bring to life Jesus' words, "Blessed are those who hunger and thirst for righteousness" (Matt. 5:6).

How can leaders help the congregation become aware of its calling to share the gospel in word and deed, embrace the church's vision for its community, and move forward in active holistic ministry? This undertaking takes place on three levels. The broadest level is an *overall holistic theology of mission* that helps people understand what the Bible says about evangelism and social action and how they fit together. The second level is a *congregational sense of mission* that describes the church's purpose and identity, including its calling to holistic outreach, captured in a mission statement. The third level is *a specific visionary plan* as to how the congregation will apply its theology and mission in its community of ministry. So there is a progression in what leaders communicate to the church: What is the ministry mandate of every Christian? What is our purpose as this local body of believers? How, specifically, does God want us to live out this calling in ministry in this place, at this time?

No technique or gimmick can replace the conviction and empowerment of God's Spirit that ultimately gives life to a church's outreach. Yet there are several ways a church can help its members embrace holistic ministry. Below are suggestions for nurturing each of the three levels of missional vision.

Cultivate the Theology of Holistic Ministry

Philippians 2:2 instructs, "Be of the same mind, having the same love, being in full accord." Church leaders need to help the congregation become of one mind regarding the theological foundations for holistic ministry.

Sermons, Sunday school classes, and Bible studies are important vehicles for sharing the biblical basis for holistic mission. However, "You can't totally communicate a vision to your congregation through your sermons," advises a lay leader at First Presbyterian. "Don't get me wrong, it's a big tool, but you've got to be doing it on every level." What church leaders *say* is only part of the theology that church members absorb. *Explicit theology* is what is taught in sermons or recorded in official documents such as the membership covenant. *Implicit theologies,* on the other hand, "inform the congregation's life but are not necessarily acknowledged or overtly expressed," explains the *Studying Congregations* handbook.[5] Implicit theologies are communicated in church rituals (such as fellowship meals or the way the church collects tithes and offerings), in songs, in congregational prayers, and in the example set by church leaders. From these aspects of church life, people learn informally about God's character and what God expects of them.

Leaders can be intentional about conveying a holistic theology through implicit as well as explicit channels. One important way to do this is to tell stories. As with Jesus' parables, stories communicate theological truths that impact people's hearts as well as their minds. David Frenchak explains the value of storytelling: "Stories open options and energize people to do new things they previously had not imagined or sometimes even resisted."[6] Herald the heroes and heroines of holistic mission, whether from your congregation or other churches and agencies. Tell tales of personal and community transformation. Relate ministry stories from the pulpit, from the pews, in the pages of newsletters, or in devotional booklets. Create a time slot during services for the purpose of sharing inspiring holistic ministry testimonies.

Changes in the church's routine or environment can also help nurture a holistic theology. We are often unaware of how external surroundings shape people's worldviews and motivate them to action (or inaction). For example, stunning murals in the sanctuary of Church of the Advocate surround all who enter with images related to the themes of liberation, justice, solidarity, and pride in the African American heritage. The words of the pastors' sermons on these themes sink in with a powerful visual reinforcement. Christian Stronghold Baptist Church makes its holistic beliefs clear every time the receptionist answers the phone: "Christian Stronghold, how may I serve you?" asks the kindly voice on the line. As you enter the church office, you can't miss the slogan, painted in big letters on the wall: "How may we serve you?" Everywhere you turn at Christian Stronghold you find reminders of the Christian calling to be salt and light in the world.

Build Support for the Church's Holistic Ministry Vision

A holistic theology is an essential foundation, but it is too general to rally the congregation's active support. Theology must be made specific to your context through a congregational sense of mission that conveys the church's purpose, calling, and values. The church needs an answer to the question, "What is *unique* about our way of fulfilling God's plan?"[7]

Tools for Communicating the Vision

A basic tool for communicating the holistic ministry vision is a *purpose or mission statement* that heralds the church's intentions: "This is who we are and what we are about!" A mission statement may be a long sentence, or it may be something shorter, along the lines of a slogan. (See the mission statements of the churches in appendix A.) It is not a theological treatise but a motivational motto that encapsulates a larger vision, which should also be fleshed out in a page or two. If your church already has a mission statement, and it makes no reference to holistic outreach—or if you have a great mission statement but no one knows what it is!—the process of rewriting and/or publicizing it is a good way of calling attention to the central importance of holistic outreach.

A mission statement and the outreach vision it represents must be clearly, creatively, and regularly, even redundantly, set before the congregation. Bulletins, newsletters, web sites, and sanctuary banners are obvious places to use your mission statement. Reading the mission statement together can also become a new tradition in worship services. Don't worry about boring people by repeating the same message. People have short attention spans and many distractions. Experts say the vision needs to be explicitly stated about once a month. Reiterate the vision on a regular basis, lest people think holistic ministry was merely a passing fad—especially if the church has tried (and moved on from) various outreach projects in the past.

Some people like words and respond well with the left side of their brains. Right-brained people, however, want and need an image. "Let me see it," they plead. Therefore, you should plan to have a *logo and/or icons* designed that imaginatively communicate the essence of your mission. Images evoke feelings, passion, and conviction. They move rather than inform people. Icons and logos fill in the blanks between words and sentences, lingering long after the words are read. "The word *vision* and the word *see* are related. If people cannot see, there is no vision," writes Calvin Miller.[8] What people see quite often at First Presbyterian Church is a logo appropriate to its mission statement: "Loved, Served, and Sent by Christ We Share Life at Its Very Best!" The logo is a towel, pitcher, and basin, inspired by the foot washing story in John 13. It appears in many places: coffee mugs, T-shirts and sweatshirts, Yellow Pages ad, baseball caps, souvenir pins, key chains, and other mementoes—all of which bring the vision into everyday life.

Artists often feel neglected in evangelical churches. Draw them in by harnessing their innovative talents to convey the vision. Engage the skills of the digital generation by taking advantage of image-creating technology: graphic design software, video recorders, Power Point presentations. The creative possibilities are endless. For example, at Word of Grace Church in Mesa, Arizona, the pastor preaches an annual sermon on the mission of the church. One year the pastor interspersed the sermon with video clips from various movies, all featuring buses. Each clip represented a different way that a congregation could relate to its mission statement (get on the bus, runaway bus, empty bus, and so on). The point—either choose a different bus or hang on for the ride—was hard to miss, or to forget.

Another way to highlight your vision for holistic mission is through *special events* such as a sermon or Sunday school series, worship celebration, mission conference, retreat, revival, concert, or drama focused on outreach. Para-church ministries such as World Vision and Compassion International can help with an event format and contacts for quality speakers and musicians such as Scott Wesley Brown. While you're at it, why not invite other churches and the community to your event and turn it into a benefit for a holistic ministry program?

One of the best ways to build members' support for a holistic ministry vision is to get them involved in doing ministry. A poster in Spanish on the wall of the New Creation Community Center summarizes this approach. Translated, it reads: "Tell me, I forget. Show me, I remember. If I do it, I understand." Onetime *demonstration projects* involve church members in low-risk, high-impact exposure to holistic outreach and allow members to glimpse the church's mission statement in action. Send a group on a short-term mission trip, such as those organized by Koinonia Leadership Mission (see its description in chapter 11). Or identify a holistic ministry of another local church or nonprofit agency that resonates with your own church's vision and round up a group of members to volunteer for a day. Or host a Christmas party or birthday party at a homeless shelter or children's hospital. The main idea is to give a group of members the flavor of reaching out, so that they can connect in an experiential way with the vision.

Tips for Communicating the Vision

As much as possible, build on your congregation's identity and heritage in communicating a new vision. Draw on denominational statements (current and historical) regarding mission. Dig deep to uncover the role of outreach ministry in your church's history. A church's origins often reveal remarkable stories of mission. Point to past pioneers in evangelism and social justice from your congregation, denomination, or ethnic group. Celebrate long-forgotten ministry accomplishments, stirring the congregation to revive and carry forward the tradition. Sometimes the holistic ministry vision does not so much need to be introduced as rediscovered.[9]

A good place to start sharing the vision is with the people who already display the vision in their lives. Look for members who quietly go about the work of sharing the Good News in word and deed—people who with no prompting are known to bring a meal to a family in crisis, hand an evangelistic tract to the clerk in the grocery store, organize a backyard Bible club, volunteer at a local soup kitchen. They are likely to be pillars of support, because for them the vision is not a new thing but a recognition of what they are already doing.

Keep in mind that the goal of communicating the vision is not just to get people to agree with it but to *participate* in it. This means challenging the mind-set of members who believe, as Rev. Bill Borror of Media Presbyterian Church puts it, that "being a Christian is a spectator event." The coordinator of the Men's Discipleship Home (substance abuse recovery ministry) at Faith Assembly of God states it succinctly: "God doesn't save us just to sit in pews." A ministry leader at Christian Stronghold describes a turning point in her church involvement.

> One day I looked up at the doorpost going into one of the classrooms, and it said: "Enter to learn and learn to serve." . . . It was a revelation to me. . . . I realized that everything that I learned [at church] was for me to use to serve. . . . Pastor Richardson had talked about service and I wanted to apply it, but I still had apprehensions. That little phrase pushed me over the edge and helped me to jump-start myself toward applying myself to ministry.

You never know what it will take to jump-start church members to do holistic mission, or how long they might have to walk past the same sign or banner before the message finally sinks in. But if you keep trying with enough clarity, persistence, vigor, creativity, and good humor, most members (though not all) will eventually catch the vision.

But what do you do if despite all efforts, the majority of the congregation simply refuses to embrace the holistic ministry vision? One response is to develop a supportive core group that is willing to get to work. Even members who don't share the vision are not likely to object if others take on the entire burden of planning and funding. Holistic ministry led by a small but energetic group can be contagious over time. Another response is to begin by collaborating with a holistic para-church agency. Such an act may feel less threatening to reluctant members than launching a project in the church's name. And persistent prayer always helps. Sometimes, all you can do is work behind the scenes and wait for God's timing. As one pastor noted wryly, his church's ministry really took off once everyone who objected either converted, left the church, or passed away. (See chapter 14 for a discussion on how to handle—and hopefully prevent—conflicts over holistic ministry.)

Case Study in Communicating a Congregational Vision: Central Baptist Church

From the moment a visitor walks in the church, Central Baptist Church's outreach-minded mission focus is unmistakable. The hallways are lined with bulletin boards with information about ministry opportunities in the church and community. Colorful banners adorn the fellowship hall, each representing one of the church's nine mission groups. In the area outside the sanctuary, stained glass windows symbolically portray the world in the embrace of the Spirit and swords being beaten into plowshares.

Outside the Sunday school classroom area is a prominent display labeled "Telling Our Story at Central Baptist Church." The display shares the stories of several people in the Baptist tradition who exemplify the church's mission. One of these heroes is Jitsuo Morikawa, a formerly interned Japanese American who became the director of evangelism for American Baptist Home Mission Societies. "His stress on both the personal and social content of the gospel of Jesus Christ dominated all that he preached and planned. . . . The gospel addresses the whole person in that person's total setting and it calls us to radical response." Another model is Maria Cristina Gomez, union activist in San Salvador, whose "senseless murder . . . is a reminder of why this church expresses its active solidarity with the poor, oppressed, and forgotten in Central America and throughout the Third World." Each Sunday school classroom bears the name of one of these leaders in the faith, a reminder that the purpose of discipleship is to follow Christ into mission.

Everything the church distributes calls attention to its vision. On the back of the bulletin is a description of the church's mission: "Central Baptist Church is a caring, concerned, and questioning congregation which supports each one's search for a personal relationship with God, a communal relationship with each other, and a mission outreach to the broader community." Other literature available to visitors affirms the church's "enthusiastic mission support for justice, witness, and healing in our metropolitan area and throughout our nation and world." Newsletters contain reports from various mission groups. The covenant affirmed annually by members concludes with a dedication to mission: "We reach out as a welcoming community of faith. We covenant as individuals and as a congregation to work with others toward peace, justice, and the wholeness of God's creation."

The church's vision is prominent throughout worship services as well. Outreach comes before the congregation's attention each week in the announcements and in the sharing time. Prayer requests highlight needs outside the church, from homeless guests in Central's Interfaith Hospitality Network ministry, to individuals in members' personal networks, to public policy and world affairs. The two pastors also consistently reinforce the mission through their worship leading and preaching. Sermons often touch on themes of seeking justice, empowering those who are marginalized, and supporting people's journeys to faith. "We know the Creator has a vision," Rev. Marcia Bailey told the kids gathered up front for the children's message one Sunday, "and we are a part of making that vision come true." Then she prayed, "May we be, God, a reflection of your vision for ourselves and for our world."

Central Baptist Church also draws on its history of "pushing the envelope," in the words of co-pastor Rev. Marcus Pomeroy. "One of the things that's exciting to me about Central Baptist Church is that we're not normal!" he remarked in a sermon. Having an identity and a heritage as a risk-taking church encourages them to embrace new ministry ventures as they arise. Reminders of past ministry ventures help sustain their commitment.

As a suburban church, Central Baptist Church sometimes struggles to reconcile its passion for seeking justice with the comfortable lives of most of its members. And evangelism could play a more prominent role in the church's outreach. But with more than 60 percent of the congregation involved in active ministry (compared with the national average of 10 percent, according to a Gallup poll), there is no question that Central Baptist Church has succeeded in communicating a compelling, unifying vision for mission.

Rally the Congregation around Specific Ministry Programs

A congregational vision bears fruit in specific ministry projects that put feet to the vision. The process of developing a holistic ministry vision may lead your church to start a new program, change an existing program to make it more holistic (such as adding a relational evangelism component to a job training program), or partner with an outside program of another church or agency. How do you recruit and equip members to connect to this new venture in holistic outreach?

The task of rallying the congregation's support for a ministry has five basic parts: inform, motivate, empower, ask, and reward.

Inform

Give the congregation the facts. What kind of program is the church sponsoring and why? Who will lead it? What does the church hope this ministry will accomplish? What commitment from the congregation will it take to make it work? Christian Stronghold Baptist Church places informational brochures about church ministries in the foyer. New Creation Lutheran hands out flyers about ministries along with the church bulletin. Bethel Temple Community Church presented their new community revitalization initiative at a congregational meeting. Pastor Jerome Simmons preaches a sermon about a new ministry at Koinonia Christian Community Church. Germantown Church of the Brethren highlights a different ministry each month during a worship service.

If the congregation is large and busy, printed or spoken announcements will not be enough to grab people's attention. Or if holistic ministry is a radical new idea for the congregation, you may need to do something radical to spotlight its advent. David Heney advises, "The best first impression to make is a bold one that says it will no longer be business as usual."[10] Smuggle new projects into familiar church territory. To launch a new outreach to single moms, for example, invite a single mom to share her story at a women's circle meeting. Or hold the Wednesday night Bible study in an unfinished Habitat for Humanity home, followed by a presentation from a Habitat volunteer.

Motivate

Motivational leaders know how to ignite a church member's ministry fire. They blend statistics, stories, Scripture, principles, and entreaties to capture people's hearts and move them to action. Because people come to holistic ministry for many different reasons, generating excitement is more like striking a chord than harping on a single note. Effective leadership draws from a palette of motivations for ministry involvement.

Compassion for individuals in need: The true meaning of compassion is to "suffer with" hurting people—to care about another's pain as if it were your own. Often it takes putting a name and a face to the suffering to get people to "suffer with" others in the true meaning of compassion. One's life can be changed by an empathetic encounter with a broken person in one's path—as were the lives of the Tenth Presbyterian Church members who found a homeless man sleeping on the church steps. The encounter helped propel the creation of ACTS outreach ministries. Such "Good Samaritan moments" happen every day in poor communities, but they require more intentional, creative efforts in comfortable neighborhoods. The needs can become more real through field trips, slide shows, skits, and interviews. Just take care not to abuse the dignity of needy persons for your own motivational purposes.

Yearning for a just society: Some people know firsthand the pain caused by twisted systems and institutions. Others need convincing that structural evils exist and that Christians are called to seek justice. Church leaders are to "comfort the afflicted and afflict the comfortable." Constantly speaking out against injustice, however, can leave members feeling discouraged and hopelessly inadequate. Motivational leaders also paint a picture of the good that God desires for every community. A vision of the shalom that is possible in God's kingdom, against a backdrop of awareness of the wrongs that now exist, is what makes people willing to put their hand to the plow rather than throwing up their hands in despair.

Longing to see people come to faith in Christ: At first, people who prioritize evangelism may see meeting social needs as a distraction from saving souls. But once they understand the connection between social action and evangelism, they may give enthusiastic support for holistic ministry. Moreover, many church members know they ought to be sharing their faith but are terrified of personal evangelism. They will be grateful for an outreach program that offers opportunities for friendship evangelism by providing guidance, structure, and support for their relationships with non-Christians.

Desire to experience God in a deeper way and grow in faith: This does not mean engaging in ministry to gain brownie points with God but to draw closer to God's heart of grace and compassion. One reason that so many families sign up for Media Presbyterian Church's annual Habitat for Humanity work camp is the testimonials that past participants share about their inspiring experience. One after another, people stand up in the worship service after returning from the trip and declare, "I thought I was just going down to help other people, but God touched my life too." People come back from the trip more sure of their faith, more excited about serving the Lord. It's contagious.

Obedience to a sense of personal calling: "A calling is empowering and sustaining, enabling us to joyfully stick to the task God has called us to through thick and thin."[11] Of course a spiritual calling must come from God, but a church leader can help prod members to discern their calling and be obedient to it.

After Eleanor, a member of Central Baptist Church, adopted two boys from Ethiopia, their schoolteacher asked her to help teach English to some new Vietnamese students. She didn't respond at first. Then she had a dream in which God spoke to her: "Feed my sheep." Later, Eleanor's spiritual mentor told her that many Albanians and South Americans were coming into the community and that they needed to be taught English. This time, convicted that this was her calling, she responded by starting an Outreach English mission group at Central Baptist Church.

Gratitude for what God has done for you: The director of outreach at Germantown Church of the Brethren sees ministry as "my opportunity to express my gratitude back to my Savior for the love he has expressed to me. . . . To be able to share that kind of peace, contentment, fulfillment, and joy with others is certainly my motivation." You can help people connect the dots between their experience of God's blessings and opportunities to bless others.

Love for the church: In a healthy church, members often feel a sense of loyalty or obligation to the congregation. In our interviews, we often heard people say, "This church has given me a lot, and I want to do something to support it in return." Members may see outreach as a way of enhancing the church's reputation in the community and attracting new people to enjoy the church's fellowship. They may also appreciate the sense of unity and bonding that team ministry brings to a congregation.[12] Once it becomes clear that the church is headed in the direction of holistic ministry, even if members do not fully understand or appreciate the vision, they may support it because of their strong attachment to the church.

Desire to meet the expectations of church leaders: Trust in the leader may precede trust in or ownership of the leader's vision. Committed followers may go along with visionary leaders without needing to understand why, at least at first. However, unless people develop ownership of the vision, a simple "because I told you to" can take a leader only so far.

Hunger to be part of a ministry that makes a difference. As the saying goes, nothing motivates like success. In a worship service, Bishop Milton Grannum was enlisting support for New Covenant's home-based Vacation Bible School program. He invited a teenage girl who had gotten saved through VBS to talk about her experience. Since her VBS host family brought her to the Lord, she reported, her life had changed. She now led a Bible study with a dozen students in her high school and directed a gospel choir. At this point Bishop Grannum turned toward the congregation. "You see how this works, don't you?" he said. "Our brother and sister opened up their home for VBS, and this young lady became a Christian. Now she has started a Bible study plus a gospel choir. And the people that she reaches will go out and reach others. So you see the multiplication of what that one family did simply by opening their home to VBS." What an incentive!

At the bottom line, each of these motivations for holistic ministry springs from knowing who we are in Christ. Holistic Christians do not just give service, they *are* servants—and to be a servant means submitting to a will other than your own. "[Christ] died for all, so that those who live might live no longer for themselves, but for him who died and was raised for them" (2 Cor. 5:15). Holistic Christians share the gospel with prisoners because they live for Christ. They build houses because Christ died and was raised for them. They create jobs in the inner city because the love of Christ compels them. As servants of the great Servant, Christians dedicate their lives to following Christ's example.

Empower

People may be motivated to get on board and yet never make the leap. The decision to get involved with a new holistic ministry requires members to overcome hurdles of inertia, inexperience, and insecurity. In Matthew 9:37–38, Jesus stirs his disciples with the vision of an evangelistic harvest waiting for workers. In the next verse, he gives them power. Then the disciples go out as harvesters, proclaiming the Good News, healing the sick, and casting out evil spirits. This pattern of empowering people for ministry still holds. With Paul in Ephesians 1:19, the church leader's prayer for the congregation is that they might know "the immeasurable greatness of his power for us who believe."

There are two dimensions to empowering the congregation for ministry: calling and equipping. First, it is essential for a congregation to understand that *each member is called and gifted for holistic ministry.* Rick Warren, author of *The Purpose Driven Church,* writes, "If we can ever awaken and unleash the massive talent, resources, creativity, and energy lying dormant in the typical local church, Christianity will explode with growth."[13] Some members, of course, are primarily called to support the church's internal ministries and administrative functions. But each Christian has some role in sharing the Good News of Christ in word and deed.

A spiritual gift inventory is an essential tool in awakening this potential in a congregation. First Peter 4:10 lays down the principle, "Serve one another with whatever gift each of you has received." For members who feel like ungifted benchwarmers, a spiritual gift inventory may assure them that they have a valued place in the church's ministry roster and give them the courage to step up to the plate.

In addition to spiritual gifts, members have skills, interests, and life experiences that can be connected with ministry needs. Sometimes churches fail to deploy the full range of talents within their congregations because they see people within the confines of church life, without looking at their roles in the workaday world. Not every congregation has an abundance of professionals. But *every* church member has some skill or hobby (baking brownies, knitting, woodworking, playing basketball) that can be unleashed for holistic ministry, if it is dedicated to the service of the kingdom. Volunteer expert Marlene Wilson suggests that you can discover members' potential by "watching when they 'light up' and get excited," and then tapping that energy for ministry.[14]

As your congregation absorbs the perspective that God has called and gifted every believer for holistic ministry, those who seem to be needy themselves will emerge as assets: youth and seniors, those with handicaps or a history.[15] Faith Assembly of God, for example, relies on residents in their substance abuse recovery program to fill volunteer positions in other ministries. At New Covenant Church, a brother and sister, ages twelve and thirteen, told their parents they wanted to lead a home-based Vacation Bible School. They gathered a team of volunteers, went through training, and ran a successful VBS in their home. Afterward, inspired by their experience, the son signed up to help with the church's preschool ministry, and the daughter became an usher. At the other end of the life spectrum, retired professionals at Media Presbyterian Church stepped forward to offer consulting and grant writing to help their sister church, Life in Christ, develop several new ministries.

Connecting members with ministry is a combination of finding people with the right gifts to fill volunteer positions and creating ministries that use the gifts of a church's members. If a ministry has consistently low involvement, this may indicate either that people have not bought into the vision or that the ministry is not well suited to the congregation. People might embrace the congregational vision but lack enthusiasm for a particular ministry project. Holistic ministry, therefore, needs support from the top down and the bottom up.

As the vision for mission takes hold, some members will likely approach church leaders and suggest, "Why doesn't the church do ____?" Such initiative should be taken as a positive sign, though too much initiative circulating at once can get out of hand. Bishop Grannum describes how he empowers "bottom-up" ministry in responding to such requests: "A person can come up with a hundred ideas that they think the church should do, and then they drop it in your lap. . . . But I think the members of this church know, generally, that if they come to me with a good idea, they've got the job." He asks the person to bring him the idea in writing—and most people, he says, never come back. Then Bishop Grannum assesses the time and funding commitment required, and asks "whether this person can run with this ball, or whether this person is just talking. . . . If the person is willing to give leadership to it, then we try to help that person get established, and we monitor their progress for faithfulness, consistency, and the ability to work with others."

The second dimension of empowerment is *equipping people for specific ministry projects*. Rev. Bill Moore of Tenth Memorial Baptist Church advises, "If members are not trained, if they're not empowered, then they cannot do the thing that keeps the church viable, and that is reaching out." Throughout this book we have stressed the importance of training. Just asking people to show up for a welfare mentoring ministry or a youth evangelism outreach or a community organizing campaign without any preparation is like tossing a child in the deep end to learn how to swim. A blend of instruction, modeling, and supervised hands-on skill development maximizes a volunteer's contribution.

Ask

As every salesperson and fund-raiser knows, all the elements of a pitch build up to the "ask." Setting up great programs without explicitly and personally asking members to participate in them is like doing good deeds in Jesus' name without ever inviting people to know Jesus. The director of Servant Development at First Presbyterian Church concludes that in her experience, "People need to be asked. . . . If I put just another memo out saying, 'If anyone wants to do this [volunteer job], contact me,' no one ever says anything." On the other hand, if she goes directly to an individual and says, "The coordinator really needs someone like you to serve, and I think you'd be good at this position," she is more likely to fill the job. The church leaders in our study were continually "fishing" for volunteers and didn't get discouraged by hearing no.

Asking directly not only produces more volunteers, but it also builds people's confidence, particularly when they lack "worldly" credentials. A ministry leader at Faith Assembly of God says that the pastor's belief in her makes all the difference. "When the pastor will say to me, 'I need you to do this,' and I think, 'I don't have a clue how to do that!' I have trust that God is talking through the pastor. Pastor Smith wouldn't have me do something important if he didn't believe I could do it. I have to believe that the Lord spoke to him, so I step out in faith."

An "ask" is more likely to be successful if you provide options for varying tasks, skill levels, and time commitment. At Central Baptist Church, for example, people can either volunteer for mission groups as "active members," with a commitment to attend meetings and take on work assignments, or join the "prayer and care circle," which "gives prayerful support and agrees to be approached for onetime volunteering." This two-tiered system encourages members to take the first step toward participation. Keep looking until you find out what someone will say yes to. David Apple has noted that members who are not involved in ACTS mercy ministries sometimes say, "Wow, I could never do what you all are doing!" To overcome people's barriers to involvement in outreach ministry, he breaks down ministry positions into small, manageable parts, such as sitting down for one meal with homeless persons at a community dinner. People reluctant to become regular volunteers may find it hard to refuse just one meal.

Getting a yes is one thing, and getting people actually to follow through with assignments is sometimes another. At the start of a project, it may be helpful to hold an event at which regular volunteers can formally "sign on" to the ministry, akin to the covenant reading ceremony in Exodus 24. People are likely to take this kind of pledge more seriously than a "well, okay" dropped in the hall after church. Such a ceremony also rehearses the vision for the rest of the congregation and provides an opportunity to bathe the ministry launch and volunteers in prayer.

Reward

A maxim in management circles declares, "What gets rewarded gets done." Sustain volunteer motivation and give glory to God by recognizing the good work done in Jesus' name by your congregation (2 Cor. 9:12). Faithful ministry calls for celebration!

First Presbyterian Church honors those who participate in the church's mission in a variety of ways. An annual banquet celebrates the contributions of volunteers. Each month a volunteer is presented with a "Serve and Tell" award—a towel monogrammed with the church's logo. A story about this "servant of the church" follows in the newsletter. This tradition recognizes members who model servant behavior behind the scenes or go beyond the call of duty in holistic ministry. Once First Presbyterian published the name of every ministry volunteer in the newsletter, inspiring members to fill even more positions.

Another way to reward volunteers is by helping them grow spiritually through their participation. Ministering to hurting people and challenging unjust structures can strengthen and refine people's faith, but this takes nurturing. An important role of ministry leaders is to help participants interpret their experience from a theological perspective. How does an evangelistic encounter help Christians better appreciate their own salvation? What can they learn about the kingdom of God from a cross-cultural church ministry partnership? How do they see Jesus in "the least of these" (Matt. 25:40)? Leaders can also encourage volunteers in their spiritual journey by connecting service with spiritual disciplines such as prayer and fasting, biblical meditation, and spiritual warfare.

Reward volunteers also with times of special refreshing and nurturing. Be sensitive to the relational, emotional, and financial needs of volunteers as well as their spiritual needs. Allow volunteers to step back before reaching the point of burnout without making them feel like a quitter. In holistic ministry, some amount of stress "just comes with the territory, so there's only so much you can do," acknowledges Rev. Lou Centeno. But, he says, "physical and emotional pit stops can help you better get through that next step." Retreats are one kind of "pit stop" for Bethel Temple ministry workers. Another are occasional breakfasts at Rev. Centeno's home, where he literally and figuratively feeds those who are doing the Lord's work.

Finally, remind volunteers of God's rewards for faithful ministry. As the adage goes, it is impossible to out-give God. "Whoever is kind to the poor lends to the LORD, and will be repaid in full" (Prov. 19:17). To those who "loose the bonds of injustice," who "share your bread with the hungry, and bring the homeless poor into your house," God promises, "Your light shall break forth like the dawn, and your healing shall spring up quickly. . . . The LORD will guide you continually, and satisfy your needs" (Isa. 58:6–8, 11). Discipling new converts, says the apostle Paul, brings to evangelists a "crown of boasting before our Lord Jesus" (1 Thess. 2:19; cf. Phil. 4:1). At times when ministry appears fruitless, servants of the Lord can be encouraged by the reminder that God "will not overlook your work and the love that you showed for his sake" (Heb. 6:10).

Case Study in Rallying the Congregation around a Ministry Project: The Burlington Center Mall Ministry

The story of the Burlington Center Mall Ministry (BCMM) (see chapter 5) illustrates the process of developing and enlisting support for a new holistic ministry. BCMM began in 1993 as a prayer project of Phil Olson, then minister of mission at First Presbyterian Church. Confronted by a lethargic period of congregational ministry and challenged by the prayer strategies of Mission 21 India (an agency that blends church planting, evangelism, and community and economic development), Phil felt a growing burden for targeted prayer and a passion for reaching unchurched people.

For several months Phil asked God where his focus should be. He felt led to pray for three townships. He colored them in on a map and prayed over them. After a month of praying, God provided a prayer partner from each township. Phil developed a calendar of neighborhoods and people groups unique to each township. The prayer partners spent a month driving around each township, praying and thinking about possible ways to minister to township residents and praying that others would be receptive to the vision. At this point, Phil conceived the idea of a ministry located off church grounds.

About this same time, First Presbyterian's session (governing board) was working on a five-year planning process. Not coincidentally, one of the goals that emerged was to develop an off-site outreach ministry. First Presbyterian's leaders realized that the church was no longer the hub of community activity in today's culture and that church services had plenty of competition on Sunday morning: soccer, the golf course, the beach, second or third jobs, or just staying in bed. Instead of asking people to find the church, First Presbyterian wanted to find the people in order to share the life-changing truths of the gospel. So the session, particularly the mission team, began considering ministry options.

Phil investigated possible ministry sites in the three townships. Each time there was some roadblock. Then Phil asked himself where Jesus would go to minister if he were walking the streets of Burlington County today. His answer: the marketplace. Phil sent a paper exploring this idea, "Let's Go to the Mall!" to fifty Christian leaders across the country for their ideas and input. A group from First Presbyterian visited two other nearby mall ministries, Echelon Mall Ministry (Voorhees, New Jersey) and the Church on the Mall (Plymouth Meeting, Pennsylvania) to learn from their successes and failures.

During a church leadership day of prayer and fasting in November 1996, the First Presbyterian mission team went to Burlington Center to talk to the mall management about the possibility of renting space. The management could not understand why anyone would want to be in the mall whose goal was not to make money. This provided the mall ministry with its first witnessing opportunity!

Phil continued to pray about funding and leadership for the emerging mall ministry. After several months he felt led to speak with a church member about paying the first year's rent. In God's amazing timing, that person had just received a lump sum and was asking God what to do with it. Also during this period, Phil and the mission team chair each prayed and made separate lists of three possible names for the mall ministry director.

Elsie Nicolette was going through a career change at the time and was pretty sure she knew what God wanted her to do. It wasn't directing the mall ministry. But each time, just when it looked as though she had a new job, something fell through. Elsie began evaluating what she really wanted in a job. She was surprised to discover that her list of things she wanted from a job matched the emerging job description for the director of the Burlington Center Mall Ministry. Her calling was confirmed when she later learned that she was the only name on *both* lists!

While the mall ministry was conceived from the beginning as a collaborative project with support from multiple churches, First Presbyterian's embrace of the ministry was crucial to its development. One way the ministry commit-tee engaged the congregation early in the process was by providing members with materials to guide their prayers as they walked through the mall. The commit-tee also kept the congregation informed through brochures and bulletin inserts that described the mall ministry's goals and listed volunteer opportunities.

What factors led to the congregation's support for the vision of a mall min-istry? First, over the years the church leadership had built up trust when it came to launching new ministries. Second, it was obvious to the congregation that care-ful thought, prayer, and planning had gone into the ministry design. Third, prior to an official vote of confidence, many people (staff, board, lay leaders, and key congregants) had already said yes to the idea, including putting their money where their mouths and hearts were. Fourth, the ministry was included as a component of the church's developing long-range plan. Fifth, leaders had already invested in laying a solid theological foundation for holistic ministry. Finally, First Presby-terian was ready for a challenge. The congregation was recovering from an inter-nal crisis, and no new major ministries had been launched in several years. Mem-bers were eager for a forward-looking project that would revitalize the church.

In October 1997, the session approved moving ahead with the mall min-istry. The ministry had one year's rent, a director, and many logistical obsta-cles to overcome. Each crisis stretched the congregation's faith and deepened their commitment to prayer. They realized that their desire to extend God's kingdom on earth had initiated a spiritual battle. The ministry committee knew they could not face the challenges on their own strength and that they needed to rely on the Lord. The committee recruited people willing to pray for every aspect of the ministry. Elsie began sending out weekly prayer concerns via fax and email. At last the doors opened, with a joyous two-day grand opening cel-ebration and consecration in mid-July 1998.

Elsie and the church's Servant Development director created job descrip-tions and began enlisting and training volunteers. Volunteers attend a one-hour orientation to learn about the ministry and volunteer requirements. Those who interact with the public also take four hours of evangelism training. The mall ministry presents many volunteer opportunities—from hosts who sit out front greeting passersby to nurses who provide blood pressure screening, from prayer intercession to grant writing and publicity. New programs, such as a children's craft time, are created when volunteers suggest, "I could do . . ." BCMM involves about two hundred volunteers from thirty-nine churches, with First Presbyterian supplying about two-thirds of the volunteers. Volun-teers cross denominational, gender, racial, ethnic, and age categories, dem-onstrating that God is bigger than any human barrier.

Probably the most powerful lesson the congregation has learned through BCMM, says Elsie, is that God "is able to accomplish abundantly far more than all we can ask or imagine" according to his power that is at work within us (Eph. 3:20). The congregation's faith, imagination, prayers, donations, and volunteer commitments are the ingredients God has used to accomplish this remarkable ministry.

Conclusion

Timothy Keller employs a useful metaphor to make it clear that sharing the vision of holistic ministry is a process rather than a pronouncement.

> Let's think of the church as a garden (as does Paul in 1 Corinthians 3). How do we get tomatoes from the garden? By rushing out on the first day of spring and throwing seeds out onto the ground? No, we must prepare the garden carefully for the seeds. . . . In the same way, ministries of mercy will only spring up if the church is prepared for them. We cannot emphasize this too much. Fertilize and "dig up" until the congregation is ready![16]

In churches that have experienced a long dry spell in their outreach, leaders must "fertilize the soil" to make it ready to receive the seeds of specific outreach programs. Long-term transformation of the congregation and its community of ministry are more important than flash-in-the-pan projects that prove unstable and ineffective. God wants every congregation to become "rooted and built up in him and established in the faith" (Col. 2:7). In Christ we are ordained to "bear fruit, fruit that will last" (John 15:16).

Keep in mind that this process takes time. It takes time to wait on the leading of the Holy Spirit. It takes time for people to absorb new ideas about the church's mission and to discover their calling and gifts for ministry. It takes time for a congregation to win the trust of the community. It takes time to establish a track record with volunteers and funders. The advice of many church leaders and consultants is that a significant congregational change takes five to seven years. Leaders must be simultaneously audacious and nurturing. "Think big, but be patient and proceed at a teaspoon pace initially." Focus on "doing small things with excellence."[17]

The key, however, is to get started doing *something*. Don't put ministry on hold until the congregation fully embraces the vision. If you want to light a fire in the congregation, "Action is oxygen!" advises Rev. Patrick Hansel of New Creation Lutheran Church. Get "prayed up," and then get going. You can always make adjustments along the way. But in the process your congregation might just bring a life-giving word or touch to someone who needs to experience the mercy of God. You might just bring your community closer to God's wholesome ideal of justice and shalom. Let this hope be your guide as your congregation takes its first steps on the journey to holistic ministry.

chapter fourteen

Dealing with Fears, Change, and Conflict in Your Congregation

Conflict and tension within a church are an occasion for maximum growth if we can stand it.[1]

Surviving Fears, Change, and Conflict: Cookman United Methodist Church

From a ministry perspective, in the mid-1990s, Cookman United Methodist Church was doing great. New holistic ministries were taking root—meal programs for children and adults, a youth entrepreneur program, and an evangelistic play that shared the gospel with hundreds of neighborhood residents. The church had even won a state contract for an extensive Christ-centered welfare-to-work program, and women in the program were coming to faith.

But under the surface, tensions and conflicts within the congregation were coming to a boil. A significant segment of the membership was unhappy with the changes initiated by the energetic new pastor, Rev. Donna Jones. The church board wondered if Cookman was stretching itself too thin and exposing itself to too many risks. The welfare-to-work program, in particular, raised misgivings. Some members did not like the idea of having so many people on the property throughout the week who were not attending Sunday services, and they feared for the safety of members and the building. Some were uncertain whether it was proper for a church to work with the state. Compounding matters, the small church had significant financial struggles. There was a danger that the church would not be able to cover its debt to the denomination, the building would be sold, and the congregation would have to merge with another church. The question was raised whether Rev. Jones was the right pastor for the church at that time.

One factor underlying the conflict was the question of the church's identity. The church had nearly closed after the original white congregation had moved out of the neighborhood. For the last fifteen years before Rev. Jones's installation in 1993, it had been considered a "mission church" by the denomination, and this influenced the congregation's view of itself as needy. The congregation was more familiar with being on the receiving end than the giving end. Some felt that their own needs were now being neglected for the sake of ministering to "outsiders." Rev. Jones promoted a different image of the church, as a ministry outpost with valuable gifts to share with the community. She pushed the congregation—too quickly, she now admits—to reorient its sense of purpose and take ownership of the hope the church could offer to the community.

Rev. Jones had been caught off guard by the strength and immediacy of the congregation's resistance and as a result had to spend a great deal of time putting out relational and administrative fires sparked by the conflicts. She reflects now that it would have been wiser to develop a stronger base of support and understanding within the congregation before moving forward with major ministry projects. As time went on, she found a better balance between taking visionary initiative and cultivating the congregation's sense of ownership and responsibility for ministry. She also strengthened relationships with core lay leaders who shared the vision for outreach.

One pragmatic response to the conflict by the pastor and lay ministry leaders was to set up a new nonprofit organization, called Neighborhood Joy Ministries (NJM), as an umbrella for the church's outreach. This measure was intended both to reassure the congregation that it would not be financially and legally liable for the programs and to protect the ministries from opposition by the church. NJM was run by an independent board, which by stipulation included the pastor and at least one officer from the church board. Everyone selected for the board was enthusiastic about its vision. This arrangement allowed the work of ministry to go forward without getting bogged down by the conflicts, while maintaining the connection between NJM and the church.

Rev. Jones took another major step toward resolving the conflict by listening more intentionally to the voices of opposition in the congregation. She explains:

> The "old guard" did not understand what the "new guard" was doing. And we had not respected and honored what the old guard had done. . . . When I started listening to all the parties—when I stopped fighting and started listening—things changed. I got into the heart of each faction and discovered that people

I thought did not have passion for ministry really did. I had made assumptions about the old guard, about how they thought about themselves and ministry. I did not see what they had done before I came. Their contributions were not lifted up.

Rev. Jones looked back through old church records and discovered ministries that had been discontinued before her arrival. She asked the members who had originally been involved, "How did you feel about what you did? How did you feel when this ministry stopped?" This helped her—and the congregation—realize the importance of community ministry in the church's history. This encouraged a shift in people's views of the new ministries, from a risky innovation to a reversal of a decline. Then she got people talking about what kinds of ministries they hoped to see develop. Says Rev. Jones, "I helped connect their past with the future."

Along with listening to members, Rev. Jones and a core leadership team also invested in reshaping the congregation's theology and self-understanding. A key theme in teaching and preaching was the central importance of holistic mission in the Christian life—that Christians are saved not only for themselves but for the sake of reaching out to others with the love of God. Another significant step was helping the congregation see how the church's community service also served them. Ministry leaders invited members to sign up for the computer lab, GED classes, and other services. This eased members' feelings of being in competition with nonmembers for the church's services and helped break down the wall between members and "outsiders" receiving services.

Along with the effort to motivate and equip the congregation for outreach, Rev. Jones addressed their need for internal nurturing as well. Pastoral teaching and counseling encouraged members to grow in the knowledge of their salvation and to rest in Jesus' forgiveness and healing. New discipling ministries were started, such as a women's group. Times of intentional reconciliation allowed the congregation—including the pastor—to confess their faults to one another and receive forgiveness. These steps helped to create an atmosphere in which people could open up to one another about the hurts and struggles in their lives and build trust.

For Rev. Jones, the crisis prompted a period of soul-searching. Was she committed to staying with the church? Was she willing to continue making outreach a priority, despite the resistance? Did she have the strength or the leadership ability to carry on at Cookman? A turning point came, she says, when she found she could "let go and trust God to be in charge of the process." Giving the church and its ministries over to God was one of the hardest things she had to do as a pastor, but it brought her peace. "I decided if I was going to stay there, that was God's will, and I would stop worrying." Her confidence grew that Cookman's mission was the work of the Lord and that by God's grace it would continue.

Despite all these constructive steps, the conflict did not entirely go away—but by the new millennium it had significantly lessened. The congregation increasingly accepted the vision for community ministry. New funding sources providentially appeared, and the threat of closure grew more remote. The congregation did lose some members, especially those who clung to the desire for a more traditional church. But slowly new members have been added to Cookman's family, some who found salvation through one of the church's ministries. The "trial by fire" strengthened Rev. Jones's leadership and brought a team of dedicated lay leaders closer together.

The growing acceptance of holistic ministry has "completely transformed the congregation. We are more capable, more confident, and more effective in what we do," says Rev. Jones. She reflects on the change the church has undergone. "We used to be a mission church—people sent us money. Now we're a church in mission."

We'd like to conclude the book by telling you that holistic ministry is easy and instantly rewarding. It's not. Holistic ministry means change, and change entails sacrifice and loss. People naturally fear and resist change, and so ministry often goes hand in hand with conflict and crises. Bishop Dickie Robbins speaks from experience about the costs: "Holistic ministry provides probably one of the greatest satisfactions that one could imagine. At the same time, it is so very costly—emotionally, psychologically, physically, and financially. . . . Holistic ministry is giving and serving above your ability, beyond your ability." Rev. Donna Jones puts it simply, "Doing holistic ministry is hard."

But what else should we expect when we follow the greatest of holistic ministers who said, "If any want to become my followers, let them deny themselves and take up their cross and follow me" (Matt. 16:24)? Fulfilling God's mission cost Jesus his life. And following Jesus into holistic ministry brings Christians to the point of dying to ourselves, dying to our own comforts and interests, even to the point of a willingness to lay down our literal lives. As Dietrich Bonhoeffer said, "Jesus bids us come and die."[2]

Counting the Cost, Looking for Treasure

As a church considers a call to holistic ministry, people will want to assess the price tag. Some in the congregation will focus on the risks associated with any new endeavor: to your membership, budget, personnel, property, facilities, or reputation. Leaders should not ignore these concerns. Rather, leaders should heed Jesus' warning and count the costs:

> For which of you, intending to build a tower, does not first sit down and estimate the cost, to see whether he has enough to complete it? Otherwise, when

he has laid a foundation and is not able to finish, all who see it will begin to ridicule him, saying, "This fellow began to build and was not able to finish."

Luke 14:28–30

Any church considering a significant investment must weigh the cost of the desired project against the potential benefits of its completion—and the risks incurred by not investing. Where a congregation often needs help is in counting the cost associated with *not* responding to a call to holistic ministry: lost opportunities to share the gospel, lost identity as a beacon of hope and transformation, lost resources and contacts from new community collaborations, lost credibility to speak prophetically to critical social issues, and the loss of the experience of hands-on ministry as fertile soil for spiritual renewal.

One of the greatest risks and rewards of holistic ministry lies in our response to the invasion of "those people." This includes new people who are moving into our community, new people coming to our church, or new relationships with people who respond to our social ministries. Rev. Jim Kraft, pastor of First Presbyterian Church, recalls hearing another pastor complain about "all those new people moving into our area," as if they were a threat to the church. By choosing to see change as a crisis and reacting negatively to it, this pastor lost a great ministry opportunity that was laid at his church's doorstep.

Learning to distinguish between crisis and opportunity and to assess risk realistically is important. As an example, let's look at the risks associated with launching a soup kitchen. Consider the risks to volunteers, church members, church facilities, and the church's ministry overall.

> *Risks to volunteers:* Volunteers may find it uncomfortable and embarrassing to have to relate to people of a different racial or socioeconomic background. Volunteering takes time away from family life. The soup kitchen might bring volunteers in contact with ex-cons, drug addicts, alcoholics, prostitutes, pedophiles, molesters, or guests infected with HIV/AIDS or other diseases. Members may become discouraged by seeing some of the same people needing a meal week after week, month after month, year after year.
>
> *Risks to church members:* Soup kitchen guests might take up increasing time and attention from staff. The church might become known as "the soup kitchen church," affecting the reputation and status of church attenders. Guests might wind up in worship services, creating disturbances and altering the "look" of the church.
>
> *Risks to church facilities:* The kitchen will need upgrading. The church will face new health and fire code requirements, bringing the church under the watchful eye of public inspectors. The program will take up space.

Equipment might be stolen or broken. Fire and other building damage is a possibility.

Risks to ministry: The soup kitchen might siphon volunteers and funds from other programs. The guests might expect other types of services besides a meal, but the soup kitchen already will stretch the church's capacity. Some members question whether continuing to feed people who express no interest in becoming a Christian compromises the church's integrity.

The above risks are real and should not be trivialized or minimized. Church of the Advocate knows this well. In twenty years of running a soup kitchen that feeds up to three thousand meals each month, as well as other ministries that serve their devastated Philadelphia neighborhood, Rev. Isaac Miller says his church has paid a price. "There have been times when it feels like you just get ripped off, like clockwork—pots and pans stolen, all of the copper in the heating system stolen." Despite the congregation's financial struggles, its service to the community has remained a priority. Sticking with the ministry through times of sacrifice and loss is part of what has kept the congregation together. The church's commitment to outreach has produced, in Rev. Miller's words, "a group of people that are remarkably resilient and courageous, and with a great ability to 'hang in there'—folks who have got a real genuine commitment to love all this place as it is, and who love the church, with the love of Jesus and his tenacity."

Church of the Advocate could make decisions about ministry based on the costs. Instead, it chooses to focus on the rewards. Many of the risks of starting a soup kitchen identified above could be rewritten as portals to new avenues of relationship and ministry:

Opportunities for volunteers: Volunteers may form genuine friendships with the guests, overcoming shyness and prejudices. Stepping out in faith may bring volunteers closer to God. They may become more empathetic, compassionate, and informed about the social issues affecting the guests. They may become more bold in sharing their faith and more committed to prayer for the lost. The children of volunteers may learn the priority of Christian service by seeing it modeled by their parents.

Opportunities for church members: New lay leaders may emerge to free up or replace staff in the soup kitchen ministry. The church may gain new members from among the guests. Members may become more faithful in giving to support the church's ministry. The new ministry focus could energize and unify the congregation. The church's emerging reputation as a caring church may attract new members with the desire and energy to be involved in transformational ministries.

Opportunities for church facilities: The improvements to the kitchen may open new possibilities for church fellowship, such as sharing a meal together after a service. The church could donate or lease use of the kitchen to other agencies when it is not used for the ministry.

Opportunities for ministry: The soup kitchen might attract new funders and donors willing to support the church's ministry. Collaborations with other agencies caring for guests' needs may develop. The church might realize that just feeding people is not enough and decide to branch out into supplemental programs of substance abuse recovery or affordable housing. The congregation may gain deeper insights into the Scriptures on caring for poor persons. Concern for guests' spiritual needs may lead to a new emphasis on evangelism training. Guests' lives might be changed!

Discussions of cost and risk reveal what people hold most precious, "for where your treasure is, there your heart will be also" (Matt. 6:21). The man who knows there is an immense treasure buried in a field is no fool if he sells all he has to buy the field (Matt. 13:44). Likewise, church leaders may look foolish for taking great risks for holistic ministry, but they consider the stakes to be light compared to the hope and joy of seeing people enter the kingdom of God. Leaders can use people's fears about holistic ministry to kindle an appraisal of the congregation's priorities and values, in light of a holistic theology.

A significant event in the history of Central Baptist Church illustrates the impact of risk-taking ministry. After the assassination of Martin Luther King Jr. and the urban tumult that followed, some of the members felt strongly that the church should take a stand in response. Soon a radical proposal was put before the congregation: Mortgage the church property for $100,000 and use the money to address the social crisis. Early on a Sunday morning, the congregation debated the proposal. The discussion lasted so long that the congregation canceled the worship service for the day in order to devote their attention to the question. At stake was not just the money and the risk of losing the church property but an understanding of the character and calling of the church. The mortgage represented, in part, a willingness to put the church's identity on the line.

After four hours, the proposal passed with a two-thirds majority vote. The resulting Martin Luther King Jr. Memorial Fund poured resources into a host of ministries in the African American community, promoting educational scholarships, job training and placement, community organizing, the arts, and housing. At a time when many white churches were withdrawing from cities—physically and spiritually—and denying any social implications of the gospel, suburban Central Baptist's investment in African American community development sent a message that some Christians believed in resisting the evils of racism and honoring the image of God in all humankind.

The risky investment has paid off within the church as well. Over the years Central Baptist strengthened its commitment to social justice. Now nine mission groups address various areas of social concern, each with the goal "to reach out beyond ourselves with God's love." One of these is an Undoing Racism group, "committed to heightening our understanding of the tragic costs of racism within and beyond our congregation and to forming partnerships to overcome the effects of racism." Through hands-on activism, the congregation continues to build on the risky resolution passed in 1968. And the church's mortgage? Repaid within seven years, thanks to the generosity of the congregation, particularly matching gifts from two church families.

Fears arise not only from the known risks but also, or especially, from the prospect of the unknown. Holistic ministry means launching out into the depths, moving out from the safety and familiarity of the harbor into the unchartered waters of the ocean. In some cases, as in the story of Central Baptist, the situation calls for a radical leap. But not all congregations need start out by taking big risks. Writes Gene Wilkes, "A leader is a pioneer because she goes to the edge of a current reality and takes the next step. Upon seeing the new reality, she invites others to join her on the edge."[3] Risk-taking leadership discerns God's leading a pace ahead of the congregation and helps the church journey "off the map" in holistic ministry one step of faith at a time.

In the end, doing holistic ministry is not a matter of making the right risk assessment but of obeying a summons. We engage in outreach in fits and starts; we incur bumps and bruises; we succeed and fail; we want more but settle for less; we get burned and we burn out; we rejoice and we grieve; we receive recognition and we get overlooked. Grants, members, and staff may come and go; equipment may be donated, broken, stolen, or given away; relationships may be forged or fractured. And yet, when we've risked it all, have we *really* risked it all? Not really. What is most important and eternal can never be taken from us. Jesus is our example, "who for the sake of the joy that was set before him endured the cross" (Heb. 12:2). God gave us so much, gave up so much for us. As followers of Jesus, "the love of Christ urges us on" to do no less in sharing God's good gifts with our neighbors (2 Cor. 5:14).

Embracing Change

No matter how unsatisfactory the status quo, how compelling the call to holistic mission, or how rewarding the goal, visionary leaders will inevitably encounter resistance to change. "Leaders realize that people will not move easily from the way things are to the way that they think they should be," writes Barbara Williams Skinner. "On the way to the promised land in Canaan, for example, the Israelites kept complaining to Moses about how good things were when they were enslaved in Egypt."[4] If people grumbled about a change from slavery to freedom, how much more tension will be generated by the transition from an inward or one-sided focus to holistic mission!

Change is both desirable and inevitable, but it is also inevitably hard. There is no easy way to help a congregation adjust to change. We recommend the important book by Jim Herrington, Mike Bonem, and James H. Furr, *Leading Congregational Change: A Practical Guide for the Transformational Journey*. This book outlines in more detail the art of navigating a process of significant change in a congregation and the necessary set of leadership skills for church transformation. Rather than plunging in, hoping for the best, and coping with crises as they arise, the authors assert the need for a strategic plan. "It is not enough to know that change is needed, or even to have a clear image of the church's future. The challenge is to create a realistic way to get there." Their Congregational Transformation Model gives "structure and sequence to the process of moving from today's reality to a distant tomorrow."[5]

One foundational step in preparing a congregation for change is to prepare the leaders. If your church lacks mature leaders, if leaders are not lit by an inner spiritual fire, or if the unity of the team is fragmented by personal squabbles, theological conflicts, or dysfunctional communication systems, now is the time to address the problems—before you make major investments in a new outreach venture. Leaders should take time at the start of a project to renew their personal spiritual life.

> Leaders who are not experiencing God's transformation in their own lives will have difficulty discerning God's vision. They are unlikely to have the courage, conviction, and stamina to lead a church through significant change. The time of personal preparation allows the pastor and other key leaders to get ready for the journey that lies ahead and become more open to hear God's voice.[6]

Another important preparatory step is to strengthen the "spiritual and relational vitality" of the congregation, or "the life-giving power that faithful people experience together as they passionately pursue God's vision for their lives," say the authors of *Leading Congregational Change*. "Authentic spiritual and relational vitality not only empowers a local body of Christ, it prepares a church to become God's instrument in the world. As the challenges of change increase, so does the demand for this well-spring of power."[7] The stresses of change are fueled by theological error, judgmentalism, egotism, and mistrust. Without spiritual maturity and healthy relationships, "the church becomes like any other organization or group of people. . . . The resistance to change and the cynicism we see may often be the consequences of people's past disappointments with the institutional church."[8] But a body of Christ with a deepening love for God and people has a fixed star providing guidance and hope through a season of intense change.

At some point in its growth toward holistic ministry, a congregation may feel that it has climbed high enough and that it is now time to settle down and enjoy the view. But "a congregation that decides to rest on its laurels is taking the first step toward decline."[9] Holistic mission always beckons a church, in the words of Aslan in the last book of C. S. Lewis's Chronicles of Narnia, to advance "further up and further in." Just as our individual calling to be holy leads us into a lifelong journey of sanctification, the church's call to holistic ministry is an unfolding transformational process as God matures, refines, and prunes his people for his purposes. That is why Christians are called disciples. The word *disciple* comes from the same root in the Greek as *learner*. The task of learning about God and learning to do God's mission in the world is never complete. But by grace, God works *through* us while God is still working *on* us.

This is why church-to-church mentoring relationships are so vital.[10] (See resources in appendix B.) Every church has a strength; therefore, every church can teach another church a thing or two. And every church can benefit from seeing another model to which it can aspire. Even the most dynamic, innovative, outward-focused, cutting-edge, seven-day-a-week church needs to be in relationship with another church as a co-learner. You can always find a church that is one step ahead of you in your area of ministry and another church that could benefit by learning from you. Seeing other models of effective ministry motivates the congregation to continue on the path of change; humbly teaching another congregation what you have learned illuminates how far you have come.

Transformational leadership can help a congregation ride change and crisis. Not ride it out, but ride it—like a surfer on a wave, like a skier on the slopes, like Peter learning to embrace Gentiles, like Saul meeting Jesus on the road to Damascus, like Martin Luther standing on salvation by faith, like the Chinese church growing despite persecution. If a church denies, resists, or passively succumbs to change, then the congregation—and ultimately, those who are in need of God's help and hope—will lose. Embrace change and transform crises into crucibles of learning, loving, and living out the gospel.

Coping with Conflict

Jesus warned his followers to expect conflict: "Do not think that I have come to bring peace to the earth" (Matt. 10:34). If holistic ministry were not controversial, more churches would already be doing it! Risks and change will inevitably "threaten those individuals within the congregation who had a deep commitment to and vested interest in the existing programs and priorities."[11] Sit in on a meeting of the elders or deacons, church staff, or the congregation at large of a church in the process of considering a shift to holistic ministry and watch the sparks fly.

Surviving Conflict

The pastor called me into his study. He informed me that the deacons had decided to vote the outreach program out of the church. I stood in his office in total disbelief. . . .

Realizing that the deacons had a sort of intimidating presence, with the ability to sway the congregation, we decided to visit the congregation individually and get their feelings about what was happening in the church. Were the deacons actually reflecting the sentiment of the whole body? . . .

We were greeted with some surprising responses. Overwhelmingly, the responses of the parishioners were positive. . . . They did believe that the congregation needed to become more community-oriented and that the children were the future. . . . We encouraged all to get out to vote.

The day of the congregational meeting arrived. The 20 or so members gathered after church. . . . About 50 children were outside the church, waiting and praying for the outcome of the vote. They were concerned that they wouldn't have a place to go after school and in the evenings, that their clubs and activities would be canceled.

One of the deacons got up to speak. A hush fell over the group as he began. "The deacons of the church feel that it is time for the outreach program to be terminated. We come here today in full confidence that you will vote in agreement."

One of the older men in the church, the normally quiet Mr. Brown, stood up. . . . "You know, in the Bible Jesus speaks about the disciples who shooed the children away. If I'm not mistaken, Jesus got a little mad. . . . If we turn away these children, I think Jesus will be real mad."

Old Joey sat down. . . . His words had gone forth with power and had made an impact. Before anything more could be added, the deacon seized the floor.

"We need to vote! All those in favor of keeping the program, raise your hands." Fifteen of the 20 hands shot up. Only the hands of the deacons did not come off their laps. The program would remain! . . . The administrating deacon now asked, "Those who oppose the program, raise your hands." Fully conscious of the stares of the congregation, only two raised their hands. The other two walked out of the church and have never returned.

Bruce Main, "I Dreamed I Was a City," *Prism* 7, no. 4 (July/August 2000): 10–11. Reprinted from Tony Campolo, *Revolution and Renewal* (Louisville: Westminster/John Knox Press, 2000).

Sources of Conflict

Conflicts often stem from competing views of the nature of the church and its mission (see chapter 7 on the battle between in-reach and outreach). Is the church a country club, with perks and privileges mainly for members only? Or is the church a community center that caters to its neighbors, whether paying (i.e., tithing) or not? Is the church a hospital, where dysfunctional, alienated, addicted, weary, disabled, hurting, needy people gather for healing and mutual support? Or is the church an outpost that recharges and resources pilgrims to "work out [their] . . . salvation" (Phil. 2:12) in ministry to the world? Which is a higher priority: caring for the flock and nurturing a thriving faith community, or expanding the church's reach and impact on those beyond its walls? Is ministry the task of the clergy and staff, with members' main responsibility being to pay their salaries? Or should church leaders stay out of the way so members can do their own ministry?

Another source of contention is the kind of ministry a church should undertake. For decades, Christians have clashed over the priority of evangelism versus social ministry. Some believe social ministry distracts the church from its mandate to preach the gospel. They may fear that social ministry represents a step down a slippery slope toward liberalism. Others want to limit outreach to social ministry, associating evangelism with aggressive, manipulative tactics or with withdrawal from social concerns. Conflict can also arise between those who hold to traditional ministry models and proponents of innovation. One example is the clash between "come here" ministries of evangelism (such as annual revivals, Vacation Bible School, or Bring-a-Friend Sundays), and "go to" ministries (such as street evangelism, workplace Bible studies, or mall ministry).

Another kind of tension exists between meeting the needs of individuals and families and confronting oppressive social institutions and systems. As Carl Dudley puts it, "Sharp disagreements between commitments to service and to justice have put many social ministry programs on the rocks of irreconcilable differences."[12] A congregation might be divided over whether to respond to poverty in the community by starting a welfare-to-work training program or an advocacy group to influence welfare policy.

Another major cause of conflict is turf wars, in which people defensively stake out "their" church territory and take any new ministry proposal as a personal threat. These battles can originate among church personnel competing for prominence, popularity, or access to church resources of funds, space, and volunteers. Conflicts can escalate if holistic ministry is seen as the responsibility of a particular staff person who is disconnected from other areas of ministry. Hostilities can also ignite between committees, boards, task forces, or classes (for example, the justice in action group versus the evangelism committee). Or warfare can spring up among the membership at large, as various individuals or groups vie for the church to support their favorite ministries.

Other sources of conflict sparked by holistic ministry relate to problems within the congregation, including:

- an unfocused or unclear vision, or competing visions
- disharmony and personality conflicts—among the staff or between clergy and laity
- theological differences
- unbiblical, unethical, immoral behavior involving ministry personnel (sexual or physical abuse, coercive evangelistic tactics, embezzlement, fraud, etc.)
- generational and cultural gaps
- dysfunctional people
- dysfunctional congregational systems
- clashing ideological allegiances

Crises in holistic ministry can also arise from external causes:

- conflict between the church and neighborhood residents, local institutions, or other churches in the community
- denominational expectations or policies counter to the church's ministry plans
- regulations, church-state issues, and pressures to secularize that arise in the context of receiving funding from secular sources
- use of church property for controversial ministries (such as those involving homeless people or ex-offenders)
- actions that bring the church into a courtroom or before a governmental board
- opposition by those in the community who feel threatened by a change in the status quo—such as established groups fearing loss to newly empowered people
- political posturing by candidates for office or government officials
- grudges held by former church members

Dealing Constructively with Conflict

How does a church move beyond fruitless either/or debates (nurture versus outreach, evangelism versus social ministry, service versus justice) to ministry that is holistically both/and? How do we prevent turf wars, overcome differing views of the role of the church, and deal a death blow to the incapacitating self-centeredness of a church that exists for "me and mine"? While every Christian has a responsibility to "live peaceably with all" (Rom. 12:18), to restore those who are in error with a spirit of gentleness (Gal. 6:1), to avoid foolish controversies (2 Tim. 2:14), and to pray for one another (James 5:16), the burden of addressing conflict falls mainly on the leadership. Following are five suggestions for church leaders.

1. *Acknowledge and accept conflict.* Conflicts over ministry are nothing new in the church. In the first century, the church nearly divided over the question, Do we minister only to the Jews, the household of faith, God's chosen ones, or do we reach out to the Gentiles, "dogs," pagans, heathen, blasphemers, and spiritual half-breeds? The early church did not try to deny or smooth over this conflict. The first Christian council faced the question head-on (Acts 15) and gained a new understanding of the global scope of mission.

Christians tend to think of conflict as a negative state to be avoided or resolved as quickly as possible. The authors of *Leading Congregational Change* say churches in the process of transformation have to toss out the prevailing belief that a healthy congregation does not have conflict. They make a distinction between "life-threatening conflict," which accompanies outright disobedience to God's commands, such as the Israelites' grumbling against Moses during the Exodus, and "life-giving conflict," or "a deeper understanding and commitment that grows out of a significant disagreement," such as the dispute over distribution of food to widows in Acts 6 that gave rise to the diaconate.[13]

The goal for leaders is not to dodge conflict but to manage it in a life-giving manner. Conflict generates energy that can be directed toward shaking up the paradigms that support an unsatisfactory status quo. Conflict can open the door to dialogue, which can give clarity to a new holistic understanding of the church's mission. Conflict accompanies the questioning of old ideas and habits and can be rephrased as an invitation to "be renewed in the spirit of your minds" (Eph. 4:23). Visionary leaders can take heart when people disagree over holistic ministry because it signals the end of "church as usual." As one pastor told the authors of *Leading Congregational Change*, "All my life, I've judged my success by how happy everyone in the church was. You are telling me that if I'm really on mission with God, one sign of my success will be the presence of conflict."[14]

2. *Listen and talk in love.* Without healthy relationships a congregation cannot survive conflict. Breakdowns in communication threaten relationships. So in the midst of a conflict, regardless of who is more reasonable or theologically correct, uphold the principles of active listening: Listen before you talk; don't talk until you can rephrase what you have heard. The goal is to foster dialogue—or in the words attributed to St. Francis of Assisi, to "seek not so much to be understood as to understand." Each party to a conflict should ask:

- What is driving or motivating the other person?
- What unspoken values, fears, and needs lie behind his or her convictions?
- What would it be like to be in his or her shoes?
- What can I affirm, support, bless, or honor in his or her position or perspective?
- What can I learn from our differences?
- What piece(s) are we each missing that we need in order to be whole?
- How can I continue to love this person while challenging his or her perspectives?

Dialogue based on sincere listening and honest communication expresses and nurtures the love within the congregation that we hope to share with others in holistic community outreach. Leaders must model this by accepting input nondefensively and taking people's suggestions seriously. The particular challenge for leaders is to hear and respond lovingly to the troublemakers, those individuals who respond to ministry proposals by being alarmist, disruptive, passive aggressive, or plain ornery. "It is helpful to remember that a heart crying to be loved lurks behind the obstinacy of many of these problem people," advises Calvin Miller. He wisely adds, "The best way to eliminate a critic is to make him or her your friend."[15]

3. *Foster unity.* In Jesus' final prayer for his disciples and those who would come after them, he pleaded for the unity of all believers: "I in them and you in me, that they may become completely one, so that the world may know that you have sent me" (John 17:23). Our unity in Christ is essential to our holistic witness. Honest disagreements, even when they turn into passionate arguments, do not compromise our fundamental oneness in the Spirit. Fostering unity does not mean seeking consensus before taking any action or squelching all divergent opinions. But a congregation intractably divided by hostility, mistrust, slander, and contention cannot effectively share the Good News of Christ in the world.

Leaders play a key role in calling Christians to "one Lord, one faith" and setting (and modeling) the standards for how Christians should disagree. As Paul urges in Ephesians 4:1–3, "Lead a life worthy of the calling to which you have been called, with all humility and gentleness, with patience, bearing with one another in love, making every effort to maintain the unity of the Spirit in the bond of peace."

Special rituals or services can help remind Christians of their "bond of peace" in a time of conflict. Cookman United Methodist Church, for example, has rediscovered the tradition of the Love Feast. The Love Feast is a rite of reconciliation and forgiveness within the church that takes place before communion, per Jesus' instructions in Matthew 5:24. Any people who have had a broken relationship can come forward to share bread and water. They can talk about their desire to be reconciled with one another, recite a liturgy of forgiveness, and embrace. Sometimes Rev. Jones has brought a smaller group together for a more informal time of sharing and relational restoration. She makes sure that the conversation focuses on forgiveness rather than rehashing the disputes. Rituals such as Love Feasts do not make the conflict go away, but they do clear the tension and help people in the congregation deal with the conflict in a godly way.

4. *Let them go.* Sometimes, despite your best efforts to hear, love, and befriend "problem people," they continue to obstruct the path of holistic ministry. Left unchecked, a particular group within the membership, or even one or two key individuals, can sap the congregation's enthusiasm and thwart ministry plans. The hope of church leaders is to see the entire congregation embrace the vision or at least go along with it. At some point, however, after the vision has been laid out and a significant core of the congregation is on board and ready to move forward, it is appropriate for leaders to make it clear that the decision has been made. The course has been laid in. Staying on the bus indicates a willingness to go where the bus is headed. If people do not like the destination, they should feel free to choose another bus. This does not mean that all dialogue is silenced—rather, that the listening and talking will continue as the bus moves forward in holistic ministry.

Bishop Dickie Robbins uses the image of constructing a tall building to describe the process of growing holistic ministry. The first thing that gets built is a scaffold that supports the construction of the real building. After a time, the scaffold comes down, but the building remains. In the early stages of Life in Christ's development, the church grew by leaps and bounds through the attraction of dynamic preaching and a powerful vision and through holistic ministries drawing new people into the kingdom of God and into the congregation. But as Bishop Robbins increasingly emphasized the responsibility of disciples to participate in outreach, many decided that the personal cost was too high. He made it clear that if people wanted a Sunday-only church, Life in Christ was not the right place for them. He explains:

> There are churches that don't have that kind of expectation [of active ministry], and [some people] would be better served in a place where they can just be comfortable going in for a worship service and then going home and not having very much else expected of them. But here, we are truly a ministry that will go out into the community.

About one-third of the congregation left. But once the scaffolding fell away, as Bishop Robbins puts it, those who had decided to stay were stronger and more committed than before. While leaders should be sorry to see people leave—and except in extreme cases should not kick people out!—leaders can let people go by trusting that the church is "God's building" and that a congregation built on the foundation of Christ will not topple (1 Cor. 3:9).

5. *Keep a healthy personal perspective.* Leaders must strive not to take personal offense when their ideas are rejected. They must have the maturity not to allow their egos to become invested in a conflict and not to retaliate on a personal level. On the other hand, in some cases leaders are personally attacked in conflicts over holistic ministry. A leader's wisdom, authority, leadership ability, and even integrity may be questioned. His or her job and reputation may be on the line. In these situations, recall Jesus' words, "Woe to you when all speak well of you" (Luke 6:26). Be assured that history bears witness that "visionary leaders are often troublemakers."[16]

A firm sense of God's calling, a strong devotional life, and the indwelling of the Holy Spirit are vital. "To survive active and vicious criticism demands that we know who we are," writes Calvin Miller. "The love of God does not keep leaders from losing, but it does keep them from seeing themselves as losers."[17] Often we need others to remind us of who we are, what we are called to do, and what God has promised to those who are faithful. Maintaining perspective requires a personal support system—a spouse, a mentor, denominational contacts, colleagues in other churches or para-church ministries, or friends within the congregation. Relationships with leaders in other emerging or experienced holistic churches are particularly helpful, because they let leaders know they are not alone.

Keeping a healthy perspective in a time of crisis also requires farsighted vision. Faith for the long haul sustains leaders through the "Joseph" years of a ministry, when they feel harassed and God's purposes seem thwarted. Leaders need to anticipate a time when they will look back on the setbacks and say with Joseph, "Even though you intended to do harm to me, God intended it for good, in order to preserve a numerous people" (Gen. 50:20).

"Where Did I Go Wrong?"

By no means are we saying that leaders are always somehow to blame when ministry plans go awry! But one sign of true leadership in a conflict is a willingness to reflect on where you went wrong and to take responsibility for your contribution to the problem. Sometimes, the root issue in a conflict over holistic ministry is simply a lack of faith, obedience, love, or maturity on the part of the antagonists. Often, however, the church's leadership has unwittingly helped to provoke or exacerbate the battle. If your vision for holistic ministry is locked in controversy, ask yourself if you have made one of the following five mistakes. Then take steps to make it right. You will learn from the experience and come away a stronger, more effective leader.

1. *Have you led ministry or done ministry?* Conflicts can arise when clergy assume total responsibility for the work of ministry, treading on or crowding out the contributions of laypeople. Many pastors "are trained to be 'doers'; thus, their feelings of turf and threat enter in where they should not. . . . Far too many pastors are burning out and leaving the ministry, while competent lay people at the same time are leaving in disaffection." Following the principle that "ministry is the work of the whole priesthood," pastors must instead "understand their role as facilitators, enablers, supporters and shepherds of the gifts of the body."[18]

2. *Has your zeal run ahead of you?* Asked what he has learned in a dozen years of holistic ministry, Bishop Dickie Robbins reflects, "Don't let your zeal get ahead of you." Sometimes, it is better to wait for the right conditions than to rush into a project. For example, Life in Christ needed transportation, so the church jumped at the chance to buy two buses from another congregation. The buses were inexpensive but in poor condition. One broke down beyond repair on a youth trip. Had the church waited until it had the money to buy a better vehicle, it would not have ended up with a bus full of disgruntled inner-city kids. Bishop Robbins has also learned to take the time before launching new ministries to develop leaders and establish sound organizational structures. His enthusiasm and compassion make it difficult to wait when surrounded by such pressing needs. But, he says, when the timing is right, "the vision will still be there."

3. *Have you left people behind—or dragged them with you?* Leaders with the vision for holistic ministry often feel forced to choose between the congregation and their calling. It is difficult—if not impossible—to get a church to move where it does not want to go. On the other hand, part of the task of visionary leadership is to influence where people want to go and then motivate them to get there. If a congregation opposes the idea of holistic ministry, leaders cannot simply "take a laissez faire approach and allow the diverse wishes of the group to provide the direction and impetus for the body."[19] But ignoring resistance and forging ahead on your own will backfire. Nor should leaders use manipulative or coercive strategies to make people go along with a ministry plan against their will. The goal is not to avoid conflict or to enforce compliance but to use the tension as a springboard for congregational transformation.

4. *Have you lost your identity?* Church members naturally cling to their church's identity. It is part of what makes up their own personal identity. When change threatens a church's essential character or heritage, people feel vulnerable and

uprooted. Their sense of belonging and ownership in the congregation diminishes. This leaves people less willing and able to throw their support behind new ministry programs. As Carl Dudley asserts, "Nothing is convincing that is out of sync with the character of the congregation, and few projects will find support if they are at odds with the kind of church the members believe themselves to be."[20]

Transforming a church's mission does not mean renouncing the past and starting from scratch. Rather, "effective leaders help church members connect new ministry approaches with well-regarded aspects of the congregation's heritage. They preserve the core values and beliefs of the congregation."[21] Look for the middle ground between being a slave to tradition and tossing valued aspects of the church's identity overboard. First Thessalonians 5:21 provides the key to this balance: "Test everything; hold fast to what is good."

5. *Have you kept people in the dark?* Says David Heney, "Resistance is strongest when change comes as a surprise, or when it is someone else's idea."[22] Minimize the surprises for your congregation. Being overly secretive can feed anxiety and the rumor mill. If leaders communicate about holistic ministry only among themselves and an "elite" group, the congregation may draw the conclusion that holistic ministry does not concern them—or worse, that something is going on behind their backs. There is a time in the early stages of developing the vision when it is appropriate to keep the decision-making process limited to the leadership team. Even during this phase, however, you should let your congregation know that God is calling the leadership to consider changes in the ministry focus and ask for the congregation's prayerful support.

When the time comes for action, be frank with the congregation about the risks and controversies entailed by a plan for ministry. Of course, it pays to be diplomatic when making the presentation! But it is better to take the time to address people's questions and concerns up front than to get derailed by conflict as people learn about the plan *after* a ministry has been launched. As Harold Fray writes:

> There is a risk to being open and candid. It will mean momentary failures when new policies and actions are put to the test and opportunity is provided for a no as well as a yes. It requires patience and endurance, and above all, it means placing all things in the hands of God, being willing to suffer defeat as well as to achieve victory, knowing there are times when he can use our defeats to accomplish his will better than the victories.[23]

Conclusion

It is no coincidence that many of the great moments in salvation history start out with a trek through the wilderness. Abraham, Moses and the Israelites, and Jesus all found themselves wandering through the desert after responding to God's calling. As your congregation answers God's invitation to join in holistic mission, you can expect to pass through the wilderness. You will most likely encounter the test of inadequate finances, personnel, and space. You will endure temptations to turn aside, turn away, slow down, speed up, and sell out. You will struggle to develop ministry leaders who share the holistic vision, are passionate servants of the Lord, and can work together as a team. As Nehemiah faced the taunts of Sanballat and Tobiah as he worked to rebuild the wall around Jerusalem (Neh. 4:1–3), you will experience opposition to the ministry, from outside as well as inside the congregation.

If your congregation (and particularly its leadership) is committed to the Lord, to one another, and to love of neighbor, these trials will not derail God's plan for your church. It is in the desert that the Holy Spirit teaches us key truths, tests our character and purpose, and strengthens us for ministry. God's strength is made perfect in our weakness (2 Cor. 12:9). Through costs, change, and conflict, God pours out on the church his boundless, all-sufficient love, power, and grace—which we then proclaim in our evangelism and demonstrate in our works of compassion and justice. A congregation that ventures into holistic ministry can thus share Paul's confidence "that the one who began a good work among you will bring it to completion by the day of Jesus Christ" (Phil. 1:6).

So "take a risk," advises Rev. Patrick Hansel of New Creation Lutheran Church. "Community ministry brings you energy. Serving people brings *you* life too. Sure, there are going to be mistakes, and you're going to fall. But you'll also be uplifted. And," he adds, "it's a lot of fun."

We Can Do It

Huge accomplishments start with small steps. Effective outreach begins with one faithful visionary.

Don't be overwhelmed or intimidated by models like Christian Stronghold Baptist Church, a congregation of over four thousand members committed to holistic outreach. Christian Stronghold did not start that way! It began with Willie Richardson finding time, in spite of his full-time job as an engineer, to pastor and preach to a few people in a small row house. Your church cannot launch a comprehensive outreach program like Christian Stronghold's by next week. But, in God's time, it *can* happen in your congregation. Whether you are the pastor, a congregational leader, or a committed layperson, God can use you to lead your congregation into exciting, expanding holistic ministry.

The spectrum of ACTS mercy ministries at Tenth Presbyterian Church developed slowly, led by one man who worked patiently for years to nurture a vision for holistic Christian servanthood in the congregation. David Apple was raised in a socially and politically active family. Following his conversion, he began to dream of a ministry that would blend social work and evangelism. In 1988, he heard that Tenth Presbyterian Church was looking for someone to direct their ACTS ministry. At that time, ACTS consisted of five committees struggling to establish a foundation for mercy ministry, hindered by the church's lack of a guiding ministry vision.

David helped give the ministry more structure and began mobilizing the congregation to expand its outreach. He embraced Tenth Presbyterian's long-standing evangelistic emphasis but longed for the church to develop an equal

311

passion for the kind of empowerment ministries that he had seen in the small African American church where he had come to faith in Christ. He wrestled with the socioeconomic and racial barriers that kept some people from feeling welcome in the church. And he challenged church leaders to invest more resources in holistic outreach. For years, he prayed and shared his vision with whoever would listen—learning to do so with more gentleness and patience along the way. Gradually, God worked change in the congregation and brought new leaders with servant hearts. ACTS has blossomed into a cluster of ministries bringing friendship, hope, resources for personal development, and a deeper knowledge of Christ to people dealing with such needs as homelessness, HIV/AIDS, substance abuse, and divorce.

The dynamic ministries of Life in Christ Cathedral of Faith exist because one couple answered God's call. When Dickie Robbins left his decaying hometown of Chester for a college education and a better future, he had no intention of returning. Ten years later, however, he and his wife, Tina, heard God's compelling call to address the problems in Chester that had made him want to leave. Obediently, they moved back to the inner city and founded a church. For the first few weeks, Tina was the only person in the congregation. They began preaching the gospel on drug corners and in public housing developments and soon were discipling a circle of converted drug addicts. Today, a growing congregation has caught Dickie and Tina's fire for evangelism and community revitalization by supporting one new outreach ministry after another. Despite many challenges and setbacks, the Robbinses continue to bubble over with ideas and energy because of their faith in God's leading. "When there is a need, rather than join in the complaints, we create an alternative," says Dickie. "God sent me here to transform a community. And that is what we are doing."

Media Presbyterian was a thriving, middle-class evangelical congregation when Rev. Bill Borror became senior pastor in 1995. The congregation gave generously to mission projects, but few members were involved in local outreach. Without neglecting pastoral care, Bill started preaching and teaching about the imperative of evangelism and God's special concern for poor people. "My hope and prayer," as he expressed his vision in his first annual report to the congregation, is that "we will individually and corporately fall deeper in love with God and in turn, seek concrete ways to love our brothers and sisters, as well as those outside the [church] community, with the profound and radical love of Jesus."

Holistic outreach began springing to life. Bill developed Habitat for Humanity mission trips, which became a powerful tool for discipling members in holistic ministry. Lay leaders who caught the vision created a Faith in Action committee to rally church members to greater involvement in hands-on ministry. Bill hired an associate pastor for holistic ministries, Rev. Deb Miller, who had a passion for both congregational care and missions. The church funded an urban intern to develop partnerships with inner-city churches and faith-based agencies. Members overcame their fear of the city to serve meals, rehabilitate houses, and lead youth programs. Members also began exploring new ways to overcome their fear of evangelism. Through these steps, Media has become a church known not only for great preaching and children's ministries but also for reaching out with the whole gospel.

The energy and dedication of one faithful layperson at New Covenant Church of Philadelphia, Ora Love, has led to an addiction recovery ministry in a network of churches. Ora became convinced of the need for a Christo-centric rehab program that would integrate Scripture and prayer. She and a friend who had recovered from a twenty-seven-year addiction to heroin adapted Alcoholics Anonymous' twelve steps, and organized the first meeting of Christians United Against Addictions (CUAA). Their vision was to develop a program that could be replicated in other churches. Ora and five others presented the ministry need to her pastor, Bishop Milton Grannum, who encouraged the idea, saying, "If it is of God, it will last." Since 1987, Ora has helped to start and coordinate roughly thirty support groups in churches and homes throughout the Philadelphia region (not all of which are still meeting). New Covenant Church has provided leadership training, funds, and oversight for the ministry. Many of the groups are led by former addicts. As those who are liberated from addictions become instruments of God's salvation for others, Ora's original vision bears fruit a hundredfold.

It is individuals like Ora Love, Bill Borror, Dickie Robbins, and David Apple who can help the church rise to the historic opportunities we face today. As we said in the introduction, top people in government, media, and academia are welcoming the social service contributions of the faith community in an astonishing new way. Biblical Christians who understand how good works and Good News together transform lives and communities have an open door. To seize this opportunity, we need tens of thousands more holistic congregations in our cititas like the ones profiled in this book. We also need holistic suburban congregations who are willling to address local needs and work as partners in the way Media Presbyterian and Life in Christ Cathedral of Faith cooperate. And for that to happen, leaders must respond faithfully to God's call.

Is God calling you and your congregation? Are you, like Jesus, moved by this vision in Isaiah:

> The spirit of the Lord God is upon me, because the LORD has anointed me;
> he has sent me to bring good news to the oppressed,
>   to bind up the brokenhearted,
> to proclaim liberty to the captives
>   and release to the prisoners;
> to proclaim the year of the LORD's favor,

> and the day of vengeance of our God;
>   to comfort all who mourn. . . .
> They shall build up the ancient ruins,
>   they shall raise up the former devastations;
> they shall repair the ruined cities,
>   the devastations of many generations.

61:1–2, 4 (cf. Luke 4:18–21)

Your church can proclaim the Good News, comfort the afflicted, build up the cities, and repair the cyclic devastations of broken communities. If you are willing in obedience and trust to take the first small step—and then the next and the next—God will take care of the big picture.

What holds you back from taking the first small step toward leading your congregation to transform your community through evangelism and social ministry? The God of the Bible wants it. Our hurting society needs it. In the power and love of the Spirit, we can do it.

Profiles of the Churches
in the Congregations, Communities,
and Leadership Development Project

Many of the stories and ideas in this book come from the churches we studied in the Congregations, Communities, and Leadership Development Project, sponsored by Eastern Baptist Theological Seminary. This project, funded by the Lilly Endowment and the John Templeton Foundation, involved in-depth case studies of fifteen churches with active community outreach in the greater Philadelphia area. These churches taught us much about how and why churches go about doing ministry and about the joys and struggles of loving your community in Jesus' name.

A brief profile of each church is listed below, including the size and age of the church at the time of our study (1999) and a mission statement. The profiles indicate the name of the researcher who was responsible for the interviews and observations. Most of our information about each case study church came from the researchers' field notes, recorded interviews, and summary reports.

Bethel Temple Community Bible Church

Rev. Joel Van Dyke and Rev. Luis Centeno (now a missionary with American Missionary Fellowship)
236 E. Allegheny Avenue, Philadelphia, PA 19134
215-423-0986
Ethnicity: Hispanic (Puerto Rican)/Anglo
Size: 250 attenders

Age: 9 years

Location: inner city

Denomination: Independent

"Discipling our members, evangelizing our community, and revitalizing our neighborhood in the name of Jesus Christ."

Researcher: Paula McCosh

Central Baptist Church

Rev. Marcus Pomeroy and Rev. Marcia Bailey

106 W. Lancaster Avenue, P.O. Box 309, Wayne, PA 19087

610-688-0664

Ethnicity: Anglo

Size: 260 members/180 attenders

Age: 101 years

Location: suburb

Denomination: American Baptist

"A caring, concerned, and questioning congregation."

Researcher: Gaynor Yancey

Christian Stronghold Baptist Church

Rev. Dr. Willie Richardson

4701 Lancaster Avenue, Philadelphia, PA 19131

215-877-1530

Ethnicity: African American

Size: 4,090 members/1,700 attenders

Age: 22 years

Location: inner city

Denomination: Independent Baptist

"Glorifying Christ, amplifying the Bible, and edifying people."

Researcher: Averil Clarke

Church of the Advocate

Fr. Isaac Miller

1801 Diamond Street, Philadelphia, PA 19121

215-236-0568

Ethnicity: African American

Size: 150 members/60 attenders

Age: 100 years

Location: inner city

Denomination: Episcopal

"An investment in the health, welfare, and spirit of our community."

Researcher: Averil Clarke

Cookman United Methodist Church

Rev. Donna Jones

12th Street and Lehigh Avenue, P.O. Box 6984, Philadelphia, PA 19132

215-229-4477

Ethnicity: African American

Size: 50 attenders

Age: 9 years

Location: inner city

"Christians responding to opportunities to witness, nurture, and serve."

Researcher: Jill Witmer Sinha

Faith Assembly of God

Rev. Richard Smith

1839 Harrison Avenue, Philadelphia, PA 19124

215-535-8581

Ethnicity: African American

Size: 100 attenders

Age: 9 years

Location: residential urban neighborhood

"Living out the gospel in our community."

Researcher: Jill Witmer Sinha

First Presbyterian Church

Rev. James H. Kraft

125 Garden Street, Mount Holly, NJ 08060

609-267-0330

Ethnicity: Anglo

Size: 700 members/500 attenders

Age: 156 years

Location: downtown

Denomination: PC (USA)

"Loved, served, and sent by Christ, we share life at its very best!"

Researcher: Averil Clarke

Germantown Church of the Brethren

Rev. Richard Kyerematen

6611 Germantown Avenue, Philadelphia, PA 19119

215-848-6501

Ethnicity: African American

Size: 70 members/60–120 attenders

Age: 10 years (as current congregation)

Location: residential urban neighborhood

"To proclaim the Good News of our Lord and Savior Jesus Christ throughout the whole world, and more particularly to the residents of the city of Philadelphia; to make known to as many people as possible the redeeming love of God; to be a light of love, hope, peace, and service in our homes, church, community, and world."

Researcher: Joan Hoppe-Spink

Koinonia Christian Community Church

Pastor Jerome Simmons

1101-03 West Allegheny Avenue, Philadelphia, PA 19133

215-227-8032

Ethnicity: African American

Size: 40 members/30 attenders

Age: 3 years

Location: inner city

Denomination: Church of God in Christ

". . . Letting our Christian light shine before men so they may see our good works and glorify our Father in heaven (Matt. 5:16)."

Researcher: Kesha Moore

Life in Christ Cathedral of Faith

Bishop Dickie Robbins

3016-3334 West 3rd Street, Chester, PA 19013

610-497-2100

Ethnicity: African American

Size: 300 attenders

Age: 12 years

Location: inner city

Denomination: Nondenominational

". . . To reach our community and the world with the true message of the gospel of Jesus Christ, proclaiming and demonstrating the love of God. . . ."

Researcher: Kesha Moore

Media Presbyterian Church

Rev. Bill Borror, senior pastor

Rev. Deb Miller, associate pastor for holistic ministries

30 E. Baltimore Avenue, Media, PA 19063

610-566-3944

Ethnicity: Anglo

Size: 880 members/400 attenders

Age: 150 years

Location: suburb

Denomination: PC (USA)

"Using time, talents, and treasures to embrace our world in the name of our Lord and Savior."

Researcher: Paula McCosh

New Covenant Church of Philadelphia

Bishop Milton Grannum

7500 Germantown Avenue, Philadelphia, PA 19119

215-247-7500

Ethnicity: African American

Size: 3,500 members/2,300 attenders

Age: 15 years

Location: residential neighborhood

Denomination: Church of God, Anderson

"Touching Philadelphia and the world by reaching and empowering individuals . . ."

Researcher: Tim Nelson

New Creation Lutheran Church/Iglesia Luterana Nueva Creación

Rev. Patrick Cabello Hansel and Rev. Luisa Cabello Hansel

162 W. Tioga, Philadelphia, PA 19140

215-426-8762

Ethnicity: Hispanic/Anglo

Size: 200 members/75 attenders

Age: 4 years

Location: inner city

Denomination: Lutheran

"Celebration, transformation, education, to all the nations."

Researcher: Paula McCosh

Tenth Memorial Baptist Church

Rev. William B. Moore

1328 N. 19th Street, Philadelphia, PA 19121

215-787-2780

Ethnicity: African American

Size: 1,500 members/600 attenders

Age: 65 years

Location: inner city

Denomination: National Baptist

". . . United in the belief of what Jesus Christ taught, covenanting to do what he commanded, and cooperating with other like bodies in kingdom movements. . . ."

Researcher: Kesha Moore

Tenth Presbyterian Church

Rev. Dr. Philip Ryken, senior pastor

Dr. David Apple, director of Mercy Ministries

1701 Delancey Place, Philadelphia, PA 19103

215-735-7688

Ethnicity: Anglo/a minority Asian, African American

Size: 1,100 members/1,150 attenders

Age: 166 years

Location: downtown

Denomination: PCA

". . . This church opens wide her doors and offers her welcome in the name of the Lord Jesus Christ."

Researcher: Tim Nelson

Holistic Ministry Resources

If you are interested in holistic ministry, you are not alone! There are many great resources out there. In fact, the challenge for busy church leaders and ministry activists is knowing where to begin. Here is our selection of the best books on holistic ministry to get you started, followed by a longer list of books and other resources. (For more contacts, references, organizations, and links, see our web site, network935.org.)

A Place to Start

Richard Armstrong, *Faithful Witnesses,* with leader's guide and participants' workbook (Louisville: Curriculum Publishing/Presbyterian Church [USA], 1997) has everything you need to offer a twelve-week evangelism training course (800-524-2612).

Jeff Arnold, *Small Group Outreach: Turning Groups Inside Out* (Downers Grove, Ill.: InterVarsity Press, 1998) shows you how to transform inward-focused small groups into centers of holistic ministry, while still helping members care for one another and grow in discipleship.

Ray Bakke, *A Theology as Big as the City* (Downers Grove, Ill.: InterVarsity Press, 1997) lays a theological foundation for holistic urban ministry. Bakke, founder of International Urban Associates, brings the insights of over forty years of global ministry experience.

Donald Dayton, *Discovering an Evangelical Heritage* (New York: Harper, 1976) highlights our nineteenth-century holistic ministry ancestors, who led the way as reformers and prophetic pioneers, before the modernist/fundamentalist battles dichotomized the gospel.

Carl S. Dudley, *Community Ministry: New Challenges, Proven Steps to Faith-Based Initiatives* (Bethesda, Md.: Alban Institute, 2001) offers guidance for church leaders seeking to develop effective community ministries, grounded in Dudley's many years of research and experience with congregations engaged in ministry (www.alban.org).

Tim Keller, *Ministries of Mercy: The Call of the Jericho Road,* 2d ed. (Phillipsburg, N.J.: P & R Publishing, 1989) provides biblical and practical guidance for ministering to "the least of these," by the pastor of one of the country's most innovative urban congregations.

319

Manuel Ortiz and Harvey Conn, *Urban Ministry: The Kingdom, the City, and the People of God* (Downers Grove, Ill.: InterVarsity Press, 2001) is thick, thorough, theological, and the best book on the subject by two scholar/practitioners.

John Perkins, *Beyond Charity: The Call to Christian Community Development* (Grand Rapids: Baker, 1993) outlines the vision and principles for holistic development ministry from the cofounder of the Christian Community Development Association. *Restoring At-Risk Communities: Doing It Together and Doing It Right* (Grand Rapids: Baker, 1995), edited by John Perkins, is its sequel.

Oliver Phillips, *The 12-Step Program: Steps to Starting a Compassionate Ministry Center* (Kansas City, Mo.: Nazarene Compassionate Ministries USA/Canada, 2001) gives an overview of the process of developing holistic ministry. See also the three-part (three hours per part) video series (800-306-9950; www.nazarenecompassion.org).

Amy L. Sherman, *Restorers of Hope* (Wheaton: Crossway Books, 1997) shows churches how to move from "commodity based benevolence" (i.e., just giving material aid) to "holistic, relational ministry" that promotes lasting transformation, with special consideration of the benefits and pitfalls of collaboration with government agencies.

Amy L. Sherman, *Sharing God's Heart for the Poor: Meditations for Worship, Prayer, and Service* (Charlottesville, Va.: Trinity Presbyterian Church, 1999) offers bite-sized, balanced, and biblical food to nourish a congregation's spiritual passion for community outreach (434-293-5656).

Ronald J. Sider, *Good News and Good Works: A Theology for the Whole Gospel* (Grand Rapids: Baker, 1993) provides a thorough examination of the theology of holistic ministry, challenging lopsided understandings of mission and exploring in-depth the relationship between evangelism and social action.

Steve Sjogren, *Conspiracy of Kindness* (Ann Arbor, Mich.: Vine Books, 1993) and *101 Ways to Reach Your Community* (Colorado Springs: NavPress, 2001) are packed with ideas for low-risk, high-impact evangelism. Sjogren also offers online resources to help churches show the kindness of God in practical ways (www.servantevangelism.com).

More Books

Abraham, William J. *The Logic of Evangelism.* Grand Rapids: Eerdmans, 1989.

Aldrich, Joseph C. *Lifestyle Evangelism: Crossing Traditional Boundaries to Reach the Unbelieving World.* Portland, Ore.: Multnomah Press, 1981.

Arias, Mortimer. *Evangelization and the Subversive Memory of Jesus: Announcing the Reign of God.* Philadelphia: Fortress, 1984.

Bakke, Ray, and Sam Roberts. *The Expanded Mission of City Center Churches.* Chicago: International Urban Associates, 1998.

Barna, George. *What Americans Believe: An Annual Survey of Values and Religious Views in the United States.* Ventura, Calif.: Regal Books, 1991.

Barrett, David B., and Todd M. Johnson. *Our Globe and How to Reach It.* Birmingham, Ala.: New Hope, 1990.

Billingsley, Andrew. *Mighty like a River: The Black Church and Social Reform.* New York: Oxford University Press, 1999.

Borthwick, Paul. *How to Be a World Class Christian.* Wheaton: Victor, 1991.

Bosch, David J. *Transforming Mission: Paradigm Shifts in Theology of Mission.* Maryknoll, N.Y.: Orbis, 1991.

Braaten, Carl E. *The Flaming Center: A Theology of the Christian Mission.* Philadelphia: Fortress, 1977.

Bradshaw, Bruce. *Bridging the Gap: Evangelism, Development and Shalom.* Monrovia, Calif.: MARC, 1993.

Bria, Ion, ed. *Go Forth in Peace: Orthodox Perspectives on Mission.* Geneva: WCC, 1986.

Bruland, Ester, and Stephen Mott. *A Passion for Jesus/A Passion for Justice.* Valley Forge, Pa.: Judson Press, 1993.

Buttry, Daniel. *Bringing Your Church Back to Life: Beyond Survival Mentality.* Valley Forge, Pa.: Judson, 1988.

Chester, Tim. *Awakening to a World of Need.* Leicester: Inter-Varsity Press, 1993.

Cheyne, John. *Incarnational Agents: A Guide to Developmental Ministries.* Birmingham, Ala.: New Hope, 1996.

Coleman, Robert E. *The Master Plan of Evangelism.* Tarrytown, N.Y.: Revell, 1972.

Costas, Orlando E. *Christ outside the Gate: Mission beyond Christendom.* Maryknoll, N.Y.: Orbis, 1982.

———. *Liberating News: A Theology of Contextual Evangelization.* Grand Rapids: Eerdmans, 1989.

Dearborn, Tim. *Beyond Duty: A Passion for Christ, a Heart for Mission.* Monrovia, Calif.: MARC, 1997.

Dennison, Jack. *City Reaching: On the Road to Community Transformation.* Pasadena, Calif.: William Carey Library, 1999.

Dyrness, William A. *Learning about Theology from the Third World.* Grand Rapids: Zondervan, 1990.

Elliston, Edgar J., and J. Timothy Kauffman. *Developing Leaders for Urban Ministries.* New York: Peter Lang, 1993.

Escobar, Samuel, and John Driver. *Christian Mission and Social Justice.* Scottdale, Pa.: Herald Press, 1978.

Evangelism and Social Responsibility: An Evangelistic Commitment. Lausanne Occasional Papers 21. Lausanne Committee for World Evangelism, 1982.

Fackre, Gabriel. *Word in Deed: Theological Themes in Evangelism.* Grand Rapids: Eerdmans, 1975.

Fuder, John, ed. *A Heart for the City: Effective Ministries to the Urban Community.* Chicago: Moody Press, 1999.

Garland, Diana S. Richmond, ed. *Church Social Work: Helping the Whole Person in the Context of the Church.* St. Davids, Pa.: North American Association of Christians in Social Work, 1992.

Glenn, Charles L. *The Ambiguous Embrace: Government and Faith-Based Schools and Social Agencies.* Princeton: Princeton University Press, 2000.

Green, Michael. *Evangelism in the Early Church.* London: Hodder & Stoughton, 1970.

———. *Evangelism through the Local Church.* London: Hodder & Stoughton, 1990.

Greenway, Roger S., ed. *Discipling the City: A Comprehensive Approach to Urban Mission.* Grand Rapids: Baker, 1992.

Grigg, Viv. *Companion to the Poor: Christ in the Urban Slums.* Rev. ed. Monrovia, Calif.: MARC, 1990.

Guder, Darrell L., ed. *Missional Church: A Vision for the Sending of the Church in North America.* Grand Rapids: Eerdmans, 1998.

Harper, Nile. *Urban Churches, Vital Signs: Beyond Charity toward Justice.* Grand Rapids: Eerdmans, 1999.

Hathaway, Brian. *Beyond Renewal: The Kingdom of God.* Milton Keynes, England: Word (UK), 1990.

Haugen, Gary A. *Good News about Justice.* Downers Grove, Ill.: InterVarsity Press, 1999.

Heney, David. *Motivating Your Parish to Change.* San Jose: Resource Publications, 1998.

Herrington, Jim, Mike Bonem, and James H. Furr. *Leading Congregational Change: A Practical Guide for the Transformational Journey.* San Francisco: Jossey-Bass, 2000.

Hunsberger, George R., and Craig Van Gelder. *The Church between Gospel and Culture: The Emerging Mission in North America.* Grand Rapids, Eerdmans, 1996.

Jacobsen, Dennis A. *Doing Justice: Congregations and Community Organizing.* Minneapolis: Fortress Press, 2001.

Kirk, J. Andrew. *What Is Mission? Theological Explorations.* Minneapolis: Fortress Press, 2000.

Linthicum, Robert. *City of God, City of Satan.* Grand Rapids: Zondervan, 1991.

McAlpine, Thomas H. *By Word, Work, and Wonder: Cases in Holistic Ministry.* Monrovia, Calif.: MARC, 1995.

McKinney, George. *Cross the Line: Reclaiming the Inner City for God.* Nashville: Thomas Nelson, 1997.

McLoughlin, William G. *Revivals, Awakenings, and Reform.* Chicago: University of Chicago Press, 1978.

Miles, Delos. *Evangelism and Social Involvement.* Nashville: Broadman, 1986.

Mitchell, Ron. *Organic Faith.* Chicago: Cornerstone Press, 1998.

Moberg, David O. *Wholistic Christianity.* Elgin, Ill.: Brethren Press, 1985.

Mott, Stephen Charles. *Biblical Ethics and Social Change.* New York: Oxford University Press, 1982.

Mouw, Richard J. *Political Evangelism.* Grand Rapids: Eerdmans, 1973.

Myers, Bryant. *Walking with the Poor: Principles and Practice of Transformational Development.* Maryknoll, N.Y.: Orbis, 1999.

Nees, Thomas. *Compassion Evangelism.* Kansas City, Mo.: Beacon Hill Press, 1996.

Newbigin, Lesslie. *The Gospel in a Pluralist Society.* Grand Rapids: Eerdmans, 1989.

———. *The Open Secret: Introduction to a Theology of Mission.* Rev. ed. Grand Rapids: Eerdmans, 1995.

Nicholls, Bruce J., ed. *In Word and Deed: Evangelism and Social Responsibility.* Grand Rapids: Eerdmans, 1985.

Nichols, Roy C. *Doing the Gospel: Local Congregations in Ministry.* Nashville: Abingdon Press, 1990.

Nouwen, Henri. *In the Name of Jesus: Reflections on Christian Leadership.* New York: Crossroad/Herder & Herder, 1993.

Padilla, René. *Mission between the Times: Essays on the Kingdom.* Grand Rapids: Eerdmans, 1985.

Pannell, William. *Evangelism from the Bottom Up: What Is the Meaning of the Salvation in a World Gone Urban?* Grand Rapids: Zondervan, 1992.

Perkins, John. *With Justice for All.* Ventura, Calif.: Regal Books, 1982.

Petersen, Douglas. *Not by Might nor by Power.* Oxford: Regnum Books, 1996.

Pierce, Bart. *Seeking Our Brothers: Restoring Compassionate Christianity to the Church.* Shippensburg, Pa.: Destiny Image Publishers, 2000.

Posterski, Don, and Gary Nelson. *Future Faith Churches: Reconnecting with the Power of the Gospel for the Twenty-First Century.* Peterborough, Ont.: Wood Lake Books, 1997.

Pullinger, Jackie. *Chasing the Dragon.* London: Hodder & Stoughton, 1980.

Roberts, J. Deotis. *A Black Political Theology.* Philadelphia: Westminster, 1974.

Samuel, Vinay, and Albrecht Hauser, eds. *Proclaiming Christ in Chrit's Way: Studies in Integral Evangelism.* Oxford: Regnum Books, 1989.

Samuel, Vinay, and Christopher Sugden. *The Church in Response to Human Need.* Grand Rapids: Regnum Books in cooperation with Eerdmans, 1987.

———, eds. *Evangelism and the Poor: A Third World Study Guide.* Oxford: Regnum Books, 1987.

———, eds. *Mission Transformation: A Theology of the Whole Gospel.* Carlisle, Calif.: Regnum Books in association with Paternoster Publishing, 1999.

Sanders, Cheryl J. *Ministry at the Margins: The Prophetic Mission of Women, Youth, and the Poor.* Downers Grove, Ill.: InterVarsity Press, 1997.

Scott, Waldron. *Bring Forth Justice.* Grand Rapids: Eerdmans, 1997.

Shenk, David W. *God's Call to Mission.* Scottdale, Pa.: Herald Press, 1994.

Shenk, David W., and Ervin R. Stutzman. *Creating Communities of the Kingdom: New Testament Models of Church Planting.* Scottdale, Pa.: Herald Press, 1988.

Sider, Ronald, J., ed. *The Chicago Declaration of Evangelical Social Concern.* Carol Stream, Ill.: Creation House, 1974 (available from ESA, 800-650-6600).

———, ed. *Cry Justice: The Bible on Hunger and Poverty.* New York: Paulist, 1980.

———. *Cup of Water, Bread of Life.* Grand Rapids: Zondervan, 1994.

———. *Rich Christians in an Age of Hunger.* 4th ed. Dallas: Word, 1997.

Skinner, Barbara Williams. *Becoming an Effective Twenty-First-Century Leader.* Washington, D.C.: Skinner Farm Leadership Institute, 2000.

Smith, Timothy. *Revivalism and Social Reform.* New York: Harper Torch Books, 1965.

Stamoolis, James J. *Eastern Orthodox Mission Theology Today.* Maryknoll, N.Y.: Orbis, 1986.

Stott, John R. W. *Christian Mission in the Modern World.* Downers Grove, Ill.: InterVarsity Press, 1975.

Sugden, Christopher. *Seeking the Asian Face of Jesus: The Practice and Theology of Christian Social Witness in Indonesia and India 1974–1996.* Oxford: Regnum Books, 1997.

Tillepaugh, Frank R. *Unleashing the Church: Getting People out of the Fortress and into the Ministry.* Ventura, Calif.: Regal Books, 1982.

Van Engen, Charles. *God's Missionary People: Rethinking the Purpose of the Local Church.* Grand Rapids: Baker, 1991.

Van Engen, Charles, and Jude Tiersma, eds. *God So Loves the City.* Monrovia, Calif.: MARC, 1994.

Van Gelder, Craig, ed. *Confident Witness—Changing World: Rediscovering the Gospel in North America.* Grand Rapids: Eerdmans, 1999.

Wallis, Jim. *The Call to Conversion: Recovering the Gospel for These Times.* New York: Harper, 1981.

Walls, Andrew. *The Missionary Movement in Christian History.* Edinburgh: T & T Clark, 1996.

WCC. *Mission and Evangelism: An Ecumenical Affirmation.* Geneva: WCC, 1982.

Wilkes, C. Gene. *Jesus on Leadership.* Wheaton: Tyndale, 1998.

Wimber, John. *Power Evangelism.* San Francisco: Harper, 1986.

Tools and Periodicals

Catalyst is the colorful newsletter for the Healing America Movement, published in partnership with the National Common Ground Coalition and World Relief (P.O. Box 43405, Atlanta, GA 30336).

CityVoices is a bimonthly newsletter for city church pastors and leaders. It contains inspiring stories of holistic ministry from around the globe (www.cityvoices.com).

ForMinistry is the web portal of the American Bible Society that provides resources from 150 leading ministry organizations. The site helps churches design their own web page and profile their church and its ministries for a national directory (www.ForMinistry.com).

The *Handbook for Urban Church Ministries*, ed. Phil Tom and Sally Johnson (Chicago: Metro Mission, 1996), is a practical workbook for planning and launching social ministry programs. It includes an extensive list of references and resources (773-478-4676).

Holistic Hardware offers a motivational life skills video series with supporting curriculum. The organization also offers consulting services to faith-based organizations seeking to establish effective public-private partnerships (800-952-6229; holiware@aol.com).

Holistic Ministry Starter Kits, available from Network 9:35, come in two levels: an introductory kit for churches just getting started, and a basic kit that helps deepen your church's understanding and shows how to take ministry to the next stage of development (800-650-6600).

Lifekeys, by Jane A. G. Kise, David Stark, and Sandra Krebs Hirsh, is a comprehensive guide (paperback, workbook, and seminars) for discovering spiritual gifts, talents, values, and personality for ministry (888-937-7591; www.life keys.com).

MARC Publications, the research and publishing division of World Vision, features some of the finest books on holistic mission from a global as well as North American perspective, including a series called Cases in Holistic Ministry from Asia, Africa, Latin America, and urban centers around the globe (www.marcpublications.org).

Network Ministries International, led by Bruce Bugbee, Don Cousins, and Bill Hybels (Willow Creek Community Church staff), offers a complete package to help churches place people in service according to their gifts, passion, and personal style (800-588-8833; www.network ministries.com).

New Focus provides training and materials to revitalize church outreach, guiding churches step-by-step in forming "Compassion Circles" that walk alongside persons seeking self-sufficiency and personal transformation (www.newfocus .org).

Prism, ESA's bimonthly magazine, offers stories about holistic ministry, biblical reflections on social and cultural issues, and analysis of public policy from a progressive evangelical perspective. ESA also offers the *Prism E-Pistle,* a free biweekly newsletter via email (800-650-6600; www.esa-online.org).

Sojourners, a bimonthly ecumenical magazine edited by Jim Wallis, examines issues of social justice from a Christian perspective, calling the church to informed action (www.sojourners.com).

Leonard Sweet, speaker and author, offers great resources (some for free, including book manuscripts) on his web site (www.leonardsweet.com).

Transformation: An International Evangelical Dialogue on Mission and Ethics, published by the Oxford Centre for Mission Studies, is the journal record of the Transformation movement in missiology (www.regnumbooks.com).

Urban Perspectives is a newsletter from veteran holistic practitioner Bob Lupton, president of the community development organization FCS (Family Consultation Service) Urban Ministries in Atlanta (www.ccda.org/fcs/index.html).

"What Is Holistic Ministry?" is a twelve-minute video produced by ESA that features interviews with leaders in holistic congregations and explores the definition of holistic ministry (800-650-6600).

World Vision's 30 Hour Famine is a complete kit for teaching youth about worldwide hunger needs and about putting their faith in action. World Vision offers many other resources for holistic ministry as well (1-800-7-FAMINE; www.worldvision.org).

Organizations and Networks

The Center for Public Justice advocates for justice by conducting public policy research and civic education from a Christian perspective. It also provides excellent materials regarding Charitable Choice (www.cpjustice.org).

Christian Community Development Association (CCDA) links nearly four hundred holistic member organizations from around the United States and offers an annual conference and other resources (www.ccda.org).

Evangelicals for Social Action (ESA) challenges and equips the church to be agents of God's redemption and transformation in the world, through publications, resources, and training in holistic ministry, and through networking (800-650-6600; www.esa-online.org).

The Gospel in Our Culture Network helps Christians and congregations move from a Christendom to a missional model in order to contextualize the gospel in neo-pagan North American society. It offers resources and conferences (www.cogn.org).

Jesus Day/March for Jesus is a day of celebration on the Saturday prior to Pentecost. It takes place in the streets of thousands of communities around the globe and connects Christians with a variety of service projects (www.jesusday.org).

The John M. Perkins Foundation for Reconciliation and Development provides cross-cultural and holistic learning as well as volunteer and internship opportunities (www.jmpf.org).

Leadership Network (LN) discerns ministry trends and connects churches with cutting-edge resources, including a free newsletter, *NEXT* (www.leadnet.org).

The Lighthouse Movement organizes Christians to pray for, care for, and share with their neighbors. Start a Lighthouse in your home, become a lighthouse church, and connect with other lighthouses in your city (www.lighthousemovement.org).

Mission America Coalition, joining eighty-four denominations and over four hundred parachurch ministries, promotes national revival and offers resources to mobilize churches to reach every person in America with prayer, caring, and witness (www.missionamerica.org).

Network 9:35 is a collaboration of Christian ministries and congregations engaged (or wanting to learn to engage) in holistic ministry. It offers resources on church-to-church mentoring, vision development, and best practices (www.network935.org).

Redeeming the Cities is a national collaboration providing funding and peer learning experiences to churches and Christian community development organizations. Covenanted members include Call to Renewal, CCDA, Council of Leadership Foundations, ESA, Habitat for Humanity, the John M. Perkins Foundation for Reconciliation and Development, Project Equip, and World Vision (651-642-4053).

We Care America is a national network that shares knowledge and resources and promotes cooperative projects in order to strengthen the compassionate ministries of churches and nonprofit organizations (404-688-CARE).

Training Programs

The Campolo School for Social Change at Eastern College is an urban-based, interdisciplinary, and cross-cultural undergraduate and graduate program that emphasizes a holistic approach to community transformation (www.eastern.edu).

The Center for Urban Studies and Ethnic Leadership at Vanguard University, directed by Jesse Miranda, is connected with the evangelical Hispanic network AMEN (Alianza de Ministerios Evangelicos Nacionales) (714-556-3610, ext. 254).

The Chalmers Center for Economic Development provides training in economic development and spiritual transformation in the context of holistic, church-based ministry (www.chalmers.org).

Partners in Urban Transformation, headed by experienced practitioner and author Robert Linthicum, offers consulting, a video curriculum, conferences, and other learning experiences (www. partnersinurbantransformation.org).

The Seminary Consortium for Urban Pastoral Education (SCUPE) specializes in teaching church leaders about urban issues, systems, and ministry (www.scupe.com).

The Urban Ministry Institute's nine-month training program emphasizes field internships with Mission Waco and other holistic ministries (urbaninst@missionwaco.org).

World Impact's Urban Institute offers on-site courses, distance learning for urban church leaders, and a kit for creating an urban leadership training center in your church (www.tumi.org).

Notes

Introduction

1. By holistic ministry, we mean first of all a wholehearted embrace and integration of both evangelism and social ministry so that people experience spiritual renewal, socioeconomic uplift, and transformation of their social context. Part 1 of the book fleshes out the definition of holistic ministry.

2. Aaron Bicknese, "The Teen Challenge Drug Treatment Program in Comparative Perspective" (Ph.D. diss., Northwestern University, June 1999).

3. Ronald J. Sider, *Just Generosity: A New Vision for Overcoming Poverty in America* (Grand Rapids: Baker, 1999), 197–98.

4. Byron R. Johnson, David B. Larson, and T. C. Pitts, "Religious Programs, Institutional Adjustment, and Recidivism among Former Inmates in Prison Fellowship Programs," *Justice Quarterly* 14 (1997): 145–66.

5. Sider, *Just Generosity,* 186–88.

6. Amy L. Sherman, "One 'Village' at a Time," *World* (19 November 1994): 10–13.

7. For a compendium of the research, see "Why Religion Matters: The Impact of Religious Practice on Social Stability," *The Heritage Foundation Backgrounder,* no. 1064 (Washington, D.C., 1996).

8. Richard. B. Freeman, "Who Escapes? The Relation of Churchgoing and Other Background Factors to the Socioeconomic Performance of Black Male Youth from Inner-City Tracts," in *The Black Youth Employment Crisis,* ed. R. B. Freeman and H. J. Holzer (Chicago: University of Chicago Press, 1986); the original study was affirmed and updated in Byron R. Johnson, David B. Larson, Spencer De Li, and Sung Joon Jang, "Escaping from the Crime of Inner Cities: Church Attendance and Religious Salience among Disadvantaged Youth," *Justice Quarterly* 17 (June 2000): 377–91.

9. "Faith-Based Funding Backed, but Church-State Doubts Abound," a survey for The Pew Forum by The Pew Research Center for the People & the Press, 10 April 2001.

10. See Ronald J. Sider and Heidi Rolland Unruh, "No Aid to Religion? Charitable Choice and the First Amendment," in *What's God Got to Do with the American Experiment?* ed. E. J. Dionne Jr. and John J. DiIulio Jr. (Washington, D.C.: Brookings Institution Press, 2000); Ronald J. Sider, "Revisiting Mt. Carmel through Charitable Choice," *Christianity Today* (June 2001): 84–89; Ronald J. Sider and Heidi Rolland Unruh, "Evangelism and Charitable Choice," *Journal of Church and State* 43, no. 2 (spring 2001): 267–95; and Heidi Unruh and Jill Witmer Sinha, "Churches and Public Funds: Risks or Rewards?" *Prism* (March/April 2001): 11–13.

11. Christian Smith, *American Evangelicalism* (Chicago: University of Chicago Press, 1998), 43.

12. The opinions expressed in this book are those of the authors and do not necessarily reflect the views of the Lilly Endowment or the John Templeton Foundation.

13. For more information about the Congregations, Communities, and Leadership Development Project, see the description on the Congregational Life and Ministry/Congregational Studies page of the Resourcing American Christianity web site (www.resourcingchristianity.org/ database.asp), or contact Heidi Unruh at ccldp@erols.com.

Chapter 1

1. Amy Sherman, "The Church as Community Asset," keynote address, Christian Reformed World Relief Committee National Conference, March 2000.

2. David S. Apple, "Wholistic Ministries at Tenth Presbyterian Church" (master's thesis, Eastern Baptist Theological Seminary, 1994), 60.

3. Glenn C. Loury, *One by One from the Inside Out: Essays and Reviews on Race and Responsibility in America* (New York: Free Press, 1995).

4. Apple, "Wholistic Ministries," 43.

5. Vinay Samuel, "Evangelicals and Racism: The Lausanne II Press Conference," *Transformation* (January 1990): 29.

6. George McKinney, *Cross the Line: Reclaiming the Inner City for God* (Nashville: Thomas Nelson, 1997), 68.

7. Spencer Perkins and Chris Rice, "Reconciliation: Loving God and Loving People," in *Restoring At-Risk Communities: Doing It Together and Doing It Right*, ed. John Perkins (Grand Rapids: Baker, 1995).

8. Rev. William Barger II, "Doing CED from a Christian Perspective without Giving Up a Sense of Ministry," in *Faith in the Community*, newsletter of the National Congress for Community Economic Development, 2000.

9. Darrell L. Guder, ed., *Missional Church: A Vision for the Sending of the Church in North America* (Grand Rapids: Eerdmans, 1998), 93.

10. George Barna, *Casting the Net: The Unchurched Population in the Mid-Nineties* (Glendale, Calif.: Barna Report, 1995), 34–35.

Chapter 2

1. David S. Apple, "Wholistic Ministries at Tenth Presbyterian Church" (master's thesis, Eastern Baptist Theological Seminary, 1994), 16.

2. See Ronald J. Sider, *Good News and Good Works: A Theology for the Whole Gospel* (Grand Rapids: Baker, 1999), 61–70.

3. See chapter 6 ("Social Sin") in Ronald J. Sider, *Rich Christians in an Age of Hunger* (Dallas: Word, 1997).

4. See chapters 5 and 6 in Sider's *Good News and Good Works*.

5. Apple, "Wholistic Ministries," 18.

6. See the marvelous book by David Lawrence, *Heaven . . . It's Not the End of the World* (London: Scripture Union, 1995).

7. Mark R. Gornik and Noel Castellanos, "How to Start a Christian Community Development Ministry," in *Restoring At-Risk Communities: Doing It Together and Doing It Right*, ed. John Perkins (Grand Rapids: Baker, 1995), 212–13.

8. For a more thorough discussion of the relationship between evangelism and social action, see Sider, *Good News and Good Works*, chap. 10.

9. John Perkins, *A Quiet Revolution* (Waco: Word, 1986), 221.

10. This definition is indebted to two sources: the motto of the Second World Missionary Conference (1928): "The whole gospel for the whole man in the whole world"; and the mission statement of Eastern Baptist Theological Seminary, where Ron Sider teaches: "The whole gospel for the whole world through whole persons."

Chapter 3

1. John Perkins, *Beyond Charity: The Call to Christian Community Development* (Grand Rapids: Baker, 1993), 80.

2. Glen Kehrein, "The Church and Wholistic Ministry," in *Caring for the Least of These: Serving Christ among the Poor*, ed. David Caes (Scottdale, Pa.: Herald Press, 1992), 94; quoted in Ronald Sider, *Cup of Water, Bread of Life* (Grand Rapids: Zondervan, 1994), chap.4 on Kehrein and Washington's ministry.

3. Christian Smith, *American Evangelicalism: Embattled and Thriving* (Chicago: University of Chicago Press, 1998), 182.

4. See Ronald J. Sider, *Good News and Good Works: A Theology for the Whole Gospel* (Grand Rapids: Baker, 1999), chap. 9.

5. Donna Schaper, "Bricks without Straw: Ministry in the City," in *Envisioning the New City: A Reader on Urban Ministry,* ed. Eleanor Scott Meyers (Louisville: Westminster/John Knox Press, 1992), 36.

6. Jimmy R. Allen, "Urban Evangelism," in *Toward a Creative Urban Strategy,* ed. G. Torney (Waco: Word, 1970).

7. Robert Wuthnow, "Evangelicals, Liberals and the Perils of Individualism," *Perspectives: A Journal of Reformed Thought* 6, no. 5 (May 1991): 13.

8. Timothy J. Keller, *Ministries of Mercy: The Call of the Jericho Road,* 2d ed. (Phillipsburg, N.J.: P & R Publishing, 1997), 112.

9. David S. Apple, "Wholistic Ministries at Tenth Presbyterian Church" (master's thesis, Eastern Baptist Theological Seminary, 1994), 19.

10. Michael N. Allen, "New Wineskin—Same Vintage Wine," in *A Heart for the City,* ed. John Fuder (Chicago: Moody Press, 1999), 224.

11. Jack Dennison, *City Reaching: On the Road to Community Transformation* (Pasadena, Calif.: William Carey Library, 1999), 169.

12. For a more in-depth examination of the biblical reasons for doing evangelism, see chapter 7 in Sider, *Good News and Good Works.*

13. Jayakumar Christian, "Toward Redefining Urban Poverty," in *God So Loves the City,* ed. Charles Van Engen and Jude Tiersma (Monrovia, Calif.: MARC, 1994), 209.

14. John Cheyne, *Incarnational Agents: A Guide to Developmental Ministries* (Birmingham, Ala.: New Hope, 1996), 22.

15. Dr. Richard Armstrong, *Faithful Witnesses* (Louisville: Curriculum Publishing/Presbyterian Church [USA], 1997).

16. Robert Linthicum, "Authentic Strategies for Urban Ministry," in *Discipling the City: A Comprehensive Approach to Urban Mission,* ed. Roger S. Greenway (Grand Rapids: Baker, 1992), 111–21.

17. Amy L. Sherman, *Restorers of Hope* (Wheaton: Crossway Books, 1997), 124.

18. Thomas Nees, *Compassion Evangelism* (Kansas City, Mo.: Beacon Hill Press, 1996), 30–31.

Chapter 4

1. Jack Dennison, *City Reaching: On the Road to Community Transformation* (Pasadena, Calif.: William Carey Library, 1999), 168.

2. "A Pooling of Resources," *Philadelphia Inquirer,* 25 April 1999, p. G7.

3. See Phil Olson, "The Eyes Have It: How to Find Out Your Church's Holistic Ministry," *NETResults,* January 2000, 8–9; also available on the Network 9:35 web site: www.network935.org.

4. Nile Harper, *Urban Churches, Vital Signs: Beyond Charity toward Justice* (Grand Rapids: Eerdmans, 1999), 5.

5. See the story in Ronald Sider, *Cup of Water, Bread of Life* (Grand Rapids: Zondervan, 1994), chap. 8.

6. Carl S. Dudley, ed., *Next Steps in Community Ministry* (Bethesda, Md.: The Alban Institute, 1996), 59.

7. For more on a Christian approach to political action and public policy, see Ronald J. Sider, *Just Generosity: A New Vision for Overcoming Poverty in America* (Grand Rapids: Baker, 1999); Ronald J. Sider, *Politics and the Bible: A Study Guide for Christians* (Wynnewood, Pa.: Evangelicals for Social Action, 1996); and David P. Gushee, ed., *Christians and Politics beyond the Culture Wars* (Grand Rapids: Baker, 2000).

8. Robert Linthicum, *City of God, City of Satan* (Grand Rapids: Zondervan, 1991), 47.

9. Ray Bakke, *A Theology as Big as the City* (Downers Grove, Ill.: InterVarsity Press, 1997), 160.

10. See Stephen Charles Mott, *Biblical Ethics and Social Change* (New York: Oxford University Press, 1982), chap. 1.

11. David S. Apple, "Wholistic Ministries at Tenth Presbyterian Church" (master's thesis, Eastern Baptist Theological Seminary, 1994), 19.

12. Bakke, *A Theology as Big as the City,* 160.

13. Ronald J. Sider addresses this argument further in *Good News and Good Works: A Theology for the Whole Gospel* (Grand Rapids: Baker, 1999), 152–54.

14. J. Andrew Kirk, *What Is Mission? Theological Explorations* (Minneapolis: Fortress Press, 2000), 113.

15. Mott, *Biblical Ethics and Social Change*, 124.

16. Jim Wallis, "The Second Reformation Has Begun," in *Envisioning the New City: A Reader on Urban Ministry*, ed. Eleanor Scott Meyers (Louisville: Westminster/John Knox Press, 1992), 63.

17. See Timothy J. Keller, *Ministries of Mercy: The Call of the Jericho Road*, 2d ed. (Phillipsburg, N.J.: P & R Publishing, 1997), 188–89.

18. Dennis A. Jacobsen, *Doing Justice: Congregations and Community Organizing* (Minneapolis: Fortress Press, 2001), 20.

19. Janet F. Spressort, "Social Action and the Church," in *Church Social Work: Helping the Whole Person in the Context of the Church*, ed. Diana S. Richmond Garland (St. Davids, Pa.: North American Association of Christians in Social Work, 1992), 110.

20. Robert C. Linthicum, "Authentic Strategies for Urban Ministry," in *Discipling the City: A Comprehensive Approach to Urban Mission*, ed. Roger S. Greenway (Grand Rapids: Baker, 1992), 118. See also Jacobsen, *Doing Justice*.

21. Keller, *Ministries of Mercy*, 189.

22. For a detailed discussion of public policy issues that are critical for churches to address, see Sider, *Just Generosity*.

23. Cal Thomas and Ed Dobson, *Blinded by Might: Can the Religious Right Save America?* (Grand Rapids: Zondervan, 1999). See Ronald J. Sider's critique, "Blinded by Fright," *Prism* (July–October 1999): 48.

24. Spressort, "Social Action and the Church," 105.

Chapter 5

1. Timothy J. Keller, *Ministries of Mercy: The Call of the Jericho Road*, 2d ed. (Phillipsburg, N.J.: P & R Publishing, 1997), 112.

2. "Whose Job Is Evangelism?" Commentary on John 16:8 in *The Word in Life Study Bible* (Nashville: Thomas Nelson, 1993), 1905.

3. For a scholarly description and analysis of this view, see Christian Smith, *American Evangelicalism: Embattled and Thriving* (Chicago: University of Chicago Press, 1998), chap. 7. Smith's term for this approach is the "personal influence strategy."

4. John Cheyne, *Incarnational Agents: A Guide to Developmental Ministries* (Birmingham, Ala.: New Hope, 1996), 21.

5. Kathyrn Mowry, "Do Good Fences Make Good Neighbors? Toward a Theology of Welcome for the Urban Church," in *God So Loves the City*, ed. Charles Van Engen and Jude Tiersma (Monrovia, Calif.: MARC, 1994), 107.

6. Christine Accornero, "A Common Ministry, a Communal Vocation," in *God So Loves the City*, 115.

7. Willie Richardson, "Empowering Lay Leadership in an African American Urban Church: A Case Study," in *Discipling the City: A Comprehensive Approach to Urban Mission*, ed. Roger S. Greenway (Grand Rapids: Baker, 1992), 154.

8. Ibid., 150.

Chapter 6

1. Don Postema, *Space for God* (Grand Rapids: CRC Publications, 1983), 159.

2. Amy L. Sherman, *Restorers of Hope* (Wheaton: Crossway Books, 1997), 170.

3. Ronald J. Sider, *Living like Jesus: Eleven Essentials for Growing a Genuine Faith* (Grand Rapids: Baker, 1996), 173.

4. Ibid., 60–61.

5. Mary Thiessen, "When We Are Dying in the City: Three Sources of Life," in *God So Loves the City*, ed. Charles Van Engen and Jude Tiersma (Monrovia, Calif.: MARC, 1994), 87.

6. Jack Dennison, *City Reaching: On the Road to Community Transformation* (Pasadena, Calif.: William Carey Library, 1999), 236.

7. Ray Bakke, *A Theology as Big as the City* (Downers Grove, Ill.: InterVarsity Press, 1997), 136.

8. Christine Accornero, "A Common Ministry, a Communal Vocation," in *God So Loves the City*, 229.

9. Sider, *Living like Jesus*, 171.

10. Bakke, *A Theology as Big as the City*, 36.

11. Jude Tiersma, "What Does It Mean to Be Incarnational When We Are Not the Messiah?" in *God So Loves the City*, 14.

12. Ibid., 18.

13. Ibid., 20.

14. Postema, *Space for God*, 160.

15. Tiersma, "What Does It Mean to Be Incarnational?" 15.

16. Ibid., 17.

17. Richard Foster, *Celebration of Discipline*, rev. ed. (San Francisco: HarperSanFrancisco, 1988), 130.

18. Quoted in Postema, *Space for God*, 159.

19. Darrell L. Guder, ed., *Missional Church: A Vision for the Sending of the Church in North America* (Grand Rapids: Eerdmans, 1998), 97.

20. Thomas Merton, quoted in Postema, *Space for God*, 171.

21. Henri Nouwen, *The Way of the Heart*, quoted in Postema, *Space for God*, 170.

22. Dallas: Word, 1997.

23. Foster, *Celebration of Discipline*, 32.

24. Thiessen, "When We Are Dying in the City," 87.

25. Sider, *Living like Jesus*, 62–63.

Chapter 7

1. Amy L. Sherman, *Restorers of Hope* (Wheaton: Crossway Books, 1997), 242.

2. Harold R. Fray Jr., *Conflict and Change in the Church* (Boston: Pilgrim Press, 1969), 21–22.

3. Sherman, *Restorers of Hope*, 23–29.

4. See Ronald J. Sider, *Rich Christians in an Age of Hunger*, 4th ed. (Dallas: Word, 1997) for a detailed biblical and social analysis of Christians' global responsibilities.

5. From email correspondence with Phil Olson.

6. David Bosch, *Transforming Mission: Paradigm Shifts in Theology of Mission* (Maryknoll, N.Y.: Orbis, 1992), 390.

7. John Driver, *Images of the Church in Mission* (Scottdale, Pa.: Herald Press, 1997), 12.

8. For more on a theology of mission, see Ray Bakke, *A Theology as Big as the City* (Downers Grove, Ill.: InterVarsity Press, 1997); Bosch, *Transforming Mission;* Darrell L. Guder, ed., *Missional Church: A Vision for the Sending of the Church in North America* (Grand Rapids: Eerdmans, 1998); Darrell L. Guder, *The Continuing Conversion of the Church* (Grand Rapids: Eerdmans, 2000); George R. Hunsberger and Craig Van Gelder, *The Church between Gospel and Culture: The Emerging Mission in North America* (Grand Rapids: Eerdmans, 1996); Lesslie Newbigin, *The Open Secret: Introduction to a Theology of Mission*, rev. ed. (Grand Rapids: Eerdmans, 1995); Ronald J. Sider, *Good News and Good Works: A Theology for the Whole Gospel* (Grand Rapids: Baker, 1999); Charles Van Engen, *God's Missionary People: Rethinking the Purpose of the Local Church* (Grand Rapids: Baker, 1991); and Craig Van Gelder, ed., *Confident Witness—Changing World: Rediscovering the Gospel in North America* (Grand Rapids: Eerdmans, 1999).

9. Driver, *Images of the Church in Mission*, 12.

10. Sherman, *Restorers of Hope*, 121.

11. See chapter 12 for more on defining and studying your church's community of ministry.

12. Jack Dennison, *City Reaching: On the Road to Community Transformation* (Pasadena, Calif.: William Carey Library, 1999), 171. The quote refers to generational groups but would apply to most other demographic subgroups as well.

13. Quoted in Mark Jobe, "Rethinking the Church to Reach the City," in *A Heart for the City*, ed. John Fuder (Chicago: Moody Press, 1999), 207.

14. Ray Bakke and Sam Roberts, *The Expanded Mission of City Center Churches* (Chicago: International Urban Associates, 1998), 54.

15. Kathryn Mowry, "Do Good Fences Make Good Neighbors? Toward a Theology of Welcome for the Urban Church," in *God So Loves the City*, ed. Charles Van Engen and Jude Tiersma (Monrovia, Calif.: MARC, 1994), 108.

16. Ibid., 117.

17. Bakke and Roberts, *The Expanded Mission of City Center Churches*, 53.

18. Carl S. Dudley, *Basic Steps toward Community Ministry* (Washington, D.C.: Alban Institute, 1991), 33.

19. Bakke and Roberts, *The Expanded Mission of City Center Churches,* 53.

20. John M. Perkins, "What Is Christian Community Development?" in *Restoring At-Risk Communities: Doing It Together and Doing It Right,* ed. John Perkins (Grand Rapids: Baker, 1995), 22.

21. Bob and Peggy Lupton and Gloria Yancy, "Relocation: Living in the Community," in *Restoring At-Risk Communities,* 83.

Chapter 8

1. Darrell L. Guder, ed., *Missional Church: A Vision for the Sending of the Church in North America* (Grand Rapids: Eerdmans, 1998), 96.

2. For a discussion of what makes the church a unique context for social ministry, see Diana S. Richmond Garland, "Church Social Work: An Introduction," in *Church Social Work: Helping the Whole Person in the Context of the Church,* ed. Diana S. Richmond (St. Davids, Pa.: North American Association of Christians in Social Work, 1992), 7–8.

3. Nile Harper, *Urban Churches, Vital Signs: Beyond Charity toward Justice* (Grand Rapids: Eerdmans, 1999), 3.

4. Amy L. Sherman, *Restorers of Hope* (Wheaton: Crossway Books, 1997), 242.

5. Guder, *Missional Church,* 181–82.

6. Ibid., 181.

7. David S. Apple, "Wholistic Ministries at Tenth Presbyterian Church" (master's thesis, Eastern Baptist Theological Seminary, 1994), 52.

8. Edgar J. Elliston and J. Timothy Kauffman, *Developing Leaders for Urban Ministries* (New York: Peter Lang, 1993), 90.

9. Sherman, *Restorers of Hope,* 230.

10. Ibid., 229–30.

11. Ibid.

12. Ibid., 29.

13. See Jeff Arnold, *Small Group Outreach: Turning Groups Inside Out* (Downers Grove, Ill.: InterVarsity Press, 1998); and Frank R. Tillepaugh, *Unleashing the Church: Getting People out of the Fortress and into the Ministry* (Ventura, Calif.: Regal Books, 1982). Also see descriptions of two churches with dynamic small group ministries in chapter 10 of Ronald J. Sider, *Rich Christians in an Age of Hunger* (Dallas: Word, 1997).

14. Christine Accornero, "A Common Ministry, a Communal Vocation," in *God So Loves the City,* ed. Charles Van Engen and Jude Tiersma (Monrovia, Calif.: MARC, 1994), 229.

15. Tony Campolo, *The Kingdom of God Is a Party: God's Radical Plan for His Family* (Dallas: Word, 1990).

16. Sider, *Rich Christians,* 218.

17. David Mann, "Pastor, Priest, Organizer: Leadership in Community Ministries," in *Envisioning the New City: A Reader on Urban Ministry,* ed. Eleanor Scott Meyers (Louisville: Westminster/John Knox Press, 1992), 69.

18. Apple, "Wholistic Ministries," 19.

19. Ronald J. Sider, *Living like Jesus: Eleven Essentials for Growing a Genuine Faith* (Grand Rapids: Baker, 1999), 124.

Chapter 9

1. C. Gene Wilkes, *Jesus on Leadership* (Wheaton: Tyndale, 1998), 19.

2. Edgar J. Elliston and J. Timothy Kauffman, *Developing Leaders for Urban Ministries* (New York: Peter Lang, 1993), 78.

3. Calvin Miller, *The Empowered Leader: 10 Keys to Servant Leadership* (Nashville: Broadman and Holman Publishers, 1995), 65.

4. Jim Herrington, Mike Bonem, and James H. Furr, *Leading Congregational Change: A Practical Guide for the Transformational Journey* (San Francisco: Jossey-Bass, 2000), 159.

5. David Heney, *Motivating Your Parish to Change* (San Jose: Resource Publications, 1998), 65.

6. Nile Harper, *Urban Churches, Vital Signs: Beyond Charity toward Justice* (Grand Rapids: Eerdmans, 1999), 229.

7. Heney, *Motivating Your Parish to Change,* 20.

8. Robert Tannehill, *The Narrative Unity of Luke-Acts: A Literary Interpretation,* vol. 1, *The Gospel according to Luke* (Philadelphia: Fortress Press, 1991), 3.

9. David J. Frenchak, "Visionary Leadership in Launching Social Ministries," in *Next Steps in Community Ministry,* ed. Carl S. Dudley (Bethesda, Md.: Alban Institute, 1996), 22.

10. Heney, *Motivating Your Parish to Change,* 80.

11. Miller, *The Empowered Leader*, 113.

12. Heney, *Motivating Your Parish to Change*, 45.

13. Means, *Leadership in Christian Ministry*, 56.

14. Carl S. Dudley, "Clergy Contributions to Mobilizing Social Ministries," in *Next Steps in Community Ministry*, 12.

15. Means, *Leadership in Christian Ministry*, 61.

16. Dudley, "Clergy Contributions to Mobilizing Social Ministries," 16.

17. Means, *Leadership in Christian Ministry*, 67.

18. Mark R. Gornik and Noel Castellanos, "How to Start a Christian Community Development Ministry," in *Restoring At-Risk Communities: Doing It Together and Doing It Right*, ed. John Perkins (Grand Rapids: Baker, 1995), 228.

19. Dudley, "Clergy Contributions to Mobilizing Social Ministries," 12.

20. Barbara Williams Skinner, *Becoming an Effective Twenty-First-Century Leader* (Washington, D.C.: Skinner Farm Leadership Institute, 2000), 6.

21. Michael N. Allen, "New Wineskin—Same Vintage Wine," in *A Heart for the City*, ed. John Fuder (Chicago: Moody Press, 1999), 219.

22. Elliston and Kauffman, *Developing Leaders for Urban Ministries*, 87.

23. Ibid., 92.

24. The story is told in more detail in Ronald J. Sider, *Living like Jesus: Eleven Essentials for Growing a Genuine Faith* (Grand Rapids: Baker, 1996), 95–96.

Chapter 10

1. Carl S. Dudley, *Basic Steps toward Community Ministry* (Washington, D.C.: Alban Institute, 1991), 77.

2. Darrell L. Guder, ed., *Missional Church: A Vision for the Sending of the Church in North America* (Grand Rapids: Eerdmans, 1998), 72.

3. Mary Thiessen, "When We Are Dying in the City: Three Sources of Life," in *God So Loves the City*, ed. Charles Van Engen and Jude Tiersma (Monrovia, Calif.: MARC, 1994), 100.

4. Thomas Nees, *Compassion Evangelism* (Kansas City, Mo.: Beacon Hill Press, 1996), 53.

5. Amy L. Sherman, *Restorers of Hope* (Wheaton: Crossway Books, 1997), 156.

6. David S. Apple, "Wholistic Ministries at Tenth Presbyterian Church" (master's thesis, Eastern Baptist Theological Seminary, 1994), 49.

7. Barbara Williams Skinner, *Becoming an Effective Twenty-First-Century Leader* (Washington, D.C.: Skinner Farm Leadership Institute, 2000), 2.

8. Dudley, *Basic Steps toward Community Ministry*, 78.

9. Ram A. Cnaan, "Keeping Faith in the City: How 401 Urban Religious Congregations Serve Their Neediest Neighbors," CRRUCS Report 2000–2001 (Philadelphia: University of Pennsylvania Center for Research on Religion and Urban Civil Society, 2000), 18.

10. Reginald McDonough, *Working with Volunteer Leaders in the Church* (Nashville: Broadman Press, 1976), 139.

11. Glen Kehrein, "The Local Church and Christian Community Development," in *Restoring At-Risk Communities: Doing It Together and Doing It Right*, ed. John Perkins (Grand Rapids: Baker, 1995), 172.

12. John R. Buzza, "Partnerships for Community Ministry-Case Study," in *Next Steps in Community Ministry*, ed. Carl S. Dudley (Bethesda, Md.: Alban Institute, 1996), 109.

13. Charles L. Glenn, *The Ambiguous Embrace: Government and Faith-Based Schools and Social Agencies* (Princeton: Princeton University Press, 2000), 211.

14. Ibid., 191.

15. Calvin Miller, *The Empowered Leader: 10 Keys to Servant Leadership* (Nashville: Broadman and Holman Publishers, 1995), 98.

Chapter 11

1. Nancy T. Ammerman, "Doing Good in American Communities: Congregations and Service Organizations Working Together," an online research report from the Organizing Religious Work Project of the Hartford Institute for Religion Research, Hartford, Connecticut, 2001, http://hirr.hartsem.edu/about/about_orw.html.

2. Robert C. Linthicum, "Authentic Strategies for Urban Ministry," in *Discipling the City: A Comprehensive Approach to Urban Mission,* ed. Roger S. Greenway (Grand Rapids: Baker, 1992), 122.

3. Jude Tiersma, "What Does It Mean to Be Incarnational When We Are Not the Messiah?" in *God So Loves the City,* ed. Charles Van Engen and Jude Tiersma (Monrovia, Calif.: MARC, 1994), 15.

4. Jack Dennison, *City Reaching: On the Road to Community Transformation* (Pasadena, Calif.: William Carey Library, 1999).

5. See chapter 11 of Amy L. Sherman, *Restorers of Hope* (Wheaton: Crossway Books, 1997), for an in-depth look at the qualities necessary for fruitful collaboration specifically between churches and government.

6. See W. Bradford Wilcox, *Salvation, Service, and Therapy in the Bowery: Lessons for Christian Nonprofits,* Crossroads Monograph Series on Faith and Public Policy, no. 20 (Wynnewood, Pa.: Crossroads, 1999).

7. Harold Dean Trulear, "The Black Middle Class Church and the Quest for Community," *The Drew Gateway* 61, no. 1 (1991): 56.

8. Sherman, *Restorers of Hope,* 226.

9. Ray Bakke, *The Urban Christian: Effective Ministry in Today's Urban World* (Downers Grove, Ill.: InterVarsity Press, 1987), 93–94.

10. Phil Reed, "Toward a Theology of Christian Community Development," in *Restoring At-Risk Communities: Doing It Together and Doing It Right,* ed. John Perkins (Grand Rapids: Baker, 1995), 44. See also Dennis A. Jacobsen, *Doing Justice: Congregations and Community Organizing* (Minneapolis: Fortress Press, 2001).

11. For more information about Koinonia Leadership Mission, visit their web site (www.KLMcrew.net), or e-mail Mark Baker at deets@esa-online.org.

Chapter 12

1. Nancy T. Ammerman, Jackson W. Carroll, Carl S. Dudley, and William McKinney, eds., *Studying Congregations: A New Handbook* (Nashville: Abingdon Press, 1998), 173–74.

2. Ronald J. Sider, Philip N. Olson, and Heidi Rolland Unruh, "Connecting the Dots: Assessing Your Congregational and Community Context to Develop a Holistic Ministry Vision," available from Evangelicals for Social Action (800-650-6600, esa@esa-online.org).

3. Ammerman et al., *Studying Congregations.*

4. See chapter 2 of Ronald Sider, *Good News and Good Works: A Theology for the Whole Gospel* (Grand Rapids: Baker, 1999) for a more detailed inventory of your congregation's beliefs.

5. Ray Bakke, *A Theology as Big as the City* (Downers Grove, Ill.: InterVarsity Press, 1997), 60.

6. Ray Bakke and Sam Roberts, *The Expanded Mission of City Center Churches* (Chicago: International Urban Associates, 1998), 55.

7. Timothy J. Keller, *Ministries of Mercy: The Call of the Jericho Road,* 2d ed. (Phillipsburg, N.J.: P & R Publishing, 1997), 145.

8. Carl S. Dudley, *Basic Steps toward Community Ministry* (Washington, D.C.: Alban Institute, 1991), 2.

9. Ammerman et al., *Studying Congregations,* 42–43.

10. Nancy Tatom Ammerman, *Congregation and Community* (New Brunswick, N.J.: Rutgers University Press, 1997), 347.

11. See, for example, Rachele Warren and Donald Warren, *The Neighborhood Organizers Handbook* (Notre Dame, Ind.: Notre Dame Press, 1977).

12. Ammerman et al., *Studying Congregations,* 48–49.

13. Ammerman, *Congregation and Community.*

14. Dudley, *Basic Steps toward Community Ministry,* 1.

15. Phil Olson, "The Eyes Have It: How to Find Out Your Church's Holistic Ministry," *NETResults,* January 2000, 8.

16. For more on what and how to learn about your community, see Ammerman et al., *Studying Congregations,* chapter 2; Bakke and Roberts, *The Expanded Mission of City Center Churches,* 51–52; Dudley, *Basic Steps toward Community Ministry,* part 1; Keller, *Ministries of Mercy,* 145–53; Olson, "The Eyes Have It"; Sider et al., "Connecting the Dots"; and Phil Tom and Sally Johnson, *Handbook for Urban*

Church Ministries (Chicago: Metro Mission, 1996).

17. Ammerman et al., *Studying Congregations,* 42.

18. For more on an asset-based approach to community development, see John P. Kretzmann and John L. McKnight, *Building Communities from the Inside Out: A Path toward Finding and Mobilizing a Community's Assets* (Evanston, Ill.: Center for Urban Affairs and Policy Research, Northwestern University, 1993).

19. Bakke and Roberts, *The Expanded Mission of City Center Churches,* 39.

20. Jack Dennison, *City Reaching: On the Road to Community Transformation* (Pasadena, Calif.: William Carey Library, 1999), 167.

21. David J. Frenchak, "Visionary Leadership in Launching Social Ministries," in *Next Steps in Community Ministry,* ed. Carl S. Dudley (Bethesda, Md.: Alban Institute, 1996), 25.

22. Gornik and Castellanos, "How to Start a Christian Community Development Ministry," 217.

23. Cornelius Plantinga Jr., *Not the Way It's Supposed to Be: A Breviary of Sin* (Grand Rapids: Eerdmans, 1995), 9.

24. Frenchak, "Visionary Leadership in Launching Social Ministries," 23.

25. Jim Herrington, Mike Bonem, and James H. Furr, *Leading Congregational Change: A Practical Guide for the Transformational Journey* (San Francisco: Jossey-Bass, 2000). This helpful book has much more to say on the process of developing and communicating vision.

26. Calvin Miller, *The Empowered Leader: 10 Keys to Servant Leadership* (Nashville: Broadman and Holman Publishers, 1995), 50.

Chapter 13

1. For helpful guidance on launching new ministry projects, see Carl S. Dudley, *Basic Steps toward Community Ministry: Guidelines and Models in Action* (Washington, D.C.: Alban Institute, 1991); Carl S. Dudley, ed., *Next Steps in Community Ministry* (Bethesda, Md.: Alban Institute, 1996); Mark R. Gornik and Noel Castellanos, "How to Start a Christian Community Development Ministry," in *Restoring At-Risk Communities: Doing It Together and Doing It Right,* ed. John Perkins (Grand Rapids: Baker, 1995); Emily Demuth Ishida and Y. Franklin Ishida, *To Serve as Jesus Served: A Guide to Social Ministry for Congregations* (Minneapolis: Augsburg Fortress, 1994); Phil Olson, "Unless the Lord Builds the House: How to Lead a Congregation into Holistic Ministry," *PRISM* 8, no. 1 (January–February 2001): 12–13; Oliver Phillips, *The 12-Step Program: Steps to Starting a Compassionate Ministry Center* (Kansas City, Mo.: Nazarene Compassionate Ministry USA/Canada, 2001); Amy L. Sherman, *Restorers of Hope* (Wheaton: Crossway Books, 1997); and Phil and Tom and Sally Johnson, *Handbook for Urban Church Ministries* (Chicago: Metro Mission, 1996).

2. David Heney, *Motivating Your Parish to Change* (San Jose: Resource Publications, 1998), 57.

3. See Phil Olson and Jim Hancock, *C2C—A Visionary Journey: Congregations Helping Congregations Launch Holistic Ministry,* available from Network 9:35 (800-650-6600, www.network935.org).

4. James E. Means, *Leadership in Christian Ministry* (Grand Rapids: Baker, 1989), 64.

5. Nancy T. Ammerman, Jackson W. Carroll, Carl S. Dudley, and William McKinney, eds., *Studying Congregations: A New Handbook* (Nashville: Abingdon Press, 1998), 31.

6. David J. Frenchak, "Visionary Leadership in Launching Social Ministries," in *Next Steps in Community Ministry,* ed. Carl S. Dudley (Bethesda, Md.: Alban Institute, 1996), 26.

7. Heney, *Motivating Your Parish to Change,* 25.

8. Calvin Miller, *The Empowered Leader: 10 Keys to Servant Leadership* (Nashville: Broadman and Holman Publishers, 1995), 71.

9. See Dudley, *Basic Steps toward Community Ministry,* part 2.

10. Heney, *Motivating Your Parish to Change,* 61.

11. Mark R. Gornik and Noel Castellanos, "How to Start a Christian Community Development Ministry," in *Restoring At-Risk Communities: Doing It Together and Doing It Right,* ed. John Perkins (Grand Rapids: Baker, 1995), 213.

12. Ram A. Cnaan and Stephanie C. Boddie, "The Secular in the Sacred: Social Services in Congregations in Seven American Cities" (paper presented at the Society for the Scientific Study of Religion Annual Conference, Boston, 6 November 1999).

13. Rick Warren, *The Purpose Driven Church* (Grand Rapids: Zondervan, 1995), 365.

14. Marlene Wilson, *How to Mobilize Church Volunteers* (Minneapolis: Augsburg Press, 1983), 90.

15. See Cheryl J. Sanders, *Ministry at the Margins: The Prophetic Mission of Women, Youth, and the Poor* (Downers Grove, Ill.: InterVarsity Press, 1997).

16. Timothy J. Keller, *Ministries of Mercy: The Call of the Jericho Road,* 2d ed. (Phillipsburg, N.J.: P & R Publishing, 1997), 133–34.

17. Gornik and Castellanos, "How to Start a Christian Community Development Ministry," 229.

Chapter 14

1. Harold R. Fray Jr., *Conflict and Change in the Church* (Boston: Pilgrim Press, 1969), 35.

2. Dietrich Bonhoeffer, *The Cost of Discipleship,* rev. ed. (New York: Macmillan, 1959), 99.

3. C. Gene Wilkes, *Jesus on Leadership* (Wheaton: Tyndale, 1998), 127.

4. Barbara Williams Skinner, *Becoming an Effective Twenty-First-Century Leader* (Washington, D.C.: Skinner Farm Leadership Institute, 2000), 5.

5. Jim Herrington, Mike Bonem, and James H. Furr, *Leading Congregational Change: A Practical Guide for the Transformational Journey* (San Francisco: Jossey-Bass, 2000), 12.

6. James Furr, Mike Bonem and Jim Herrington, *Leading Congregational Change Workbook* (San Francisco: Jossey-Bass, 2000), 29.

7. Herrington et al., *Leading Congregational Change,* 4–5.

8. Ibid., 16.

9. Ibid., 93.

10. See Phil Olson and Jim Hancock, *C2C—A Visionary Journey: Congregations Helping Congregations Launch Holistic Ministry,* available from Network 9:35 (800-650-6600, www.network935.org).

11. Herrington et al., *Leading Congregational Change,* 8.

12. Carl S. Dudley, *Basic Steps toward Community Ministry* (Washington, D.C.: Alban Institute, 1991), 100.

13. Herrington et al., *Leading Congregational Change,* 8–9.

14. Ibid., 8.

15. Calvin Miller, *The Empowered Leader: 10 Keys to Servant Leadership* (Nashville: Broadman and Holman Publishers, 1995), 140.

16. David J. Frenchak, "Visionary Leadership in Launching Social Ministries," in *Next Steps in Community Ministry,* ed. Carl S. Dudley (Bethesda, Md.: Alban Institute, 1996), 29.

17. Miller, *The Empowered Leader,* 36.

18. Marlene Wilson, *How to Mobilize Church Volunteers* (Minneapolis: Augsburg Press, 1983), 91.

19. Herrington et al., *Leading Congregational Change,* 161.

20. Dudley, *Basic Steps toward Community Ministry,* 43.

21. Herrington et al., *Leading Congregational Change,* 98.

22. David Heney, *Motivating Your Parish to Change* (San Jose: Resource Publications, 1998), 95.

23. Fray, *Conflict and Change in the Church,* 47.

Ronald J. Sider, president of Evangelicals for Social Action (ESA) and professor of theology and culture at Eastern Baptist Theological Seminary, is the author of over twenty books, including *Just Generosity* and the best-selling *Rich Christians in an Age of Hunger.* **Philip N. Olson** is vice president for church relations at ESA and director of Network 9:35. **Heidi Rolland Unruh** is associate director of the Congregations, Communities, and Leadership Development Project at Eastern Baptist Theological Seminary.